# Humanism
### and the
# Social Order
### in
# Tudor England

# Humanism
*and the*
# Social Order
*in*
# Tudor England

*By* Fritz Caspari

THE UNIVERSITY OF CHICAGO PRESS

THE UNIVERSITY OF CHICAGO PRESS, CHICAGO 37
Cambridge University Press, London, N.W. 1, England
The University of Toronto Press, Toronto 5, Canada

TO

E.W.C.

# Acknowledgments

I AM grateful to many teachers, colleagues, and friends for the generous help and encouragement they have given me over a number of years in the preparation and writing of this book. Any virtues it may possess are due to them, and no one but the author should be blamed for its inadequacies. I cannot, in the following lines, name all those whose suggestions are reflected in it, but I wish to express my sincere gratitude to them all.

Earlier studies preparatory to the present work—a thesis written at Oxford University and a dissertation submitted to the University of Hamburg—greatly benefited from the advice of Sir Ernest Barker, Sir David Keir, the late Dr. A. J. Carlyle, and the late Professor Emil Wolff. Professor W. K. Jordan and Mr. A. L. Rowse contributed much to the present work by their constructive suggestions and criticism; the encouragement and inspiration of Professor Arnold Bergstraesser have accompanied it from its inception. Professors Louis Gottschalk and Edward Shils were kind enough to read the completed manuscript. The discussion of early English humanism is indebted to the advice of Professor Roberto Weiss; that of Erasmus benefited from suggestions made by Professors Richard P. McKeon and Helena M. Gamer; and that of Sir Thomas Elyot has profited from the advice of Professor Ronald S. Crane. My wife, Elita Walker Caspari, shared the labors of final revision and proofreading, and her judgment in matters of substance and style has been most valuable.

I am very grateful to the readers of the University of Chicago Press for their critical reading of the manuscript and for several suggestions that have been embodied in this book. It has been a pleasure to work with the staff of the University of Chicago Press, whose admirable thoroughness has saved me from a number of pitfalls. I am much obliged to Miss Judith Lucas for preparing the index. My gratitude is due also to the staffs of the University of Chicago libraries, of the Newberry Library, of the Henry E. Huntington Library, and of the British Museum for their ready assistance in assembling materials.

To the Newberry Library, and especially to its librarian, Mr. Stanley Pargellis, as well as to the University of Chicago, I am indebted for the practical encouragement they have provided toward the completion of this book by giving me some leisure for my work on it. I gratefully acknowledge the assistance given by the College of the University of Chicago in connection with the typing of the manuscript, and I wish particularly to thank the Social Science Research Committee of the University of Chicago for its generous subsidy to the cost of printing the book.

The editors of the *Journal of the History of Ideas* have kindly permitted me to reprint the major part of my article "Erasmus on the Social Functions of Christian Humanism," which was published in that *Journal* in 1947. It appears here, with certain alterations, as part of chapter ii.

Fritz Caspari

Chicago, Illinois
June 8, 1954

## NOTE

Except where modernized titles and texts are cited, the original spelling has been retained in quotations from old texts. For greater convenience in reading, however, the letters *v* and *u* have been brought into conformity with modern usage in all quotations except those from the poetry of Edmund Spenser, where the original spelling is entirely observed. In first citations of titles of sixteenth-century books, the original spelling is reproduced exactly; thereafter, *v*'s and *u*'s are adjusted.

# Contents

# I

# Social and Intellectual Foundations
# of English Humanism

Humanism was an intellectual movement that sprang from a longing for the revival of classical antiquity.[1] The humanists advocated a rational and largely secular education based on the study of the Greek and Roman classics, and from it they expected great benefits to the individual and to society. A specifically humanistic ethos developed, which influenced, in different ways and degrees, the thought, education, and social order of the countries which came under its spell. We shall here be concerned with investigating the development and influence of this ethos in Tudor England.

Throughout most of the fifteenth century, humanism in England was predominantly a formal, scholarly movement modeled on the imitation of Ciceronian Latin which then flourished in Italy. In this outward form it found a limited degree of acceptance. Thus, the new Latin style became increasingly the language of diplomacy, and men who could write and speak it could hope for employment in diplomatic functions. The inner core of humanism, the ethical, pedagogical, and political values that had so vitally affected Italian life, was but dimly perceived.[2] Humanism did not play a decisive part in English intellectual life until, toward the end of the fifteenth century, these values began to be assimilated, and, in the sixteenth century, took firm root as a definite body of doctrine.[3] It was then recognized that the precepts of Greece and Rome were relevant to the new and special needs of state and society in England.

During the sixteenth century, English humanists evolved a social doctrine with which they tried to defend and improve the existing order of society. They used their knowledge of Plato and Aristotle, of Cicero and Quintilian, to justify the aristocratic structure of English society, the hierarchy of "order and degree" in the state.

1

Their particular concern was to devise means whereby, in the social and political framework of Tudor England, the ruling members of society would also be its "best" men. Under the Tudors, the country gentry emerged as the leading and most active element in society. The nobility, which had lost much of its former power through the Wars of the Roses, was partly re-created by the Tudors, who raised men into it from the gentry. The merchants in the cities, increasingly wealthy and powerful, particularly in London, could not measure up to the landed classes in prestige and influence. The humanists did not forget the nobility, often mentioning nobility and gentry in the same breath, nor did they overlook the needs and importance of the urban citizenry; but the particular social and political condition and development of Tudor England caused them to concentrate their thoughts and efforts mainly on the gentry. The improvement and transformation of this most important class, and the firm establishment and justification of its position, came to be one of their major concerns.

The particular course of humanism in England can be partly explained by the historical circumstances in which it became effective. If humanism helped to form a theory of society and influenced the growth of its structure, it was in turn influenced in its own development by the conditions which it encountered, and to which it adapted itself. In our treatment of humanism and the social order in sixteenth-century England, we shall be primarily concerned with the first type of influence, with the effect of English humanism on the order and ideals of society. For the purpose of indicating its character, however, we must first single out certain aspects of the complex structure of that society which particularly affected the nature and course of English humanism. Most important among these were the various factors which contributed to the rising importance of the English gentry.

The new Tudor monarchy, established in 1485 on the battleground of Bosworth, was insecure against rival claims to the Crown. It centralized much of the government in its own hands, prohibited private feudal armies, was suspicious of the nobility whose power had been shaken by the preceding wars, and found its most reliable ally in the gentry. That term was used to designate the lower landed aristocracy, below the nobility but above the yeomanry. It included all those groups in the social hierarchy that belonged to the upper middle class of the countryside, the knights, esquires, and gentlemen. The term "gentleman" was used to describe not only individual members of the lowest group within the country gentry, but was applied to members of all its social groups, often to members of the nobility, and extended to professional men such as lawyers. The humanists expanded and changed the meaning of the term "gentleman" to describe their ideal type of man; it could thus be used to describe any person who met their demands, and was not necessarily restricted in its use to a definite caste.[4]

The gentry provided the Crown with some of its ablest servants; it was favored in elevation to high office, numerically predominated in the privy council, and was preferred over the nobility in such an anti-feudal body as the King's Council in the North.[5] The connection of the gentry's interests with those of the new monarchy became even closer after the dissolution of the monasteries when, to a larger extent than other classes, it increased its wealth and power by the acquisition of monastic lands. A number of its members were raised to the peerage, so that a considerable proportion of the Tudor nobility owed its position to the ruling house. Meanwhile members of the lower rural classes and merchants from the cities were finding their way into the gentry, and townsmen, sometimes of "obscure" origin, also found employment and advancement with the Crown. These latter did not share the widespread aristocratic prejudice against "bookish" learning, had better opportunities for attending schools, and found that their talents and learning were rewarded by a state which was developing its central organs of government and needed alert and educated men for them. Thomas Wolsey and Thomas Cromwell are the most obvious examples of men who rose from lowly origins to the highest offices of state; Thomas More, the son of a "gentle" but undistinguished London family,[6] had a similar career. (It may be noted, incidentally, that all three ended in disgrace, with two losing their heads on the scaffold.) It is certainly indicative of the alertness of the urban, as contrasted with the rural, groups around 1500, that both John Colet and Thomas More, the leading figures of the "New Learning," were London citizens, and that most of their fellow-humanists came to live in London. The first school to be established on humanistic principles, Colet's foundation of St. Paul's, was located in London and intended to provide for the education of the sons of her citizens. The wealth and influence of merchants, tradesmen, and lawyers in the urban communities was growing, although by no means was it equal to that of the landed gentry. Prodded on by the government, the humanists, and its own self-interest, that class soon remedied its intellectual backwardness and invaded the institutions of higher learning to equip itself for its duties in the state.

The privileged status of the gentry was not without its obligations. The gentry was responsible for the bulk of local government, and it was charged with an ever growing number of duties which resulted from the expansion of the sphere of state intervention, from the increasing complexity of social problems, and from the recession of feudal institutions in government. The members of the Tudor gentry have, therefore, rightly been described as the "unremunerated agents" of the central government.[7] They were not, however, agents in the sense of being members of a bureaucracy, mere tools of an administrative absolutism. On the contrary: the characteristic quality of their position is to be found in their comparative independence, in the measure of autonomy which they enjoyed.

Neither at the center nor on the local level did there exist a strict separation of political, administrative, and judicial functions; in the country, the gentry performed administrative duties in judicial offices. The one office which a country gentleman was most likely to hold was that of Justice of the Peace; he might also have to take on the burdensome office of High Sheriff. Almost everything pertaining to administration and jurisdiction in the counties came to be concentrated in these offices. (The only other significant county office, and the most distinguished of them all, was that of the Lord Lieutenant, usually reserved to the nobility.) As justices of the peace, members of the gentry enforced the laws of the land and ruled the countryside. They might, in simple cases, act either as single justices or in conjunction with one colleague; for more complex matters, a number of them met in Sessions. When, in the reign of Elizabeth, William Lambard wrote his famous guide for them, the *Eirenarcha, or of the Office of the Iustices of Peace* (London, 1581),[8] he could speak of "stacks of statutes"[9]—some three hundred enactments—which the justices were expected to execute. Among other things, a single justice was then empowered to prevent breaches of peace and riots, to arrest beggars and criminals, to enforce attendance at church; two justices could enforce the laws regulating work and apprenticeship and the legal wages for servants and laborers which were fixed by the assembled J.P.'s in their quarterly meetings, the Quarter Sessions. On these occasions, the justices, with the aid of a jury, dealt with most of the criminal offenses. They were controlled by the justices of assize who came through the counties on circuit, and who had jurisdiction in certain

4

cases and in civil suits; the privy council also kept a watchful eye on them, interfering directly when necessary. The justices of the peace nevertheless enjoyed a considerable measure of autonomy in their administration; up to a point, they were able to represent their own and local interests against the centralizing tendencies of the government. Country gentlemen might represent these interests in Parliament: the two county seats were virtually monopolized by the gentry, and borough seats were frequently held by its members.[10] A seat in Parliament became increasingly desirable during the sixteenth century.[11] The High Sheriff controlled the county court, where the election of the members of Parliament for the county took place.[12] His office was more onerous and expensive than that of J.P., and more directly under the supervision of the privy council.

The gentry thus held a central position in the administration of the country—at the center in the privy council and in Parliament, locally as justices of the peace and sheriffs. As the scope of these offices widened under the Tudors, the gentry continued to preserve a considerable degree of independence in the face of the government's tendency toward centralization. The attempt to set up a royal absolutism did not come until the ensuing century, and met with disaster: the Tudor monarchs, on the whole, recognized the elements of power in their kingdom and were more politic and skilful than their Stuart successors in manipulating, rather than subduing, them. The gentry, "brave halfe paces between a Throne and a people," as Fulke Greville described it early in the seventeenth century,[13] assumed a position in the country which was not paralleled elsewhere. While preserving some feudal features, it became an essentially civil governing class. It was not turned into a caste of officials or into the ornament of an absolutist court, but retained its roots in the countryside. The new demands made on this group required new qualifications; the study of law, which many of the future justices of the peace found it necessary to take up, partially met this need. But the change of its functions in society demanded more than that; it called for a new social ideal. That of the knight had paled because it no longer fitted the requirements of society.

Another ideal had been produced by classical antiquity and revived by the humanists of the Italian Renaissance. It could be and, as we shall see, actually was adapted to the needs of the English ruling class by the theoretical works and practical efforts of some English humanists. Athens and republican Rome, where the conceptions of the ἄνθρωπος πολιτικός and of the *cives* were formed, were democracies with aristocratic social systems and aristocratic elements in their constitutions. Their upper classes were inextricably connected with public life; in the "classical" periods of these states, most of the important positions in peace and war were occupied by their members, and their voices—like that of Pericles— were heard in popular assembly and senate and often decided the course to be taken. In Rome, the higher judicial and administrative offices—the quaestorship, the aedileship, the praetorship, the consulate, and the censorship—were, since the fourth century B.C., open not only to the nobility but to plebeians as well; in practice, however, and particularly in the last century of the republican era, they were mostly filled by members of the new nobility, the *optimates*. Augustus reorganized the lower nobility, the equestrian order, and employed it in the magistracies and as an imperial civil service. In both Athens and Rome, the ideal of the orator, of the man who could sway court and assembly by his speeches, had its appeal. It was thought that, in order to be a good orator, the individual had to be a good man and that, to be a good man, his good potentialities had first to be developed by a careful and comprehensive education. The ideal of such a man retained its appeal into the days of imperial Rome, when Quintilian described his education and character in *De Institutione Oratoria*.

In some respects, conditions in sixteenth-century England resembled those of the classical states. There was a definite similarity between the functions of the Roman and the English aristocracy, of *equites* and knights; both groups tended to occupy the important judicial and administrative offices, and both preserved a certain degree of independence in their positions. The education of the Greek and Roman aristocracy could thus provide a most useful example, even if the need for oratory was not as great in England as it had been in Greece and Rome; the great men of these states, and the ideals according to which they had lived, could serve as prototypes in sixteenth-century England.[14] The ideas of the humanists, derived as they were from the ideals of classical antiquity, thus fell on fertile ground, and owed their peculiar growth to its special conditions.

The English humanists did not create a new structure of society. They largely accepted what they found and infused their ideas into the society that surrounded them. Humanistic ideas thus became a powerful element in the predominant sixteenth-century belief in

6

a social hierarchy which it was the duty of the ruler and of the aristocracy to maintain and in which every man had his place, high or low. This hierarchical conception of society and the state contained many traditional elements. The organic analogy by which it was frequently illustrated—the comparison of the functions of various members of society with those of different parts of the human body—had often been used in medieval thought, and the idea that the terrestrial order among men should correspond to the celestial hierarchy had been a commonplace. Feudal society had corresponded to such ideas: everyone in theory had had his place in it, with his duties balanced by privileges, his services by protection, his rule by obligations. These ideas continued to have their appeal in sixteenth-century England and to be voiced frequently; the order of society still was in large measure based on them. The principle of "order and degree," proclaimed with great vigor by Elyot and Shakespeare[15] and approved by most of their contemporaries, thus had many of its roots in medieval thought, just as the aristocratic social order, with the monarch at its head, descended directly from the order that had prevailed in the preceding centuries. Yet it would be wrong to see merely a restatement of medieval doctrine in the works of sixteenth-century English humanists and poets, just as it would be a mistake to consider the social and political order of Tudor England as nothing but a continuation or a revival of the medieval feudal monarchy. In theory and in practice, new elements became amalgamated with the old heritage and gave it new emphasis and content. Humanistic ideas came to be a powerful constituent element of Tudor social thought.

The medieval belief in the divine institution of the social hierarchy was fervently restated by sixteenth-century English political theorists, especially when its validity was attacked by "Anabaptists"—a name rather freely bestowed on various types of sectarians—by other social equalitarians, and by ordinary common men who rose in protest against this order. Yet, while the old doctrine continued to be preached with undiminished fervor, subtle changes were taking place in its character. It could no longer be maintained with the same strength of conviction as before that a man belonged to that place in the hierarchy to which he had been born, that his station was permanently fixed since at the time of his birth it had been assigned to him by the will of God. The theorists could not entirely close their eyes to the fact that there was considerable social mobility in sixteenth-century England.[16]

Some flexibility had always existed in the social system—for instance, in the cities and towns, or in the Church, where lowly men might rise to positions of power and dignity. The system had been more rigid in the countryside, and it was there that its softening became evident during the sixteenth century, and posed problems for the defenders of the aristocratic order. There were yeomen who expanded their holdings until they or their children could call themselves "gentlemen"; there were some wealthy men from the cities who bought their way to eventual gentility by the acquisition of large enough holdings of land; there were members of the gentry who were advanced, for services rendered to the young Tudor monarchy, into the depleted ranks of the nobility. Finally, there were men drawn from all these groups and even "obscure" men of "vile" blood whose sheer ability, knowledge, and sometimes ruthlessness, recommended them to a dynasty which valued such qualities. In their endeavors to concentrate the powers of government in their own hands, to strengthen the governmental system, and to keep the nobility subdued, the Tudor rulers—particularly Henry VII and Henry VIII—picked loyal and efficient crown servants where they could find them. They freely rewarded men who served them well with possessions and rank. (In fairness, it must be added that they also freely discarded them.) Elizabeth, in the later part of the century, was less ready to advance "new men" than her father and grandfather had been; she largely relied on the services of men whose families had come up under her predecessors, whose fortunes were closely connected with those of the Tudors, and whose social positions were already well consolidated.

The lines separating the different groups in the social hierarchy were thus more elastic than they had been in the past. The partial commercialization of land, as manifested in the enclosure movement —so bitterly denounced by Thomas More in 1516[17]—indicated the weakening of the ties that had held medieval society together and, by impairing the old "organic" relationship of the social groups, itself contributed to their greater fluidity. The event which produced the greatest chances for sudden enrichment and a consequent improvement of social status, however, was the dissolution of the monasteries from 1536 on.[18] Henry VIII and his successors used the spoils not only to improve their own and the government's finances, but also to reward their most faithful servants and supporters. The gentry emerged with the lion's share, and as a result was able to establish itself more firmly than before as the most influential class in the state. Some of its members acquired enough property to maintain themselves in a manner befitting noblemen, and they were in a number of cases raised to the peerage; others, of lower origin, obtained the means which enabled them to live like gentlemen and to be accepted into the gentry. In short, the composition and relative position of the various classes, and in particular of the gentry, underwent a considerable change as a result of all these factors which culminated in the wholesale redistribution of land after the break with Rome.

The social order was still hierarchical, but the hierarchy itself, whatever its defenders might say, was less rigid than before, and it had undergone a change of character. It could no longer be maintained that a man was tied to the station to which he was born, and that only military prowess could qualify him and his descendants for a leading position in society. Factors other than heredity, qualities other than chivalrous valor, had come to be important. A man with a good sense of business, with an eye for enlarging and exploiting his land, had a fine chance of improving his lot, of becoming not a "knight"—although he might still receive that title—but a "gentleman." If the accent had here shifted from military to civilian aptitudes, the same shift had occurred in other spheres. A man with a good practical knowledge of political affairs in his own and in other countries, with a knowledge of "letters" and the law, was more useful to his monarch than a chivalrous warrior. The knight on horseback had ceased to be a decisive military figure, and England no longer was involved as deeply in military affairs on the Continent as she had been during the Hundred Years' War. The Crown, which was trying to replace the old, largely indirect feudal system of government by more direct methods of rule and control, needed men skilled in the arts of government and administration, both on the central and the local level, and was ready to recognize and reward their talents. Inevitably, those members of the old ruling classes who stubbornly clung to the standards of a former age, who refused to acquire such ignoble qualifications as "bookish learning" (which they considered fit for "clerks" but not for themselves), lost prestige and influence to others who, irrespective of their origins, could offer what they themselves were unable or unwilling to supply. The aristocracy of the pen began to invade and even to displace that of the sword, eliciting the latter's bitter complaints.

This was precisely the point where the humanists intervened, and where they were able to inject their ideas most effectively. The social and economic situation made the time especially propitious

9

for an infusion of the educational ideas which had come out of the Renaissance. It is the character, growth, and acclimatization of these ideas which we here propose to investigate through some of their protagonists—Erasmus and such English humanists as Sir Thomas More, Sir Thomas Elyot, and Thomas Starkey. These humanists urged gentlemen and noblemen to shed some of their outmoded prejudices and predilections, and to prove their worth by showing that they were equal to the tasks that men of power and influence were expected to perform. They had to acquire learning if they wished to maintain their traditional position.

This demand was destined to meet with a very wide and favorable response in the course of the century. The appeal of the humanists was so great because they showed how the position of the aristocracy could be preserved, because they replaced no longer adequate criteria with adequate standards, because they helped to adapt the social ideal to the needs of the age. But if the appeal of the humanistic postulates was so successful because it was practical, the motivation of the humanists was essentially idealistic. They brought to bear the ideas and ideals which they had imbibed from their studies of classical and humanistic authors. With the exception of Thomas More, they did not create a theoretical, abstract vision of an ideal society; rather, they adapted the ideals of Athens and Rome to suit the needs of their own society.

Plato's thought had a special attraction for them and greatly influenced their own ideas. Before the fifteenth century, most of Plato's works had been unavailable in western Europe, but in the course of that century, Plato had come to occupy the dominant position, hitherto held by Aristotle, of *the* philosopher. That is not to say that Aristotle's influence vanished: the Aristotelian tradition continued strong at most universities, and a study of the works of Aristotle continued to form an important part of higher education. His teachings on ethics and politics, for instance, were closely intermingled with those of Plato in much of humanistic thought. Yet, with the introduction of Plato's work into western Europe, the emphasis tended to shift from Aristotle to Plato, and this shift was of decisive importance for the further development of humanistic political theory. The change took place first in Italy, where the most outstanding representatives of humanism were active in promoting it, and then spread to other countries in the later part of the fifteenth and in the early sixteenth century. The Platonic Academy, founded by Cosimo de' Medici in 1462,[19] provided a center for Platonic studies and was the basis for Ficino's translation of Plato.[20] While some of Plato's works, among them a manuscript of the *Republic*, had been brought to England under the auspices of Humphrey, Duke of Gloucester, as early as the 1440's,[21] the full impact of his thought was not felt there until the last decade of the fifteenth and the beginning of the sixteenth century, when men like Grocyn, Linacre, and Colet, who had studied in Italy and come in touch with the work and teachings of the Florentines, had returned to England. Thomas More, their friend and pupil, was deeply impressed by the Platonic image of the good and just state. He tried to equal and even surpass its example with his *Utopia*. English thought did not remain Utopian, however, and More's successors, notably his younger friend Thomas Elyot, brought Plato's precepts back from the Island of Nowhere onto the solid soil of England. It should be definitely noted, however, that none of the English humanists here under consideration were "pure" Platonists or Neoplatonists: they were all, in varying degrees, indebted to Platonic philosophy, but they used it eclectically, and mingled with it concepts derived from Aristotle's *Politics* and *Ethics*, from Cicero, Quintilian, and other favorites of the humanists. Much of what they had to say, furthermore, was undoubtedly derived from secondary works rather than from a study of the texts themselves, and was often not distinguished by much originality.

Whatever their shortcomings, it is clear that English humanists were deeply affected by the Platonic ideal of a good and just state which is ruled by an elite of guardians and philosophers. They chose from this conception what they felt could be fitted into contemporary English society, what could be used to meet its needs and to improve it. Plato's description of the state had certain elements which resembled existing conditions: thus, he had postulated an aristocratic order of society, and English society was ruled by an aristocracy, though by one very different from what he had envisaged. His guardians were trained as warriors, as were the knights. There also were elements which were radically at variance with English practice; only More followed him, and went beyond him, in his communism, but he wisely placed his communist society on an imaginary island. Other humanists were opposed to this form of economic organization, and neither More nor they approved of Plato's proposals for the community of women and children. They tended to temper their acceptance of the Platonic world of ideas by combining it with the Christian idea of God, thus following Christian and Neo-

11

platonic traditions. The crucial point, however, was the Platonic scheme for the selection and training of future rulers. As in the chivalrous code, physical prowess and the training of body and character by sports and arms was a prerequisite in Plato's scheme. But his ideas differed from the chivalrous code in his insistence on high intellectual qualifications in his future guardians and philosophers, and in his provision of a very exacting scheme of education in the disciplines of the mind, particularly in philosophy. In successive steps, the future ruler is to be led out of the cave of ignorance until he may be ready to perceive the divine world of the eternally good and beautiful ideas. It is his task to transform reality, and especially the reality of the state, so that it may conform as closely as possible to the order of perfect goodness and justice which he has come to know, and to safeguard that order.

The education of the future rulers is Plato's primary concern: through it alone can the "right" order of the state be established and maintained. Following him, the humanists demanded that future "governours" partake of a rigorous education in the intellectual disciplines, and they stated that only such training would qualify them for leading positions in the state. With the exception of More, they were less radical than Plato with regard to the selection of those to be educated as future rulers. Plato had insisted on a method which would insure that only those qualified by character, intellect, and physique would be chosen; not all the children of guardians and philosophers would automatically be included, and on the other hand children from the lower classes were not excluded. More made similar provisions for the selection of future members of the Utopian "order of the learned," but those English humanists who addressed their hereditary aristocracy could not entirely follow Plato and More in these respects. They omitted or modified these important features of the Platonic system in adapting it to the existing order of society. In order to improve this society they provided a scheme of education for those who were traditionally considered qualified to rule it by inherited position and wealth. While the humanistic movement also supported the education of "poor scholars" and the establishment of schools and scholarships for them, the English authors under consideration here were mostly concerned with the education of the aristocracy rather than with that of men of low social origin.

Erasmus also faced the need of improving society through the better education of its ruling members. He provided plans for the education of the "Christian Knight" and the "Christian Prince" which were designed to reform aristocracy and princes through Christian ethics and classical letters, and his plans were widely imitated in England, where they were adapted to the special conditions of the country, and where they assumed a very concrete and practical form. The main point was that a member of the aristocracy now was supposed to add to his traditional qualifications that of "learning"; the right kind of learning was expected to make a good and "virtuous" man of him, and to provide him with the knowledge necessary for fulfilling the functions of government.

Learning did not eliminate the other attributes of aristocracy, but it shifted them more into the background. It also created a number of problems which were only partly solved. What was to be done with a nobleman or gentleman who was too stupid or lazy to learn? What, on the other hand, was to be the fate of a common man who possessed the necessary intelligence and acquired the knowledge considered prerequisite for high office? Most of the English theorists shrank from following the Platonic position to its logical conclusion: if knowledge led to virtue, and virtue alone qualified a man to rule, then, according to Plato's and More's plans, those who were devoid of knowledge and virtue had to be eliminated from the ruling group, and men from the lower orders of society who proved their abilities had to be brought into it. Clearly, no such plan could be expected to receive prompt acceptance in England; it would have meant a complete upheaval of the established order. Yet, as we have noted, a process remotely resembling it was actually taking place: gifted "new men" were establishing themselves in the ruling group, and noblemen were complaining that they were being pushed into the background by such men.

The humanists who concerned themselves with these problems arrived at compromise solutions which would accommodate, in so far as that was possible, the exigencies of the traditional order, the changes that were taking place in it, and their own scheme of values, in which knowledge occupied the most prominent place. They placed the main emphasis on the education of the existing aristocracy: if inherited position and an illustrious ancestry could be joined with learning and virtue, then that was the best combination. Their exhortations were principally directed to the aristocracy; but, they warned, if noblemen and gentlemen did not educate their children properly, then mean men's sons would take the positions that ought to be theirs. Since this warning had an uncomfortably close correspondence to actual happenings, it was effective, and with surprising speed learning came to be considered the attribute of a gentleman.

This change in attitude began in the 1530's. The old prejudice against learning decreased without vanishing altogether; the question still remained what was to be done with those who would not acquire this new attribute of gentility, who were "gentle ungentle"?[22] Their attitude was loudly deplored, they were warned of dire consequences, but usually that was all. And what was to be the situation of the gifted man of ordinary parentage who acquired learning and virtue, the "ungentle gentle"? Here the views ranged from the almost complete rejection of such men to their more or less grudging acceptance. The author of a tract on *The Institucion of a Gentleman* in the middle of the century took a rather liberal view of them and felt that their advancement was justifiable; Elyot before him, and Spenser after him, while not entirely excluding the possibility of such advancement, were evidently highly reluctant to grant it, and made it very clear that they considered a combination of blue blood and learning superior to learning alone.

We need not here go into the many nuances with which different interpreters varied this doctrine. In all cases, the humanistic emphasis resulted in learning taking its place beside the traditional qualifications as a prerequisite for "governours"; it was the most recent and dynamic element among these qualifications, was stressed constantly, was in great demand, and thus naturally came to be pre-eminent among them. It should be noted that it was always, at least in theory, associated with a corresponding growth in character or virtue. Men like Elyot tried to effect a conciliation and combination between the ideals of chivalry and of classical antiquity, and the result of this fusion was the figure of the "governour," the new type of "gentleman." The hierarchical, organic conception of society that had prevailed in the later Middle Ages was accepted but given a new content. While the humanists did not make the degree of knowledge, of understanding or *episteme*, the only criterion by which a man's "degree" in that hierarchy was to be determined, they made it, in combination with other factors, a highly important one.

That, together with the social changes that were taking place, meant a loosening of the structure's former tightness, since the qualities of intellect and character stressed by the humanists were not confined to, or necessarily found in, any single class. If what they defined as an individual's "virtue" became ultimately more important than the chivalrous deeds of his distant ancestors, then their concep-

14

tion of the social order moved away from the medieval-feudal in the direction of the Platonic ideal. They were not democrats, but by stressing the function of knowledge in society their theory opened the way *aux talents,* irrespective of whether they actually approved of this development or not. To members of the aristocracy, they showed how they might preserve their position, to the parvenus how they might legitimize that of their family, and to ambitious young men without the right kind of parentage, how they might advance legitimately. For all of them, they provided a new social norm which filled the void left by "the waning of the Middle Ages," of feudalism and chivalry. And, while modifying it in important respects, they revitalized the aristocratic conception of society by infusing classical ideas into it. The pattern which they gave to English thought on education and society was to remain characteristic, though not unchallenged or unchanged, for centuries to come.

We have described the most effective impulse which influenced the English humanists in the formulation of their ideas as "Platonic." Thomas More would not have written the *Utopia* without the example of Plato's *Republic,* and his friend Erasmus, in describing the education of a Christian prince, borrowed more heavily from Plato than from other classical authors. Elyot greatly admired Plato and wrote a Platonic disputation,[23] and Starkey's *Dialogue* is much indebted to Plato in both form and content. However much they might deplore the impracticability of Plato's scheme, which they felt could never be implemented in actuality, they were powerfully attracted by his vision. Like most humanists everywhere, however, they drew their inspiration not only from Plato but from a variety of sources. Aristotle might no longer be *the* philosopher, but his *Ethics* and *Politics* were freely used and quoted. The Roman conception of the leading citizen, as formulated in Cicero's *De Oratore* and *De Officiis* and Quintilian's *De Institutione Oratoria,* had combined the precepts of Greek philosophy with Roman political experience: in order to be able to take part in political affairs, a man had to be an orator, and only the philosophically educated, virtuous man could be a good orator.

This latter conception had exerted a powerful influence on all humanistic thought, an influence somewhat overshadowed, but also deepened, by that of the Greeks, notably that of Plato, when their works became more fully available. Homer's and Plutarch's heroes, rulers like Alexander, Caesar, and the stoical Marcus Aurelius, were

15

considered by the English humanists as didactic examples of "good governours" who should be imitated. The works of humanists, especially of the Italians, who made use of these and other classical authorities, were in turn widely read and imitated, and the Neoplatonic philosophy of Florence had a strong appeal. The educational methods of such fifteenth-century humanists as Vittorino da Feltre and Guarino da Verona represented the practical implementation of much of what humanism stood for; they became known to Englishmen who studied in Italy and were admired by them. Finally, the greatest humanist in the North, Erasmus, spent some of his best years in England and was connected by close friendships with several of his English contemporaries; his Christian-humanistic ideals of man and society communicated themselves to England both through these friendships and for decades and centuries through his works.

Typical humanists, the Englishmen copied and plagiarized freely from the works of their remote and immediate predecessors, partly to show their wide reading, partly to bolster and amplify their own ideas. Our concern here is not so much to show the nature and extent of their collective and individual borrowings from, and indebtedness to, classical, medieval, and humanistic authors, as to present and investigate English humanistic doctrine as the historically effective synthesis which it was. The materials for this structure were taken from many quarries and old buildings; we shall be interested primarily in the structure itself, in its growth, and some of its details, and shall only occasionally indicate the origins of the materials that went into it. The plan of the structure and many of its materials are preponderantly Platonic in origin, either directly or through derivation.

The history of English humanism between the early fifteenth and the late sixteenth century may be divided into four periods. Like all periodizations, this division is somewhat arbitrary, but it is convenient for the purpose of bringing out some significant features in that development. The first period is that of a nascent humanism which lasts into the last decade of the fifteenth century. The second begins in that decade with the return to England of Grocyn, Colet, and Linacre, and with Erasmus' first visit there, and ends in the 1530's. During it, the great programmatic works of English humanism were produced: More's *Utopia*, Elyot's *Governour*. The circle around More, with Erasmus a frequent visitor, flourished. Humanism was placed on a firm foundation, first at Cambridge, then at Oxford, through the efforts of men like Fisher, Erasmus, Fox, More, Wolsey;

through the collaboration of Colet, Erasmus, and Lily, it was introduced at St. Paul's School in London, from which it spread to other schools. The third period begins with the separation from Rome and the upheaval caused in the educational system by the distribution of Church properties and the large-scale reorganization and partial secularization of education, particularly on the elementary- and grammar-school level. It includes the unsettled years that followed, the changes of rulers and official religious doctrines, until the re-establishment of more settled conditions with the accession of Elizabeth in 1558. During this period, humanism developed and spread in an unspectacular but effective and practical manner. No work comparable in importance to More's *Utopia* appeared, but the pedagogical plans and principles of the humanists were widely introduced in the new or reorganized schools. Humanistic learning was able to expand its hold on the universities at the expense of the conservative, scholastic elements, particularly at Cambridge, where it flourished during the 1540's. The men who were to play a prominent part during Elizabeth's reign, and Elizabeth herself, were educated in conformity with humanistic principles during those years, and an increasing proportion of the nobility and gentry was sent to schools and universities and thus came under the influence of the new learning.

During the second and third periods, the foundations were laid for the fourth, the age of Elizabeth. By that time, humanistic learning had become virtually a prerequisite for political and social advancement, and it was a basic constituent of the amazing literary creativeness of the age. Humanism achieved the same kind of social respectability that it had achieved in Italy; the Elizabethan court, in a late flowering of Renaissance life, consciously imitated the courts of Italy. The court drew much of its inspiration from the description of the life at the court of Urbino as given in Castiglione's *Courtier*, a work published in English translation at the beginning of Elizabeth's reign.[24] In taking up this fashion, in establishing close contacts with Italian civilization, the Elizabethans put the finishing touch to their social ideal. We shall later try to show why it cannot be maintained (as has been argued) that the supposedly "dark" period of the middle third of the century caused a complete break in the humanistic tradition in England, and that the Elizabethans had to make an entirely new start for which they relied on the example of Italy. The Italian example was indeed very stimulating, but it had such great effect precisely because the minds of the generation that

17

had grown up with Elizabeth had been prepared for it through the ideas of the older humanists.

One significant development will illustrate this point: A great crop of translations into English of the works of Greek, Latin, Italian, French, and other authors appeared during the first two decades of Elizabeth's reign.[25] These translations were the work of men who, for the most part, had been educated at the schools, universities, and Inns of Court during the preceding period. Generally, they were "gentlemen" who tried to obtain preferment by showing their learning. They translated a considerable portion of the available classical literature and many humanistic works into English—the outstanding examples are North's translation of Plutarch's *Lives* and Hoby's translation of the *Courtier*—and thus made them available to a wide circle of readers. It is due to the efforts of these translators and to the wide diffusion of humanistic learning through schools and universities that Elizabethan literature is so saturated with the classics. The pervasive influence of the classics is evident in works which range from the translations and English imitations of Seneca's tragedies to Shakespeare's Roman plays. The members of the ruling class that furnished Elizabeth's statesmen, courtiers, and administrators were inevitably and often deeply affected by the humanistic ideal— an ideal which found its artistic expression in the "heroic poems" of Spenser and Sidney, *The Faerie Queene* and the *Arcadia,* in Lyly's *Euphues,* in the speeches of Shakespeare's heroes in *Coriolanus* and *Troilus and Cressida.*

A remarkable change in the intellectual caliber of the English ruling class took place between the beginning and the end of the century, between what we described as the second and fourth periods in the development of English humanism. The postulates of Erasmus and his contemporaries, which had begun to be translated into reality during their lifetime, found widespread acceptance in the third period, in the time of Cheke and Ascham, and bore fruit in the Elizabethan age. Theory and practice were not static, but developed as they were implemented, as political, religious, and social changes took place, as new influences from the outside were felt and accepted. Yet, from beginning to end, there was the belief in an aristocracy made good and virtuous through knowledge, enabled to perform its task through education in the classics; and there was the firm faith in the superiority of an aristocratic order of society, which this group was enjoined to maintain over all other forms of social organization. Medieval ideas of chivalry and images of the

18

organic state were blended with these conceptions, but the emphasis had shifted from them to the classical inspiration.

Humanism became a vital force in England in the second period, when the generation of humanists under Henry VIII applied its knowledge to the evolution of a theory of society and to the problem of education. Weiss, who in his investigation of *Humanism in England during the Fifteenth Century* has amplified and corrected Schirmer's pioneering work on the first period,[26] comes to the conclusion that humanism did not establish a firm foothold in England until approximately the last quarter of the fifteenth century. He shows that during most of the fifteenth century humanism was a means rather than an end.[27] Only certain formal elements, such as the collecting of books, an improved Latin style, and, late in the century, the study of Greek, the art of writing polished letters and making elegant diplomatic speeches, were adopted by some more or less scattered and amateurish individuals in England who had studied in Italy or had come in contact with visiting Italian humanists. Such elements, Weiss argues, were taken into an essentially medieval intellectual and social framework in England, so that the humanistic forms still were at the service of a pervasive scholastic system. In contrast to their Italian contemporaries, the early English humanists—most of them churchmen—did not perceive any fundamental difference between scholasticism and humanism, and they did not adopt a humanistic philosophy. Weiss's characterization of Thomas Chaundler, who had been warden of New College since 1454, also vice-chancellor and chancellor of Oxford University, illustrates the character of much of the movement: "His efforts to give a humane character to some of his writings, and his use of neo-classical and ancient texts while pursuing typically scholastic studies, indicate clearly his conception of modern learning merely as a means by which the old learning could be improved. . . . If he encouraged classicism he did so in order to further the advancement of medieval rather than of Renaissance culture."[28] This, surely, cannot be compared with the beginnings of Italian humanism: early English humanism lacked the enthusiasm, the vital *élan* that animated the Italians in their search for a new view of the world. As yet, it was not connected with a re-evaluation of life, of theology, of society. It was in conformity with the character of this earlier development that the transition from the old to the new learning was gradual when it actually came—as it did in the theology and pedagogy of John Colet, for instance; that traditional theology and hu-

19

manistic learning continued to exist side by side, often in the same persons; that the break between the two was less radical in England than it had been in Italy or than it was depicted in that classic satire, Erasmus' *Praise of Folly*, which itself was written on English soil.

Early English humanism, on the whole, confined itself to a limited imitation of the classicism of the Italians, lacked their larger aesthetic and philosophical interests, and introduced very little of their pedagogy. Its importance should not, however, be underestimated. Patrons of learning like Humphrey, Duke of Gloucester, imported Italian humanists and their books: thus, Pier Candido Decembrio's Latin translation of Plato's *Republic*—a thorough revision of that made by Chrysoloras and his father, Uberto Decembrio—reached Humphrey in 1443,[29] and he asked (but did not pay) Leonardo Bruni for a translation of Aristotle's *Politics* which he also received.[30] Through Decembrio and others, he bought a large number of manuscripts of classical works, many of which had not been available in England at all or only in inadequate texts. During his lifetime, he gave more than two hundred and fifty such manuscripts to Oxford University, and he left more at his death.[31] Although this legacy may not have reached the university, what did reach it was of great importance in providing tools for the slow growth of the New Learning in the second half of the century up to the time when printed editions became available. Humphrey himself seems to have had a genuine interest in the classics, with Plato, Aristotle, and Plutarch among his favorites. His imitation of Italian princes in the patronage of scholars encouraged an interest in humanism. The activities of John Tiptoft, Earl of Worcester, were similar in character and importance. Tiptoft spent some time around 1460 at the "school"— really a part of the university—of Guarino da Verona at Ferrara.[32] Guarino's importance for the development of early English humanism was considerable since a number of Englishmen—such as William Grey, Robert Flemmyng, John Free, John Gunthorpe[33]—were pupils of this famous humanist whose teaching methods enjoyed an international reputation.

It is not our intention here to enter into an investigation of the streams and trickles by which humanistic learning reached England during the fifteenth century. We shall only briefly point to the main features and results: Italian and, later, Greek scholars came to England, while a number of Englishmen studied in Italy. Humanistic Latin was cultivated by a few persons, and some Greek began to be taught around 1470.[34] A number of the classical works preferred, rediscovered, or newly edited by Continental humanists were brought to England. No major scholarly or artistic work was produced. All this shows that some formal elements of humanism were introduced over a period of time, that the foundation was laid for later developments, but that the period itself was fairly barren. That there was some continuity between the humanism of this and the later period is evident; one example may serve to illustrate it. William Sellyng worked at Oxford under Chaundler, the warden of New College who has already been mentioned; he studied Greek in Bologna, where he stayed in 1466, and taught it at the monastery of Christ Church at Canterbury, whose prior he became in 1472.[35] Thomas Linacre is supposed to have been taught by Sellyng there, and to have accompanied him to Italy in 1487.[36] Linacre, in turn, was Thomas Elyot's teacher, if, as seems most likely, Elyot was referring to him when he stated that he had been taught by "a worshipful physician and one of the most renowned at that time in England."[37] This intellectual pedigree from Chaundler to Elyot cannot be established with absolute certainty, but is probably correct and typical of similar developments. A new stage can be noted in each new generation: first the rudiments of Latin humanism, then the beginnings of the study of Greek, followed by Linacre's close connection with Florentine and Venetian humanists, and finally Elyot's application of humanistic doctrine to the problems of education and society in his original and widely influential works.

One final observation about the character of early English humanism and its significance for the further development of that movement in England is in order here. The fact that, in its early stages, humanistic learning in England was largely subordinated to traditional theology, taken in conjunction with certain aspects of the later development of English humanism, has led W. F. Schirmer to postulate his thesis that English humanism was "pedagogic-theological" and thus very different from its Italian prototype. Schirmer sees in the particular quality of English humanism, which he thus tries to establish, its essential and typically English character; in his interpretation, the whole humanistic movement is a decisive step toward Puritanism, and traces of Puritanism are to be found in English humanism from its beginnings.[38] Such an interpretation would seem to involve an overextension of the term "Puritanism," both with regard to chronology and with regard to the kinds of attitudes it is made to cover. If the early English humanists did not become pagans, and if they accepted only some formal elements of humanism, they were not therefore pre-Puritans. If the later humanists generally remained Christians, they shared this religious attitude with most of their fellow-humanists in other northern countries, without becoming precursors of Milton in their religion. Schirmer's interpretation undervalues the truly humanistic elements in Henrician and Elizabethan thought and literature, with some of which we shall here be concerned. It is our contention that the generation of humanists under the first two Tudors, especially under Henry VIII, differed essentially from its predecessors, departed from their theological preoccupations, and made its humanism a vital force in England by applying its knowledge to the education of the leading men in the state, and to the evolution of a theory of society. This very emphasis was indeed pedagogical, but with a social and political rather than a religious or "puritanical" accent.

Our treatment of the growth of a humanistic theory of education and society is not intended to be all inclusive. It is selective, but the choice of subjects should prove representative of the major stages in the development of this doctrine. It has been thought best to treat separately each of the men whose thought is presented. Such a procedure should bring out the individuality of the man and of his contribution more clearly than would be possible in an analysis organized on the basis of a scheme of ideas and with little respect for the persons who produced them. The choice of Erasmus, More, Elyot, Starkey, Sidney, and Spenser as major representatives of humanistic doctrine does not imply that other men could not have been added to advantage. Our investigation stops short of Shakespeare, and it does not include all the relevant humanists who come within its chronological limits. It leaves out the constitutional lawyers and theorists, and with them some of the more strictly constitutional aspects of More's, Elyot's, and Starkey's work. It does, on the other hand, concern itself with the thought of Sidney and Spenser, to whom not enough special consideration has been given in this context. The inclusion of Erasmus in a treatment of English humanism needs no justification: he was personally very closely connected with, and in part responsible for, its first real growth, and his works had a lasting effect on later thought and practice. The omission of any detailed treatment of the classical sources and of the Italian antecedents—of Vittorino da Feltre and Guarino da Verona, of Patrizi and Castiglione—may be regretted, but it is caused by the decision to limit the scope of this discussion to the

English humanists as such, and to pay attention to the specific influences of the works of others on theirs only where this is particularly relevant.

A principle of selection and rigid limitation also applies to the presentation of introductory and connecting materials. Thus, we can here touch only briefly and by way of introduction to the following chapters on some of the major figures of what we have termed the second period of English humanism, on the men who were teachers and friends of Erasmus, More, and Elyot. We have already referred to Thomas Linacre as a kind of connecting link between the first and second periods of English humanism. With him, we have reached that great generation of English humanists which Seebohm has described as *The Oxford Reformers*.[39] A definitive account of that group, amplifying and correcting Seebohm's and other older works, and gathering the results of recent studies, still has to be written. We shall see how in the thought of Erasmus and of More a new emphasis on educational and social problems arose, an emphasis destined to remain a characteristic preoccupation of their English followers. This interest is not yet so evident in their seniors and contemporaries, in Linacre, Grocyn, Latimer, and Colet, in whom humanism found its first great representative scholars and thinkers in England.

According to Leland, Thomas Linacre was introduced in Italy by his teacher Sellyng to Politian,[40] who in turn introduced him to Lorenzo de' Medici. Lorenzo permitted him to share the Greek instruction given by Chalkondylas to his sons Piero and Giovanni. A letter written much later (in 1521) by Linacre to Giovanni Medici, who by that time had become Pope Leo X, supports this assumption, since he there alludes to having been Giovanni's companion in playing games.[41] Linacre thus entered into the group which was at the center of Italian humanism, and which had done most to revive the Platonic philosophy. After a sojourn in Rome in 1490 and 1491,[42] he became a member of Aldus' Neacademia in Venice and translated the *Sphaera* of Proclus from Greek into Latin. He may also have participated in the Aldine edition of the works of Aristotle.[43] In 1496, he took his degree in medicine in Padua.[44] After his return to England, he was made tutor to the young Prince Arthur and became court physician. His later scholarly works included translations of some works of Aristotle and of the medical works of Galen into Latin. (His pupil Elyot was to take up this latter interest as a sideline, and to popularize Galen further by partly translating

23

him into English.) Linacre thus was one of the first Englishmen to master the Greek language, and to make serious use of this knowledge. He could measure up to the Italian humanists in the thoroughness of his learning and in the universality of his interests; he was proficient both in the literary and philosophical disciplines and in the natural sciences.[45] His presence at court presumably stimulated the interest in the New Learning there. He was More's "studiorum praeceptor" in 1504,[46] and his influence on this student must have been profound. While he worked with Linacre, More translated the *Life* of Pico della Mirandola, written by Pico's nephew, into English.[47] The interest in the Neoplatonic philosopher may well have been aroused in him by his teacher, who represented a direct link with the circle in which Pico had lived; More's other mentors, Grocyn and Colet, may also have shared responsibility for this predilection.

Like Linacre, William Grocyn (born 1442)[48] is reputed to have worked under Politian and Chalkondylas in Florence. Linacre had been a fellow of All Souls, Grocyn of New College (under Chaundler) and Magdalen, after going to school at Winchester. It seems that Grocyn had learned some Greek at Oxford before he went to Italy in 1488—not, as Seebohm and others assume, from Vitelli, but probably from Emanuel or Serbopoulos,[49] two Greeks whose presence in England in the 1470's Weiss has established. During his three years in Italy, his knowledge of Greek may have improved sufficiently to permit him to lecture on it after his return to Oxford in 1491.[50] He thus appears to have been the first English scholar to have taught Greek at an English university. Erasmus and Linacre provide us with brief accounts of him, but since almost nothing from his pen is preserved,[51] the direction of his thought and the extent of his influence cannot be definitely established. It is worth noting, however, that he made his pilgrimage to the land of humanism when he was close to forty years of age. Like almost all the other "Oxford Reformers," he did not stay long at his university but went to London after some years.

William Latimer, another member of this group and like Linacre a fellow of All Souls, was in Italy during approximately the same years as Linacre; he too returned to England an accomplished humanist, with a knowledge of Greek. He was a renowned scholar in his day, but his stature too is difficult to assess since he did not commit his thoughts to paper. He is interesting to us mainly because he was the tutor of Reginald Pole at Magdalen around 1513;[52] it seems

24

most likely that Pole's later travel companion, Thomas Starkey, who went to the same college at about the same time, also benefited from his instruction. It is not improbable that Pole's and Starkey's humanistic interests were first aroused by this teacher, and that the strong Platonic strain in Starkey's thought had its origin in this source.

We know more about John Colet (1467–1519) than about Grocyn or Latimer, since many of his writings and lectures have come down to us; his interests and attitudes are reflected in the statutes of St. Paul's School, which he established, and in Erasmus' extensive account of him.[53] Like the other members of his group, he went to Oxford and then to Italy, where he spent the years from 1493 (?) to 1496; he probably was in Rome in 1494[54] and did not go to Florence until 1495, if he went there at all.[55] Pico and Politian had died in the preceding year, and it thus is most unlikely that (as has been asserted) he met these men and came under Pico's influence; there is also no proof for Seebohm's assumption that he met Ficino and Savonarola, although he later frequently quoted Ficino in his works. Unlike the other members of his group, he did not come back to England with much knowledge of Greek, and his interests remained predominantly theological. Erasmus, who heard and met Colet at Oxford in 1499, testifies that his lectures attracted great attention. He later lectured in London, where he, the son of a wealthy London citizen and former lord mayor, became dean of St. Paul's, in 1505. Among his lectures are expositions of St. Paul's Epistle to the Romans, and of his first Epistle to the Corinthians. In contrast to the prevailing allegorical interpretation of the Scriptures, he emphasized their literal and spiritual meaning. He was clearly influenced in his approach by Neoplatonism and mysticism, most notably so in the two treatises on the *Hierarchies of Dionysius*.[56] There are frequent quotations from Plato, Plotinus, Cicero, Origen, Pico, and long passages from Ficino's *Theologia Platonica* in his works,[57] which indicate that the Platonic tradition, particularly its religious side, played a considerable part in his thought.[58] Colet's discussions with Erasmus were instrumental in turning Erasmus' interests and energies toward what became a major part of his life's work, the restoration and interpretation of the texts of the New Testament and of many of the Church Fathers. In 1504, young More described Colet as his *vitae magister*,[59] i.e., his confessor, and Colet's guidance must have been very important for him at that time when he was debating whether to take holy orders. There are, however, as we shall later discuss in more detail, very considerable differences in the thought and development of Colet on the one hand and Erasmus and More on the other. Colet's interest remained primarily theological,[60] whereas Erasmus and More were at least as interested in the *bonae litterae* as in theology. (For More, this interest probably predominated during the middle, the "Erasmian," period of his development in which he produced the *Utopia;* toward the end of his life theological issues again preoccupied him.) Colet was skeptical of the value of pagan authors, and apparently incorporated them with some hesitation and only to a limited degree in the curriculum of St. Paul's. Despite its inclusion of such authors and its indebtedness to humanistic principles, Colet's plan of education placed greater stress on Christian values, and was on the whole less humanistic in character, than the plan advocated by Elyot some years later, or the curricula adopted in other English schools in the following decades. Still, the establishment of a school which was much indebted to Erasmus' advice, and the choice of William Lily, an accomplished Greek and Latin scholar, for its high mastership, provided a definite starting point for the introduction of humanistic training in other institutions on the grammar-school level, and gave considerable encouragement to humanistic studies.

What the establishment of this school meant to the cause of humanism can be gathered from Richard Pace's *De Fructu qui ex doctrina percipitur,* an important treatise on education which he dedicated to Colet. Pace was the King's secretary, Colet's, More's, and Erasmus' friend, and formerly a student at Padua and Oxford. He extols Colet for establishing and maintaining the school, Lily for being a splendid living example to his students and for introducing "politiorem latinitatem, atque ipsam Romanam linguam, in Britanniam nostram. . . ."[61] The lively advice he gives to the schoolboys of St. Paul's on the content and purpose of their studies not only shows Pace's strong humanistic convictions but also his belief that his ideals were being realized at St. Paul's.

Colet's and Erasmus' attitudes certainly differed, and the former's preoccupation with faith and theology may be contrasted with the latter's more rational humanism. This difference is real and important, but it is overstressed by Hyma when he describes Colet as the true Christian humanist and forerunner of Luther and contrasts him with Erasmus, whom he classes with more or less pagan rationalists like Valla and Voltaire.[62] It should be remembered that Erasmus combined a simple Christian piety with his humanism, and that he wrote devotional works to foster such piety in others. Nevertheless, it is true that there was considerable divergence between the views not only of Colet and Erasmus but also between those of Colet and other Englishmen like Linacre and More.

Seebohm's picture of the Oxford Reformers, the happy little band of scholars, working hand in hand to promote the New Learning and through it a reform of religion and the Church is too undifferentiated to do justice to the various individualities and aims of its members. If in some respects Colet still resembled the fifteenth-century humanists who subordinated their learning to theological ends, several of his contemporaries no longer shared this orientation. With Colet's friends Erasmus and More, both of whom were much less reserved than he in their appreciation of pagan authors, humanism in England assumed a new dimension. It turned its major attention to social and political problems, and began to emphasize education in relation to these problems. The generation of humanists under Henry VIII made its major contribution by applying its knowledge to the education of the leading men in the state and to the development of a theory of society. It was to take another half-century before the aesthetic and artistic elements of humanism came to full fruition in the England of Elizabeth.

# II

# Erasmus

Erasmus was almost thirty years old when he first visited England in 1499.[1] He paid at least five other visits to that country during the next eighteen years, extending one of them for nearly five years, from October, 1509 to July, 1514.[2] From the beginning, he was kindly received there, and from 1512 to the end of his life in 1536, an English parish provided him with a dependable source of income.[3] Earlier than elsewhere, his genius found appreciation in England, and this appreciation has continued into the present century which has seen P. S. Allen's monumental publication at Oxford of the eleven volumes of Erasmus' correspondence.[4] The great Dutchman received much from England, and gave much in return. Almost from the moment he arrived in England, he occupied a prominent position in the small circle of English humanists.[5] Deep and lasting friendships developed between him and John Colet[6] and Thomas More; his accounts of their lives and characters are vivid testimonials of the spirit which animated the relationships between them.[7] Colet's foundation of St. Paul's School in London was greatly indebted to Erasmian advice. More's *Utopia*, the greatest literary monument of early English humanism, is in large measure the fruit of his friendship with Erasmus. Through these and similar personal relationships with Grocyn, Linacre, Lily, Lupset, and others, and through his works, Erasmus exerted a very great influence in England on education and political thought as well as on religion and literature.[8] His close connection with Englishmen and the lasting influence of his works in England justify the inclusion of Erasmus in an account of humanistic political thought in that country. The difference between Erasmus' cosmopolitan idealism and his friends' and successors' practical adaptation of it to the demands and needs of England should serve to give clearer contour to the individual character and development of English humanism.

The story of Erasmus' first visit to England, which lasted from

June, 1499 to January, 1500,[9] of his meetings with such men as More and Colet, of his subsequent visits and of their joint activities, has often been told. Erasmus came to England from Paris, where he was a student of theology, and where he had already developed a definite interest in humanistic studies. Lord Mountjoy, one of the students he was tutoring there, invited him to come across the Channel and introduced him into some of the first houses of the realm—houses of ecclesiastical dignitaries and wealthy London citizens, country houses of the nobility, and even the royal court. For the first time in his life, Erasmus was accepted by the wealthy and powerful and moved freely among them, and it was here that he began to transform himself from a studious, poor Dutch monk into the urbane humanist with a definite taste for the agreeable aspects of a more affluent life. If "he was thoroughly in sympathy . . . with the highly aristocratic tendency of the Renaissance," as one of his best biographers states,[10] it is reasonable to assume that he acquired this attitude not only from the books of the Greeks and Romans and his fellow-humanists, but also from his experiences in England, where he was fortunate in coming into contact with many of those members of the London citizenry, of the Church, and of the aristocracy who combined wealth and power with love of classical learning.

Shortly after his arrival in England, Erasmus met Thomas More. Despite the difference in age—More was over eight years younger than Erasmus[11]—they immediately became friends. More soon took Erasmus to Eltham Palace to meet the royal children, among them Prince Henry, later Henry VIII, then eight years old.[12] When Erasmus went to Oxford in the autumn of 1499, he kept in touch with his new friend by correspondence,[13] a habit which they continued during the rest of their lives. At Oxford, Erasmus first met John Colet. Colet, of approximately the same age as Erasmus,[14] had been to Italy, where he had come in contact with the Neoplatonists, and had already made a name for himself by his lectures on the Epistles of St. Paul which, according to Erasmus' testimony, were attended by a large and distinguished audience.[15] Colet's method of exposition and his unusual approach to theology as well as his personality attracted Erasmus, and there immediately began a lively interchange of ideas between the two men, both in writing and in conversation. It has often been claimed that the friendship with Colet decided the course of Erasmus' intellectual development,[16] that under its impact the light-hearted humanistic *poeta* changed into the serious scholar who began to see that his lifework lay in the interpretation, not only of the works of pagan antiquity, but particularly of the sources of Christian thought, in the editions of the New Testament and of the Church Fathers which he undertook in the ensuing decades. How much of this development was due to Colet's influence, and how much to that of Valla, and what, on the other hand, Erasmus' friendship meant for Colet, has not been definitely established. Intimately connected with these questions is the problem of how important for Erasmus' whole outlook was the *devotio moderna,* the practical imitation of Christ that he imbibed from his early teachers, the Brethren of the Common Life,[17] as compared with the teaching of a man like Colet. What were the factors that determined his interpretation of Christian teachings? The influence of Neoplatonic philosophy has usually been stressed in that connection, but it offers only a partial explanation, since Colet's thought is more definitely Christian than is that of the Italian Neoplatonists.[18]

If *pietas* was the more characteristic element of Colet's attitude and *humanitas* appears to prevail in Erasmus' thought, this difference in emphasis should not cause us to forget that both did, up to a point, share the ideals of piety and humanity, and that this common ground made their lifelong friendship significant and fruitful.

Erasmus was impressed with the atmosphere at Oxford. He described fully a dinner there, in writing to a friend, and he compared the group that was present, and which included Colet, to an "Academy."[19] On another occasion, he likened Colet to Plato and, incidentally, gave a vivid account of the impression England and his new friends there had made on him:

> ... I never liked anything so much before.... I have met with so much civility [*humanitatis*], and so much learning, not hackneyed and trivial, but deep, accurate, ancient, Latin and Greek, that but for curiosity I do not now much care whether I see Italy. When I hear my Colet I seem to be listening to Plato himself. In Grocyn, who does not marvel at such a perfect world of learning? What can be more acute, profound, and delicate than the judgment of Linacre? What has nature ever created more gentle, sweet, or happy than the genius of Thomas More? ... It is marvellous how widespread and how abundant is the harvest of ancient learning which is flourishing in this country. ... .[20]

Even if we make allowance for the humanist's usual exaggeration, this praise has the ring of sincerity and fairly represents Erasmus' reactions at the close of his first visit to England. Despite his claim that there no longer was any real need for him to go to Italy, he did spend three years there, from 1506 to 1509. Before that, however, he devoted himself to an intensive study of Greek and paid another visit to England in 1505–6 during which he and Thomas More translated some of Lucian's *Dialogues* into Latin.[21] Thomas More had, meanwhile, also learned Greek, apparently from Grocyn and Linacre, and become interested in Neoplatonism, the *Life* of one of whose main exponents, Pico della Mirandola, he translated around 1505 from the account given by Pico's nephew Gianfrancesco.[22] The lively contact that was maintained among the group of English humanists whom Erasmus had met during his first English visit, and who all came to live in London, is illustrated by a letter written by More to Colet in October, 1504: "Meantime, I pass my time with Grocyn, who is, as you know, in your absence the guide of my life, with Linacre, the guide of my studies, and with our friend Lily, my dearest friend."[23] With William Lily, who was later to be appointed High Master of St. Paul's School by Colet, More was translating epigrams from Greek into Latin.[24]

Erasmus' most extended visit to England began under happy auspices. Mountjoy, who had first brought him to England, wrote to Erasmus, who was then in Rome, that with the accession of Henry VIII to the throne (April 23, 1509) "heaven laughs and the earth rejoices." He held out high hopes of royal patronage, claiming that Henry would say: "Accept our wealth and be our greatest sage."[25] This invitation, which implied the dawn of a golden age of letters, coupled with the invitation of Warham, the Archbishop of Canterbury,[26] brought Erasmus back to England in the autumn of 1509. He first stayed with Thomas More, whom he had once called "the sweetest of all my friends, with whom I am always pleased to join in any employment grave or gay."[27] The first task in which he engaged was indeed gay: he wrote what proved to be his most lastingly popular work, the *Moria* or *Moriae Encomium*, the *Praise of Folly*, whose title was clearly a pun on More's name. Part of the next one and a half years he lived in More's house. In the summer of 1511, he was made lecturer in Greek at Cambridge through the intervention of John Fisher, bishop of Rochester and chancellor of the university, and later that year he was appointed Professor of Divinity.[28] Altogether, he spent over two years at Cambridge. During this time, he received the living of Aldington in Kent from Archbishop Warham which was later transformed into a pension that was paid for the rest of his life.[29] (It may have been at this period that he and John Colet went on a pilgrimage to the shrine of St. Thomas at Canterbury; his amusing account of it in the *Colloquies* is full of their sarcasm about the relics they were shown and expected to venerate.)[30] Although Erasmus was well treated by his patrons, the royal appointment for which Mountjoy had held out such hopes was not forthcoming, and he left England in 1514, after almost five years there, to return again for three visits in each of the following years. During all these years, he certainly was frequently Thomas More's guest, as for instance in July, 1516,[31] and he later compared More's house to Plato's Academy.[32] During this latter visit, More was finishing his *Utopia,* begun in the preceding year in Flanders,[33] and there can be no doubt that Erasmus took great interest in the work. More sent the manuscript to him for correction on September 3, 1516,[34] and the book appeared at Antwerp, with Erasmus' annotations, in December, 1516. Earlier in the same year, Erasmus had finished his own *Institutio Principis Christiani.*[35] The completion of these two works of humanistic political thought and, in addition, the publication of Erasmus' Greek and Latin New Testament in 1516 have caused More's foremost biographer to call this "The Wonderful Year of Erasmian Reform."[36]

The *Utopia* and the *Institutio,* published in the same year, appear like the end products of the period of closest association between More and Erasmus which had begun seventeen years earlier. In their similarity, they show the mutual indebtedness of the two friends;[37] in their differences, they testify to the diversity of their characters, experiences, and positions in life. Erasmus' work is written for a concrete situation in that it addresses itself to a young ruler to whom he tries to show his duties and functions; More, on the other hand, constructs an imaginary ideal society on the Island of Nowhere where he is free to disregard all the institutions and conditions existing in the Europe of his day and to create a radically new scheme of things. Nevertheless, despite the very different settings of their works, both authors are concerned with showing the need for the humanistic education of rulers; both are convinced that the well-being of their respective societies depends on the successful inculcation of humanistic knowledge and ethics into the minds of princes and aristocracy.

Erasmus actively contributed to the practical implementation of his ideas on humanistic education in England. The humanistic reforms introduced in Cambridge by his friend John Fisher after 1505 show Erasmus' influence.[38] We have already noted that Erasmus himself was later brought to Cambridge to strengthen the cause of the new learning there. The founding in 1516 of Corpus Christi College, Oxford, by Bishop Richard Fox, with his introduction of a radically humanistic curriculum that led to the quarrel between the "Greeks" and the conservative "Trojans," and Wolsey's similar grandiose activities, received Erasmus' warm praises. While in these cases his influence was less direct, he wrote to Wolsey of his satisfaction that "good letters are triumphing in England."[39] He aided his friend Colet in the establishment of the curriculum of St. Paul's School, London. Colet used Erasmus' works, in part written specifically for this purpose, such as his description of a course of studies, the *De Ratione Studii*, published in 1512, *De Duplici Copia Verborum ac Rerum*, a work on composition, and his poem, *Institutum Christiani Hominis*. In his statutes for the school, Colet mentions specifically that the *Copia* and the *Institutum* are to be read by its pupils.[40] Furthermore, Erasmus certainly had a hand in the composition of at least part of Lily's grammatical works that were written for St. Paul's and later used for centuries in all English schools in the combination known as "Lily's Grammar." From St. Paul's, Erasmus' writings passed into the curricula of many other schools in sixteenth-century England. Thus, pupils at Canterbury Cathedral Grammar School were required to study the *Copia* after the school was refounded in 1541, and those at Westminster were entertained by Erasmus' *Colloquia*, according to that school's statutes of 1560.[41] Virtually all English sixteenth-century works on pedagogy were to advocate the reading of these and other works of Erasmus.[41a] If the plan of studies at St. Paul's, and later elsewhere, emphasized Latin and Greek literature, this humanistic orientation was in no small measure due to the work of Erasmus.

After this brief indication of Erasmus' influence in England, we must turn to an analysis of his ideas on politics and education and the relation he established between them. Our investigation will be based partly on the *Institutio Principis Christiani*, and we shall also draw on other works, including his earlier *Enchiridion Militis Christiani*.[42]

Erasmus was a Christian humanist, a liberal rationalist, an individualistic cosmopolitan. He meant to lead humanity toward a peaceful and harmonious order of the world based on Christ's principle of brotherly love. His lack of clarity and consistency in practical matters and a certain vagueness with regard to actual aims made it difficult to follow him. Unlike his friend Thomas More, Erasmus was not a lawyer, and he had little understanding of, or interest in, the legal framework of states. He was mainly concerned with the ethics that should underlie the conduct of individuals and societies, and much less with the practical details, with the legal provisions and the constitutional framework needed to translate ethical postulates into political practice.[43]

In various places and at different times, Erasmus advanced opinions on such matters as the ideal Christian world, the perfect state, the kind of man that was to embody that perfection and to make it a living reality, the education necessary to create this ideal type. These elements of Erasmus' thought have been the subject of much discussion, but the basic unity of purpose in his thought has not perhaps been sufficiently recognized.[44] His humanism is not limited in its functions to the field of education but tries to encompass the whole organism of human society, which it seeks to mold into a better and more harmonious shape. Whatever shortcomings his conception may have should be seen in their proper perspective, as blemishes and imperfections of the larger picture Erasmus had in mind. While he was not a systematic philosopher and created no system comparable in completeness to Plato's *Republic*, he must himself have felt his ideas to be interdependent and complementary—to form a whole. The functions he assigned to a militant humanism in education, national government, and international relations were conceived as similar means in different fields leading to the same end. Certain basic contradictions between the Christian and the pagan worlds were glossed over rather than resolved in both his aim and his methods. This burdens his argument. A further difficulty, as we have noted, is his lack of concern with the forms of actual social and political organization, and at the same time an overestimation of the efficacy of education. These factors explain the practical limitations of his influence, but they do not detract from the greatness of his vision.

Erasmus hoped that the education of all individuals, especially of princes and nobles, in the spirit and disciplines of antiquity and Christianity would bring the rational element in them to full fruition. *Ratio*, reason, was, in his mind, almost synonymous with "goodness" and "kindness." The rule of reason, achieved through education, would therefore result in men's living together in universal peace and harmony in accord with the lessons of Christ's Sermon on the Mount. This briefly was what Erasmus envisaged. Spirit, virtue, reason were important to him, more important than outward forms. The latter, he was confident, would evolve logically from the former. It was perhaps due to this attitude that Erasmus was frequently vague and sometimes contradictory when he came to positive suggestions for the organization of society. The core of Erasmus' interest was the individual, and his image of man as expressed in his ideas on education must therefore be our first concern. Society and state, their national and international organization, are secondary to this central theme. Erasmus seems to test the institutions of communal life by asking whether they enable man to grow and exist in accordance with his humanistic ideal. Organized forms of human life, such as states, are not seen as ends in themselves, but are always subordinated to the needs of the individual, as postulated by the humanist.

Like most humanists, Erasmus was most optimistic concerning the educability of man. He goes so far as to say that "homines non nascuntur, sed finguntur,"[45] that men are shaped by education rather than by birth. Like many of his dicta, this phrase should not be taken too literally; it is, however, indicative of his general emphasis. He obviously does not attach much importance to hereditary or other natural differences between men. Such differences can presumably be overcome by education, which in his opinion is so potent a force as to "overcome everything"[46] and to form the individual completely.[47] The power of education is based on the highly formative effect which Erasmus attributes to *ratio* in man. It is possible for man to follow reason, after the right kind of education has enabled him to recognize it. Once he sees its light, he will make it his guiding principle and become good by following it.

Since all men are endowed with liberty of will by their Creator,[48] according to the stand taken by Erasmus in his famous controversy with Luther, there can be no natural badness that will not yield to the force of reason. It must therefore be the aim of a Christian society to educate its members in accordance with reason and, through this process of education, to achieve universal goodness. This in itself would solve all the problems of the political organization of mankind, which to him were "merely a matter of personal morality and intellectual enlightenment."[49] A recent critic remarks that with his "enunciation of the creed of education and perfectibility, of warm social feeling and of faith in human nature, of peaceful kindliness and toleration," Erasmus was a precursor of the eighteenth century.[50] He probably would have been happier in the enlightened and tolerant atmosphere of that period than he was in his age of violent religious convictions. It is interesting to note that the most complete edition of his works, which remains the standard one to this day, was printed in the eighteenth century.

The predominance which Erasmus usually assigns to reason over nature, to rational education over characteristics inherited at birth, and the emphasis he places on the power of the spirit to form men, are obviously exaggerated and frequently betray a typical neglect of natural factors. Human nature in its perplexing and often crude variety seems to have appalled him so much that he often refused to face it, even though he was able to describe it most vividly, with all its faults and follies, in works like the *Praise of Folly*. On the whole, he preferred to take refuge in his vision of a purely rational and, therefore, good man, which he opposed to the unpleasant reality.

The central position reason assumed in the work of Erasmus reflects the preponderant role it played in his own life and thought. His scholarly, detached, and noncommittal attitude restricted his practical effectiveness: it is not an unfair criticism to say that his conceptions of man, society, and the state, admirable as they are in their burning idealism, often seem lifeless because, while they have much *esprit*, they lack body. It is, of course, a moot question whether he should have been more "realistic," or whether instead of accusing him we would not be more justified in blaming mankind for being selfish, crude, vulgar, violent, and therefore unable to live up to his ideas. This question is already raised in Plato's problem of how to make reluctant philosophers consent to be kings. Erasmus, in his own practice, decided that philosophers should be philosophers rather than spoil their ideas and soil their hands by being kings or their helpers. While thus keeping himself pure, he advised rulers to turn to philosophy.

Despite his abstract tendencies Erasmus can be very lively and practical. Nevertheless, the general impression of idealistic detachment prevails. His humanistic friends and followers, pursuing more limited aims, evolved more practical systems of education and society; but they depended for their conceptions on Erasmus' superior vision. They adapted his ideas to their own specific purposes. Erasmus also furnished them with an enormous collection of practical tools for transmitting classical erudition. He was a mentor of teachers rather than a teacher himself.

The humanism of Erasmus was diametrically opposed to the doctrine enunciated by his contemporary, Machiavelli, in *The Prince*. That doctrine of realistic and ruthless power politics, which made

Machiavelli famous, undoubtedly shows only an isolated aspect of his thought,[51] but it was his fate that his name should become virtually synonymous with the practices he advocated in *The Prince*, with the attitude of cynical realism which permeates that particular work. It is unlikely that Erasmus could have known *The Prince* when he published the *Institutio Principis Christiani*. *The Prince* had then just been written but was not available in printed form;[52] yet some of Erasmus' remarks sound as if they had been written in flat contradiction of certain tenets of the Florentine. The explanation is very simple. Machiavelli in *The Prince* described objectively and reduced to a rational system the political practices of the *condottieri* and princes of his day, whereas Erasmus attacked these very practices from an ethical point of view. It is not surprising then that the two works, the *Institutio* and *The Prince*, should seem like two opposite poles. *The Prince*, when taken by itself as it usually was, and not in conjunction with Machiavelli's other works, reveals a basic ethical antagonism between Machiavelli and Erasmus. The author of *The Prince* takes a cynical view of human nature; his premise is the badness of man. Erasmus, despite skeptical moments and utterances, generally holds to the premise that man is or can be made good. The *raison d'état* of Machiavelli's disciples and the moral humanism of Erasmus and his followers derive logically from these opposite convictions.

The key to Erasmus' position is his ideal of humanity. As Pfeiffer has shown, it is based on the classical Roman conception of *humanitas*.[53] In this *humanitas*, Greek ideas had been harmoniously blended with the traditions of conduct of the Roman aristocracy. Romans of the classical period held to the conviction that education based on the *litterae* leads to *virtus*, to *morum integritas*. This pagan ideal could not be entirely acceptable and complete for the Christian Erasmus, yet he regarded it as the only comprehensive system of human erudition. He did not consider scholasticism to have provided such a system, nor did he believe that Christian education necessarily had to follow scholastic lines. He was convinced, on the other hand, that Roman humanism contained nothing alien to Christianity, but that the two elements formed an organic unity—both as regards their historical growth and the way in which they complement each other systematically. Only with the aid of classical *humanitas* had Christianity originally been spread, for according to Erasmus it was the synthesis of ancient wisdom with the new creed into the *philosophia*

*Christi,*[54] as achieved by Fathers of the Church like St. Jerome and Origen, which won the battle for Christianity.

Erasmus clearly saw the crisis through which Christianity was going in his own time. He insisted that only the aid of *humanitas* could save Christian civilization. Thus Erasmus conceived it as his lifelong task to reconcile and tie together the *sacrae* and the *humanae litterae*. It was his conviction that humanistic studies must of necessity lead to Christian *pietas*, just as ancient philosophy led to the Christian religion and was crowned by the gospel. In Erasmus' reasoning, *paideia* would revive *pistis;* the combined study of both would result in *pietas litterata*, the Christian and therefore highest form of *humanitas*. To achieve such perfection lies within the free will of man, and is his task in this world. The purpose of human society must be to assimilate the world to the divine as closely as it is within man's mortal powers to do so. In this manner, Erasmus Christianized classical erudition and at the same time humanized Christian education. He transformed Christian *humilitas* into Christian *humanitas*.[55]

In arriving at this conception of Christian *humanitas*, Erasmus assumed that the pagan writers of antiquity had contributed to its growth, and that there was nothing unalterably opposed to Christianity in their writings. It was the task of the Christian humanist, as he conceived it, to find the philologically exact meaning of their writings and of the Bible, to interpret them accurately, and to derive from them the true philosophy of Christ, first by rational means and then, if these proved insufficient in the case of the Bible, by inspired intuition and faith. This method had two consequences: (1) his "Christian philosophy" contained many truly pagan elements and was not much concerned with questions of Christian doctrine, such as the problems of the Trinity and of transubstantiation; (2) philological discrimination and rational understanding ultimately became more important than repentance and prayer. Even though he advocated that the gospel be made available to all in the vernacular so that they might read and understand it, the learned man appears to take a higher place in Erasmus' hierarchy, and to approach God more closely, than the humble man, the poor in spirit. In his philosophy, the degree of knowledge determines man's position: he who knows most approximates the divine most closely.

This Erasmian stand was powerfully challenged by Luther. For Luther, the only way to God is through devotion and prayer, through the invocation of His grace, and Erasmus seems to him to rely too much on human judgment, too little on grace. Trust in mere human knowledge, unaided by grace, can but lead to sinful pride, to eternal perdition; only through God's grace can man find salvation, and that salvation can probably be attained by the poor in spirit more easily than by conceited philologists. *Humanitas*, the perfection of human nature as such, which Erasmus advocates, has no place in Luther's theology. It must have appeared to him like wicked temerity, like sheer *superbia*. Believing in inspiration and guidance, Luther detested Erasmus' rationalism. Where Luther was convinced of the utter helplessness of the human creature, Erasmus believed in the perfectibility of man by his own effort. He came close to paganism when he exclaimed that in our efforts to reach the limits of humanity and approximate God we should imitate Prometheus[56]—the greatest symbol of man's rebellious ambition and pride!

Such pagan statements are not the rule with Erasmus, however, even if on another occasion he does invoke "Saint Socrates" to pray for us.[57] He usually reiterates the more conservative opinion that Christ alone is to be imitated in every respect[58] as the absolute example of all virtue and wisdom, the ultimate goal of all education.[59] In a very real and personal sense, Christ as a human figure embodied Erasmus' ideals. The study of the gospels is to lead to the imitation of His life, to the practice of His teachings. He is seen, not through the haze of scholastic doctrine but in an unbroken light, as the eternal living example of goodness, kindness, and charity. The early Christians and St. Francis beheld a similar image.

It was to show his fellow-men how to educate themselves and their children and students, how to model their lives according to this prototype, that Erasmus wrote such works as the *Enchiridion Militis Christiani* (1501–3) and the *Institutio Principis Christiani*. The law for the education and behavior of Christian princes and noblemen as well as the moral principles which they are to follow are laid down in these works. The *Enchiridion*, in particular, stresses that, above all, they are to imitate Christ, and in that emphasis it reflects more strongly than the later *Institutio* the tradition of the Brethren of the Common Life. Whoever is of noble stock, he states in the *Enchiridion*, will increase his honor if his manners are worthy of Christ, if he reads and follows the gospel.[60] Education is to produce an aristocracy[61] which is superior to that of the states of pagan antiquity on account of its Christian faith.

Among the writings which form the basis of his educational scheme, Erasmus includes some biblical and patristic texts, but he later places his emphasis increasingly on the classics. Plutarch, Aristotle's *Politics*, Cicero's *De Officiis* should be studied; "sed sanctius his de rebus locutus est Plato."[62] Plato is his favorite philosopher, and Plato's influence on Erasmus' work is evident everywhere. He and after him the other classical authors were the *"fontes"* of knowledge for Erasmus.[63] They are not to be read by the young merely as intellectual and philological exercises: it is their ethical content to which Erasmus attaches the greatest importance. This is to inspire and transform the student so that he may become capable and worthy of his function as a *miles Christianus*. It is his task to fill a high position in the state and there to employ to the common benefit rather than to keep to himself what he has learned.[64] Erasmus thus hoped to fashion the humanistic Christian nobleman who in every respect distinguishes himself honorably from those below him in the social scale, and who gives an example of Christian life to those in his charge.[65] Rulers and nobility must be reformed in order to be justified in occupying their elevated positions. In Erasmus' view the transformation of these greedy, rapacious, and violent groups should be brought about by Christian humanism.[66]

Erasmus failed, however, to solve one important problem inherent in his conception of *humanitas Christiana*. Since Christ above all others is to be the ruler's prototype, the question arises to what extent His life can be the guiding example for a man who has to exercise worldly power. Christ, unlike the worldly ruler, did not have to command and punish and use force. Erasmus tries to solve this dilemma in the traditional manner: spiritual authority is exercised by the clergy, secular authority by the princes who protect good men and frighten bad ones, paralleling the efforts of the Church.[67] This does not answer the question how a ruler is to act in situations for which the life of Christ provides no examples. Erasmus says that the Christian ruler should follow the example of Christ and, with important limitations and exceptions, the precepts contained in the literatures of Greece and Rome, and the examples of certain classical figures. This can only be considered a superficial solution of the problem since it glosses over the antinomies between the teachings of classical antiquity and Christianity without basically reconciling this.[68] In this, Erasmus reveals the dualism that has run through the history of Western civilization since the end of antiquity, a dualism that neither he nor any of the other "Christian humanists" could overcome. We also see this inherent paradox when, on the one hand, Erasmus calls Socrates a "Saint," states that "with slight qualifications the whole of attainable knowledge lies enclosed within the literary monuments of ancient Greece,"[69] affirms that a man becomes educated by reading these and some Roman authors; and yet, on the other hand, declares that Christ should be man's guide and example.

An amalgamation of the two attitudes had been attempted by the scholastic philosophers who adopted an inexact and Christianized version of antiquity. As a humanist, Erasmus saw classical life and thought more accurately than his scholastic predecessors.[70] He had better and fuller texts of Greek and Roman works and of the Bible at his disposal. This made contradictions more evident and their solution more difficult. While not neglecting Aristotle, Erasmus, like other humanists, shifted his emphasis to Plato. The combination of classical and Christian elements thus had to be effected on a new plane in line with the efforts of the Neoplatonists. The form in which it was achieved by Erasmus was not a complete fusion of the two elements; as we have noted, many unresolved divergences reveal that his *humanitas Christiana* does not present an entirely harmonious synthesis of the two systems.[71] Sometimes, as in the *Praise of Folly*, one has the feeling that he saw the thinly veiled dichotomy that runs through his humanism and is apparent in his injunctions. It comes out most strikingly in the moving description of "Christian folly" at the end of that work.

Even if we take into consideration the various tutoring jobs of Erasmus' earlier days and his university lectures, the actual education of men according to his ideal played only a subordinate part in his life. He was much more interested in the theoretical exposition of the methods of pedagogy than in actual teaching.[72] He laid down practical and detailed rules for the training of children in the classical languages and literatures in *De Ratione Studii* (which he sent to his friend Colet), and therein established a concrete curriculum of humanistic studies for the young.[73] In his later treatise, *De pueris statim ac liberaliter instituendis,* he advocates a very liberal, humane, almost "progressive" method of instruction. He provides young pupils with a book of exercises, *De copia verborum,* and directs them to other treatises on pure Latin such as Valla's *Elegantiae.*[74] He teaches everybody how to write letters by innumerable epistles that were immediately reproduced by the printing press, and in his work, *De conscribendis epistolis.* How to make polite conversation and write elegant compositions one learns from the *Colloquia.* In the *Adagia,* the *Parabolae*, and the *Apophthegmata* he provided the world with what Huizinga describes as a retail shop of classical knowledge.

These works were very effective and successful in spreading humanistic refinement throughout Europe; and yet, when reading much of Erasmus, one comes to wonder on what image of man, society, and the state his eyes were ultimately focused. There seem to be different pictures, changing with circumstance; they have strong colors but not very clear lines. When he rises above the textbook and grammar level and considers the ultimate objectives of his educational suggestions in terms of an ideal society, his ideas are not very clearly defined or always consistent in detail. When he discusses the education, character, and duties of the princes and noblemen who will be the decisive elements in society, he is apt to indulge in general moral injunctions. In their moral loftiness and practical vagueness these statements are similar to those on the state, society, and politics, which we shall discuss later. Neither in the *Enchiridion Militis Christiani* nor in the *Institutio Principis Christiani* does Erasmus elaborate in detail how his knights and princes are to discharge their functions, although it is made abundantly clear that they are to be paragons of all the virtues. Erasmus often seems to assume that the spirit which animates him and to which he gives expression will create, by its own impetus, the institutions it needs to propagate itself. His rational idealism, his frail constitution, his great intellectual ability, and capacity for work led him to an overestimation of the power of pure intellect, of *ratio*, in man. An educational optimist, he failed to see the limitations to the effectiveness of education.

Nonetheless, Erasmus' impact on the humanistic scheme of education was profound. For centuries his pedagogical works were quoted and imitated. They served both as guides to the authors and teachers of classical Latin and as examples of it. Being written in Latin and completely cosmopolitan in outlook, they were not limited to any particular country or religion. Thus Erasmus was the teacher not of one country, like Melanchthon who is still remembered as the *Praeceptor Germaniae*, but of all Christendom, whether Catholic or Protestant.[75] He held this position despite the fact that neither side was very fond of him, and that some of his works were until recently on the Index. While his contemporaries and successors used his precepts, thus giving them even wider currency,[76] they were apt to neglect Erasmus' ultimate cosmopolitan and Christian aims. They limited their appeals to their own nations and religions and created the different national and religious forms of humanistic education, the vestiges of which exist to this day. We shall observe the adaptation of his ideas to the particular conditions of their country by English humanists.

The less universalistic humanists in the various nations of Europe, then, were narrower in outlook but more realistic than Erasmus. While Erasmus had an ideal Christian order among men and nations before his eye, and wrote with this end in mind, they paid more attention to the immediate needs that had been created in their particular countries by the dissolution or alteration of the medieval system of education and the medieval structure of society. They founded schools and taught in them as schoolmasters or professors; they became officials, princes' councillors and ministers or they held important positions in their respective churches. They became practical pedagogues, specialized scholars, apologists for their faiths, or patriots appealing to the nationalism of their countries. In short, they lost the breadth of Erasmus' vision and used the tools he gave them for their more limited aims and special interests. Erasmus, it is true, was nominally an imperial councillor; he lectured in several universities, gave advice on the founding of schools, and belonged to the Catholic clergy. But he kept as far aloof as possible from all activity connected with these functions, from any kind of permanent association with institutions of learning or education or religion.

This aloofness, which distinguishes him from most other humanists, kept him socially, politically, and ideologically independent. It was the essential basis for the characteristic liberty with which he acted in contemporary issues of all kinds. He was "essentially a critic and an intellectual,"[77] and his real effectiveness came out in oral disputations and controversies of the pen, in his penetrating, sharp, often constructive criticism. That his own words can be contradictory is not surprising, considering the size of his literary output; they shimmer in so many colors that one has to observe the whole picture from some distance in order to appreciate its outlines.

As in educational practice, Erasmus took little part in actual politics, although he was in frequent contact with rulers and statesmen. He served the pure idea, and as a philosopher did not want to contaminate or falsify it by becoming absorbed in political action. Whereas Machiavelli assumed the amoral political practices prevailing at the time to be natural and inevitable and rationalized them into an eminently practical and realistic political system, Erasmus opposed these same practices by his humanistic idealism. His goal in politics was a moral humanity; he refused to divorce the realm of power from that of ethics. Where Machiavelli deduced his *raison d'état* from his striking conviction that in dealing with men the principal factor to be taken into account is their inherent badness, Erasmus, maintaining his faith in the goodness of man, never tired of attacking the practical application of such a *raison d'état* and never ceased to demonstrate its disastrous consequences for Europe. There are many treatises and letters in which he complains of power politics and confronts them with his moral ideal. His view is clearly expressed in the *Principe*'s contemporary, the *Institutio Principis Christiani*. Here we have his basic educational idea that, if all those who call themselves Christians follow Christ, there will be no need for the use of force among them;[78] by right education, they can all be induced to lead such truly Christian lives that force will be replaced by reason and brotherly love. Mutual friendship will then animate the life of society and nations[79] and make the state superfluous in all but its purely administrative functions. Force will become meaningless, since it will be used neither in internal nor in external affairs. The whole Christian world will be one peaceful Christian universe, without disturbing political divisions. Roman *philanthropia* and Christian *agape* will rule men and states in their mutual relations and be the basis of Christian life in the occident.

Erasmus seems at times to suspect any form of secular hierarchy among Christians. The ultimate logical consequence of his reasoning would be a state without domination of men by men—a condition in which there is no longer any need for government. If the pagan Stoics held all men capable of being good, free, and equal, certainly Christians should be capable of living in freedom. When Erasmus thinks along these lines, all authority, any sovereign power, seems bad to him.[80] If the state for Erasmus is a necessary evil, the form in which it is least bad is a republic. Did not the greatest philosophers, such as Plato, Aristotle, and Cicero, live in republican communities? If there has to be a monarchy, it should not be absolute; at least the people should be able to express their opinion and consent in a constitutional form,[81] and certainly grave matters such as war should not be undertaken without such consent.[82] Although Erasmus did not directly advocate government without royalty, he often showed strong democratic tendencies,[83] defended the freedom and self-government of the people against princely encroachments,[84] and vigorously attacked the abuses of monarchical power.[85] He did not concern himself, however, with the way in which opinion and consent were to be expressed and transformed into political action. Since the "practical details" of institutions did not interest but rather annoyed him, he made hardly any serious suggestions with regard to constitutions, laws, and political bodies. His argument is concerned with ethics rather than with the incorporation of such ethics into the actual organization of society. "He wrote not as a politician, but as a moralist."[86]

Occasionally, Erasmus seemed to favor a popular democracy, but on the whole, he tended to have a low opinion of the rule of the people. Because it lacks true education, the crowd is unreasonable and inclined to badness; like the men in Plato's cave, it mistakes the shadows for the real things,[87] easily acclaims the worst and follows it.[88] After the Peasants' War in Germany, Erasmus came to the conclusion that even a bad monarchy is preferable to anarchy: "Princes must be endured, lest tyranny give way to anarchy, a still greater evil. . . . Lately the insurrection of the German peasants has taught us that the cruelty of kings is better than the universal confusion of anarchy."[89] It is not surprising to see him apparently disregard, in some of his works, as for instance in the *Institutio,* his usual demand for a "mixed" government, for a constitutional monarchy which needs the consent of the people. In the *Institutio,* he assumes that the ruler can do anything he chooses to do, without any apparent limitation to his powers.[90] This clearly shows a misunderstanding of political realities. Erasmus justifies this absolutism with the theory that the ruler is to be the embodiment of all that is good.

It might be objected that this is nothing but flattery on the part of Erasmus, and that, while praising individual princes, he still condemns them in general.[91] There certainly is no lack of flattery when he addresses princes or other men of influence whom he wants to lead in his direction or to use for his purposes.[92] But his theory of "good absolutism" is at times put forth quite enthusiastically and recurs too frequently to be brushed aside. Thus, in one of his adages, there is the most exuberant exaltation of the good prince, whose function is compared with those of the eye, the sun, the soul, even of God.[93] These comparisons are taken from classical and medieval sources; they show his esteem for an absolute monarchy with an absolutely good prince.[94]

The apparent contradictions between his statements in favor of monarchy and those for republican liberties are explained by the fact that in Erasmus' scale of values the ethical good takes first place. Since this good cannot be definitely connected with any particular form of government, good and bad forms of monarchy, of aristocracy, or of democracy appear to Erasmus to be equally possible. The form of government was less important to him than the degree to which it made realization of the ethical good possible, and his conclusion on the whole was that a good ruler and an intellectual aristocracy, properly educated, would provide the best way for achieving this aim.

In the light of Christianity, Erasmus qualified the requirements for a good ruler. He attacked the prototypes of secular monarchs, such as Alexander and Caesar, and Christian princes who tried to emulate these pagan heroes rather than Christ. As the greatest and best of all kings, Christ, and Christ only, was to be imitated by Christian princes.[95] Erasmus apparently thought that this injunction should in itself suffice to make a good ruler. He neglects to elaborate his postulate in detail, and fails to think about the mechanism of a truly Christian empire. This omission is caused in part by Erasmus' disregard of institutions. Moreover, it reveals a fundamental difficulty: did not Christ say that His Kingdom was not of this world?[96] That being the case, how is He to be the example for the worldly ruler? There was no king to whom Christ could give His laws, and to whom He could prescribe a Christian order of the state. Christ asked for brotherly love, and Erasmus wished to use this love, the *concordia* of all men, as the basis of his ideal society. He had only to look around, however, in the world in which he lived to become imbued with the gravest doubts as to whether this code would ever be sufficient to replace power as the basis of social order.

With his distinctively Christian conceptions, Erasmus combines a number of political ideas that are derived from medieval, Hellenistic, and classical Greek political thought. Thus, he turns to the essentially medieval notion of a natural law that is thought to represent the will of God, a law that is to guide the state and its ruler.[97] When he says that a good monarch actually embodies the law so that he is a living law he repeats the famous definition of the king as ἔμψυχος νόμος which had been developed in Pythagorean and later Hellenistic philosophy.[98] With this conception, he combines the Platonic idea of the philosopher-king who by contemplation of the eternal finds the right order of things, incorporates it in his person, and imposes it on the world. Erasmus specifically refers to and agrees with this Platonic conception.[99] In order to be able to rule, the king must be ruled by reason.[100] If he does act according to reason, the most divine part of his soul, he is God's image on earth, comparable to the sun in the heavens. This last comparison again has Hellenistic and ultimately Persian origins.[101] Monarchy, which imitates the divine order, is the best form of the state if the prince excels all in wisdom and goodness, only strives for the advantage of the state, and is entirely unselfish.[102]

It is interesting to note that Erasmus did not consistently adhere to a purely Christian order of the state in the sense described above, but again and again turned to Hellenistic and Platonic ideas, advocating a hierarchical order rather than the egalitarian order of brotherly love. Christ did not give instructions to rulers how to manage worldly affairs, whereas the Greek and Roman authors recommended and quoted by Erasmus did, although their teachings were by no means always consonant with the Sermon on the Mount.

For Erasmus as for Plato, the well-being of the state depends on the human quality of the ruler, which in turn is largely the result of education. The education of the Christian prince, therefore, is of the utmost importance, because it determines whether he will rule as a good monarch or as a tyrant. The young prince is to be shown the way to goodness, virtue, wisdom, unselfishness, and justice.[103] There is a direct connection between his education and the quality and welfare of the people over whom he rules: if a bad teacher corrupts him, he will corrupt the entire nation.[104] If he is stupid he is most apt to do harm to the whole world, just as if he is wise his knowledge may be to everybody's advantage.[105] The worst thing that can happen is the perversion of knowledge by the ruler who abuses his intelligence to further his own ends by clever falsehood and injustice. He is a tyrant and nothing less than a public pestilence.[106]

It is to man and his perfection that the humanists devote their efforts; and since government, to them, is largely a process of education as well as its result, the virtues or vices of the princely pedagogue necessarily have the most far-reaching effect. Unfortunately, if one draws the balance of Erasmus' eulogies and condemnations of princes, if one weighs his flatteries and bitter blasts, one cannot help feeling that the vices were more frequently to be found in reality than the ideal virtues. His praises of monarchy are counterbalanced by tirades against tyranny, his defense of popular freedom by attacks on the stupidity and incompetence of the crowd.

One comes to the conclusion that a patriarchal government, animated by the spirit of Christian love, and therefore able to dispense with force in both internal and external affairs, comes closest to his ideal. The ruler of his state is always "under the law"; he may be a good *paterfamilias*,[107] like his Roman prototype endowed with absolute authority, but ruling his family in the spirit of Christian love; or he may be a monarch limited in his powers by the nobility, the magistrates, and the necessity of obtaining the consent of the people. Some of Erasmus' views are derived from medieval images:[108] when he compares the state to a large monastery, he is thinking of the prince in terms of a good shepherd, of a paternally benign abbot.[109] Platonic and Aristotelian ideas are blended with medieval ones into his conception of an organic society, when he describes the state as an enormous human body:[110] the head of the state, which is farthest removed from the passions and partakes most of wisdom, should govern the limbs and the body in the same manner as the upper part of the soul governs its lower spheres, and the soul in turn rules the body. Between the "head" and the "body" of the state are the magistrates, who correspond to the middle part of the soul, and thus both obey and command.[111] Like the authors of most "mirrors of princes," Erasmus addresses his injunctions with equal force to princes and to "subordinate rulers," to nobility and magistrates, and with slight modifications his educational scheme is valid for all of them.

The magistrates and nobility are, next to the prince, the most important members of the social organism. They fulfil a function similar to that of the Platonic guardians.[112] In the *Enchiridion Militis Christiani* Erasmus follows the Platonic doctrine closely when he makes the degree of knowledge the criterion of man's position in society.[113] He combines this with a conservative esteem for high birth, but condemns the choice of magistrates according to their monetary power.[114] He demands that the best citizens and nobles be heard in councils, at least in an advisory capacity.[115]

The outline Erasmus gives of the Christian prince and the Christian nobleman lacks the clarity of feature that distinguishes Plato's philosopher-king and guardian; or, to draw on a contemporary for comparison, Erasmus gives us not nearly as succinct a picture as Castiglione does of his exemplary courtier in the *Cortegiano*. Yet he established an educational ideal of man, and this ideal both occupied a central position in his philosophy and influenced his followers. Erasmus devoted much of his educational and literary work to the attempt to inject his humanistic idealism into the manifold social and political organization of Europe.

While on the whole he concludes that such organization is necessary, he does not arrive at a definite and clear conception of its machinery. On the one hand, he desires to replace all sovereignty by Christian love; on the other, he wants to resuscitate the medieval empire under a Christian monarch; again, he advocates constitutional monarchy. Geldner concludes that "Erasmus is in theory a democrat, an aristocrat by inclination, and in the face of [contemporary] reality a monarchist."[116] This statement needs some modification and amplification.[117] It is Erasmus' idea of the fundamental goodness of man which is essentially democratic. His emphasis on intellectual and ethical excellence is aristocratic in the sense of quality rather than of privilege.[118] Finally, Geldner's statement indicates that Erasmus was aware of monarchy as the form of government coming to prevail in his age, and that he held the modern prince perfectly capable of becoming his ideal statesman. As we have noted earlier, Erasmus' efforts to achieve a society based on ethics are put into proper perspective when we realize that in his scale of values the particular forms of government are subordinated to the ethical wisdom and conduct of their representatives. Any form of society seems acceptable to him if it brings mankind closer to the realization of his educational ideal.

In consequence, it is in Erasmus' philosophy of education that we find his hope greatest and his ideas most constant. An aristocracy educated according to these ideas, and therefore good by his standards, may one day be the ruling element in Christendom. Knight and scholar shall be welded into a new type of man, the Christian prince and the Christian knight, and to that end Erasmus gave fruitful advice. His advice was taken up, and his ideas were further developed by his English friends.

# III

# Sir Thomas More

THOMAS MORE wrote *Utopia*[1] in that period of his life[2] in which he was most closely connected with Erasmus.[3] At that time, he largely shared the latter's optimistic faith that humanistic idealism might be the vehicle for far-reaching reform, a faith which in More's case was in later years overshadowed by his preoccupation with immediate political and religious problems. In *Utopia*, More drew a picture clearer and fuller than anything his friend Erasmus had produced, of a humanistic state, of a society which was inspired by the central ideals they held in common. Where Erasmus, in the *Praise of Folly*, had portrayed the rule of unreason, More replaced the negative signs by positive ones, turned the picture around and depicted the rule of reason. A society ordered according to reason and ruled by reasonable men: that is the principal humanistic feature of this work.

The question immediately arises: Is not *Utopia* more justly famous for its revolutionary social and economic features, for its portrayal of a communistic society? That is indeed its most striking aspect, and it is perhaps this aspect of More's work which has exerted the greatest influence.[4] Quite apart from the questions whether or not the social and economic system of *Utopia* actually represents More's ideal, and whether he seriously hoped for the practical implementation of his theory, it seems to me that in *Utopia* the economic order is a means to an end rather than an end in itself.[5] The economic organization of the island, interesting and original as it is, is not the author's primary concern but is introduced as a means toward the solution of his central problem, the achievement of the rule of reason. In order to carry out the experiment in which he was interested—to see how a society could be organized on the basis of reason alone, and ruled by those who possessed it in the highest degree—he eliminated such factors as property, inherited social position, and, within limits, revealed religion. Thus

50

he was able to "isolate" reason, and to investigate how it could serve as the only basis of society, without interference from any of the other factors which traditionally influenced societies. More was primarily concerned with presenting a state ruled by humanists in accordance with humanistic precepts; the particular form of social organization he chose was important but secondary to that aim. *Utopia* and, to a more limited extent, some of More's other writings will here be considered with regard to this central aspect of More's thought.

*Utopia* has been interpreted in many different ways and from the most varied points of view. I return essentially to the interpretation supplied by More's contemporary, Jerome Busleyden, who wrote to More from Mechlin in November, 1516:

Your ideal state . . . devoted its energies not so much to forming laws as to training the most approved magistrates . . . , because after their likeness, the pattern of their virtue, the example of their conduct, the picture of their justice, the whole state and right course of any perfect commonwealth should be modelled. . . .[6]

A work which is a mixture of fact and fancy, of serious proposals for reform and *jeu d'esprit*, has confronted its interpreters with the very perplexing task of disentangling the serious elements from the whimsical and playful aspects. Thus, different interpreters hold opposite positions with regard to More's attitude to communism, and it has been elaborately argued both that he did and that he did not seriously believe in, or approve of, the economic system outlined by him.[7] Such confusion could hardly arise over his unequivocal attitude to humanism and to humanistic reform. While there is no indication that More ever made an effort to give practical reality to the Utopian economic doctrines in the England of his day,[8] he was active in advancing the cause of humanism, both in his private sphere and in his official functions. From the close agreement between his emphasis on humanism in the *Utopia* and his activity in its cause, we may properly infer that More meant what he said in *Utopia* about the importance of the humanistic education of rulers and magistrates. That does not mean that he necessarily wished or hoped to introduce the entire Utopian scheme of education and government in his own country. In *Utopia*, he presented such a scheme in isolation, completely outside the historical traditions and limitations with which he was familiar; in practice, he took account of these factors and attempted to promote humanistic reform within their framework. The Utopian methods of selection of officials evidently could not be fitted into that framework without revolutionary changes. Since there is no evidence that in practical politics More was a revolutionary, I do not take the Utopian practices to represent proposals which More thought could be introduced in the England of his day. In his emphasis on the function of humanism in the life of society, however, More was as serious as Erasmus, and *Utopia* represents a major part of his effort to strengthen the position of humanism in England and Europe.

More stresses the close connection between education and politics, the paramount importance of the preparation of the future rulers by the right kind of education, the ideal of a society in which the "learned" rule. Trained as a humanist and lawyer, he displayed an uncommon devotion to the service of his country. Where Erasmus kept his scholarly distance from the affairs of the day, More employed his abilities and learning in the *vita activa* of legal and political service. He served first the City of London, then the government, eventually rising to the highest legal position in the realm, that of Lord Chancellor.[9] The problem how humanistic ideals might be translated into practical reality, or how service of the government might at least be reconciled with such ideals, was weighing on his mind when he was writing the *Utopia*. Probably in the year 1516, in which he finished it, he became committed to the service of the Crown.[10]

The first part of *Utopia*, most of it composed later than the bulk of the second,[11] in 1516, gives much evidence of More's concern with the question of how philosophical idealism may be reconciled with political service. Having been on that mission to Flanders for the City of London and the King[12] which provided the setting for the work,[13] and probably aware that Wolsey and the King were interested in his services, his interest in that question was more than purely academic; it was an acute problem for him. Raphael Hythlodaye, the traveler who appears in *Utopia* as Vespucci's companion,[14] as visitor to the fabulous island, and as the reporter on it, discusses with More and Peter Giles the question whether the wise man, the philosopher who is engaged in the search for truth, may actively participate in the political life of his country. Which takes precedence: his duty to learning and truth or to his country and fellow-citizens? And is it possible to reconcile the two? Raphael's arguments sound as if Erasmus might have uttered them,[15] and we can well imagine conversations between More and Erasmus similar to this fictitious discussion of the problem in the first part of *Utopia*.

More draws on Plato's ideal of the philosopher-king[16] to support his contention that the wise man should go into politics.[17] He carefully adapts his argument to prevailing circumstances by stating that the same felicitous state of affairs that Plato had expected from the rule of philosophers turned kings or kings turned philosophers would be brought about "yf philosophers wyll vouchsaufe to enstruct kinges with their good counsell."[18] Since there already is a king and a hereditary monarchy, More, like Erasmus, Castiglione, and many others, in this manner adapts Platonic theory to sixteenth-century reality. Instead of becoming kings themselves, the philosophers become instructors and advisers of kings, hoping thus to achieve indirectly by their influence what Plato would achieve more directly. The shrewd Hythlodaye, however, is not convinced by this argument, which seems to him like wishful thinking. After pointing to Plato's own failure in his attempt to pursue the course suggested by More by becoming adviser to Dionysius, the tyrant of Syracuse,[19] he describes an imaginary and very Machiavellian meeting of the French king's council in order to prove his point that there is no place for the philosopher and his advice in such company, that he will only be thrown out or become a laughingstock if he adheres to his convictions and tries to "plucke out of [the king's] mynde the pernicious originall causes of vice and noughtines."[20] In Hythlodaye's opinion, then, the true philosopher can achieve nothing as adviser to a king—unless that king himself is a philosopher[21]—and he only endangers his own sanity: "Whyles that I goe aboute to remedye the madnes of others, I shoulde be even as madde as they."[22] Any participation in the government of contemporary European countries inevitably corrupts the philosopher, since sooner or later he will have to agree to actions and laws which run counter to his philosophical convictions: "Noughtye counselles muste be openlyc allowed and verye pestilent decrees muste be approved."[23]

More does not deny that such situations may arise, but, Hythlodaye notwithstanding, he feels that the philosopher's place is in politics. He takes the skeptical yet cautiously optimistic attitude that the philosopher may at least be able to avert the worst: "Yf evel opinions and noughty persuasions can not be utterly and quyte plucked out" of the hearts of princes, "if you can not even as you wolde remedy vices, which use and custome hath confirmed: yet for this cause you must not leave and forsake the common wealthe: you muste not forsake the shippe in a tempeste, because you can not rule and kepe downe the wyndes."[24] It is your duty to play a part in the public life of your country, he argues, convincing himself but not Hythlodaye, "and make the best of it."[25] The active life demands compromises, and you may have to make them; you must endeavor "that whyche you can not turne to good, so to order it that it be not verye badde."[26]

More acted accordingly. At the end of his own career, he gave an interesting piece of advice to Thomas Cromwell which illustrates the tenacity with which he held to his conception of the moral duties of a royal adviser, and, by implication, to his belief that such an adviser's activity had some good effect and therefore could presumably be justified morally. Roper, More's son-in-law and biographer, informs us that More told Cromwell: "You shall, in your councell gevinge unto his grace, ever tell him what he owght to doe, but never what he is able to doe. So shall you shewe yourself a true faithfull servant and a right worthy councelour."[27] Harpsfield, the later biographer, repeats the same story but adds that Cromwell failed to heed this advice and, by not acting like "a good Counsailour," became partly responsible for the "greevous enormities" that befell king and realm and for the ruin and destruction that ended his own career.[28] More was preaching good humanistic doctrine to Cromwell. For many years, More himself faithfully carried out what, in the first part of *Utopia*, he had declared to be his duty, and he thus seems to have adhered to the position outlined there. He had indicated that, in order to achieve a limited amount of good, or at least to prevent things from becoming thoroughly bad, a royal councillor would have to make compromises; he undoubtedly realized before he committed himself to serve Henry VIII that such service would demand considerable flexibility. There was a limit to his adaptability, however, which finally forced him to resign his position and, in so doing, to abandon the principle he had enunciated in his Utopian discussion, that one must not forsake the ship in a storm because one cannot keep down the winds. This limit was reached when he decided that his conscience would not let him subscribe to Henry VIII's breach with Rome.[29] In devoting himself to the active life, he had made a practical compromise between its demands and those of pure contemplation, a compromise of the kind advocated in *Utopia*. But was not Hythlodaye finally vindicated in a tragic manner? More eventually found it impossible to give his explicit approval to what he felt were "pestilent decrees" and, as a result, rather than sacrifice his ultimate convictions, he chose to die a martyr's death.[30]

There is another aspect to the discussion between More and Hythlodaye which requires some comment. If Hythlodaye is as opposed to participating in the government of a country as he claims to be, why does he describe the government of Utopia (where philosophers have to busy themselves with affairs of state) with such enthusiasm[31] that he would gladly wish "this fourme and fashion of a weale publique . . . unto al nations"?[32] The answer is obvious: on that isolated island, all men, and particularly those destined to rule, have been brought up so that they permit reason and goodness to prevail among themselves. In the absence of private property, very few laws are needed to make sure that "vertue is had in pryce and estimation."[33] In his discussion with More, he does, by implication, agree that in a state which gives reality to the Platonic demand for the philosopher-king, the philosopher may devote himself to politics[34]—and Utopia represents such a state in ideal purity. So Utopia fulfils the demands of the absolute idealist Hythlodaye. More represents himself as not approving of all the aspects of the picture painted by Hythlodaye; nevertheless, he seems to regard it as an image of the rule of reason and virtue which the practical statesman may emulate and use as a guide even though he may not approve of it in its entirety. Whether for reasons of the real More's personal security or out of genuine conviction, the More of the Utopian dialogue repeatedly dissociates himself from the system of communal ownership,[35] that feature which he recognizes in Hythlodaye's account of the Utopians as "the principal foundation of al their ordinaunces."[36] On the other hand, he never criticizes that feature of Utopia which is here emphasized: the rule of virtue, achieved through humanistic training.

In his actual life, More took the realistic position that had been advocated by his likeness in the dialogue; behind the arguments of Hythlodaye in the first part of *Utopia* in favor of the *vita contemplativa*, we may surmise the voice of Erasmus. In his life, More bore witness to what he considered to be the duty of the learned man, and in the second part of *Utopia*, through the voice of Hythlodaye, he described a state in which the learned could rule effectively, unhampered by tyranny or outside interference. In contrast to Hythlodaye, he was ready to serve a state in which these conditions did not exist. He contrasted the peace, well-being, happiness, and virtue of Utopia with conditions prevailing in the Europe of his day and, particularly, with the evils that were infesting the body politic of his own country.

More's piercing analysis, in the first book of *Utopia*, of the social and economic troubles of England, and of the injustices of her legal system, remains a famous document of social history. He presumably meant his comments and criticisms to suggest some lines along which reforms should be undertaken. There is, however, no evidence that Henry VIII followed his advice,[37] or that More himself later carried out to any extent the reforms he had indicated. He must have hoped that his more immediate criticisms might lead to some changes, but he knew that, at best, he would have to be content with a very partial and inadequate response to them.[38]

The picture of the ideal commonwealth on the Island of Nowhere, outlined in the second part of *Utopia*, might also suggest to his fellow-countrymen and to the Christians of Europe some ideas which they could adopt to their advantage from a society that had solved the problems of communal life so much more successfully than they, on the basis of reason alone and without the aid of the Christian religion.[39] More was sufficiently disillusioned about contemporary Europe to separate his ideal state completely from its troubles and entanglements. He constructed this ideal state on an imaginary island which in some respects resembles England, but which, on the whole, is clearly a product of the age of discoveries; on it More introduced features of such novelty and originality that it is hard to attribute them all to his imagination. Hythlodaye, the raconteur, is introduced as having been on one of Vespucci's voyages of discovery,[40] and More did base his story in part on the reports—both true and fanciful—of the customs and manners of the newly discovered inhabitants of America. He used, altered, mixed, and enlarged upon these reports freely. There have been ingenious efforts to find an actual prototype for the society that More describes in such detail in *Utopia*, and one recent interpreter has gone so far as to argue extensively "that More's book in the main is not a fictitious story, but a record of a trip to Peru and what was observed there."[41] In order to make this thesis plausible, its proponent, A. E. Morgan, insists—without proving his contention—that accounts of the Inca Empire, usually thought to have come to Europe long after *Utopia* had been published, were available to More when he was composing that work.[42]

The suggestion that More was stimulated into writing *Utopia* by accounts of the fabulous Inca state, with its planned, money-less economy and its hierarchical social organization, sounds very alluring, but the explanation by Donner is much more solidly supported and defensible: Vespucci's *Quattuor . . . nauigationes*, published in 1507, and the first part of Peter Martyr's *De Orbe Novo*, published in 1511, were available to More.[43] The natives of the New World are described in the first of these works as being very kind and helpful; they despise gold, do not buy or barter, have communal habitations, live in liberty, and follow a kind of Epicurean philosophy. Peter Martyr stresses the West Indians' common ownership of the soil and their general community of property; he also ascribes to them an intuitive knowledge of the essential moral and philosophical truths. These accounts of unfamiliar peoples, plus the *Germania* of Tacitus, which had recently become available, are taken by Donner[44] to represent More's major descriptive sources. He argues very convincingly for this view which makes it unnecessary "to assume that More was in possession of any occult knowledge of the Incas of Peru."[45]

More derived from such works many factual details and ideas which he incorporated in his own account, and they may even have suggested to him the writing of *Utopia*. Nevertheless, *Utopia* is his own creation; materials from different sources went into it, were combined with his own inventions and organized by his own ideas and intentions into a systematic and original structure. There would be little point to touching on these probable sources of *Utopia* in a discussion of its author's humanism if it were not precisely this humanism which distinguishes his work from these sources, which provides its unity and makes it unique. Utopia is organized to provide an equal distribution of work, material goods, and amenities for all its citizens; these aims, however, important as they are, are subordinate to the main purpose of making the pleasures of learning and knowledge available to everyone, and all these aims are achieved in turn by the rule of the most erudite members of this society. The meaning which is thus given to the life of the entire community—its orientation toward intellectual and spiritual values, and its organization according to such values—distinguishes Utopia from the actual societies whose traits More incorporated in his work.

A state in which intellectual values are counted supreme, and in which everyone has access to them; a state where scholars rule, and where they can rule without compromising their intellectual and moral honesty—surely the ultimate hopes of the humanists were crystallized in its symmetrical shape! Even the incorruptible and uncompromising Hythlodaye could give an enthusiastic account of it, and thus, by implication, approve of the scholar's active participation in the political life of a state of this kind.

When *Utopia* is seen in this light, Plato's *Republic* clearly emerges as its most important inspiration and prototype. It is in that sense that Peter Giles shrewdly remarks to More, who has just noticed the strange-looking Hythlodaye for the first time, that this stranger "hath sailed in deede, not as the mariner Palinure, but as the experte and prudent prince Ulisses: yea, rather as the auncient and sage Philosopher Plato."[46] The whole idea of establishing an ideal commonwealth can be directly traced to the example of Plato's work. In fact, More reveals on several occasions that he is competing with the *Republic*. His claim to have outdone his source is based on the contention that he has portrayed his Utopian state more realistically. He felt that he had given flesh and blood to his society, and in this vein he speaks of "those thinges that Plato faynethe in his weale publique: or that the Utopians doe in theires."[47] More illustrated many aspects of the practical, everyday life on his island very plastically and in considerable detail; he describes the structure of the entire Utopian society—the lives, duties, work, and pleasures of the mass of the people—which Plato neglects. The insistence on the "practical" side is demonstrated in the statement which, it is claimed, is translated from the Utopian language:

> I one of all other without philosophie
> have shaped for man a philosophicall citie.[48]

Perhaps More's pride in the realistic character of his philosophical city was occasioned by his use of the actual or purported institutions and practices of various societies. Partly to maintain the fiction that Utopia actually exists, but also to indicate its superiority, "A shorte meter of Utopia, written by Anemolius poete laureate, and nephewe to Hythlodaye by his sister" precedes the 1518 text of *Utopia:*

> . . . . . . . . . . . . . . . . . .
> Nowe am I like Platoes citie,
> Whose fame flieth the worlde throughe,
> Yea like, or rather more likely
> Platoes platte to excell and passe.
> For what Platoes penne hathe platted briefely
> In naked wordes, as in a glasse,
> The same have I performed fully,
> With lawes, with men, and treasure fyttely
> . . . . . . . . . . . . . . . . . .[49]

In contrast to Machiavelli, More did not reject Plato, but aimed to surpass him. Both criticized the imaginary character of Plato's *Republic;* but whereas Machiavelli rejected all such idealistic constructions[50] and, in the *Prince,* undertook to investigate the functioning of men and states from a purely practical point of view, More defended the product of his own imagination by claiming real existence for it, and by supplying it with all the lively details that he felt were missing in Plato's work. Nevertheless, he was admittedly following Plato's example in creating the picture of an ideal state, even if he did argue for *Utopia*'s difference and superiority on the grounds that it was more realistic and complete.

More held up his ideal state against the reality of the Renaissance state as Machiavelli—and More himself in the first part of *Utopia*—described it. A moral and spiritual ideal, embodying the hopes of the humanists, is poised against unscrupulous acquisition and exploitation of property and power for their own sake, against that *raison d'état* which Machiavelli had just analyzed and systematized. More did not know *The Prince,* but some passages in *Utopia,* like some in Erasmus' work, sound as if they were written in direct answer to it:

> . . . the comminaltie chueseth their king for their owne sake, and not for his sake: to the intent, that through his laboure and studie they might al live wealthily sauffe from wronges and injuries: and that therfore the kynge ought to take more care for the wealthe of his people, then for his owne wealthe, even as the office and dewtie of a shepehearde is in that he is a shepherde, to feede his shepe rather then himselfe. . . . And yf any Kyng were so smally regarded, and so lightly estemed, yea so behated of his subjectes, that other wayes he could not kepe them in awe, but only by open wronges, by pollinge and shavinge, and by bringinge them to beggerie, sewerly it were better for him to forsake his kingedom, then to holde it by this meanes: wherby though the name of a king be kepte, yet the majestie is lost. . . . But let him rather amende his owne lyfe, renounce unhonest pleasure, and forsake pride.[51]

If "parts of *Utopia* read like a commentary on parts of *The Prince,*"[52] it can also be said that More's *History of Richard III*[53]—begun before, and finished after, the *Utopia*[54]—"is an attack on the non-moral statecraft of the early Sixteenth Century, exactly as *Utopia* is."[55] Richard's abuse and tyranny of the state is contrasted with the good rule of his predecessor, Edward IV;[56] it is also the direct antithesis of the conditions prevailing in the state founded by the Utopian king Utopus. Pointed comparisons, reminiscent of Erasmus, between good rulers and bad ones, are made by More in his epigrams: good rulers are like sheepdogs, bad ones like wolves,[57] and the character of their kingdoms is determined by their natures.

In the *Utopia,* More does not admit any distinction between private and public morals.[58] He does not admit that men may act according to two different standards, whose coexistence makes it possible to sanction and justify as permissible actions considered immoral in the private sphere if they are performed in the so-called "public interest." He undoubtedly advocates a single moral standard for the internal relations of the Utopians among themselves. It has been argued that, when it comes to foreign relations, More introduces the double standard of the *raison d'état* to justify imperialistic expansion.[59] This is not the place to discuss that much debated question; I have elsewhere presented some arguments to modify this interpretation.[60] In the present context, we are concerned with the internal structure, organization, and standards of Utopia rather than with her foreign relations.

In Utopia, there is little need for compulsion on the part of the state because most citizens not only in theory subscribe to a basic system of morals but are in practice guided by its precepts in their relationships with each other. "The startling differences between Europe and Utopia exist because in Utopia every free citizen is a philosopher whose life perfectly exemplifies [More's] conceptions that, for uncorrupted men, the good life can be only that led strictly 'according to nature' or 'reason.' . . ."[61] R. P. Adams, the author of this statement, has investigated More's use and interpretation of the terms "reason" and "nature," which he considers to be the central elements of More's Utopian philosophy. He arrives at the following definition of their significance for the social life of Utopia:

After reason the Utopians held the divine "nature's" greatest gift to be man's capacity for and strong inclination toward a close-knit, harmonious family and communal social life, a life distinguished . . . by . . . man's mutual benevolent solicitude for the common welfare. . . . "Reason" itself . . . prompts man . . . to lead a joyous Epicurean life, not in selfish privacy, but actively aiding other men to equal felicity.[62]

Nature and reason determine the morals of the Utopian citizens, which are both their private and public morals. In accordance with the dictates of nature and reason, Utopian society has been constructed as a large living organism based on mutual co-operation, friendship, and peace. Ideas derived from Plato and from the reports on strange, newly discovered societies are blended with medieval and monastic codes and More's original inventions into the unique structure of the Utopian state. Everybody eats in common refectories, similar to those in the monasteries, although there is no compulsion to do so.[63] Work is strictly organized and assigned, not for isolated groups of the population only (such as the inhabitants of a monastery) but for everybody; yet the individual does have the freedom to choose his occupation and to change from one to another.[64] In order to keep the sizes of families fairly uniform, children may be shifted from one family to another.[65] While this is not as rigorous a measure as Plato's community of children, it does involve, to a limited extent, an inroad into the natural family structure, justified here by economic reasons and an infatuation with the statistical average size. For the same reasons, larger segments of the population may be moved from one city to another in order to keep their sizes equal.[66] A scheme for the rotation of town and country population is introduced.[67] The authorities see to it that everybody works the prescribed six hours.[68] One might say that the rules of Plato and St. Benedict are modified, combined with other elements, and extended so as to cover not merely selected groups but the entire community. There are considerable limitations on personal liberty—no journey is possible without permission, for instance[69]—and there is no private property.[70] All work is performed for everybody's need and benefit rather than for private gain. Communism is not limited to the elite, as in Plato, but embraces everyone.[71] The state is, so to speak, extended in breadth and depth as compared to the *Republic*: it is not confined to a city-state, but extends over a whole island with fifty-four cities "or shiere townes"[72] and their adjacent agricultural districts. In describing its life and social structure, More is not, like Plato, concerned almost exclusively with the ruling class; rather, he describes the life and activities of the whole people. Furthermore, he puts much greater emphasis on economic aspects. From an economic point of view, there are, with the exception of a small number of "bondemen,"[73] no class differences. Although all citizens participate in military exercises,[74] military prowess is not, as it is for Plato's guardians, a prime prerequisite for those who hold administrative positions in a state which relies on foreign mercenaries and only in an emergency resorts to the military action of its own citizens.[75]

Both Plato and More insist that natural intellectual ability and a thorough education are indispensable for rulers and magistrates, but while Plato's philosophers and guardians are the authoritarian rulers in an aristocracy, More portrays his magistrates as the elected officers of a democratic state. This last-mentioned difference, however, is not as great as might appear because the group from which the higher officers can be chosen is very limited in number, although more flexible in its composition than Plato's, and because, once elected, these officers have very considerable authority and powers.

Utopia's democratic institutions owe their origin not to a popular revolution but to the short, decisive period of enlightened despotism of King Utopus in the distant past, 1,760 years ago,[76] which established them on firm foundations. (This closely resembles Machiavelli's account, in the *Discourses*, of the first establishment of republican institutions by dictatorial rulers and lawgivers.)[77] Utopian democracy is tempered and modified by the patriarchal authority of heads of families and magistrates; the whole state is likened to a family: it "is as it were one familie, or housholde."[78] Whereas Plato thinks that only the few are capable of recognizing the idea of the good, and that only they should therefore have the task of shaping the reality of political life, More believes that every citizen can live "consciously according to 'reason' or 'nature,' as a virtuous philosopher whose life exemplified his philosophy."[79] It is a prerequisite for the smooth functioning of the Utopian system that not only a small group but the whole people should be raised to a high intellectual and moral level by general education. The fact that work is limited to six hours a day gives everybody a chance to achieve greater perfection by devotion to study and attendance at public lectures. The elimination of money and the profit motive, the provision of a secure and equal material basis of life for every citizen, and the consequent general unimportance of material things, combine to make a man's moral qualities and intellectual achievements the only criteria which determine his social and political position. The Utopian form of communal organization is instituted as the basis of a highly civilized life. Its purpose is to bring out the best human potentialities and to make them the decisive element in society.

The political system established in Utopia is a democracy with patriarchal and aristocratic features. Great emphasis is placed on the family unit or clan whose members—never less than forty in the countryside[80] and between ten and sixteen adults plus children in the cities[81]—form one household. This is the basic political and social unit. It is presided over by its oldest male member, unless he is senile, in which case he is replaced by the second oldest.[82] Thirty of these families are under the authority of one "syphograunte" or "philarch." In the countryside, this man has the functions of a head bailiff;[83] we are not told how he is appointed there. In the city, he is chosen annually by the thirty families.[84] The philarch's main functions are to see to it that everybody works,[85] and that production, consumption, and labor are properly regulated and distributed. In the cities, he is also the magistrate for his ward and the resident warden of the large halls where his thiry families take their meals in common.[86] The heads of the households and the philarchs rule their families and wards with patriarchal authority.[87]

There are 200 philarchs in each city,[88] which means that a city consists of 6,000 families. This indicates a population of between 60,000 and 96,000 adult citizens per city.[89] The cities are divided into four major quarters or districts. The *princeps* or mayor of the entire city is the one official who is chosen for life,[90] but with the provision that he may be removed if he is suspected of trying to assume tyrannical powers. When a *princeps* is to be elected, each quarter of the city nominates one candidate. Then the two hundred philarchs constitute an electoral college which, in a secret session, elects the mayor from the four candidates. The chief governmental powers rest with this *princeps* and the council of twenty "tranibores" or "chief philarchs."[91] Each of these chief philarchs is elected annually by three hundred families, i.e., there is one for every ten philarchs. Their council or senate assembles every third day, or oftener if necessary, with the *princeps;* also, two philarchs—different ones for each occasion—take part in these assemblies, evidently as a precaution against possible oligarchic desires on the part of the mayor and the chief philarchs. There are other safeguards against usurpation of power by this group: matters of great importance are referred to the council[92] of philarchs, who in turn consult the families. Furthermore, it is provided not only that the princeps may be removed "for suspition of tirannie" but that "it is deathe to have anye consultation for the common wealthe oute of the counsell, or the place of the common election. This statute, they saye, was made to the entent that the prince and Tranibores might not easilye conspire together to appresse the people by tyrannie, and to chaunge the state of the weale publik."[93]

A considerable measure of constant popular control over the government is thus insured, not only by the system of annual elections, but also by the functions assigned to the philarchs, who are the most immediate representatives of the people, and who occupy an intermediate position between it and the higher authorities. On the other hand, incumbents may be re-elected, and since the Utopians are a conservative people, it is their custom to continue the chief philarchs in office, and "lightlie they chaunge them not."[94] There is then a good deal of continuity in the governing group, and we shall see that this continuity is assured by other means as well.

Many details of the Utopian constitution are left to the reader's imagination or are only vaguely indicated. The method of voting is not described, except that officers are chosen by secret vote.[95] The precise functions of the different bodies and officers are not always explained. More outlines the government of the capital, Amaurote, which, he says, is identical with that of the fifty-three other cities.[96] We are told that a kind of national senate[97] meets in Amaurote annually, consisting of three "old men wyse and well experienced"[98] from every city, a total membership of 162. Matters of common concern are debated in the "senate"; also, it serves as a central agency for the equal distribution of products throughout the island[99] and receives ambassadors.[100] Sometimes, matters of great importance are referred to this council from the individual cities. More is, however, much vaguer about the national than about the local institutions of Utopia. It has usually been assumed that there is a king or prince of the entire island; however, when talking of a *princeps,* More generally refers to the local mayor or prefect rather than to a national monarch, although he may sometimes use the term in the latter meaning.[101] Since the Utopian constitution was established by a king, his office presumably continues to exist, but nothing is said about the manner of his appointment or his duties.[102] Some interpreters have suggested that there is no king at all in Utopia, and that the whole island is a republican city-league.[103] If that were the case, it seems to me that More would not have reported dreaming that he had been made perpetual prince of the Utopians by being crowned with a diadem of wheat, and that in this capacity he received foreign ambassadors and princes.[104] Yet it is strange that More neglects to describe the sovereign of Utopia; in the absence of evidence to the contrary, we may assume that what More had in mind for the whole country was similar to the pattern he set for the cities: parliamentary government with an elective but permanent ruler at the head.

There is one other group of officials, the priests, who, like the magistrates, are chosen "by secrete voices"[105] of the people. There are thirteen priests and as many churches in a city; a *pontifex* presides who may have up to seven additional priests in his entourage, so that there can be altogether twenty priests in a city.[106] "They be overseers of al divine matters, orderers of religions, and as it wer judges and maisters of maners,"[107] and "both childhode and youth is instructed, and taught of them."[108] As judges of manners and teachers of youth, they play a vital part in the Utopian scheme.

In contrast to Platonic, monastic, or modern conceptions, More places his primary emphasis on the family group or clan as the basic political unit. Within this group, discipline and obedience are demanded and enforced by its patriarchal head, and his rule is backed and controlled by the higher officials. This domestic government extends to the most minute details of daily life, to proper behavior, good manners, and morals. Chambers goes too far when he claims that "the ideal of Utopia is discipline, not liberty,"[109] and underemphasizes the liberties that do exist; but it is true that liberties in Utopia are both limited and well regulated. The discipline in the family is moderated by paternal kindness of the sort More exhibited in his own very large household; the same is true of discipline in the body politic. As the father is a king in his family, the king is like a father of the people—like its shepherd—and the people resembles a large family.[110] It must be evident that in a society that has such a patriarchal structure as part of its political system the citizens cannot be really equal. Young men and women are definitely subordinated to their elders, and it is hard to see how decisions within the clan could go contrary to the opinion of the head of a family. Economic equality is assured, but not political or social equality. There is potential equality of opportunity for everyone to rise to the higher offices, inasmuch as there are no hereditary prerogatives of caste, blood, or wealth; but since only those of superior mental ability are eligible for the higher offices, and since these endowments are very unequally distributed by nature, equality of opportunity for all is nonexistent. It exists only for the few to whom nature has been particularly kind in this respect. Of all the possible arguments for the rule of an aristocracy, More uses the one that is most readily defensible—superiority of character and intellect—and builds the structure of his society around it. Utopia has many aspects of an equalitarian democracy, but it is actually ruled by an intellectual aristocracy. While the paterfamilias controls the small units of society, the higher offices in the state are open only to the members of the "company"[111] or "order"[112] of the learned. This order is an aristocracy of the mind and, as such, an embodiment of the hopes and desires of the humanists.

Out of this *literatorum ordo* "be chosen ambassadours, priestes, Tranibores, and finallyc the prince him selfe."[113] Only the highest officials and the priests are included in this listing; philarchs and heads of families are not among them. The philarchs occupy a kind of intermediate position between the order of the learned and the rest of the population. They are included in the number of five hundred able-bodied persons whom the law exempts from ordinary work: "yet they exempte not themselfes; to the intent that they may the rather by their example provoke other to worke."[114] As we have noted, they are the overseers of work, and the course they are described as taking would result naturally from their occupation. But Hythlodaye does not tell us that the highest officials similarly engage in ordinary labor; it is they who really take advantage of their freedom from it, and who constitute the "order of the learned." They have been "geven a perpetual licence from laboure to learninge,"[115] and make use of it.

The total group in the city and the surrounding countryside that is thus exempt from work has no more than 500 members; if we deduct the 200 urban and perhaps 50 rural philarchs, we arrive at a figure of 250 as the membership of the order in each city. Now we have noted that there are 20 protophilarchs, 20 priests, and a *princeps* in each city, i.e., a total of 41. Even allowing for additional functionaries in the country and the youthful members who are still studying, this leaves a considerable reserve: presumably, the people may choose substitutes from it if they decide they want a change in magistrates. In any case, considerably less than 1 per cent of the adult population is thus exempt from labor duty, and less than $\frac{1}{2}$ per cent belongs to the order of the learned.[116]

Like Plato, whose guardians and philosophers he had in mind when he was describing the position of the "learned," More feels that a state, if it is to make the good life possible, must be ruled by a group of philosophers. There are important differences between More's and Plato's concepts, however. Military training is universal in Utopia,[117] and the "learned" do not appear to be singled out for the special training, duties, and privileges of the Platonic guardians in this respect. In another sense, too, More is more democratic than Plato: he advocates a scheme of liberal education for all children and provides for adult education for everyone who wants it,[118] whereas Plato is concerned only with the education of the ruling class. The provisions made for the general election of magistrates also serve to make More's constitution more democratic than Plato's.

Democracy is limited, however, by the fact that in order to fill the higher offices a person has to be a member of the order of the learned. Except for the lowest officials, the philarchs, membership in this order is a prerequisite for candidacy.[119] The philarchs share with the "learned" the privilege of exemption from practical work, but they do not usually take advantage of it and presumably only have it for the duration of the term of their office. While all children are given a liberal education, and while all adults may continue this education, a particularly intensive and comprehensive training is provided for the members of the order;[120] otherwise there would be no reason for singling them out in childhood. The kind of education given to everyone would seem to be identical; the difference lies in the degree of intensity and comprehensiveness, which obviously can be much greater for those who have no other duties.

How does a Utopian become a member of this select and privileged society, of this "réservoir naturel de l'aristocratie utopienne"?[121] The priests, who are also teachers and who are members of the order, suggest the candidates for membership; actual membership is conferred, on their recommendation, by a secret ballot of the philarchs.[122] As in the *Republic*, the candidates are generally already singled out in childhood; they are persons in whom the authorities have "from theire very childhode . . . perceaved a singular towardnes, a fyne witte, and a minde apte to good learning."[123] In addition, however, adults may also be admitted if their accomplishments warrant the conferring of this privilege.[124] Although this procedure is less restrictive than that advocated by Plato, and although the vote of the philarchs and the sanction given by the people introduce some measure of democratic control, the ruling body is still essentially self-perpetuating, both in the choice of new members and in their education. Persons who do not live up to the expectations placed in them may be "plucked back to the company of artificers"[125] and thus be deprived of their privileged status. Only those who continue to prove their intellectual and moral superiority can stay in this group; furthermore, presumably only those who are in agreement with the fundamental religious, ethical, and social doctrines of Utopia can belong to it. Thus, by perpetuating itself and the values for which it stands, the *literatorum ordo* makes sure that the lives of all Utopians will continue to be governed by it. In any case, long tradition has developed a high degree of uniformity. This does not, however, mean that the Utopians live in a state of mental stagnation: the ideas of visitors, the customs of other civilizations, other religions and philosophies, are carefully investigated, and what seems good and complementary to the Utopian system is amalgamated into it.[126] While a wide divergence of opinion is permitted,[127] it seems hardly likely that anyone who would, for instance, deny that learning and virtue are the indispensable prerequisites for holding high office has the slightest chance of ever gaining influence in Utopia.

67

The education of the Utopians in general and of their future rulers in particular proceeds along humanistic lines. To judge from More's account, the Utopian system of education has always been closely akin to humanism. We are told that the Utopians had learned all the crafts and sciences of Rome from the Roman and Egyptian crew of a ship that was wrecked on the coast of Utopia 1,200 years before;[128] the knowledge of Greek literature and philosophy came to them only when that learned traveler, Raphael Hythlodaye, appeared among them.[129] But while they had not even known the names of the European philosophers, they had independently developed virtually identical disciplines and conclusions: "in Musike, Logike, Arythmetyke, and Geometrye they have founde oute in a manner all that oure auncient Philosophers have tawghte."[130] That goes far toward explaining the amazing rapidity with which—to judge from Hythlodaye's account—the writings of the Greeks became the backbone of their curriculum, once had communicated these writings to them. The Utopians very rapidly developed a preference for Greek literature and philosophy; while they did read Latin poets and historians, they turned to the Greeks for deeper philosophical insights.[131] This of course reflects More's own attitude, and shows that he and his northern fellow-humanists, foremost among them Erasmus, had been seized by that same enthusiasm for things Greek which had sprung up in Italy a century before. Furthermore, the Utopians' special appreciation of Plato is indicative of More's predilection and shows his great indebtedness to the Platonic renaissance, of which *Utopia* itself is one of the most vivid documents.[132]

Following the example of the *Republic*, then, More establishes an ideal commonwealth. It is carefully constructed so as to provide for the "good" life and the rule of the "best." The criteria for what is "good" and who is "best" are similar to those found in the *Republic*, although not as fully argued and elaborated. High intellectual capacity and the right gifts of character, the proper education with virtue as its goal, are present in both Plato's and More's conceptions. The rule of the "best," in both instances, is carefully safeguarded and perpetuated. In the *Utopia*, the "best" are classically educated humanistic philosophers and statesmen. This radical and theoretical postulation of a commonwealth ruled by scholars represents the application of Erasmus' and More's humanism to the problems of society. While there is no indication that More thought he could transplant the Utopian order of the learned into the Europe or England of his day and thereby supplant the existing hierarchy, he did presumably hope that the character of the ruling groups could be changed so that they would come closer to his Utopian ideal.

This brings us to the details of the Utopian educational scheme. More provides only a fairly general outline. The Utopians study music, logic, arithmetic, and geometry;[133] in their study of philosophy, they concentrate on Plato and Aristotle, with the greater part of whose works Hythlodaye has acquainted them.[134] They read such poets as Homer, Euripides, Sophocles, and Aristophanes and are "delyted wyth Lucianes mery conceytes and jestes"[135]—some of the latter had been translated by More and Erasmus,[136] and this judgment evidently reflects More's own pleasure in them. "Of the historians they have Thucidides, Herodotus, and Herodian," and "they sett greate stoore by Plutarches bookes."[137] They also study some medical works of Hippocrates and Galen. The core of Utopian education would seem to be Greek philosophy, literature, historiography, and science; in the particular context in which More enumerates these "basic" works, not a single Latin author is mentioned. The Utopians are also interested in Latin historians and poets,[138] but it is clear that Latin works are second in importance to those of the Greeks.

While More does not give a very full description of Utopian education, we are surely justified in assuming from what he does say that he would expect the Utopians to follow in their teaching materials, methods, and aims such works as Erasmus' *De Ratione Studii* and *De Copia*, or William Lily's Latin grammar. These provided the basis for the curriculum of St. Paul's School in London, which had been recently established by his friend John Colet.[139] (More was closely associated with the Mercers, whom Colet put in charge of St. Paul's; William Lily, also a friend of More, was its first headmaster.)[140] To amplify the picture he gives of Utopian education, we may also take into consideration More's own pedagogical achievements and attitudes. Since there is every reason to believe that More was in agreement with what he describes as the education of the Utopians, and since it very closely resembles his own practical efforts,[141] we are justified in using the latter to elucidate the former, and vice versa.

In his own household and "school," More gave a practical demonstration of the application of Utopian educational principles and methods, and an example which others might follow.[142] In his letter to Oxford University,[143] with which he intervened in the dispute between the reactionary "Trojans" and the humanistic "Greeks," he made his program and position clear. There is other evidence, such as his letter to Dorp,[144] which helps fill in the picture of his vigorous fight for humanistic scholarship and education. Like the families he describes in *Utopia*, More's own large family lived with him in his house: "The saide three daughters, with their husbandes, and his sonne and heire, with eleven nephews and neeces of his foresaide children, continued in house with him untill suche time as he was sent to the towre."[145] Among a number of others who were educated there, was "Margaret, daughter of John à Barrow . . . who some time after 1522 married Thomas Elyot."[146] The circle which centered in this household came to constitute the most civilized group in the England of Henry VIII; a number of its members rose to legal or parliamentary office or were active as writers.[147] Erasmus compares More's house with the Platonic Academy, and in a letter to Budé, he gives an enthusiastic report on the scholarly achievements of More's children.[148] Harpsfield, More's biographer, repeats that More brought up his "children from their youth . . . in vertue, and knowledge both in the latin and the greeke tonges."[149] Like many others, Harpsfield particularly praises the accomplishments of Margaret, More's daughter,[150] and points with particular emphasis to the custom which More had established in his household, but which was then very unusual in England, of educating women thoroughly in the classics. He states that Margaret's daughter, Mrs. Bassett—i.e., the third generation—translated Eusebius from Greek into English.[151] Stapleton tells us that More's "first care was the religious training of his children: second only to this was his zeal for their advancement in learning."[152] He goes on to enumerate the various tutors who taught the family, such as John Clements, William Gunnell, Richard Hirt (or Hyrde),[153] and the astronomer, Nicolaus Kratzer.[154] William Gunnell had been in Erasmus' circle in Cambridge; some letters from Erasmus to him are extant.[155] Stapleton continues: "The subjects of study were not only Latin and Greek literature, but also logic and philosophy, in which subject formal disputations were arranged, and also mathematics. Sometimes, too, the writings of the Fathers were read. . . ."[156] In what has remained of More's correspondence with his "school," we see him as a firm but gentle and patient teacher, practicing Erasmus' injunctions that children should be lured and guided in their studies rather than prodded and beaten, precepts that are later repeated by Elyot.

In a letter to William Gunnell, More expands both on the humanistic education of women and on the aims of education in general. He states that learning is not to be pursued for its own sake and for the attainment of empty glory but for practical reasons:

Among all the benefits that learning bestows on men, there is none more excellent than this, that by the study of books we are taught in that very study to seek not praise, but utility. Such has been the teaching of the most learned men, especially of philosophers, who are the guides of human life, although some may have abused learning, like other good things, simply to court empty glory and popular renown.[157]

In *Utopia*, the priests instruct the children in learning as well as in virtue and good manners, and put into their heads "good opinions and profitable for the conservation of their weale publique."[158] And in his letter to Oxford University concerning the struggle of "Greeks" and "Trojans"[159]—probably written shortly before the letter to Gunnell—More expounds further on the aims which the scholastically benighted Oxford dons ought to be pursuing in educating the young, but which they appear to be sadly neglecting:

Although no one denies that a man can be saved without a knowledge of Latin and Greek or of any literature at all, yet learning, yea, even worldly learning . . . prepares the mind for virtue. Everyone knows that the attainment of this learning is almost the only reason why students flock to Oxford. . . . The State needs men learned in the law. A knowledge of human affairs, too, must be acquired, which is so useful even to a theologian. . . . And this knowledge can nowhere be drawn so abundantly as from the poets, orators and historians. There are even some who make the knowledge of things natural a road to heavenly contemplation, and so pass from philosophy and the liberal arts . . . to theology.[160]

He goes on to discuss the usefulness of classical learning, of the knowledge of Hebrew, Greek, and Latin, for theologians—was not the New Testament, were not the works of the Church Fathers written in Greek?—and states what he had already declared in *Utopia:* that all good philosophy is Greek, and that (with the exception of Cicero and Seneca) there is nothing worth while in Latin in this field.[161] Finally, he tries to put Oxford to shame by his remark that in Cambridge ("cui vos praelucere semper consucvistis"!)[162] Greek studies are being supported. The views expressed by More in this remarkable letter to Oxford were shared by the king, and we can assume from the fact that More became High Steward of Oxford University in 1524 and of Cambridge University in 1525 that his opinions on education carried some weight.

Knowledge of human affairs, contemplation, active virtue are the aims of liberal education, and the main vehicle of this education is the study of poets and orators, historians and philosophers. This education, which seems to be much the same in England and in Utopia, prepares men for positions in the state, as More explicitly says in his letter, and for the Church. (We have noted that the priests in Utopia are prominent members and teachers of the order of the learned; More would like the priests in England to be similarly learned in human letters since this would make them better theologians.) The kind of education which More introduced in his own home, advocated for England, and described as being universal in Utopia has the essentially practical aim of preparing a man for a useful function in society. It is derived from humanistic doctrine, and More elaborated it in close conjunction with Erasmus.[163] The classical authors provide both practical knowledge of human affairs and a road to heavenly contemplation. They lead the reader to that public-minded, unselfish activity described by the term "virtue."

To be good through humanistic knowledge is the Utopian ideal. More implies that, from a philosophical point of view, this is the highest ideal that can be imagined, but he indicates that a religious ideal of life based on divine revelation may be higher than the Utopian ideal. What he strives for is what the Utopians are about to achieve—if only a priest will go to Utopia![164]—and what he advocates in his letter to Oxford: the combination of classical wisdom and Christian piety. In *Utopia*, More presumably describes the highest kind of life possible to pagans, that is to men who are guided solely by the light of reason and not by that of faith. "The good life in Utopia is represented as achieved by man's wisdom and energy alone, whereas the wretched conditions in Europe were the sorry accomplishment of Christians, who possessed not only the same 'natural' gifts as the Utopians but above all the aid of divine revelation."[165] If the Christians were to follow the lead of the Utopians, More may have felt, and were to add their revealed religion to that of reason, they could even outdo the Utopians.[166] Meanwhile, however, More develops a comprehensive philosophical religion which is independent of the Christian faith and complete in itself. This philosophy is the dominant force in Utopia; it does not suppress the great variety of religious faiths that are tolerated there, but rather provides a common denominator for them. As far as dogma is concerned, the only articles of faith which Utopians are expected to believe in, on pain of losing their rights of citizenship, are that the soul is immortal, and that there are rewards and punishments after death for good and bad deeds.[167]

Their religion is in happy agreement with their Epicurean philosophy that they should direct their activities toward the attainment of pleasure, and that virtue consists in living according to this doctrine: "Very nature saye they prescribeth to us a joyful life, that is to say, pleasure as the ende of all oure operations. And they define vertue to be lyfe ordered accordynge to the prescripte of nature."[168] When investigating the nature of true felicity, they always "ioyne unto the reasons of Philosophye certeyne principles taken oute of religion,"[169] because reason alone is insufficient for that purpose— although they use it to prove their religious principles—and because their religion itself is centered around the concept of happiness.[170] However, not all kinds of pleasure lead to felicity: through religion, investigation, experience, and observation they have learned to distinguish true from false pleasures: "they thinke not felicitie to reste in all pleasure, but only in that pleasure that is good and honeste."[171] The Utopians, fortunately, are in agreement as to what pleasures are good or bad. The principal criterion of pleasure, it would seem, is its social usefulness rather than personal self-gratification.[172] Man is prompted by reason "to lead a joyous Epicurean life, not in selfish privacy, but actively aiding other men to equal felicity."[173] To act according to nature by recognizing and pursuing true pleasures, one must be guided by reason: "He dothe followe the course of nature, which in desiering and refusinge thinges is ruled by reason."[174]

While the Utopians define pleasure as "every motion and state of the bodie or mynde wherin man hath naturally delectation,"[175] the actual pleasures that reason allows them to indulge in are clearly very much more restricted than this definition would seem to indicate. Furthermore, there are degrees and kinds of true pleasures. They count the pleasures of the mind "the chiefist and most principall of all,"[176] and enjoy them more than pleasures of the body. The greatest of these pleasures "come of the exercise of vertue, and conscience of good life";[177] and the soul enjoys "that delectation, that commethe of the contemplation of trewth."[178] The recognition of truth and the realization of the good in their communal life by the process called "exercise of vertue" are the highest joys a Utopian is capable of experiencing. This felicity is open to all who aspire to it; it is achieved to its fullest degree by those who have the tasks of devoting themselves to the pleasures of the mind and of "exercising virtue" in government, i.e., to the order of the learned. The pleasures of the body, however, are not neglected. More enumerates them all, including eating, drinking, and scratching.[179] Beauty, strength, nimbleness[180] are pleasant gifts of nature to which the Utopians pay much attention; their estimation of these qualities is reminiscent of the Greek attitude toward them. The Utopians enjoy riding and fencing, dancing and music. Pleasures that are good and do not arise from false desires and passions lead to the perfect life and are part of it.

Man's task is to find the good and pleasant order of this world. The *princeps*, the chief philarchs, and the priests, who through their natural gifts and the discipline of a rigorous education have become members of the ruling group, guard this order which makes the good and pleasant life possible. Like Plato, More creates an aristocracy of the mind which, in contrast to the ruling group in Plato's *Republic*, is partly chosen through democratic processes. As noted earlier, there are explicit safeguards against tyranny and oligarchy. Those against ochlocracy and demagogy[181] are not so explicitly described, but are equally stringent: obviously one who is insufficiently educated or who holds wrong opinions is not eligible for higher offices. In order to be eligible, a person first has to be taken into the order of the learned, and to be educated by it. It should be kept in mind that it is not the electorate that suggests who should be taken into that group, but it is the priests, who are themselves members of it, who initiate the proceedings, by suggesting the candidates among whom the philarchs then make their choice. Thus, despite popular elections and other democratic features, it is impossible for a demagogue or a dissident of whom the ruling group disapproves to gain influence and power in Utopia. By these methods the rule of reason is carefully established and elaborately protected in Utopia, with the character and position of the humanistic aristocracy as the cornerstone of the entire structure.

From the point of view of humanism, the decade in the middle of which *Utopia* was composed was the most fruitful in More's life. It was a period during which he and Erasmus were frequently together, and during which the latter produced some of his most influential works; More's children received their education at this time, and the important letters to Dorp and to Oxford University were written. This productivity of both More and Erasmus is not a coincidence but the result of a joint effort born of convictions common to these men and their friends. The ideas that originated in their circle during this period were taken up and developed further by younger men, in England notably by Sir Thomas Elyot.

Later, More became preoccupied with affairs of state and with the religious issues raised by the Lutheran reform. Recent biographers, notably R. W. Chambers, have claimed that More's actions and thoughts in this later period are entirely consistent with those of his earlier, "Utopian" period,[182] and have found a complete and heroic unity in his words and deeds, in his life and martyr's death. Without wishing to argue the point here, I see a definite change of emphasis in More's life after the Reformation began to threaten his faith, a turning away from the humanistic problems that had occupied him earlier, to the religious problems that then became more urgent, and a concurrent change in his attitude. Thus, despite Professor Chambers' skilful effort to demonstrate, for instance, the consistency of More's views with regard to religious toleration, it seems to me that there is a distinct divergence between the spirit of *Utopia* in this respect and More's later attitude toward toleration and heresy. As Professor Conyers Read has said, "It is hard to believe that More could have written *Utopia* after the Lutheran revolt and impossible to believe that . . . he did not . . . lose a great deal of his sweet reasonableness in the heat of the fight."[183] The humanism which had produced the picture of a state based on reason and education eventually receded into the background of his thought and was largely overshadowed by a concern with theological issues; in his later period, More became more conservative and dogmatic than he had been when he wrote *Utopia*.

The spirit which created *Utopia* lived on in the work of his friend, Sir Thomas Elyot. We have noted that Elyot's wife went to More's "school," and we know that More and Elyot himself were friends. Elyot specifically adapted the ideas of Erasmus and More concerning the functions of a humanistic upper class to English conditions. In *The boke named the Gouernour*, he showed how the Utopian "order of the learned" could be transferred into the reality of contemporary England.

# IV

# Sir Thomas Elyot

IN HIS treatises on education and government, Erasmus tried to create models for the perfect humanistic ruler and the good society. He intended these models as guides for any individual and nation that shared the classical traditions of Greece and Rome and embraced the Christian faith, for the whole of Christendom rather than for any specific country. While his cosmopolitan attitude was advantageous for the diffusion of his ideas and influence throughout Europe, it involved at the same time a detachment and lack of concreteness which often stood in the way of a practical application of his ideas. Erasmus had investigated the ethical foundations of a humanistic society, and he had provided a system of education which should serve as the basis of such a society; but the picture of the kind of society and individual which he would regard as a fulfilment of his wishes remained so vague that it could hardly serve as a guide for the construction of a social order. On many problems, Erasmus' advice was eagerly sought and followed: philological and pedagogical questions are typical instances. But his name does not evoke the picture of a distinctive social and political order, or of a definite type of man—unless it be that of the scholar. It remained for other humanists—some under his direct or indirect influence—to create the images of Utopia, of the *cortegiano*, the *honnête homme*, the "governour" and gentleman.

Sir Thomas Elyot (1490[?]–1546)[1] was more than twenty years younger than Erasmus, more than ten years younger than Sir Thomas More. Erasmus' and More's ideals of an intellectual aristocracy were crystallized in his figure of the "governour" which adapted them to concrete English conditions. Elyot does not seem to have known Erasmus personally, but a close personal relationship between him and More certainly existed. He knew such Erasmian writings as the *Institutio Principis Christiani*, which he used and recommended,[2] and he apparently followed Erasmus' precepts in the style of his English translations from the classics.[3] The information concerning his relationship with More is unfortunately very scanty, but, besides mentioning that Elyot's wife went to More's school, Stapleton tells us that among More's "friends and companions in the pursuit of polite literature" was "Thomas Eliot, a well-known English writer."[4] Elyot himself corroborates this statement in a letter written to Thomas Cromwell, probably in the autumn of 1536, in which the following passage occurs: "I therefor beseche your goode lordship now to lay apart the remembraunce of the amity betwene me and Sir Thomas More, which was but *usque ad aras,* as is the proverb, consydering that I was never so moche addict unto him as I was unto truthe and fidelity toward my soveraigne lorde as godd is my juge."[5] This letter, written after More's execution, was intended to persuade Cromwell to intercede with the king so that he "might reward me with some convenyent porcion of his suppressid landes,"[6] i.e., with some expropriated church property. Apparently, Elyot's friendship with More had been such a well-known fact that at this point that past relationship became a danger or at least a considerable impediment to Elyot and his ambitions.

Elyot did not disclaim his friendship with the executed More, but evidently defended himself against the imputation that he might have shared More's political attitude which had aroused Henry VIII's violent hostility. That, at least, is Croft's very plausible interpretation[7] of the words "usque ad aras": what Elyot probably had in mind when quoting these words was Erasmus' interpretation in the *Adagia* of a saying attributed by Plutarch to Pericles, who, with the Greek equivalent of "usque ad aram amicus sum," refused to perjure himself by giving false testimony on behalf of a friend. The sense of the remainder of Elyot's passage bears out Croft's contention that, by referring to this proverb, Elyot meant to indicate that the limits of a private friendship were reached when they conflicted with what he considered to be his duty toward God and his sovereign. This attitude would agree with Elyot's vigorous support in his treatises of the royal authority. Nevertheless, the request "to lay apart the remembraunce" of his friendship with More has an unpleasant ring when it comes from a man who, in his writings, extolled the virtues of heroic, classical friendship, and particularly so since it is coupled with a request for material benefits.

Apart from Elyot's own reference to his friendship with More, there is evidence of his close relationship with the younger members of the More circle. Roper, More's earliest biographer, concludes his account of More's life with the story[8] which, he claims, Elyot himself told him, that the emperor, Charles V, sent for the English ambassador, Sir Thomas Elyot, to tell him the news of the execution of Sir Thomas More, and to take that occasion to express his admiration for More. Professor A. F. Pollard has made it clear that Roper's recollection was inaccurate,[9] for Elyot was not at Charles's court when More was executed: in fact, he had left it more than three years before that event, even before More had resigned his office. Professor R. W. Chambers argues[10] that, nevertheless, Roper's story—which is repeated by Harpsfield and Stapleton[11]—is not altogether devoid of factual basis: Charles did have advance news of More's impending resignation, and at some occasion expressed his admiration for More to Elyot, who repeated the emperor's words to some of More's friends when he came back to London shortly after More had resigned. If we accept Chambers' explanation, the following factors with regard to Elyot's relationship to More and his group emerge: (1) Charles probably was aware of Elyot's friendship with More; otherwise he would not have extolled More and, by implication, criticized Henry, to the latter's ambassador at that particular critical juncture. (2) Elyot was on terms of considerable intimacy and mutual confidence with More's friends; otherwise he admiration for More to Elyot, who repeated the emperor's words not only to Roper but to the whole group. Roper is very emphatic in declaring that the "matter was by the same Sir Thomas Eliott to my self, to my wife, to maister Clement and his wife, to master John Haywood and his wife, and [unto] divers other his Freinds accordingly reported."[12] Roper clearly had such a meeting in mind, and even if he confuses the occasion and Elyot's words, a close connection between Elyot and More and his group emerges from this account. Elyot and More were friends and shared the same humanistic interests; their ways parted when More chose martyrdom and Elyot made the accommodation necessary for survival in Henrician England.

Some proofs for the existence of a close relationship between More and Elyot have here been rather fully examined because that relationship seems to me to be a very important link between Elyot's ideas and those of More and Erasmus, and because in the accounts I have seen there is usually no more than a passing reference to its existence.[13] In consequence, Elyot's dependence on Italian thought, though no doubt very great, is generally allowed to overshadow his very considerable indebtedness to Erasmus and More, and the close connection of his thought and program with theirs.

There is one important and typical difference between More's and Elyot's humanistic works: More, like Erasmus, wrote his humanistic works in Latin, whereas Elyot wrote his in English. The *Utopia* was neither published in England, nor translated into English, during More's lifetime, whereas *The boke named the Gouernour* was written in English, published in London, and went through eight editions within fifty years of the time of its first publication in 1531.[14] Elyot, rather than More, was the great popularizer of humanism in England, and, to judge from the continued demand for his works, his efforts were popular and successful. He blended the ideas of More and Erasmus with those of a number of other humanists, mostly Italian, to arrive at his own conceptions of man and society, in which the postulates of the various humanists were so selected and modified as to become directly applicable to existing English conditions.

While Elyot was strongly influenced by the ideas current in the circle of Erasmus and More, the influence of Italian humanism[15] is also evident in his portrayal of the perfect "governour." The courtier, as described in Italian courtesy books, was a more distinct type than Erasmus' Christian prince and Christian knight, had a wider appeal, and was more readily imitable. As a social type, he also bore a closer relationship to contemporary reality than did More's Utopian "order of the learned." The practical concreteness of the Italian model appealed to Elyot and other sixteenth-century Englishmen who copied and transformed it to suit the needs of their own country.

Italian authors of courtesy books, such as Patrizi,[16] Palmieri,[17] and Castiglione,[18] quite naturally aimed their precepts at Italian conditions. They were narrower and often shallower, more concerned with immediate, practical situations and more limited by their national horizon than Erasmus. Palmieri's *optimo cittadino* could only exist in the city states of Renaissance Italy, and Castiglione's *cortegiano* only in her courts. But the writings of classical antiquity, foremost among them those of Plato, Aristotle, Cicero, and Quintilian, formed the basis of these conceptions. In so far as the Italians revived and re-formed the classical ideal of humanity, their work was a model and a challenge for all European nations. If those features of the *cortegiano* which were suited only to his local environment could be modified, he could serve as an example in any occidental country.[19]

The pattern of the *cortegiano*, evolved by humanists since the days of Petrarch,[20] achieved its *locus classicus* in the work of Castiglione. It replaced the medieval conception of man, though some medieval elements remained in it. In the feudal order of medieval society, military achievements and inherited dignity had determined a man's rank in the world, unless he had chosen to dedicate his life to pious contemplation and work, in which case he was expected to find his proper place in the ecclesiastical hierarchy according to his piety and talents. The knight and the cleric lived in two different worlds, each with his own functions: the one led the *vita activa*, the other the *vita contemplativa;* the one was to perform valorous deeds, the other to please God by devotion to religion and letters. The clergy was the only erudite group in medieval society, and it was from this group that the higher political and administrative positions which demanded its skills were apt to be filled. It is true that with those members of the clergy who occupied themselves with the affairs of church and state, the contemplative life was apt to give way to the active, but this was a situation created by practical necessities and represented a deviation from the ideal. It was only the Renaissance which brought a conscious return to the classical fusion of the active and the contemplative aspects of life, a revival of the Greek conception of the "political man." True nobility was no longer derived from birth and knightly valor alone, but was supposed to be based on man's essential quality, his ἀρετή and to be expressed in deeds inspired by virtue and guided by learning. While this conception retains some medieval elements, the emphasis on "virtue" and the requirement of learning as prerequisites of nobility are distinctly new demands, derived from the example of classical antiquity.[21] Action not based on knowledge was thought to be worthless; knowledge without resulting action was thought to be wasted. In this amalgamation of the active and the contemplative, the Platonic ideal was reborn: only he really fulfils his role in the world who, through learning and contemplation, attains the knowledge of the divine good, realizes it within himself and reproduces it in his sphere of activity.

This, briefly, was the ethical foundation underlying the conception of the *cortegiano*. The Italian courtier's environment was the small court typical of the Italian Renaissance, which was frequently based on the most iniquitous tyranny. Far from realizing Plato's demand for the highest self-realization of the individual in a just state, this kind of court was apt to bring out a man's worst qualities. Often the courtier's activities under a tyrannous regime were turned into social and aesthetic rather than into political channels, and that, in part, is Castiglione's way out of the dilemma. According to him, the courtier was to mold the life at court into a beautiful pattern, and to be an example of its perfection. Despite such preoccupations, however, the courtier did have definite political duties: while he could not exercise any independent governmental functions, because all power was usually concentrated in the hands of the prince and exercised at his arbitrary whim, Castiglione suggested that the courtier should use his influence to show the prince the path of virtue, and to assist him in making the right decisions. Not only was the courtier to advise the prince, but his most essential and fruitful task was to educate the young prince in conformity with humanistic precepts. If goodness were planted in the heart and mind of the young prince, it should eventually prevail in the state through his just and virtuous action.[22]

The Renaissance epigones of Plato's guardians in Italy probably had to be courtiers because the courts were the political and cultural, social and artistic, centers of her states. Able and ambitious men could put their talents to the best use in the vicinity of princes, for only there could they hope to gain political influence. At first sight, the courtier as described by Castiglione would seem to bear little resemblance to his classical prototype. He is burdened with a bewildering mass of ceremonial, "courteous" manners which he has to learn carefully and observe strictly. The enumeration of the rules of polite behavior in almost every courtesy book seems to overshadow, or to eliminate completely, any evaluation of the real nature and of the ethical function of man. That is true to a certain extent even of Castiglione's book, the most famous of them all. His courtier at times has an air of shallow formality and playful elegance which curiously contrasts with the ethical justification for his elevated position provided by the author. If we disregard all the petty and superficial rules of courtly behavior, however, and compare Castiglione's work with other books of the same literary genre, Castiglione seems quite convincing because of the seriousness with which he treats the philosophical foundations of his conception, and because of the integrity of his purpose: he wanted to adapt the classical type to the conditions of his own time and place. His elaborate description of the courtier's education and functions could easily be used, since it showed clearly how to become, and behave like, a perfect *homme du monde*.

Erasmus went more deeply into the philosophy of humanistic education than did Castiglione. He had not, however, painted a portrait which could become the pattern of a courtly society. That pattern was provided by Castiglione and his predecessors and imitators. Castiglione's writings were destined to have a widespread influence in England, but the pattern supplied by him was not at first directly applicable there. The structure of the country was very different from that which had produced the Italian figure of the courtier. While the court was the center of national activity under Henry VIII, political life even under the "Tudor despotism" was not concentrated exclusively in the prince and his court. The larger size of England—larger, that is, than the Italian principalities—the continued relative importance of the "country" as against the cities, and the persistence of traditional elements caused political power to be balanced and distributed between Crown and gentry. The latter class had to discharge ancient judicial, administrative, and political duties which were constantly being augmented. While some of its members lived at court, most of them continued to reside in the country, where they exercised the functions of local government. Even those who temporarily came to the capital to sit in parliament or work in the central government usually retained their roots in the country.

The office most frequently held by country gentlemen was that of justice of the peace, a judicial office upon which fell the main burden of the more centralized and efficient administrative system that was being set up by the Tudors. The average gentleman in the reign of Henry VIII had little formal education and little, if any, training in the law—which he was supposed to administer. If he wished to discharge his obligations as a justice of the peace properly, he needed the kind of technical advice on legal questions that was provided in various manuals describing his office.[23] These books gave dry enumerations of his duties, but they could not be expected to provide a new social code which might take the place of the vanishing and no longer adequate medieval code of knighthood. Castiglione's *Cortegiano* could not fill this need because its precepts were suited to the utmost refinement and elegance of the Italian courts and held little that could appeal to, and serve the needs of, a rustic, unpolished, and rather independent landowning gentry. It is significant that Hoby's English translation of the *Cortegiano* appeared more than thirty years after the original,[24] at the beginning of Elizabeth's reign. It was under Elizabeth that the court reached its climax as a social and cultural center, and that, in consequence, Castiglione's doctrines became more directly relevant.

The English gentry of the earlier Tudor period could not yet use Castiglione's rules, and Erasmus' exhortations were too vague. Their need was filled by Sir Thomas Elyot. In *The boke named the Gouernour*, the best known of his works, and in his other writings, such as the *Image of Governance*[25] and *Of the Knowledge Which Maketh a Wise Man*[26] (described as *A disputacion Platonike*) he was concerned with the problem of creating and educating a governing class. A typical representative of that class, Elyot lived mostly in the country, and held such offices (in Oxfordshire, Berkshire, Cambridgeshire, etc.) as justice of the peace and sheriff;[27] we have noted, however, that he was at one time (1531/32) Henry's ambassador to Charles V—an appointment perhaps connected with the success of the *Governour*.[28] He had other experience in the central government: for more than six years (from 1523), he had been performing the duties of clerk of the council on Wolsey's recommendation,[29] but had been "discharged without any recompense, rewarded only with the order of knighthode, honorable and onerouse, having moche lasse to lyve on than bifore."[30] He also probably served as a member of Parliament in his later years.[31] The rules he set down in his books were the answers he found for the problems and questions that arose in his own life; they constitute a system that he felt would be valuable for many who were in a position similar to his own.

In the figure of the "governour," Elyot amalgamated such chivalrous traditions as were still alive in England with humanistic ideas to form the English counterpart of the *cortegiano*. The title of Elyot's main work significantly points to the need for a man different from the Italian courtier, for an independent individual, capable of governing, able to act and decide on his own.[32] While it is undoubtedly true that Elyot wrote the *Governour* because there was need for such a work, it is still interesting to speculate whether any specific impetus started him and furthermore what men and works influenced him in its composition. These questions have been investigated, and certain theories concerning them have been advanced.[33] The general conclusion seems to be that Elyot was a well-read humanist who, like his learned contemporaries, used his knowledge of classical and contemporary works freely and without the scrupulous acknowledgment which a modern scholar would be expected to make. While he was not especially profound or original, he did think for himself and came to his own conclusions. Like a painter, he took his colors freely where he found them and mixed them to his own taste for his picture. Like all humanists, he may, therefore, justly be accused of constant and flagrant plagiarism, but he plagiarizes so well that it is sometimes difficult to catch him in the act. His modern interpreters, beginning with Croft, the nineteenth-century editor of the *Governour,* can assign a number of passages to the sources from which he presumably took them, but they are at odds as to what sources might have served him as examples for other portions of his work. To quote one instance: there is the question whether Elyot followed Francesco Patrizi's *De Regno et Regis Institutione* in his work. Croft assumed that Elyot was dependent, for certain passages at least, on Patrizi's treatise. Schlotter, the author of a recent dissertation on the subject, sets out to prove that Croft had no factual basis for his assertion. He claims that there is no similarity in the plan of the two works,[34] and arrives at the conclusion that a close textual collation shows corresponding passages only where quotations taken from other authors and common to both works are concerned. Strong similarities in these quotations, and other occasional correspondences, lead Schlotter to agree in the end that Elyot probably read and used Patrizi,[35] but he maintains that most of the similarities in their works are due not to Elyot's copying but to the fact that both were Platonists.[36] In another recent dissertation, Warren claims that Elyot actually used Patrizi's work as a model for Books I and III of the *Governour*[37] and gives a long list of parallel passages.[38] None of these passages, however, are original with Patrizi[39]—a fact which would seem to strengthen Schlotter's claim that Elyot may have made use of some passages which Patrizi had taken from another source, but that he is otherwise not really dependent on him. Warren also finds striking similarities between Elyot's ideal "governour" and Palmieri's *optimo cittadino,* and suggests, without being able to prove it conclusively, that Elyot made use of Palmieri's *Della Vita Civile.* The only point which Warren thinks he can definitely establish in this case is the fact that they pursued similar studies and developed similar political ideas. They both read Quintilian and Plato and used the Platonic conception of the ruling class.[40]

Warren tries to find sources for all the different parts of the *Governour.* He thinks that Book II of that work shows traces of Erasmus' *Institutio Principis Christiani,*[41] and was influenced particularly by Petrarch's *Lettere senili.*[42] The third book, according to Warren, is indebted partly to Plato, partly directly to Cicero, and partly to Patrizi.[43] Much of this indebtedness cannot be established beyond all possible doubt, but Warren makes his theses very plausible. While it seems very likely that Elyot used the work of these authors, the fact that often he cannot be conclusively convicted of literary theft from them proves that he was able to use his authorities with discrimination, that if necessary he could go back from contemporary to classical sources, and that he was capable of making the writings from which he borrowed serve his own ends. He was eclectic in appropriating passages and ideas that might be useful to his conception. We can safely say that Elyot followed the Platonic tradition in humanism which Palmieri, Patrizi, and Erasmus had represented before him. Since he wrote on a theme which had occupied these and other writers—on the education of the ruling class and the kind of society in which such a class should predominate—it is natural to expect certain similarities in his work and theirs, and it is most likely that he made use of whatever guidance he could find in their writings when he was composing his own books.

A more detailed discussion of Castiglione's *Cortegiano* as a probable contemporary source of the *Governour* seems relevant. That work was published three years before Elyot's, and may have been his incentive to compose something equivalent in English. While again there is no incontrovertible proof that Elyot knew the *Cortegiano*, there is fairly good circumstantial evidence that he read Castiglione before or while composing the *Governour*.[44] Thomas Cromwell, with whom Elyot was well acquainted, appears to have had the *Cortegiano* in his possession shortly after the book came out in Italy.[45] As Van Dyke has ingeniously pointed out, this book was much on Cromwell's mind, and so it is very likely that he discussed it with friends such as Elyot.[46] Even if we do not go so far as to assume, with Warren, that Cromwell practically commissioned Elyot to write the *Governour*[47]—in which case he would have suggested the *Cortegiano* to the prospective author as the outstanding example of a similar work—their common interest in political and social questions would naturally have caused Cromwell and Elyot to discuss a book like the *Cortegiano*. There is no conclusive proof by which Elyot's knowledge of that work can be confirmed. Warren makes the strong point that Elyot, in recommending the inclusion of painting and sculpture in the young governour's course of studies, was following Castiglione.[48] At the same time, he rightly points out that some of the assumptions that have been made as to the extent of Castiglione's influence are extravagant.

Whatever the degree of Castiglione's influence,[49] Elyot's *Gov-*

*ernour* is the English counterpart of the *Cortegiano*—a crude counterpart, it is true, with much that sounds ponderous, commonplace, and mediocre, and without the Italian's superb mastery of form and matter; yet it is a genuine creation of Elyot's mind, not without orginality, sincere in its aims and, as it turned out, highly influential in his country. The two writers are truly representative of their respective civilizations: Castiglione was the end product of a highly urbane and refined civilization and wrote with a corresponding brilliance almost brittle in its perfection; Elyot stood at the beginning of a great period in the civilization of his country and had not quite shaken off what might be termed a certain archaic heaviness in style and thought. His great achievement was the adaptation of the humanistic ideal of man and society to English needs and conditions: he created a new social norm which the English ruling class, then in its most formative period, could and did adopt as its own. The thought of Italian and northern humanists is fused in his conception.

The *Governour* is written as a guide and example for those who are appointed to some responsible position by their king. Elyot implies that the education of a king and that of one who is called to rule in a less exalted position must be based on the same principles, and that the criteria by which their characters may be judged are identical.[50] He thus helps us to explain the great popularity of books concerned with the right education of princes: they were written not so much for the princes, whose virtuous images they were supposed to mirror, and to whom they were formally addressed, but for the ruling classes in general. In his *Image of Governance*, Elyot makes this quite clear: the life of the Roman Emperor Alexander Severus, which that work describes, ". . . maye worthily be a paterne to knyghtes, an example to iudges, a myrrour to prynces, a beautifull ymage to all theym that are lyke to be governours. . . ."[51] All prospective governors, then, should shape their lives after the example of the emperor and follow him in their actions.[52] With the same educational end in mind, Elyot writes most of his other works. To show the range of his ideas, we shall bring the *Image of Governance* and other comparatively unknown writings into the discussion, but our main concern will be with the *Governour*.

In that work, Elyot proposes to describe "the beste fourme of education or bringing up of noble children from their nativitie, in suche maner as they may be founde worthy, and also able to be governours of a publike weale."[53] The formation of the future governour must begin at his birth. Comparing himself to a gardener who fosters the growth of a precious plant and protects it from weeds,[54] Elyot declares that he is anxious to shelter the growing child from the beginning, and to develop in him the aptitude to rule from the very moment he is born.[55] Strangely enough, the first step in this direction is Elyot's stringent injunction that men be kept away from the nursery, and that the child be surrounded entirely by women carefully selected for their virtue and good manners.[56] (Men, it seems, are liable to corrupt the young mind with their crude vulgarity!) Carrying the analogy with the gardener further, Elyot declares that every care should be taken to prevent a poisonous dew from penetrating into the small and tender bud—otherwise the fruit may grow wild and poison entire states.[57] Therefore, great care is to be taken in the selection of playmates and similar matters.[58] Sweet manners and virtuous customs are to be "instilled" into the child by "most pleasaunt allurynges";[59] Elyot thus follows Quintilian and Erasmus and anticipates Pestalozzi and Froebel. His whole method of teaching is based on the conviction that kindness is preferable to the inhuman methods of cramming and punishment prevalent at this time: the boy should be lured into learning with "praises and . . . praty giftes," rather than forced into it by harshness and flogging.[60]

Even before he is seven years old, he should learn to speak, read, and write pure and elegant Latin. Elyot suggests that nurses, capable of conversing fluently in that language, should be chosen for this purpose. It seems hardly likely that he could have met with much response to this particular suggestion![61] His other injunction, that the father should teach the boy Latin, is much more likely to have been followed, although it certainly never became the accepted practice. In his day, Elyot still had to defend it against the prevailing attitude of his contemporaries by declaring that it does not hurt a gentleman's reputation to do this[62] rather than to instruct his child in the art of playing dice and cards.[63]

At the age of seven, the boy should be removed from the company of women and intrusted to the charge of an "auncient and worshipfull" tutor.[64] His primary concern is to be the formation of the boy's character; formal instruction in the various branches of knowledge is subordinated to this end. If the boy shows a natural inclination to be courteous, charitable, and open minded, such qualities are to be encouraged, whereas bad ones should be suppressed.[65] The teacher should not burden the pupil with too much work, because

87

that would "dull or oppress" his tender and delicate wit. The lessons should be interspersed with some pleasant recreation, such as the playing of a musical instrument. The teacher, following Plato, will use even this playful exercise to endow his pupil with a better understanding of the state. In fact, the knowledge and understanding of music is essential "for the better attaynynge the knowlege of a publike weale: whiche . . . is made of an ordre of astates and degrees, and by reason therof, conteineth in it a perfect harmony."[66] Elyot does not describe the relationship between musical and political harmony in any detail, but refers tutor and pupil to Plato and Aristotle for an explanation.

Like Castiglione, Elyot suggests that other artistic abilities in the young man should also be stimulated. Among them, he mentions painting and sculpture.[67] After apologizing for falsely appearing to make of a nobleman "a commune painter or kerver,"[68] he defends his injunction by pointing to the practical uses of these arts—drawing might be useful in war—but cautions his governour against practicing them in public. While it is remarkable that Elyot goes as far as he does in the defense of these arts, his reasons for advocating their practice are mostly utilitarian. He does not betray any great aesthetic appreciation, and one wonders what he may have thought of a man like Holbein who, when Elyot sat for him, undoubtedly was so "common" as to be "openly stained or embrued with sondry colours!"[69]

Between the ages of seven and thirteen, the boy reads first Greek, then Latin literature. He is not sent to school, but instructed by a private tutor—a suggestion that reflects Elyot's own education at home rather than at a school. Besides insisting on a high scholarly standard of instruction, Elyot emphasizes the importance of the tutor's human quality. By his example as much as by his teaching, the tutor is to draw out and develop the good qualities of his pupil. At this stage of the educational curriculum, the greatest value attaches to the study of the poets.[70] Poetry, Elyot insists, has the strongest formative power: it presents inspiring examples which inflame the young mind with the desire to imitate them. He recommends Aesop, Lucian, and Aristophanes, but above all others Homer, "from whom as from a fountaine proceded all eloquence and lernyng. For in his bokes be contained, and moste perfectly expressed . . . instructions for politike governaunce of people: with the worthy commendation and laude of noble princis: where with the reders shall be so all inflamed, that they most fervently shall desire and coveite, by the imitation of their vertues, to acquire semblable glorie."[71] Some Latin poets, like Virgil, Ovid, and Horace, may similarly inspire their readers. Poetry, then, is not to be read merely for aesthetic enjoyment, but has a definite didactic function: the great classical poets mold the soul of man and inspire him with zeal to imitate the ideal represented by them.

At the age of fourteen, the pupil should learn logic. Then he should study rhetoric, aided by the treatises of Isocrates, Quintilian, and Erasmus, and by the examples of Demosthenes' and Cicero's speeches. As for an Athenian or Roman, it is necessary for an English nobleman to master the art of speaking before a large and critical audience. He may have to argue in council or to speak to "strange ambassadours of great princes," and in doing so will have to "bestowe [wordes] aptly and in their places."[72] "Cosmography" comes next in the curriculum, then history. Like poetry, history has a didactic function. It is to be studied less for objective reasons, for its own sake, than for the lessons it can teach, for the "example of lyvynge" it gives.[73]

Elyot's insistence on the reading of poetry and the study of history as principal formative powers represents a change in emphasis from Erasmus' preoccupation with grammar (in its widest sense), from the humanistic love of rhetoric, and even from More's emphasis on philosophy, although all are present in, and form part of, Elyot's pedagogy. The new importance of history in his scheme probably reflects the prominent position it had assumed in the studies of the Italian humanists; the view of poetry as a moving force and moral example anticipates Sidney's theory and the pedagogical reasons Sidney and Spenser adduce to justify the writing of "heroic poems."

In recommending that the study of history should begin with Livy, Elyot advances a remarkable reason for the choice of this writer: apart from the fact that his elegant style flows "like a fountaine of swete milke," he teaches "howe the mooste noble citie of Rome, of a smalle and poure begynnynge, by prowes and vertue, litell and litell came to the empire and dominion of all the worlde."[74] Elyot really sounds as if he had hoped that a similar imperial expansion of England might ensue if his future governours would read Livy properly. It is interesting to speculate how much the knowledge of Roman history, in the practical manner postulated by Elyot, may have contributed to the establishment and policies of the

British Empire, and it would seem that this influence has been and perhaps continues to be considerable.[75]

The study of Livy and other historians is to be the young man's main preoccupation until he has reached the age of seventeen. Elyot is by no means content to terminate his curriculum at this point, however. While he does not go as far as Plato, whose educational plan extends into mature manhood, Elyot does insist on a continuation of formal education far beyond the age of seventeen and thus advocates a scheme of education very much more thorough and extensive than that prevalent in his own day. At seventeen, the young man may be presumed to be prepared for the study of philosophy, which will teach him how to bridle his courage with reason. More specifically, "moral philosophy," or ethics, is to be the young man's principal preoccupation for the next four years.[76] Its study should begin with such works as Aristotle's *Nicomachean Ethics* and Cicero's *De Officiis*.[77] After these have been studied, and after the student's judgment has "come to perfection," the course in philosophy is to culminate in Plato's works, which "wolde be most studiously radde."[78] In declaring that Plato is "for his divine wisedome and eloquence named the god of Philosophers,"[79] Elyot displays typical humanistic exuberance, but undoubtedly at the same time describes his own evaluation of Plato. The above-mentioned treatises of Aristotle and Cicero, and Plato's works—he does not state which works—"be almoste sufficient to make a perfecte and excellent governour."[80] As an afterthought, Erasmus' *Institutio Principis Christiani*, the only modern work in this list, is mentioned and praised: all gentlemen should always be as familiar with that "lytell boke" as Alexander was with Homer, or Scipio with Xenophon.

For the first time, the Bible appears in this context as part of the "required reading." Surprisingly enough, however, it is not to be studied for theological or even philosophical reasons as much as for the historical lessons the Old Testament can teach: "All the historiall partes of the bible be righte necessarye for to be radde of a noble man, after that he is mature in yeres."[81] The New Testament is not to be read, but to be revered like "a celestiall iewell or relike."[82] This injunction, which seems extraordinary to the modern reader when contrasted with his insistence on the perusal of Plato, shows that Elyot had not adopted a Protestant attitude toward the Bible.[83] The Bible certainly is not very essential in his scheme of education; it is not even as important for him as it is for Erasmus.

In Elyot's educational plan, the formation of the mind is inter-connected with, and dependent on, that of the body. Proper physical exercise is necessary for the maintenance of health, and at the same time it strengthens the spirit.[84] From the age of fourteen onward, the boy is instructed in various sports which make him strong and hard, nimble and quick.[85] Elyot derives many of his recommenda-tions from *De sanitate tuenda*,[86] Linacre's Latin translation of Galen's work, and refers his readers to it. Apart from wrestling, running, and swimming, Elyot recommends some chivalrous exercises like fencing with sword and battle-ax, hunting, and hawking. Above all, it is necessary to learn to ride on horseback at an early age,[87] because riding is the one exercise that most clearly distinguishes a gentleman from the common lot: "the most honorable exercise . . . and that besemeth the astate of every noble persone, is to ryde suerly and clene on a great horse and a roughe, which undoubtedly . . . im-porteth a maiestie and drede to inferiour persones, beholding him above the common course of other men. . . ."[88] Another exercise which he esteems highly, and which he defends vigorously and extensively against the clergy in general and St. Augustine in par-ticular, is dancing. In a long but occasionally very charming treat-ment of the subject,[89] he discusses the different movements and figures of the dance and describes their significance: they are all symbolical of various human characteristics. To justify it as a serious discipline he adduces numerous classical authorities in true human-istic manner. He argues that the dance is beautiful, demands skilful and balanced movements, teaches a sense of proportion, and fashions the body well.[90] Therefore, all those who desire to gain honor and perfect nobility should learn to dance well, "kepynge iuste measure and time."[91] Like Ascham, in his *Toxophilus*, and other writers of the period, Elyot recommends "shootinge in the longe bowe," which "incomparably excelleth all other exercise, passetyme, or solace,"[92] but laments the steady decay of this national sport.

At the age of twenty-one, the young gentleman who has followed Elyot's curriculum should be universally educated. Mentally and physically, he has grown into a real "human" being in the sense in which the humanists used the word, a man who has developed and matured all that is best in him by following the precepts of the ancient Greeks and Romans. After he has reached this stage, he may proceed to study jurisprudence. We see that Elyot insists on the completion of the full humanistic curriculum before he permits the future governour to acquire the restricted and narrow technical knowledge of the law,[93] which he regards mainly as a tool necessary for the job of governing, not as an education in itself. At the same time, he does not disapprove of jurisprudence as such; on the contrary, he is proud that both he and his father have occupied honorable positions in the legal profession,[94] and thinks that the wisdom contained in good laws rivals or surpasses that of the philosophers:[95] While he criticizes the Common Law for being inadequately organized and written in a bad Latin-French-English mixture, he thinks that English law would equal the Roman if these defects were remedied, since it has sifted the best from the laws of all countries.[96]

He does, however, vigorously object to the practice of studying law too early, before the future governour has completed the full humanistic course as set out by him. Coupled with this particular objection is a strong protest against the entire educational system prevalent in his time. Generally speaking, a gentleman's son would be lucky if he received any extended formal education. At best, after being taught the elements of Latin and rhetoric by an inferior teacher, he would be sent to the Inns of Court at the age of fourteen to be crammed with the dull technicalities of the law. An alternative to the study of law was the practice of sending the boy to the household of some great nobleman, where he had no time for further intellectual pursuits because he had to be in continual attendance.[97]

Elyot's suggestions are entirely at variance with these practices, and it is therefore not surprising that he found it necessary to defend his system by a vigorous attack on them. Their inferiority he believed to be due to "the pride, avarice, and negligence of parentes, and the lacke or fewenesse of suffycient maysters or teachers."[98] He had to contend with "that pestiferous opinion" that learning makes a man unfit for important political or administrative positions, and fought against the snobbish prejudice "that to a great gentilman it is a notable reproche to be well lerned."[99] Against all such objections, which sound so genuine that we can almost hear some country squire raise them, he adduces Plato's conception of the philosopher-king: that state would be blessed in which either philosophers ruled or kings became philosophers.[100] He argues that, since Plato and other great philosophers have thus defended the value of education, such noblemen are entirely unreasonable who pay their children's tutors hardly better than their servants, who, out of sheer avarice and prejudice, "desyre to be father rather of a pece of flesshe, that can onely meve and feele, than of a childe that shulde have the perfecte fourme of a man."[101] The perfect form of man—that is the humanistic ideal. The children will not achieve it if they learn only Latin and the dry and hollow rules of medieval rhetoric, and are then plunged into the study of law or into attendance at a big household: if their education is confined to this customary curriculum, they will "like to a trumpet . . . make a soune without any purpose."[102] It is not a sign of education if a man can compose meaningless verses in accordance with all the rules, if he makes high-sounding but empty speeches, or if he produces elegant and inane letters. Neither the scholastic system nor even a superficial veneer of humanism—such as had been acquired by a number of Englishmen in the generations preceding Elyot's—are considered sufficient by him: a man can be truly formed only if he learns to recognize the model of humanity in antiquity and makes it an active force by re-creating it in his own life.

Typical of Elyot's attitude is the high esteem in which he holds Homer and the other poets. We have noted the importance of the poets in his scheme of education. Since he truly believes in a regeneration of man through poetry, he assigns to it a central function. The Greeks and Romans are quoted as believing that poetry is the first philosophy known to man, and that it comprises all wisdom, poets being inspired by "celestiall instinction."[103] Poetry, therefore, according to the philosophers of antiquity, moves man to lead the good life. There is no justification for the philistine belief of Elyot's contemporaries "that in the warkes of poetes is contayned nothynge but baudry":[104] like Sidney half a century after him in the *Apologie for Poetrie*,[105] Elyot defends poetry against this misrepresentation and comes to the conclusion that "none auncient poete wolde be excluded from the leesson of suche one as desireth to come to the perfection of wysedome."[106] He effectively contrasts scholastic rhetoric, which has become an empty outward form,[107] with real understanding of poetry which creates new life.

Thus, Elyot established his educational ideal and a system to implement it, and denounced the inadequate type of education that still prevailed in his day. He warned that, even if his plan were followed and a good beginning had been made under a competent teacher, it would be of no consequence and come to nought unless carried out to the end. If a boy has to go through the "grose or unpleasaunt" study of the Common Law at his most receptive age, when he should be reading poetry and philosophy, his human and intellectual development will be crippled and misdirected.[108] Many of those who are sent to the Inns of Court soon take to gambling and loafing;[109] even if they do not succumb to these temptations and actually pursue their legal studies, they remain narrow-minded and only acquire a partial knowledge which has nothing in common with real wisdom. In a sentence in which he obviously follows Plato's simile of the cave, Elyot condemns the exclusive occupation with purely technical subject matter: "as if they beyng longe in a derke dungeon onely dyd se by the light of a candell, than if after XX or XXX yeres studie they happen to come amonge wyse men, hering matters commened of concerning a publike weale or outwarde affaires betwene princes, they no lasse be astonied than of commyng out of a darke house at noone dayes they were sodaynly striken in the eyen with a bright sonne beame."[110]

If the young gentlemen of his country are educated according to his plan, the result, he thinks, will be that "undoughtedly they shuld become men of so excellent wisedome that throughout all the worlde shulde be founden in no commune weal more noble counsaylours" than in England.[111] In this proud phrase, Elyot clearly shows the way in which humanism and patriotism had become fused in his mind: in contrast to the "internationalist" Erasmus, Elyot and most of his contemporaries among the humanists of all countries made the new learning serve patriotic ends.

Elyot's argument clearly illustrates the application of general principles to the particular problems of his country, and the manner in which humanistic learning is adapted to English purposes. The future governours must first learn to comprehend the origin and nature of states. Through the works of Plato, Aristotle, and Xenophon, they become acquainted with different kinds of states and constitutions or, as we should say, they study philosophy and political theory. When they have acquired this philosophical foundation which enables them to see things in a wider context, they will devote themselves to the study of English jurisprudence with much greater insight and zeal.[112] General knowledge must precede the specialized knowledge of the Common Law; the occupation with universal problems must precede the study of technical questions valid only in particular cases and in one particular country. The thorough erudition thus attained will enable them to put their best qualities at the disposal of king and country; eventually, through its medium, there will be established in England "a publike weale equivalent to the grekes or Romanes."[113] Elyot's ambition to raise his own country to the level of the great states of antiquity shows up in the most vital passages of his work; his patriotism and humanism had fused into a burning desire to make England the equal of Greece and Rome. It should be noted here that Elyot sees the erudition of the individual as the only method by which such greatness can be achieved: this is one of the main factors that distinguish humanistic nationalism from the various diseased collectivistic nationalisms of our own age. There is no other way to Elyot's goal except through the process of perfecting the single personality. At the same time, it is evident that the perfection of the individual is not only seen as an end in itself but has as its ultimate motive the greatness of England.

In his suggestions for study and teaching, Elyot adopts a number of points from Erasmus, but he places greater emphasis than the more rational Erasmus on "intuition" as a vital factor in these processes. He considers human *ratio* without recourse to something beyond it inadequate as a means of attaining knowledge. In this insistence on suprarational means of cognition, he is indebted to the Italian Neoplatonists.[114] Elyot's ideas on the subject are scattered, but appear in their most complete form in his dialogue, *Of the Knowledge Which Maketh a Wise Man*.[115] In that "Platonike" dialogue, he describes the attainment, function, and nature of knowledge. He declares the intuitive comprehension of spiritual things to be the last step on the way to wisdom, thus following the interpretation that had been given to Plato's doctrine at the Florentine academy. The form, as well as the subtitle, of the dialogue itself indicates his Platonism. Elyot imitates the maieutic method of discussion, Plato's famous dialectical and pedagogical device: the master leads the pupil to understanding and finally to the intuitive recognition of ultimate truths through inspired discussion. Thus Elyot speaks of the sparks by which the master lights the fire of true wisdom in his pupil.[116] Ultimate understanding cannot be taught; it can only be aided by a wise friend and master. Socrates, Elyot says, did not teach anything to men, "but rather brought furthe that which all redy was in them."[117] Elyot agrees with him when in the *Governour* he compares himself to the gardener who watches over the free development of a precious plant,[118] and he uses the same comparison in his "disputacion Platonike," *Of the Knowledge Which Maketh a Wise Man*, where his Plato says to Aristippus: "... the sedes which Socrates had sowen in thy minde, do begyn nowe to sprynge with this lyttell waterynge: ... thou shalte shortly perceive the frutes of wysedom . . . spryng abundantly."[119] The intimate connection between maieutic method and inspiration is finally seen in a passage of the *Governour* adapted by Elyot from Plato's *Theaetetus*, where Socrates says: "Never man lerned of me any thinge, all thoughe by my company he became the wiser. I onely exhortynge and the good spirite inspyringe."[120]

Intimately connected with Plato's theory of education is his doctrine of love. Like Plato, Elyot considers *eros* as a central formative power. *Eros* comes from God, and nothing that emanates from God should be more highly valued than "love, called in latine *Amor*, whereof *Amicitia* commeth, named in englisshe frendshippe or amitie."[121] It should be noted that Elyot, by this little philological stratagem, ties love and friendship very closely together, as indeed for Plato *eros* pervades both kinds of human relationships. Elyot feels that, if friendship is taken from a man's life, the sun seems to have gone out of it. Besides basing his argument on Plato, he invokes Aristotle and Cicero to prove that true friendship is a virtue. One should strive to attain it in an age when, owing to the evil influence of ambition, it has become very rare. True friendship is possible only between good men, whose nature reveals a definite affinity of character, manners, and interests.[122]

The value of friendship was a favorite humanistic theme. Elyot does not, as one might suspect, merely reiterate standard phrases and sentiments, but shows by original remarks and interpretations that he has thought about the question independently. In the *Governour*, he tells of various famous friendships of antiquity and dedicates a whole chapter to the story of Titus and Gysippus[123] as a "right goodly example of frendship."[124] It has been demonstrated[125] that Elyot deviates to a considerable extent from Boccaccio, his source, with the obvious intention of assigning a more prominent function to the story's *eros*-element. In his revision, Elyot changes a number of details and achieves the desired effect.

His nearest approach to Plato's theory of love as enunciated in the *Symposium* is to be found in the *Image of Governance*, where the following passage appears in a fictitious letter of the Roman Emperor Alexander Severus: ". . . where before we dyd favour you, nowe do we most hartilye love you, and have no lasse ardant desyre to have the fruition of your vertue & lernyng, than hath the true lover of his wyfe or companyon. What suche love is, ye that have ben at Socrates banket, do knowe most certaynely."[126] Elyot is aware of the productive tension which exists both in the friendship of equal men and in the relationship between master and pupil; he, like Plato, considers it important for the harmonious formation of man. In his *Governour*, he gives a disproportionately large amount of space to the description of friendship. By his treatment of the theme, he wishes "to persuade the reders to enserche therfore vigilauntly, and beinge so happy to finde it . . . to embrace and honour it . . ." as an "incomparable treasure."[127]

Active knowledge cannot be acquired by mere learning, but must be embodied in the living example of the teacher and friend, with whom it is found in the joint search for ultimate truth. In the community created by inspired discussion, the ashes which hide the "sparks of true wisdom" are cleared away. At the culmination of this process, man attains to an understanding of the true nature of things, and divine reason becomes supreme in his being. The true knowledge which has thus been attained must become an active force. In his insistence on this point, Elyot follows the Platonic doctrine: the value of purely abstract knowledge is limited,[128] unless as living knowledge it becomes a formative power within the knowing man.

Elyot explains that he uses the word "understanding" as a translation of the Latin *intellectus* or *mens;* he actually uses it in the sense of the Greek $\epsilon\pi\iota\sigma\tau\dot{\eta}\mu\eta$—which he renders by these Latin and English terms—since he implies not only the faculty of reasoning but the active process of search and cognition.[129] Understanding, he says, is "the most excellent gyfte that man can receive in his creation, wherby he doth approche most nighe unto the similitude of god";[130] it is "that portion of divinitie, whiche is in man, wherby he is made to the image and similitude of god."[131] Man's understanding is perfect as long as he rests in the contemplation of the divine, and man's soul is like God in this state.[132] "In beholdynge the goodnesse of Godde, manne dothe perceyve, that therof procedethe vertue . . . he that is vertuouse, is . . . lyke unto god."[133] To sum up: contemplation of the divine and eternal good makes man similar to God. From it derives his virtue; virtue is active application in the world of the divine good which he has beheld.[134] The whole process is like a circle: after quietly contemplating the divine, man descends into the world. He is active there, trying to approximate the world to the divine. That very activity, which is virtue, again makes him "lyke unto god."

Contemplation in its highest form, then, makes man similar to God, both directly, and indirectly through the resulting virtuous

97

action. The latter is an essential part of the doctrine: since man cannot remain in the blissful state of beholding the divine but has to return to the world and its imperfections, he must reascend toward the divine by trying to perfect the world, by virtuous activity. Only such virtue ennobles man. Elyot warns: "In vayn were your longe travaile in study and lernynge, yf actuall experience dydde not shewe forth their fruites."[135] (His insistence on activity rather than pure contemplation would seem to be reflected in the motto on his coat of arms which he liked to parade in his books: "*Face aut tace*"[136] —"Do or be silent.") By going back to Plato's doctrine, Elyot tries to reconcile the medieval opposition of world and spirit, as well as to resolve the philosophic doubt whether contact with reality will not contaminate or pervert pure truth. We have already encountered the same problem at the beginning of *Utopia*, where, as in Elyot's work, it is resolved in favor of the *vita activa*.

The intimate connection between the spirit and the world explains Elyot's confirmed opinion that "preeminence in degree shulde be amonge men according as they do excell in the pure influence of understandynge."[137] The degree of $\epsilon\pi\iota\sigma\tau\eta\mu\eta$ should determine man's social and political rank, as in Plato's *Republic*. The difference in human ability to understand results from the fact that God chooses to distribute his gifts of grace and nature unequally.[138] This rules out an equalitarian order of society, and demands a hierarchy among men. God has ordered the world in accordance with the value of its parts; he has "set degrees and astates in all his glorious warkes,"[139] in nature and among men.

In several of his plays, notably in *Coriolanus*[140] and *Troilus and Cressida*,[141] Shakespeare proclaims his faith in the same hierarchical system. The ringing lines of Shakespeare's Coriolanus and Ulysses bear a remarkable resemblance to Elyot's words. The insistence on a stratified, monarchic society—on hierarchy, order, degree, and vocation—was perhaps as common and widespread in Renaissance thought as has been that on democracy—on liberty, equality, and fraternity—from the days of the American and French revolutions to our own. Nevertheless, there is enough similarity in their reasoning and choice of words to make it highly probable that Shakespeare was familiar with Elyot's work, and that he molded his poetic image out of Elyot's prose. The likelihood of Shakespeare's philological dependence on Elyot's *Governour* has been demonstrated by Starnes, who provides a detailed juxtaposition of the relevant passages;[142] his general agreement with Elyot's political philosophy has been analyzed by Phillips.[143]

We may content ourselves here with comparing two passages, with the object of showing Elyot's influence, and the perfection into which Elyot's heavy, potent prose is transformed by Shakespeare's majestic language.

First, Elyot's statement at the beginning of the *Governour:*

... *Plebs* in latin, and comminers in englisshe, be wordes only made for the discrepance of degrees, wherof procedeth ordre: whiche in thinges as wel naturall as supernaturall hath ever had suche a preeminence, that therby the incomprehensible maiestie of god, as it were by a bright leme of a torche or candel, is declared to the blynde inhabitantes of this worlde. More over take away ordre from all thynges what shulde than remayne? Certes nothynge finally, except some man wolde imagine eftsones *Chaos:* whiche of some is expounde a confuse mixture. Also where there is any lacke of ordre nedes must be perpetuall conflicte: and in thynges subiecte to Nature nothynge of hym selfe onely may be norisshed; but whan he hath distroyed that where with he dothe participate by the ordre of his creation, he hym selfe of necessite muste than perisshe, wherof ensuethe universall dissolution. . . . Hath nat [God] set degrees and astates in all his glorious warkes? . . . Beholde the foure elementes wherof the body of man is compacte, howe they be set in their places called spheris, higher or lower, accordynge to the soveraintie of theyr natures. . . . Beholde also the ordre that god hath put generally in al his creatures, begynnyng at the moste inferiour or base, and assendynge upwarde . . . so that in every thyng is ordre, and without ordre may be nothing stable or permanent; and it may nat be called ordre, excepte it do contayne in it degrees, high and base, accordynge to the merite or estimation of the thyng that is ordred. Nowe to retourne to the astate of man kynde, . . . hit semeth that in [man] shulde be no lasse providence of god declared than in the inferiour creatures; but rather with a more perfecte ordre and dissposition. And therefore hit appereth that god gyveth nat to every man like gyftes of grace, or of nature, but to some more, some lesse, as it liketh his divine maiestie.[144]

This line of reasoning is continued a few pages further on, where Elyot points to the monarchical organization of nature:

For who can denie but that all thynge in heven and erthe is governed by one god, by one perpetuall ordre, by one providence? One Sonne ruleth over the day, and one Moone over the nyghte; and to descende downe to the erthe, . . . the Bee is lefte to man by nature, as it semeth, a perpetuall figure of a iuste governaunce or rule. . . .[145]

Shortly thereafter, as Starnes has pointed out, Elyot discusses the situation of the Greeks before Troy,[146] with which Shakespeare's Ulysses deals in his great speech in *Troilus and Cressida;* he begins with a reference to the bee-state, the last point mentioned by Elyot:

When that the general is not like the hive
To whom the foragers shall all repair,
What honey is expected? Degree being vizarded,
Th' unworthiest shows as fairly in the mask.
The heavens themselves, the planets, and this centre
Observe degree, priority, and place,
Insisture, course, proportion, season, form,
Office, and custom, in all line of order;
And therefore is the glorious planet Sol
In noble eminence enthron'd and spher'd
Amidst the other; whose med'cinable eye
Corrects the ill aspects of planets evil,
And posts, like the commandment of a king,
Sans check, to good and bad. But when the planets
In evil mixture to disorder wander,
What plagues, and what portents, what mutiny,
What raging of the sea, shaking of earth,
Commotion in the winds, frights, changes, horrors,
Divert and crack, rend and deracinate
The unity and married calm of states
Quite from their fixture! O! when degree is shak'd,
Which is the ladder to all high designs,
The enterprise is sick. How could communities,
Degrees in schools, and brotherhood in cities,
Peaceful commerce from dividable shores,
The primogenity and due of birth,
Prerogative of age, crowns, sceptres, laurels,
But by degree, stand in authentic place?
Take but degree away, untune that string,
And, hark! what discord follows! . . .

. . . . . . . . . . . . . .

Force should be right; or rather, right and wrong,
Between whose endless jar justice resides,
Should lose their names, and so should justice too.

. . . . . . . . . . . . . .

    . . . Great Agamemnon,
This chaos, when degree is suffocate,
Follows the choking.[147]

So Ulysses, to conclude the circle, ends on the note of chaos with which Elyot begins—"chaos, when degree is suffocate." There is the reference to music—"untune that string"—which occurs elsewhere in Elyot's book.[148] Both the general sense and many specific points of the two passages are strikingly similar. Elyot's and Shakespeare's images of the world, of the state, and of man, of their cosmic order and unity, are ultimately derived from Plato. The gradation of nature and of men recalls the Platonic comparison of gold, silver, and iron with men of corresponding values.

100

While some of the more radical Christian reformers were preaching with revolutionary fervor that all men are equal, Elyot insisted that men are unequal because God's order is hierarchical and anti-equalitarian. God creates different kinds and higher and lower types of men. The degree of understanding, and the extent to which such understanding rules the individual and his actions, are the factors which determine a man's worth and position. As Elyot puts it in his archaic manner, understanding is "the principall parte of the soule: it is therefore congruent, and accordynge that one excelleth an other in that influence, as therby beinge next to the similitude of his maker, so shulde the astate of his persone be avanced in degree or place where understandynge may profite: whiche is also distributed in to sondry uses, faculties, and offices, necessary for the lyving and governaunce of mankynde."[149] The individual's position in the organism of human society is to be determined by his intellectual ability and a concomitant sense of responsibility.

In the manner of the Neoplatonists, Elyot compares those of the highest intelligence—and therefore most qualified to rule—with the angels, and with fire, the purest and highest of the elements. The angels, being most fervent in their contemplation, occupy the highest and most glorious place next to God. Similarly those mortals who most clearly partake of divine wisdom should occupy an elevated position "where they may se and also be sene," so as to be able to order human affairs in accordance with the precepts of divine reason. They show the right way to those of lower intellectual capacity and inferior social status: "by the beames of their excellent witte, shewed throughe the glasse of auctoritie, other of inferiour understandynge [are] directed to the way of vertue and commodious livynge."[150]

Turning to the economic aspect of the question, Elyot finds it right and proper that men of such great virtue should not only be honored but maintained "according to their merites" by other people's work.[151] There may be a faint echo of Plato's and More's Utopian commonwealths in this argument: both exempt the ruling class—More's "order of the learned"—from ordinary labor, and see to it that the necessities of life are provided for its members by the work of the rest of the community. They also do away with economic differentiation—Plato explicitly only between members of this class, More between all—and establish communism, but while Elyot, of course, heartily agrees that the rulers should be maintained by the others, and points with great satisfaction to the beehive, where this system prevails,[152] he is certainly far from giving any hint of communism in his scheme. He uses Plato's and More's argument, but changes it to defend the existence of a traditional aristocracy, and justifies its wealth with the hope and contention that its members have superior morals and intelligence. Being less visionary and more conservative than Plato and More,[153] he chooses to apply his doctrine in a practical manner to the existing social order, which he does not wish to change, rather than to invent a completely new Utopian society. What he hopes is that, in addition to their wealth and social power, persons "avanced in degree" will acquire and practice the kind of virtue he postulates.

That virtue becomes apparent in the good qualities and characteristics of a man's nature. Elyot devotes approximately half of the *Governour* to an exhaustive description of these qualities, or individual virtues. With the aid of moral tales and examples usually drawn from antiquity, he establishes a catalogue of virtues which is not distinguished by great originality. As with Plato, Aristotle, and Cicero, the highest virtue is justice. Without it, "all other qualities and vertues can nat make a man good."[154] The essential prerequisite for the attainment of justice is the knowledge of one's self. Elyot attributes great value to the adage "nosce te ipsum"—γνῶθι σεαυτόν. He who knows himself learns to know and judge other people and thus becomes just in his dealings with them.[155] There can be no justice without faith, honesty, and truthfulness.[156] Justice therefore prevails only in that commonwealth in which those who rule possess these and similar characteristics and practice the corresponding virtues. It is the task of the rulers to establish and maintain the divinely ordained order of society by holding their inferiors "within the bounds of reason." They preserve the organism of the state, which, like the cosmic order, is proportioned according to the value of its parts.

While Elyot defends the existing social system and its ruling class, he makes very high demands of that class. Virtue, not title, wealth, or favoritism, justifies an exalted position,[157] and such a position "in very dede . . . is a burden and losse of libertie." As a means to bring about a state of affairs where these criteria really prevail, he advocates evolution through good education. Any idea of revolution is repulsive to him. We might ask what should be done to a governour who is wealthy and noble but wicked. I have not found that Elyot anywhere in his writings goes beyond general statements deploring such a situation. The forcible removal of an unworthy member of the aristocracy, which is advocated by Plato and More, apparently is not envisaged by Elyot. He insists only that those who rule should make every effort to educate themselves and their children in a manner which will render them more just, wise, and virtuous. If they take his advice and learn to "know themselves" as Elyot demands, they will realize that a gentleman is made of no better clay than a poor carter. They will then be aware of the fact that in certain respects the poor shepherd and the rich emperor are equal: since they are both men, they are alike in having soul and body, and in having free will.[158]

In the great controversial issue of *liberum* versus *servum arbitrium*, Elyot follows the traditional doctrine and the defender of free will, Erasmus, and not Luther, its opponent. It is free will, in Elyot's opinion, that makes it possible for a man to distinguish himself from others; it enables him to choose to follow the path of truth and goodness, the only way to true nobility. The divinely ordained hierarchy among men is determined by the degree to which different individuals succeed in being virtuous. The dogma of the "evangelicall persones,"[159] in particular that of extremist sects like the Anabaptists, insists that man, being sinful, can only be saved by God's grace, not by his own works. All men are equal when they face their Creator on doomsday, so they should also be equal in this world where they have only one task—to prepare for the day when they shall face their Creator. Elyot, who considers the good and just, the hierarchical, ordering of the world to be man's noblest task, turns sharply against this doctrine. In his opposition to sectarian equalitarianism, he agrees with the position of the Catholic and Anglican churches and, incidentally, with Luther's attitude during and after the Peasants' War.

Elyot denies that the Anabaptists can justify their democratic communism by reference to Holy Scripture, and claims that they twist God's words for their purposes.[160] He does not, however, indulge in any prolonged theological debate, but summarily dismisses the arguments of his opponents as nonsensical. His defense of aristocracy against "evangelicall persones" does not prevent him from admitting the validity of certain biblical injunctions on which they base their claims. Reason, society, and knowledge bid man: "Love thou thy neighbour as thou doest thy selfe." He comments that "that sentence . . . came from hevyn, whan societie was firste ordayned of god."[161] Elyot recognizes the validity of this biblical injunction for utilitarian and practical, rather than for religious, reasons, and considers it as the dictate of something like divine common sense. That is a far cry from making it the basis of a revolutionary social movement. In any case, he violently contradicts the claim that this and similar biblical phrases are part of a divinely sanctioned doctrine of general social equality and democracy.

So much for his opposition to sectarian demands for equality. On the affirmative side, Elyot explains very clearly the form of state he wants. To avoid any possible misunderstanding, he begins *The boke named the Gouernour* with the unequivocal description, already quoted in part, of what he calls the natural order of society.[162] He introduces there the term "publike weale" instead of the customary "commune weale" for "state" or "commonwealth," and gives as his reason for the use of that word—which despite his efforts was not taken into the English language—his desire to reproduce the meaning of the Latin *res publica*.[163] *Res publica*—"publike weale"— to him denotes not a democratic republic but an aristocratic polity, whereas "commune weale" sounds suspiciously like communism.[164] That objectionable term might give the deplorable impression "that every thinge shulde be to all men in commune, without discrepance of any astate or condition. . . . "[165] Such a state of affairs, Elyot thinks, would call for the Latin term *res plebeia* rather than *res publica*,[166] and that would represent the principle opposed to the divine order, pure chaos.

After these preliminaries and a short description of aristocracy and democracy, Elyot boldly and dogmatically asserts the superiority of monarchy over all other forms of government, and thus implicitly defends the rule of Henry VIII.[167] He advocates a benevolent monarchy, but not the kind of despotism into which his monarch's rule degenerated in its later years. He supports his argument in favor of monarchy by a comparison of the king to God, the sun, the moon— and to the queen bee! Having established the monarchical principle, he elaborates his conception by pointing out that part of the weight and responsibility of government must be borne by the aristocracy, that in practice a combination of monarchy and aristocracy will be most likely to provide good government. In keeping with the constitutional practice of his day, Elyot does not make gentry and nobility equal partners with the king in the job of governing the country. The monarch really is supreme, not just *primus inter pares*. Nevertheless, Elyot assigns very important functions to the upper class, which bears the main burden of governmental work. Its members have the duty to aid the king in performing the functions of government, primarily in "the distribution of iustice in sondry partes of a huge multitude."[168]

Elyot always has English conditions in mind. When he speaks of "sondry meane authorities" who should help the "capitall governour"—the king—in the administration of the country, he means the English country gentlemen, who, as justices of the peace and in other judicial and administrative functions, maintain and enforce the king's peace, or advise the king in Council and Parliament. For their instruction, Elyot writes practically all his works; their proper training is his constant concern. He frequently expresses this, in terms similar to the passage that introduces the *Image of Governance:* ". . . which boke I do dedicate unto you noble lordis, gentil knightes, and other in the state of honour or worshyp, as beinge moste redy to be advanced to governance under your Prince: so that your vertues be correspondent unto your fortunes."[169]

His educational plan presupposes a certain amount of wealth and can be carried out only in the house of a country gentleman who can afford to pay for all the requisite nurses and private tutors. Here, the interplay of actual social conditions and ideas is particularly evident; the whole system is based on the fact that a fairly wealthy landed class is the leading political group. Elyot sees this connection of economic and political power and approves of it: "It is of good congruence that they, whiche be superiour in condition or haviour, shulde have also preeminence in administration."[170] He goes on to state that he favors this situation because "they have competent substaunce to lyve without takyng rewardes,"[171] or, in other words, because they can perform the duties imposed on them by the government without having to be paid or bribed for their services. Elyot does not think in terms of a modern, salaried civil service, but of a class which performs the functions of government essentially on an honorary and voluntary basis, which regards such service as a responsibility incident upon it on account of its wealth and superior social position. When talking of "takyng rewardes," Elyot means that men with a secure economic basis are less easily bribed than others.[172] In any case, he described the existing situation: the duties of local government, on its higher level, were performed almost in their entirety by the unpaid country gentry. Sir Thomas Elyot himself is a good example of such service to the community. He repeatedly mentions that he works "without hope of temporall reward, only for the fervent affection, whiche I have ever borne toward the publike weale of my countrei."[173] His claim that he has spent his own "commodity" in the process of writing books for his fellow-countrymen[174] is probably accurate enough; but it is clear that he actually did hope for temporal rewards, and that he obtained some, for his public services.

Elyot esteems inherited position and wealth as very valuable attributes of a governour; they are not absolutely essential, however, and they are not the main factors that determine a man's fitness to rule. Of greater consequence than the material wealth needed to insure his unselfish devotion to the service of the state, and more important than an inherited title, is a man's human quality as defined by the term "virtue." Since virtue derives from true knowledge and understanding, and since knowledge and understanding are not the special privileges of one class, a man of low birth presumably may also develop them, and thereby become qualified to serve his country in high positions. Such a parvenu, however, often lacks the aristocratic attitude and dignity necessary for one who is "above the common course of other men." He is apt to be a harsher and less kind ruler than one who has inherited the habits of tolerance and affability from family tradition.[175] Elyot probably did not have much difficulty in arriving at this conclusion through his own observation: he must have been irked by the behavior of contemporary *nouveaux riches* and opportunistic hangers-on of the recently "arrived" house of Tudor. One wonders what he really thought of a friend like Thomas Cromwell who agreed with Elyot on the need for a strong monarchy but who definitely was not famed for noble lineage or kindness or the kind of virtue advocated by Elyot.[176] Whatever his thoughts on that subject may have been, he did not have them perpetuated by printer's ink. Suffice it to say that the actual process of rapid social rise was not necessarily achieved in his time via the educational curriculum and moral superiority advocated by him, but by means more closely associated with strong elbows and a mind not unduly weighed down by moral scruples.[177]

Although Elyot believed that gentlemen's sons were more desirable as governours than the social and political climbers fostered by the new monarchy, the latter might at least educate their sons properly, and *The boke named the Gouernour* is presumably designed for them, too. However, the characteristics required of a true gentleman, such as courage, perseverance, continence, incorruptibility, moderation, self-control (called "inwarde governaunce" by Elyot), are more likely to be found in a person who has inherited them from chivalrous ancestors than in a man of "very base linage" who has grown up without such a tradition. The people will bear the rule of one who was born a gentleman more readily and with fewer objections than that of a man who has risen from its ranks.[178] Furthermore, a gentleman's son has the advantage of being able to obtain a better education, and therefore a better preparation for public life, than a poor man's son.[179] However able the latter may be, he starts out with a handicap that is hard to overcome. Elyot offers no feasible remedy for this situation—he never conceived of universal, free, equal, and public educational facilities for all—but is content to state the situation as he sees it. He admits that a gentleman's son may be incapable of assimilating the kind of education to which he is subjected, and that a poor boy may be more capable. He strongly condemns those who are unworthy of their title and position, and agrees that very gifted persons of the lower classes may properly become governours. That, however, is as far as he is prepared to go: he always views the latter possibility with considerable skepticism, and is instinctively in favor of those who inherit wealth and position.[180] He does not stand for a strictly hereditary principle of aristocracy, but reluctantly admits those into the ranks of the upper class who are properly qualified by the standards he sets. All in all, it can be said that the natural security and gentle bearing of the born aristocrat, and the esteem due to his estate, are more important to Elyot than great knowledge accumulated in a person of low parentage whose learning is not balanced by "manners." Elyot neither likes to see the poor scholar in a responsible position, nor does he approve of the man of low birth who rises by clever and forceful application of Machiavellian *virtù*.[181] If he had to choose between the two, Elyot would favor the former over the latter even though it was the application of the latter method which made some of the more spectacular careers of his day.

His governours should always bear in mind that aristocracy does not mean privilege, but responsibility.[182] They are examples to their people, and must realize that they are being observed in all their actions, for "they sitte, as it were, on a piller on the toppe of a mountaine, where all the people do beholde them. . . ."[183] The "noble example of their lives"[184] and the way in which they rule is decisive for the nature of their state. "Such as be the governours . . . suche be the people."[185] A certain attitude and corresponding manners are to be so consistently observed by a gentleman that they become part of his nature. Elyot calls this basic attitude "majesty," and describes it, the "fountaine of all excellent maners," in these words: it "is the holle proporcion and figure of noble astate, and is proprelie a beautie or comelynesse in his countenance, langage and gesture apt to his dignite, and accommode to time, place, and company."[186] This description resembles the definition of *grazia* given by Castiglione[187] and others in Italy; it is derived from, and forms the counterpart of, such Italian conceptions. The gentleman should be affable, "shewyng to men a gentil and familiare visage,"[188] so that he is "easie to be spoken unto."[189] He always controls himself and never rages in uncontrolled anger. He is placable, merciful, and beneficent, and spends liberally on the right occasions.[190]

Reason must lead him in all his actions and rule over his emotions: a governour must practice both inward and outward "governance"— self-control and authority.[191] Self-control enables a man to find the mean between extremes, to see both himself and the world in which he lives with objective justice, and to apply such justice. If he thus permits reason to rule, his abilities will become virtues. If, on the other hand, he is driven by the lower part of his soul, if his emotions and passions rule without the bridle of reason, his abilities will become vices. The constant aim and goal of all his actions should be the advantage of the commonwealth, yet he must not pursue that advantage blindly and fanatically. If his actions are to be in the public interest, they should be the result of his mature and considered judgment, and should be carried out firmly but with tolerant moderation. If he acts with too much foolhardy bravado, he cannot be called reasonable or valiant, but is "rather to be rekned with bestes savage."[192] He must learn by experience to judge what course of action will bring the greatest benefit to the community, and act accordingly. Elyot insists that the care for the well-being of the state must take precedence over attention to any particular interests.[193]

The "publike weale" for Elyot is always England, and it is to her greatness that he hopes to contribute. All his books are written for this purpose. Even where he does not specifically refer to it, the English background with its particular conditions is perceptible. His work is based on it and fits into it. He hopes to improve the state of England by his suggestions to such a degree that his country may measure up to the greatness of the states of antiquity. In his noble patriotism, he speaks of "the fervent zele that I have to my countrey," and adds that he desires "only to employ that poure lerning, that I have gotten, to the benefite thereof."[194] This he did both in his judicial, administrative, and political activities, and by creating the figure of the governour in which he amalgamated what was left of chivalrous tradition with the human norm of antiquity.

Elyot's governour is not a courtier who only too frequently acquires knowledge for the sole purpose of showing off in elegant conversation, nor is he a scholar to whom knowledge is an end in itself; he makes it his task to realize the good in this world by administering true justice—the good which he has come to know through study and intuition. For this task Elyot wishes to prepare the noble youth of his country. Each one has to contribute his share toward the realization of this humanistic ideal, whether he serves the king in Council, in Parliament, in an embassy, as a judge, as justice of the peace, as sheriff, or in any other of the functions that the Tudor state assigns to its governours. This is Elyot's aim, and his lively literary activity is always determined by it. We may let him sum it up in his own words, as they appear at the very end of the *Governour:*

Nowe all ye reders that desire to have your children to be governours, or in any other authoritie in the publike weale of your countrey, if ye bringe them up and instructe them in suche fourme as in this boke is declared, they shall than seme to all men worthye to be in authoritie, honour, and noblesse, and all that is under their governaunce shall prospere and come to perfection. And as a precious stone in a ryche ouche [brooch] they shall be beholden and wondred at, and after the dethe of their body their soules for their endevour shall be incomprehensibly rewarded of the gyver of wisedome, to whome onely be gyven eternall glorie. . . .

# V

# Thomas Starkey

THOMAS STARKEY is the last member of the group of humanists active during the reign of Henry VIII with whose thought we shall be concerned. He is the least well known among them, owing to the fact that his major work, *A Dialogue between Reginald Pole and Thomas Lupset,* remained unprinted for almost three and one-half centuries. It was first published by J. M. Cowper in 1871,[1] and this was followed in 1878 by S. J. Herrtage's biographical work, *Starkey's Life and Letters.*[2] Starkey has in recent years received attention in some general histories of political thought[3] and in a few more detailed studies.[4] The text of the *Dialogue* is now available in a modernized edition by Kathleen M. Burton; this is the edition we shall use in our discussion.[5]

Starkey was born not later than 1499 and died in 1538.[6] He was thus some years younger than Sir Thomas Elyot and slightly older than his friend Reginald Pole. His *Dialogue* was probably finished in 1535. *An exhortation to the people instructynge theym to unitie and obedience* was printed in 1536.[7] "What ys pollycy aftur the sētēce of Arystotyl,"[8] as well as most of the other writings and letters that have come down to us, were written during his last five years.[9] It was during those years that his fortunes first reached their highest point and then suffered an irremediable relapse.

Starkey had been a student at Oxford as a member of Magdalen College.[10] He took his B.A. in 1516,[11] his M.A. in 1521,[12] becoming proctor, on Wolsey's appointment, in 1522.[13] At the university he studied Latin, Greek, and philosophy,[14] and he continued his studies in Italy, where he probably first went in 1525[15] to join the circle of which Reginald Pole was the center. Starkey had presumably already met Pole during their Oxford days.[16] Pole, a Plantagenet on his mother's side and kinsman of Henry VIII,[17] promoted and himself engaged in humanistic studies, and maintained a large household in Padua which included a number of English scholars.[18] He broke

110

with the king over the latter's controversy with Rome, was made a cardinal, and eventually, under Mary, became Archbishop of Canterbury. The friendship with Pole was to become of decisive importance for Starkey; after 1525, he was in Padua, Paris, England, Avignon, and again in Padua as Pole's secretary and friend.[19] When Starkey returned to England in December, 1534, he became chaplain to Pole's mother, the Countess of Salisbury.[20] (He had held a church living since 1530.[21])

From his earlier philosophical studies, Starkey turned to theology for some years, "aftur the wyche, bycause my purpos then was to lyve in a polytyke lyfe, I set my selfe now thes last yerys past to the knolege of the cyvyle Law."[22] He obtained the degree of Doctor of Laws in Padua.[23] These scholarly qualifications eminently fitted him for that "polytyke lyfe" which he was keen to enter, but probably what most aroused Henry's and Cromwell's interest in him was his friendship with Pole, whose support they were anxious to win. Promptly after his return to England in December, 1534, when he was chaplain to Pole's mother, Starkey approached Cromwell, outlined his qualifications to him, and asked whether he "coude in some parte helpe" the king in "the restitutyon of the true commyn wele,"[24] that is, whether he could obtain a position in the king's service. As a sample of his qualifications, he wrote for Cromwell, at the latter's request, the treatise, "What ys pollycy aftur the sētēce of Arystotyl."[25] Soon thereafter, before February 15, 1535, Starkey received his appointment as royal chaplain.[26] The treatise on Aristotle provided the basis for part of the *Dialogue*, which cannot have been finished before October, 1535.[27]

*A Dialogue between Reginald Pole and Thomas Lupset* was written for the king; in it, Starkey held out the hope that Pole might be persuaded to return to England to help promote the royal policies. In the letter with which Starkey dedicated the *Dialogue* to the king, he says: "I trust hit shalnot be long before [Pole] shall declare unto your grace of his wysdome and Iugment playne and manyfest argument."[28] Starkey was right in this assumption, but, to his unpleasant surprise,[29] Pole's argument was very different from what he and the king expected. Starkey's hopes and his career were shattered when, in June, 1536, Henry VIII received from Pole his *Pro ecclesiasticae unitatis defensione*,[30] which for the first time revealed Pole's real attitude and, with its vigorous attack on Henry's break with Rome and on his character, marked Pole's defiance of and opposition to the royal policies. This meant the end of Starkey's political career and his relegation to comparative obscurity,[31] even though he had evidently been animated by good faith and loyalty to the king in the attempt to enlist Pole's support that failed so suddenly and completely.

The *Dialogue*, however, remains an impressive presentation of Starkey's humanistic views. Like Plato, he uses the dialogue form as a vehicle for his own ideas. He is concerned with the political and ethical reformation of the state of England. The disputants introduced by him are his friends; the views expressed by them do correspond, at least in part, to the views actually held by their prototypes.[32] Moreover, there is probably a factual basis for the setting of the *Dialogue*. Thomas Lupset, a humanist taught by Colet and William Lily,[33] at one time Erasmus' assistant,[34] later Reader of Humanity at Oxford, and a member of Pole's household in Padua, apparently visited Pole in 1529 to persuade him to take an active part in English politics.[35] Lupset died in the ensuing year, and Starkey succeeded to his living at Great Mongeham.[36] Writing at a time when the question of obtaining Pole's support was very much on Henry's and Cromwell's minds, Starkey implied that the conversation with Lupset had taken place on such an occasion in 1529, and, through the mouth of Lupset in the *Dialogue*, he again tried to persuade Pole to devote himself to the *vita activa* in England. Thus, while the *Dialogue* was partly an attempt to indicate Pole's attitude and show how his support might be gained, its real content goes much deeper. Starkey himself expresses his major intention in writing it in the words with which he presented the work to the king:

I went streyght in to the cuntre of Italy, as to the place most famyd both with grete lerning and gud and just pollyci, by the reson wherof glad I was ther certayn yiris to be conversant as dilygently as I cowd observing ther lerning ther in hye philosophy as ther manerys and practyse in commyn pollysi, by the whych observatyon I was somewhat better instructe at my return into myn owne cuntrey . . . well notyng the manerys here usid at home and comparyng them with other usid in straunge natyon I have fund grete correctyon with much abuse in law and pollyci wherof by long observatyon I have geddryd a certayne commentary and compylid as hit were a lytill boke of the same . . . for as much as [I] perceyve your highness now nothing more curith and hath in mynd than the extyrpatyon of all abusys both in custume and law . . . in this your commynwelth, by the reson whereof grete hope I have onys yet to see that veray and true commyn wel whereof I have with myselfe fansid here in your reame to have place and by your high wysedome and polyci here to be stablyschid . . . my porpos ys in this commentary to tuch the maner and mean of the restytutyon of this true commyn wele and Iuste pollyci. . . .[37]

Starkey goes on to say that since Henry already has "utterly plukkyd up the rote of all abuse, this utward powar and intolerabull tyranny of rome,"[38] God will guide him in the eradication of other "abuses" which he lists in the work. But the *Dialogue* is more than a tract that enumerates certain faults in the social and political structure of his country and suggests remedies for them; as Starkey states, his studies of philosophy and politics in Italy—the center of classical learning—have led him to "fancy" or postulate a "veray and true commyn wel," an ideal state which can be realized in the England of his day. In contrast to More in the *Utopia*, Starkey applies his theory directly to English conditions. The *Dialogue*, then, is a statement of his political theory, complete with its ethical and philosophical basis, and of its practical application in England.

Starkey himself declares this when he discusses the plan of his book. He informs the king that the *Dialogue* is divided into three parts. In the first of these he establishes his ideal: "what thing hit ys that men so much speke of and call a commynwele or a gud and Iust pollicy, and wherein hit principally stondith and chefely is grondyd"; in the second part he enumerates "the most commyn and notabull abusis, both in manerys custummys and all commyn lawys . . . wereby we are slippyd from that gud and iuste pollicy"; in the third he makes suggestions for the reform of these abuses and the restoration of "the treu commyn wele a-mong us."[39]

We shall be mainly concerned here with the humanistic aspect of Starkey's thought, which comes out most strongly in his description of the good "commyn wele" and in some of his suggestions for bringing it about. It will be seen that his ideas are very closely related to those expressed by Elyot and More, and that he can be considered one of the outstanding English representatives of humanistic political thought in the first half of the sixteenth century. The fact that his *Dialogue* was not published—no doubt because the real Pole took such a radically different attitude from that hopefully ascribed to him by Starkey—combined with the disfavor into which Starkey fell shortly after he wrote it, makes it certain that it was not read by many persons, and greatly limited its possible range of influence on the thought or action of others.[40] The *Dialogue* cannot be compared in popularity to the work of his more famous contemporaries, but it is itself a vivid testimony of the effect of humanistic thought in England.

We shall confine our discussion to the *Dialogue*, and in considering it we shall not, on the whole, be concerned with its strictly constitutional and legal aspects. Like Starkey's views on the religious question, these aspects are not essential for our discussion, and they have been investigated by others.[41] We shall concentrate on the philosophical and ethical foundations of Starkey's ideal state and on the educational measures he advocated for making that ideal a reality. Baumer has shown the very considerable indebtedness of Starkey's ideas on constitutional government to Marsilius of Padua's *Defensor Pacis*,[42] as well as the origin of much of the political thought of both authors in Aristotle.[43] Schroeder and Dannenberg have emphasized Plato's influence on Starkey's ideas.[44] It seems evident from a number of similarities in the two works that Starkey must have known the *Utopia*,[45] whose author was a friend of his friend Pole.[46] From all these and other influences emerge Starkey's own synthesis and creation.

Since his whole training had been humanistic, as he indicates in the letter to Cromwell in which he describes his education at Oxford and in his dedication to Henry VIII where he refers to his sojourns and studies in Italy, it is not surprising that the fruit of his studies, "in leyser and quietnes geddrid . . . by long observation,"[47] should be essentially humanistic. Tillyard claims that "Starkey's whole scheme, the correspondence between the body politic and man's microcosm, is a medieval commonplace,"[48] and J. W. Allen makes a similar, though more differentiated, statement in his chapter on "The Very and True Commonweal." Speaking of Robert Crowley, Starkey's *Dialogue*, and More's *Utopia*, he says: "Men were considering the actual structure of society and asking how its parts are related and what binds it together and what should be its animating purpose. In this there was nothing whatever that was new. It is true to say that, under Henry VIII and Edward VI, there was formed a conception of what the commonwealth should be, or, if you like to put it so, of what it really is. It would be more fully true to say that medieval conceptions received at that time a fresh expression."[49]

A certain inconsistency seems to be involved in the statements that "there was nothing whatever that was new" and that "medieval conceptions received . . . a fresh expression," since the "fresh expression" presumably involves a new approach. The idea of an "organic society," though outwardly similar to the medieval conception, received a new content and significance as a result of the humanists' return to the authors and values of classical antiquity, particularly to Plato. The principle which justifies the hierarchical order, and on which that order is organized, is knowledge and virtue. This is

114

Platonic rather than medieval. It would be more accurate to say, then, that this "medieval commonplace" was very thoroughly revitalized and transformed by Starkey and other humanists under the direct impact of classical philosophy.

"A renaissance of the antique form of good living often appears as the high and unremitting purpose of those who studied with Pole at Padua," Zeeveld states. He argues that "the pattern of a fixed social order had been outgrown, and expediency required a new social theory to accommodate the current situation" in the 1530's, a theory which was developed "on a broad humanistic level."[50] This statement, which is meant to indicate the accommodation made by a number of political theorists who worked for Cromwell, needs some modification as far as Starkey's own position is concerned. Starkey did not break with the principle of "order and degree," but adapted it to current conditions by emphasizing knowledge and virtue, and an education designed to produce them, as the principal factors which should ideally determine a man's position; he wished to maintain the social hierarchy by reforming it. The adaptation carried out by Starkey was soundly based on his philosophical and ethical convictions,[51] and on his study of contemporary societies. It represents his solution of the problem how humanistic ideals may be brought to bear most effectively on contemporary English society. In writing his *Dialogue*, Starkey intended to do exactly what his friend Edmund Harvel had asked of him some years before, to "come forth to teach others, and make all the land know *quam sit humaniter vivendum*," to "help to take out all barbarous customs, and bring the realm to an antique form of good living."[52] The occasion seemed auspicious; his years of learning and travel promised to come to fruition with the prospect of an important part in the shaping of the policy, and perhaps even of the very structure, of the state. With slight rhetorical exaggeration, Zeeveld correctly describes the situation: "Never had the opportunity been greater for men solely on their merits as scholars to influence national policy, and never did scholars live up to their opportunities more brilliantly."[53]

*Quam sit humaniter vivendum*: that we may take as the motto of the *Dialogue*. How does Starkey translate it into his own terms? He is concerned with finding out and describing how we may "attain to such end and perfection as, by the providence of God, is ordained to the excellent nature and dignity of man."[54] The "excellent nature and dignity of man"—a brief, definite statement of the humanist's optimistic belief in man—is reminiscent of the title of Pico della Mirandola's famous *Oration on the Dignity of Man*. Starkey repeats similar phrases on several occasions throughout his work. He is not unaware that the emphasis on worldly prosperity, happiness, and beauty, which he connects with his conception of man's dignity and power, may create certain problems with regard to the teaching of Christ. Lupset, who in the *Dialogue* does most of the listening, but interrupts Pole's arguments to raise pertinent questions, at one point refers to "the doctrine of our Master Christ, which calleth them blessed which ever be in wordly [worldly] adversity, patiently suffering it for his sake; and, contrary, those which be in wordly prosperity he noteth to be miserable and wretched."[55] Pole rightly considers this objection a "rigid knot" and struggles with it for some time. He emerges with a statement which hardly answers Lupset's question regarding the blessedness of the rich and fortunate. He bases his reply on Aristotle, whose authority in this case is plainly considered superior to that of Christ and Plato by Starkey's Pole: if we follow Plato in considering only the soul, and Christ in despising "the vain pleasures of the present life" and thinking only of the life to come, then it is true "that man, though he be troubled with all wordly adversity, yet may right well attain to high felicity."[56] This, however, is not the highest felicity for Pole: "But, contrary, if we have regard not only of the soul but also of the body, saying with Aristotle that man is the union and conjunction togidder of them both, and if we have regard also not only of the life to come but also of the life present, then it is true that I say, that felicity in the highest degree is not without wordly properity [prosperity]."[57] Thus he really contradicts Lupset's formulation of Christian doctrine by using Aristotle to emphasize the values of this world and emerging with a scale of values that is definitely weighted on the classical side.

Starkey's view of Christ is expressed by Pole: "He came to make perfit man" and has left to him His "celestial doctrine . . . to conduct all Christian minds to their perfection."[58] This interpretation is similar to that of Erasmus, who saw Christ's teaching as the culmination of ancient philosophy. Man, it is true, is not self-sufficient, according to Starkey. God's aid is needed to help him achieve perfection, but man's own effort is indispensable: he "shall have nothing that is good, nothing perfit, without his own labour. . . ."[59] Starkey is principally concerned with man's "own labour," with guiding his effort to achieve the perfect order in this world; the need for divine aid is acknowledged and briefly defined,[60] but the main emphasis of the *Dialogue* is on the shaping of his own life by man. *Quam sit humaniter vivendum* is thus conceived by Starkey in a way which is reminiscent of Pico and Erasmus, with a humanistic emphasis on the perfectibility of man and his society.

*A Dialogue between Reginald Pole and Thomas Lupset* begins with the same problem which we have encountered at the beginning of Thomas More's *Utopia:* Should the philosopher take part in the political life of his country? In this case it is Lupset who urges Pole that it is his duty to do so, and Pole finally sees his point and expresses an attitude which, in the situation in which the *Dialogue* was written, Henry VIII was anxious to find in the real Pole: he declares his readiness "ever to apply and endeavour myself to the maintenance and setting forward of the true common weal." He then immediately proceeds to present his, that is really Starkey's, ideas "touching the order of our country and common weal."[61]

The discussion on the merits of the active versus the contemplative life begins with Lupset's reproach to Pole: "You see your country, as me seemeth, require your help, and as it were cry and call unto you busily for the same, and you—as drowned in the pleasure of letters and private studies—give no year [ear] thereto. . . ."[62] Pole answers by voicing his doubts about Lupset's position that the perfection of man is to be found in the active participation in public life, and argues that since "the perfection of man resteth in the mind and in the chief and purest part thereof, which is reason and intelligence, it seemeth without doubt that knowledge of God, of nature, and of all the works thereof should be the end of man's life, and the chief point therein of all men to be looked unto." He cites the philosophers of classical antiquity who, he claims, "forsook the meddling with matters of common weals" and preferred to investigate God and nature.[63] This, they felt, according to Pole, was on a higher level than the practical or even the theoretical occupation with political questions. Lupset disagrees: Aristotle, he points out, insisted on the combination of the active and the contemplative life. It is the duty of man "first to make himself perfit, with all virtues garnishing his mind, and then to commune the same perfection to other" by devoting himself to the affairs of the common weal, "for little availeth virtue that is not published abroad to the profit of other."[64] "Virtue" is seen by Starkey as the immediate emanation of knowledge;[65] man attains perfection only if his knowledge is translated into active virtue: ". . . the perfection of man standeth not in bare knowledge and learning without application of it to any use or profit of other; but the very perfection of man's mind resteth in the use and exercise of all virtues and honesty, and chiefly in the chief virtue . . . , the communing of high wisdom to the use of other. . . ."[66]

This view of the function of the philosopher is intimately connected with Starkey's interpretation of man's position in the world. There is a definite analogy between God and man: as God rules heaven, so He has appointed man to rule the earth. Their tasks in their respective spheres are identical: "man by nature far excelleth in dignity all other creatures in earth, where he is by the high providence of God set to govern and rule, order and temper all to his pleasure by wisdom and policy, none otherwise than God Himself doth in heaven govern and rule all celestial things immediately. Wherefore he was of the old philosophers called a earthly god. . . ."[67] Man's task is both to rule over nature with its creatures, and to find the perfect form of man and state. He approximates God by aiding in the realization on earth of an order which corresponds to the celestial order. It is in this creative activity that man lives up to his potentialities, to his divinely ordained destiny. "Like as the body of man is then most perfit in his nature when it hath power to gender another like thereunto, so is the mind then most perfit when it communeth and spreadeth his virtues abroad to the instruction of other. Then it is most like unto the nature of God. . . ."[68] This "instruction," as conceived by Starkey, consists in political activity, in the establishment of the right commonwealth; its result should be "to bring the whole country to quietness and civility, that every man, and so the whole, may at the last attain to such perfection as by nature is to the dignity of man due. . . ."[69] These points are presented by Starkey as Lupset's argument; they serve to convince Pole, who finally agrees, that "it is undoubtedly . . . best of all to help a whole country, insomuch that man so doing nearest approacheth to the nature of God. . . ."[70]

In the course of this argument, Lupset demonstrates at length that man is "born to common civility,"[71] i.e., that he is essentially a political being "inclined and stirred to civil order and loving company."[72] There are certain ethical values which underlie all political organizations. These are implanted in the hearts of men by "the universal and true law of nature."[73] They are not, as Pole interjects, relative and arbitrary, determined by "the judgment and opinion of

man."[74] All men have an innate knowledge of the good and the bad;
the virtues "by the benefit and power of nature in [man's] heart
are rooted and planted, inclining him ever to the civil life, according to the excellent dignity of his nature."[75] There is then one absolute and unalterable standard which is the foundation of all political societies, Christian or pagan, however much their particular
provisions may differ:[76] for all of them, "the civil life is a politic
order of men conspiring togidder in virtue and honesty."[77] To this
kind of civil life "man by nature is ordained."[78]

Lupset feels that after this extensive demonstration Pole ought
to see where his duty lies. He exhorts him: "apply yourself to the
handling of the matter of the common weal, which you know right
well is the end of all studies and, as you would say, the only mark
for every honest mind to shoot at."[79] Pole, however, still has an
objection which echoes that voiced by Hythlodaye in *Utopia:* the
wise man only wastes his time and makes himself ridiculous if he
tries to take part in politics under a bad or tyrannous government,
for "hard it is daily to be among thieves and be not a thief."[80] To be
of real service, he must keep himself in the background and pick the
time and place of his activity more carefully than, for instance, Plato
did in Sicily. Lupset is very scornful of this cautious "wait and see"
attitude which, he says, "hath caused many common weals utterly
to perish."[81] Like More in the *Utopia*, he takes the view that the
wise man should serve his commonwealth as best he can by "amend-
ing" tyranny, for instance, and not keep away from political service
to await the kind of ideal conditions which will probably never
materialize in his lifetime. Men who act in this manner "look, I
trow, for Plato's common weal; in such expectation they spend their
life, as they think, with great politic wisdom, but indeed with
great frantic folly."[82] Lupset points out that Pole's argument does
not, in any case, apply at the moment: England, with such an excellent and just king who is ready for instruction "by his wise
counsellors and politic men,"[83] offers outstanding opportunity for
his service, and Pole finally consents to at least offering his advice.

When Pole proposes to begin his exposition by examining and
describing the nature and character of his ideal state, Lupset again
cautions him not to be overly idealistic: "But here of one thing, I
pray you, take heed: that in this your device of your communica-
tion you follow not the example of Plato, whose order of common
weal no people upon earth to this day could ever yet attain."[84] This
statement is reminiscent of the similar censures leveled against

Plato's *Republic* by such different authors as More and Machiavelli, but it cannot obscure the fact that Starkey, like More, is deeply indebted to Plato. Thus cautioned, Pole proceeds to expound Starkey's political theory. Men are born to live together in society and form a social organism which is likened to the human body. The human body is in perfect condition when it is endowed with health, strength, and beauty;[85] similarly, "health, strength, and beauty of this body politic" are "the foundation of the common weal."[86] Health consists in the right proportion between the size of the country and of its population. The "strength of this politic body standeth in every part being able to do his office and duty. For this body hath his parts, which resemble also the parts of the body of man. . . . The heart thereof is the king, prince and ruler of the state, whethersoever it be one or many. . . . To the head . . . resembled may be right well the under-officers by princes appointed. . . . To the hands are resembled both craftsmen and warriors. . . . To the feet, the ploughmen and tillers of the ground. . . ."[87] The beauty of the body politic "standeth in the due proportion of the same parts togidder, so that one part ever be agreeable to another in form and fashion, quantity and number. . . ."[88] (Starkey's emphasis on the beauty of the human and the political body has rightly been singled out by Schroeder as indicating his strong Platonic leanings.)[89] The parts of this body should all work together harmoniously; they should all be "coupled togidder, unite and knit as members of one body by love, as by the common band of all politic order and good civility."[90] It is essential that "concord and unity" prevail; tensions and disagreements between the different social groups, "discord" between the parts of this body, are symptoms of deadly pestilence which "shortly destroyeth all good order and civility, and utterly taketh away all health from this politic body. . . ."[91]

Starkey's organic analogy is fully and vividly elaborated. As might be expected, his most vital, though not his exclusive, concern is with the "heart" and "head," the ruler and officers who administer the state. As man has both body and soul, so "there is in every commonalty, city and country . . . a politic body, and another thing also, resembling the soul of man."[92] The soul of man "far passeth and excelleth the body"[93] since there is "a sparkle of the godly and eternal reason" in it.[94] God has endowed man with this "right reason" in his soul so that with its aid "he should govern himself in civil life and good policy."[95] The analogy between individual man and the state is close: the "body is nothing else but the multitude of people, the number of citizens. . . . The thing which is resembled to the soul is civil order and politic law administered by officers and rulers. For like as the body in every man receiveth his life by the virtue of the soul, and is governed thereby, so doth the multitude of people in every country receive, as it were, civil life by laws well administered by good officers and wise rulers, by whom they be governed and kept in politic order."[96]

Starkey makes a fine point here: he does not simply equate the rulers with the soul, but defines the soul of the state as "civil order and politic law administered by officers and rulers." This careful formula is important for his concept of constitutional rule. The law in the state corresponds to divine reason in the soul of man; it is based on universal natural law and is implemented in each state by a special body of law which corresponds to its particular needs and conditions. The rulers of the state are not above but under the law, and it is their duty to administer it. Starkey feels that here his views differ from those held by Plato, however similar they are in other respects; his Pole remembers Lupset's advice to be careful not to follow Plato too closely. "The wise philosopher Plato," he says, "in all his common wealth chiefly laboured to see good officers, heads and rulers, the which should be, as it were, lively laws; for the which cause also, after mine opinion, he thought nothing necessary to write any laws to his commonalty; for if the heads in a common weal were both just, good and wise, there should need none other laws to the people."[97] When Pole asks whether this ideal situation could be achieved in England, he promptly draws Lupset's denial to the effect that this dream could only be realized if God were to send down his angels "and of them make a city." Pole agrees with Lupset: "We look not for such heads as Plato describeth in his policy, for that is out of hope with us to be found, nor yet for such wise men as the Stoics describe, and ancient philosophers. But after a more civil and common sort we will measure they wisdom of them whom we would to rule. . . ."[98] He does concur with Plato that it is "the ground of all felicity in the civil life" to have a good prince,[99] but, "seeing . . . that princes commonly are ruled by affects [emotions] rather than by reason and order of justice, the laws, which be sincere and pure reason without any spot or blot of affection, must have chief authority; they must rule and govern the state, and not the prince after his own liberty and will."[100]

We cannot here enter into the very interesting constitutional provisions with which Starkey would safeguard the rule of law. It should be pointed out, however, that he favors an elective monarchy for England in which a prince may be chosen who "is both wise and just," and that he does not hesitate to advocate the deposition of tyrants.[101] It follows as a logical corollary from his insistence on the rule of law that he is a relativist with regard to constitutional forms: as long as the supremacy of law is maintained, it does not matter too much which form of state any given country may choose if the form chosen suits the conditions of the country in question.[102] For England, he prefers a "mixed state," a constitutional monarchy.[103] Those who rule should in any constitutional form play their part in the functioning of the "soul" of the state by administering the laws. These laws, as he states, are "sincere and pure reason without any spot or blot of affection" and thus correspond to divine reason in the individual human soul. In their administration, the rulers must always be guided by the interest of the community as a whole: "So long as they which have authority and rule of the state look not to their own singular profit, nor to the private weal of any one part more than to the other, but refer all their counsel, acts and deeds to the common weal of the whole, so long, I say, the order is good and directed to good civility, and this is good policy."[104] It follows, of course, that those who rule by following their own ambitions and particular interests break up the state and turn "this good order . . . into high tyranny." Such a situation must not be allowed to develop, and where it has developed the tyranny must be eradicated. Real "politic rule" and "civil order" should be established, the end of which is "to induce the multitude to virtuous living, according to the dignity of the nature of man"; people can be "directed in virtue and honesty" under different constitutional forms, "whether they be governed by a prince or common counsel,"[105] but direction by the best men who "commune" their "perfection to other" is needed if the civil life is really to be "a politic order of men conspiring togidder in virtue and honesty."

What Starkey has in mind, then, is essentially an aristocratic order of society. This order may be realized under different forms of government, since in his view the basic structure of all healthy social organisms can be likened to a human body with its hierarchy of heart, head, hands, and other parts. In this "very and true common weal," as he calls such an organism, every part does "his office and duty appointed."[106] He describes this in detail: "When all these parts thus coupled togidder exercise with diligence their office and duty, as, the ploughmen and labourers of the ground diligently till the same, for the getting of food and necessary sustenance to the rest of the body, and craftsmen work all things meet for maintenance of the same, yea, and they heads and rulers by just policy maintain the state stablished in the country, ever looking to the profit of they whole body, then that common weal must needs flourish."[107] Starkey makes a number of suggestions designed to enable the various social groups and professions in England to play their parts better. He suggests, for instance, proper education and training of future craftsmen for their jobs, limitation of the number of idle servants of the nobility, reform of the monasteries, restriction of luxury imports, revival of the cloth industry, and other economic and social measures.[108]

All such provisions, however, will come to fruition and improve matters only if the "chief and principal" need is met, which is that "the good order and policy by good laws [be] stablished and set, and by heads and rulers put in effect, by the which the whole body, as by reason, is governed and ruled,"[109] and by which, as we noted earlier, "the multitude of people" receives its very "civil life."[110] God has imparted reason, "that celestial light," to different men in different degrees, and education has accentuated this difference: "to some man this light is more communed, to some man less, according to the nature of his body and according to his education and good instruction in the common wealth where he is brought forth of nature."[111] It is evidently the task of those who have more of this light to rule and administer justice, "for the which purpose they are thus maintained in pomp and pleasure and in quiet life, without all travail and bodily labour" so that they may "diligently . . . apply themselves to their labours and pains for the sustaining of the whole body. . . ."[112] (More had justified the exemption of his rulers from ordinary labor in a similar way, although he had not advocated that they live in pomp.) The argument concerning the qualities and functions of the rulers is summarized and concluded by Pole in the following words: "A country, city or town then is well governed, ordered and ruled when the heads or rulers thereof be virtuous and wise, ever having before their eyes, as a mark to shoot at, the wealth of their subjects, every one of them also doing their office and duty to them appointed and determed."[113]

The question now is: does England have such virtuous and wise rulers, and if not, how can she obtain them? In speaking of the aristocracy and its duties, Starkey is clearly thinking of the English nobility and gentry and their functions in the Tudor state. He evidently has in mind such offices as that of justice of the peace and sheriff when he expresses the hope that "the nobility and gentlemen of every shire would consider their office and duty therein, which is chiefly to see justice among their servants and subjects and to keep them in unity and concord."[114] He feels that they, in turn, need supervision by the central government to keep them from abusing, or going beyond, their powers: all "inferior lords, knights and gentlemen which did not their office and duty in administration of justice with equity toward their subjects . . . should be called to count," and "any man" has the right to bring charges against them.[115] In all his suggestions for the improvement of the nobility, Starkey, like Elyot, addresses himself specifically to the Tudor aristocracy and keeps in mind its particular social and legal position and its obligations within the framework of the common weal. The wealth and pre-eminence of this class should be maintained because "our people . . . by nature be somewhat rude and sturdy of mind, insomuch that if they had not in every place some heads and governors to temper their affects rude and unruly, there would among them be no order at all."[116] His suggestion that lawyers should not have to "look . . . for all their living of their clients," but should be "gentlemen which have other land, office or fee sufficiently to maintain themselves withal,"[117] recalls the similar suggestion made by Elyot that those holding legal office should be gentlemen of independent means.

While Starkey is a strong defender of the aristocracy, he is not blind to its faults, such as ignorance, excessive eating and drinking, gambling, display and waste of wealth,[118] and he advocates a number of measures designed to remedy the situation. Before we turn to the most essential remedy, education, we may briefly single out one suggestion for the reform of nobility and gentry, which evidently reflects his study of conditions in contemporary Italian city-states: "Our gentlemen must be caused to retire to cities and towns . . . and there to see the governance of them. . . . They may not continually dwell in the country as they do. This is a great rudeness and a barbarous custom used with us in our country . . . the which surely is a great ground of the lack of all civil order and humanity." Lords and gentlemen must be compelled to build houses in the cities "and sometimes there to be resident."[119] He apparently does not want the aristocracy to become an urban class as in Renaissance

Italy, since its members are not expected to reside permanently in their town houses. What he hopes to achieve by this measure is to make the aristocracy less rustic—presumably to raise it to the level of the civic aristocracy in Italy—as well as to improve the standards of cities and towns. He conceives of the nobility and gentry as essentially a rural aristocracy in "every shire," but he would like them to be more urbane and "humane."

Like Plato, Starkey sees the education of the future rulers as the crucial problem which ultimately determines the character of the state: "It is not for nought, be you assured, that the most wise philosopher Plato in his common weal that he deviseth laboureth so much to instruct the officers and governors thereof."[120] Like More, however, Starkey is concerned not only with the education of the future rulers but demands general compulsory education for all children: after they have reached the age of seven years, they should be brought up in letters or in a craft, "according as their nature requireth."[121] Boys who want to prepare for the learned professions are to be chosen with particular care, and only those thought to be really suited for the professions are to be admitted to the curriculum that leads up to them.[122] Starkey advocates the creation of "conservators of the common weal" whose functions would correspond to those of the Roman censors; they are to be charged with the selection of candidates for higher education and with the supervision of their education.[123] Education is the cure for all ills: "This good education of youth in virtuous exercise is the ground of the remedying all other diseases in our politic body."[124] This corresponds to Starkey's conviction that "ignorance, as Socrates said oft, is the fountain of all ill, vice and misery, as well in every private man's life as in every commonalty."[125] It is the characteristically humanistic view that the banishing of ignorance by education eliminates evil tendencies and ambitions, that knowledge makes man good and "virtuous." In order to be able to discern such absolute values as "the good" and "the just," and to govern himself and others in accordance with them, man must attain true knowledge through right education.

Starkey's description of the education of future "governors" differs from the system outlined by More in the *Utopia*, and resembles that advocated by Elyot in the *Governour*. Starkey concentrates on the established aristocracy and, although he does not seem to exclude members of other groups specifically, he makes special provisions for them. He proposes to set up a separate and distinct system of education for the sons of the nobility which prepares them for their future functions. They are badly in need of being educated, if we are to believe his complaints which echo those voiced by Erasmus, Elyot, and other learned contemporaries: "First and most principal of all ill customs used in our country commonly . . . is that which toucheth the education of the nobility, whom we see customably brought up in hunting and hawking, dicing and carding, eating and drinking, and, in conclusion, in all vain pleasure, pastime and vanity."[126] Their fathers indulge in the same vices (particularly gluttony!), and so it is not surprising that "with us . . . gentlemen study more to bring up good hounds than wise heirs."[127]

Starkey has a definite plan for remedying this situation. Like More and Elyot, he advocates a humanistic scheme of education, but in one respect his scheme is closer to Plato's suggestions than either of theirs: he demands that the children of the nobility be brought up together in schools specifically organized and reserved for them. This provision and its implementation are closely related to Plato's plan for the joint and exclusive education of the guardians. More had not been specific on this point, and Elyot had recommended private instruction at home by a tutor. While Starkey's scheme presumably exerted no direct influence on the actual course of events, it closely corresponds to that actually evolved in the English "public schools" which were to develop into institutions largely reserved for the sons of nobility and gentry.

Like Elyot, Starkey envisages a fusion of humanistic and chivalrous education, a fusion which these schools should accomplish. He describes his whole scheme and its motivation as follows: there is "not only in our country but also in all other which ever yet I knew, a great lack and negligence of them which rule in common policy, and that is this: that in no country there is any regard of the bringing up of youth in common discipline and public exercise, but every man privately in his own house hath his master to instruct his childer in letters, without any respect of other exercise in other feats pertaining to nobility no less than learning and letters, as in all feats of chivalry. Therefore there would be some ordinance devised for the joining of these both togidder, which might be done after this manner. Likewise as we have in our Universities colleges and common places to nourish the childer of poor men in letters . . . so much more we should have . . . certain places appointed for the bringing up togidder of the nobility, to the which I would the nobles should be compelled to set forward their childer and heirs, that in a number togidder they might the better profit. To this use turn both Westminster and St. Albans, and many other. And to this company I would have appointed rulers certain of the most virtuous and wise men of the ream, the which should instruct this youth to whom should come the governance, after, of this our common weal. . . . Here they should be instruct not only in virtue and learning but also in all feats of war pertaining to such as should be hereafter, in time of war, captains and governors of the common sort. This should be the most noble institution that ever was yet devised in any common weal; of this, surely, should spring the fountain of all civility and politic rule . . . like . . . monks and religious men . . . living togidder exercise a certain monastical discipline and life, so they nobles, being brought up togidder, should learn there the discipline of the common weal . . . here I would have them . . . first to . . . learn what they be, and what place they occupy in the common weal, and what is the office and duty pertaining to the same . . . to be instruct in the administration of justice both public and private. . . . And thus they should be worthy of the name which we now unworthily give unto them commonly; then they should be nobles indeed . . . true lords and masters; then they people would be glad to be governed by them. . . ."[128]

Certain conclusions emerge from this statement. One of the principal values of these schools, as Starkey conceives their function, is the reproduction in them, on a small scale, of the social organism of the state, thus giving the students an opportunity to experience there "the discipline of the common weal" on a preparatory, experimental level. Other important features which emerge clearly are the limitation of these schools to the higher ranks of society, and Starkey's insistence that they provide for their pupils a complete liberal education corresponding to that provided for others at the grammar schools and universities; he insists on legal training as well, and includes the "administration of justice" among the subjects to be taught. Starkey wishes to combine this legal training with the introduction of the Roman civil law, and he expects great benefits for his country if not only poor men but also noblemen are trained in that law.[129] Evidently, Starkey assumes that universities are limited to the education of the poor. Another passage in the *Dialogue* bears out this interpretation: the function of the universities is there described as the training of future preachers in the liberal arts, and university education and the education of the nobility are definitely treated as two separate curricula.[130] In this respect, Starkey proved a bad prophet: he did not anticipate that the sons of the nobility and gentry would soon be crowding the universities, taking away places that were thought to belong to poor men's sons. He predicted more accurately what was going to happen in another respect: his suggestion that some existing schools should be taken over for the education of the nobility forecast a development which was actually to take place. While such schools were not formally limited to the education of the sons of the nobility and gentry, they began in practice to draw most of their pupils from this group.

One point touched upon by Starkey is that the nobles, now unworthy of their position, will become worthy through proper education. He hardly deals with the intricate problems raised by this observation; he does not investigate the question what is to be done with those scions of noble houses on whom this education is wasted, or with poor but able boys who might be expected to become qualified by it for public service in responsible positions. Starkey does not include the latter among those to be educated in the schools for future governors, although he must have been aware that in his day men of low birth were in high positions. Like Elyot, he worked closely with Cromwell, an upstart, and he himself was not of noble origin.[131] He probably felt that such problems would take care of themselves. In any case, he does not state that those educated in ordinary schools and universities may not rise to positions of importance. He apparently implies the opposite when he talks of "this good education of the nobility and of clerks, of whom we should after have they heads and rulers."[132] This may be presumed to mean that "clerks"—who are educated in ordinary schools and universities—may become qualified to occupy such positions, and it is reasonable to suppose that he would include lawyers in this category, since in another context, when he talks of the selection of those who may prepare for learned professions, he lumps "priests, clerks and learned in the law" together.[133] Since legal training is included in the curriculum of the nobles, others may presumably also become qualified for high office through it. Starkey undoubtedly prefers to see noble or at least wealthy men as lawyers —he once goes so far as to say that "a great ruin of all good order and civility" results if only "popular men which are born in poverty" practice law[134]—but, since he provides for the legal education of gifted commoners as well as of noblemen, he clearly thinks that members of both groups may become qualified for high office. He does not say so explicitly, but he does not exclude this possibility when he describes the composition of the two highest councils in the realm, the "little parliament" and the king's council. The former is to consist of "four of the greatest and ancient lords of the temporalty; two bishops, as of London and Canterbury; four of the chief judges; and four of the most wise citizens of London";[135] the latter is "to be of ten persons: two doctors learned in divinity, and two in the civil law" (did Starkey envisage himself in that position?) "and two of the common law . . . and four of the nobility, expert and wise men in matters of policy."[136] In both cases, the nobility only furnishes a part of the membership of these bodies. While nothing is said about the social origins of the other members (except in the case of the most wise citizens of London), Starkey stresses their academic qualifications, particularly in the king's council, in which the lawyers and divines actually have the majority over the nobles. He cannot have expected that they would all be noblemen or perhaps even gentlemen by birth, but he certainly hoped that the noble lords in both councils would be properly qualified for their responsible positions by the right education.

While Starkey thus allowed for a certain fluidity, he was on the whole a strong supporter of a social order based on the maintenance of separate estates. He comes to the defense of the principle of primogeniture, which he considers essential for the continuity of "nobility and ancient stocks"; its abolition would "confound the nobles and commons togidder," erase the nobility, and thus "take away the foundation . . . of all our civility."[137] He favors the principle of a hereditary aristocracy, of an aristocracy, however, which no longer bases its claims solely on blood and inherited wealth but has to justify its position by living up to standards similar to those established by Plato for his guardians and philosophers.

One important point is left out by Starkey both in his statement concerning the education of the nobility and in his remarks about the education of others: he does not tell us what plan of studies he wishes them to pursue. He is aware of this omission, which he justifies with the remark that the description of each type of curriculum would "require a whole book, and, beside this, there be wise and learned men which have writ in the same matter."[138] One of these wise men is Jacopo Sadoleto, to whose *De Liberis Recte Instituendis* he refers the reader.[139] In another context, when he discusses the establishment of a "good order of studies in the uni-

versities," he refers to Erasmus' "Instruction of a Christian Man."[140]
He indicates the need for humanistic reform in universities and
grammar schools of the "manner of studies which are confused."[141]
We are safe in deducing from this statement, from his references
to humanistic writers on education, and from his own convictions,
that he would have his students brought up on lines closely resembling those outlined by such men as Erasmus and Sadoleto,
More and Elyot.

While Starkey does not describe in detail the kind of education
he wishes to see introduced in England, he does give some indications of its character and results. We have noted the obvious indebtedness of much of Starkey's scheme for the education of
future rulers to Plato's *Republic,* and also his protests that Plato's
demands are impossible of realization. Since it "is out of hope with
us" to find "such heads as Plato describeth in his policy," he sets
his sights lower and suggests that the "wisdom of them whom we
would to rule," i.e., of "governors," be measured "after a more civil
and common sort."[142] In the choice of the criteria which he employs, he is indebted to Aristotle: he wants "such as will not in
all things nother follow their own affections, nother yet in whom
all affects are drowned and taken quite away, but, observing a
certain reasonable mean, ever have their eyes fixed to the common
weal. . . ."[143] Here as elsewhere Starkey displays what may be
described as a common-sense attitude which, without lowering his
standards unduly, keeps him from striving for the unattainable.

His insistence that the rulers "ever have their eyes fixed to the
common weal" is not just a commonplace saying; in his view, this
attitude is a token of their true nobility: "when men desire to bear
office and to rule to the intent they may stablish and set in their
country this common weal . . . it is the highest virtue that is in any
noble stomach, and is a certain argument of true nobility; for
sluggish minds live in corners and content themselves with private
life, whereas very noble hearts ever desire to govern and rule to the
common weal of the whole multitude."[144] Such a desire to rule is not
motivated, in Starkey's idealistic view, by selfish ambition or the
quest of power and wealth. If such motives should predominate, they
represent a perversion of man's innate tendencies and lead to the
destruction of the state. The right attitude which Starkey desires
can and should be fostered by education. The qualities which this
attitude comprises are indeed "by the benefit and power of nature
in [man's] heart . . . rooted and planted," but they need diligent

cultivation if "these seeds and virtues . . . shall . . . bring forth their fruit" and "bring man to his perfection."[145] Elyot had used a similar comparison with the gardener to describe the proper function of the teacher.

Education, however, is not enough. Man must choose of his own free will to seek out and follow the good, and only his constant initiative and effort will help him attain it. Lupset raises this issue in the discussion, after Pole has described his constitutional and pedagogical scheme: "But whether yet all these ordinance, yea, or all the power of law be able to bring man to this perfection, I somewhat doubt, forasmuch as the perfection of man standeth in reason and virtue, by the which he both knoweth that which is truth and good . . ."; but there is nothing to impel him to follow this except "his free will and liberty. With prudent knowledge and perfit love moved, he ever applieth his mind to such thing as shall bring him to his perfection. And to this methink no law is sufficient."[146] The "perfit love" which moves man in his efforts clearly recalls the Platonic *eros*. Lupset is doubtful whether man's free will suffices to let him achieve this goal; he is reassured by Pole's advice that we must follow Christ who "came to make perfit man, and supply the defect of the law by his celestial and divine doctrine."[147] (We have already noted that this is a very Erasmian interpretation of Christ.) The achievement of perfection, then, demands man's free decision to seek it and divine aid: "albeit . . . to stablish this doctrine in any common weal [is] the only work of God and not of man, yet this is not amiss: to show somewhat the mean how man may dispose himself and make himself meet to receive this heavenly doctrine"[148] by following virtue "for love only of virtue" and Christ "for love of Christ."[149]

The right education of the future governors is, in Starkey's view, the most vital need if his ideal is to be achieved. "This should bring forth in few years, I trow, Plato's common weal, or else, rather, the true institution of Christian doctrine."[150] Those who have passed through it should "as stars . . . light in all parts of the ream hereafter,"[151] and make a reality of Starkey's ideal in Tudor England. "Then shall there be stablished . . . that thing which we so long have sought: that is to say, a very and true common weal . . . governed virtuously in civil life, according to the dignity and nature of man."[152]

# VI

# Humanism and the Rise
# of the Gentry

ALL THE humanists whose thought we have investigated so far
lived and wrote in the reign of Henry VIII. With the exception
of Starkey, their major work was done before the impact of the
break with Rome was felt. That break and the measures growing
out of it, particularly the dissolution of the monasteries and the
distribution of their properties, were to have far-reaching effects in
religion, scholarship, education, and literature, in the economic life
and social structure of England. The changes and reversals in religious doctrine that came with the reigns of Edward VI, Mary, and
Elizabeth certainly had a very unsettling effect on the religious
and general intellectual life of the country, forcing clerics, scholars,
and other men either to conform to the changing forms of religion
or to seek refuge abroad. The middle third of the century is comparatively barren in intellectual and artistic creations, and is, in
retrospect, largely overshadowed by the extraordinary creativity of
the Elizabethan age. Some scholars have maintained that there was
an almost complete break between the literature and scholarship of
the period of Henry VIII and Elizabeth, that, with the executions of
Fisher and More, Henry dealt a blow to learning and the arts in
England from which it took her more than a generation to recover.
Chambers, one of the main upholders of this view, claims that
Henry "axed" classical scholarship, destroying its greatness for two
hundred years to come, that he grievously spoiled the universities,
and that, in general, "all learning felt the blow, and shrank."[1] If
this interpretation were correct, we would be forced to consider the
humanistic tradition of Erasmus, More, Elyot, and even Starkey, a
closed chapter of little further significance in the development of
English thought; the thought and civilization of the Elizabethan
period would be separated from the period of Henry VIII by a

"gap of more than a generation," by a "blank,"[2] and would, so to speak, have to start anew.

Humanistic learning in the middle third of the sixteenth century was not, in the opinion of this writer, as barren as Chambers would have us believe. The political and educational ideas of the earlier humanists were very much alive during that period, and much of their advice on the proper education of future "governours" was translated into practical reality. It was during this period that many of the men who were to be the statesmen, courtiers, and writers of the Elizabethan period received their humanistic education, that the seeds were planted which bore such splendid fruit in the last third of the century. Douglas Bush, in challenging Chambers' thesis, has furnished ample proof of the continuity of English humanism during the supposedly barren years after More's execution.[3] He concedes the obvious fact that the changing religious climate was not favorable to the free development of learning. Thus he finds that, for instance, "the history of most of the colleges throughout the period reveals continued disturbance and continual changing of masters, according as the reforming or the conservative party got the upper hand,"[4] but he argues convincingly that humanism not only did not suffer as much as might be expected in such a situation, but actually had a vigorous growth. Bush rightly points to "an unbroken succession of eminent classical scholars throughout the long blank period that Mr. Chambers deplores," and he considers the twelve years after More's death "the one period in English history before Bentley when classical studies in an English university were a matter of international fame, when Sir John Cheke taught Cambridge and King Edward Greek."[5] In the 1540's when, according to some interpreters, the English universities went through a period of great depression and sterility, we have "Ascham rejoicing in a golden age at Cambridge, and . . . Walter Haddon declaring that he had never seen the university more affluent or more thronged."[6] John Lyly, the author of *Euphues,* was later to compare Oxford to Athens; Edmund Spenser's ideas were to be formed in the active intellectual atmosphere of Cambridge.

Bush attributes the flowering of humanistic studies largely to the activities of Henry himself, whom he considers the patron rather than the destroyer of the new learning. He points to the numerous new foundations or refoundations of grammar schools and colleges that took place during Henry's reign, so numerous that he feels Henry should be called the greatest of school founders.[7] He stresses

Henry's active encouragement of classical studies in the universities by specific suggestions, by requests for lectureships in classical subjects, and the establishment of Regius Professorships. Among the latter, the provision for chairs of Greek and Hebrew shows the emphasis given to humanistic studies. There can, of course, be no question that only a small portion of the property that was taken away from the church was used to endow educational institutions. Very many schools were destroyed by the distribution of church properties, and elementary education in particular was very adversely affected by the spoliation of the chantries, where much of it had been imparted.[8] Yet large numbers of schools, especially on the more advanced or grammar-school level, were re-established or newly founded, often by laymen, and "it is probably fair to say that there was a greater rate of school foundations in this than in any other period" of English history.[9] Among the schools that were founded in the sixteenth century, after Colet's early establishment of St. Paul's, were Harrow, Merchant Taylors', Shrewsbury, Rugby, Tonbridge; Westminster and Canterbury were thoroughly reorganized.[10] There were 360 grammar schools in the country by 1600.[11] The new schools took their places beside older institutions like Eton and Winchester. Eton, Winchester, and Shrewsbury seem to have acquired their particular attraction for young noblemen and gentlemen in the second half of the sixteenth century, but other schools too attracted them in varying degrees.

The institutions that were newly created or reorganized under Henry, Edward, Mary, and Elizabeth, from grammar schools to colleges, were required to promote humanistic studies and to center their programs of teaching in them. This is clearly recognizable from the new charters, statutes, and courses of studies of the grammar and "public" schools: they show the great change that was taking place in the entire educational system of England. We have noted elsewhere the significance of Erasmus' advice in the establishment of St. Paul's School by Colet; about fifteen years later, in 1528, Wolsey reformed the Ipswich Grammar School, and planned for it "a much more liberal intellectual *menu* than that provided by Colet" for St. Paul's.[12] The time-tables of Winchester and Eton for 1530 reflect a limited degree of humanistic influence; Erasmus' *Copia*, for instance, was read at Eton, but no provision was as yet made for the teaching of Greek.[13] When Elizabeth refounded Westminster School thirty years later, the time-tables of that school looked very different: from the fourth through the seventh forms, Greek works, to be read in the original, constituted a major part of the curriculum, and in the seventh form, even Hebrew was studied.[14] Greek grammar and Lucian's *Dialogues* were read in the fourth form, Isocrates and Plutarch in the fifth, Demosthenes and Homer in the sixth and seventh forms; the titles of the Latin works prescribed reveal that the compilers of the curriculum were making humanistic choices here too: among the writings to be studied were not only those preferred and edited by humanists, such as Sturm's selection of Cicero's letters, but also writings of the humanists themselves, such as Erasmus and Vives.

On the university level, St. John's College, Cambridge, had been devoted to the new studies since its foundation in 1511. With Sir John Cheke and Roger Ascham, Princess Elizabeth's tutor, among its many distinguished members, it reached its greatest fame in the 1540's. Near the end of his reign, Henry founded Trinity College, which drew its inspiration and many of its men from St. John's.[15]

At Oxford, Fox's foundation of Corpus Christi College in 1516 had provided the first firm institutional basis for humanism. Wolsey's Cardinal's College, later refounded as Christ Church by Henry VIII, was another center of humanistic interests.[16] Thus, the changes in the direction of learning and the content of education that Fisher had initiated at Cambridge and Fox at Oxford, and that More had vigorously supported when he intervened in the struggle between "Greeks" and "Trojans" at Oxford in 1518, had been successfully incorporated into the structures of universities and schools by the middle of the century; the new learning existed side by side with the old. If the humanists of the "middle" generation did not leave many major works of scholarship, this fact may be attributed largely to their preoccupation with the reform of studies and religion and with actual teaching. The education of youth in the spirit of classical antiquity and of Christianity rather than the production of scholarly works was their primary purpose. Bush rightly reminds us "that the purpose of Tudor humanism was education. The broad aim was training in virtue and good letters, the special aim was preparing young men for public life. It was these Tudor humanists who established what was to remain the ruling motive of English classical study down to the days of the 'Jowett mind.' "[17]

These aims had been postulated by the earlier humanists, notably by Elyot and by Starkey. The training of men for the church and the education of future "clerks," which had been the major function of the universities before this time, continued to occupy part of

their energies, but the emphasis changed to the new role assigned
to them by the humanists and by the needs of the state. It matters
little that this development differed in some details from what Elyot
and Starkey had advocated: Elyot's suggestion that future governors
be educated privately, and Starkey's plan for the education of the
sons of the aristocracy in special academies did not prove practi-
cable. (This latter plan, incidentally, was revived early in Elizabeth's reign by Sir Humphrey Gilbert, but the scheme which he
outlined for a *Queene Elizabethes Achademy*[18] for noble wards and
other noble children was also destined to remain on paper.) Instead,
the ideas of the humanists were carried out in existing or newly
established institutions of learning which were not restricted to any
one class.

Since the later part of Henry's reign the sons of the nobility and
gentry had been attracted to schools and universities in growing
numbers, in a movement that continued to gain momentum throughout the rest of the century. The loud complaints that these young
men were crowding out poor men's sons and appropriating the places
meant for them[19] indicate that a considerable change was taking
place in the social composition of those attending schools—especially "public" schools like Eton and Winchester—and the universities
of Oxford and Cambridge. Even if we make allowance for exaggeration in the complaints of contemporaries like William Harrison and
Humphrey Gilbert about the displacement of the poor, the change
must have been very noticeable.[20] This change meant a thorough
reversal of the upper-class attitude toward learning: in the fourteenth and fifteenth centuries, aristocrats had drawn a sharp line
between their own chivalrous and clerkly education.[21] If some
members of the nobility and gentry, such as younger sons who were
destined for the church, had devoted themselves to "bookish"
studies and gone to the universities during that period, they proved
the rule by the exception. The arrogant upper-class prejudice against
learning is vividly illustrated by Richard Pace, Henry VIII's secretary of state, in his description of this argument which took place
at a banquet. A gentleman who betrayed his predilections by wear-
ing his hunting horn even at the dinner table reacted furiously
against another's discussion of the training of children in letters:
"All learned men are beggars; even Erasmus, that most learned man,
is poor, I am told." After swearing that he would prefer to see his
son hang than to have him study letters, he ended by declaring that
"gentlemen's sons ought to be able to blow their horn skilfully, to

hunt well, and to carry and train a hawk elegantly; but the study of letters is to be left to the sons of peasants." Pace reports that he was unable to restrain himself at this point; he broke into the discussion, and his reply, apart from silencing his immediate opponent, explains why most gentlemen sooner or later changed their minds. If the king were to receive the representative of a foreign power, Pace asked, and someone had to respond to this emissary's oration, "your son would but blow into his horn, if he were educated according to your wishes, and the learned sons of peasants would be called upon to reply. And they would be placed far ahead of your hunting or hawking son"; and they would say to your face that they would rather be learned than boast of stupid nobility. Camden repeats the story; in his version, "Richard Pace replied: Then you and other noble men must be content, that your children may wind their hornes and keepe their Haukes, while the children of meane men do manage matters of estate."[22]

The same reasoning was behind a memorandum for a plan to be submitted to Parliament early in Elizabeth's reign: its anonymous author intended to propose

that an ordinance be made to bind the nobility to bring up their children in learning at some university in England or beyond the sea from the age of twelve to eighteen at least. . . . The wanton bringing up and ignorance of the nobility forces the Prince to advance new men that can serve, which for the most part neither affecting true honour, because the glory thereof descended not to them, nor yet the commonwealth (through coveting to be hastily in wealth and honour) forget their duty and old estate and subvert the noble houses to have their rooms themselves.[23]

In order to provide for the inclusion of "the poorer sort of gentlemen's sons" in this scheme for the compulsory education of the aristocracy, the author of the memorandum proposed that one-third of all the free scholarships at the universities be set aside for them. He strongly advocated instruction in schools and universities, and proposed to limit the private education of children by preventing anybody below the rank of baron from keeping a schoolmaster at his house.[24]

Nobility and gentry, in any case, understood that it was not enough for them to complain against the rise of "mean men" to positions of eminence in the state, that they had to compete with "poor scholars" in those studies which led to the management of "matters of estate." If they swallowed their feudal pride and sent their children to places where they might acquire that much despised bookish learning, they were motivated at least as much by self-interest as by the moral admonitions of Erasmian humanists. They could not hope to maintain their position by adhering stubbornly to a social code that no longer met the needs of the state; with some exceptions, they adapted their code to the requirements of the age, shedding antiquated notions and accepting humanistic ideas. Elyot and the many authors of books on the education of the aristocracy who followed him showed them the way, creating their ideal of the "gentleman" out of a combination of chivalrous and humanistic ideas. That is not to say that the old ideals immediately lost their appeal: a nostalgic longing for the glorious past manifested itself in the great popularity which romances of chivalry enjoyed throughout the sixteenth and into the seventeenth century. It is significant, however, that these stories were ridiculed by the fashionable element of Elizabethan society and retained their popularity mainly among backwoods squires and the lower classes.[25] Sidney's *Arcadia* and Spenser's *Faerie Queene* retain certain elements of these romances in their subject matter, but they are distinguished from them by their purpose, "to fashion a gentleman or noble person in vertuous and gentle discipline"; an ideal which combines classical and chivalrous virtues.

The aristocracy was quick to recognize that the wind had turned, and adjusted itself to the new situation with amazing speed, as the following episode will show. Canterbury Cathedral was reorganized in 1541, and with it the Grammar School. At the meeting of the commissioners[26] for that purpose,

it came to pass that when they should elect the children of the Grammar School, there were one or two who would have none admitted but sons or younger brethren of gentlemen. As for other, husbandmen's children, they were more meet, they said, for the plough and to be artificers than to occupy the place of the learned sort. So that they wished none else to be put to school but only gentlemen's children.

Archbishop Cranmer objected to this brazen attempt of the commissioners to capture the school for their class—an attempt much more radical than the later plan to set aside one-third of the university scholarships. He argued that

poor men's children are many times endued with more singular gifts of nature, which are also the gifts of God, as with eloquence, memory, apt pronunciation, sobriety, and such like, and also commonly more apt to apply their study than is the gentleman's son delicately educated.

But his rejoinder did not end the argument:

138

Hereunto it was on the other part replied that "it was meet for the ploughman's son to go to plough and the artificer's son to apply the trade of his parent's vocation, and the gentleman's children are meet to have the knowledge of government and rule in the commonwealth."

Cranmer accepted part of this argument "as needful in a commonwealth," but invoked Christian doctrine to defeat the exclusion of the poor: to exclude them would involve the presupposition that "they were utterly unworthy of having the gifts of the Holy Ghost bestowed upon them," and this would be tantamount to saying "that Almighty God should not be at liberty to bestow his great gifts of grace upon any person." This appeal to theology seems to have won the day for Cranmer's final compromise, which still gives a slight advantage to the gifted gentleman's son over the gifted poor boy, but puts the latter before the "very dull" or lazy gentle-born: "If the gentleman's son be apt to learning let him be admitted; if not apt, let the poor man's child being apt enter his room."

The statutes as adopted show the effect of Cranmer's pleading: they provide for the free education of "fifty boys, poor and destitute of the help of their friends,"[27] as long as they prove their aptitude, and they state that "others" may also come to the school.[28] Sir Ernest Barker's interpretation of Cranmer's position on this occasion describes an attitude which was on the whole to prevail in England:

He sees that a commonwealth needs a differentiation of social functions. . . . But he also sees the other and greater side of the matter: that if God has made a world of degrees, like an ascending ladder, He has not fixed men irrevocably to the rung of their father's birth. . . . Any of us, wherever we are born, may be called by His will to a higher state, and prove that we are gentlemen.[29]

In order to put the Canterbury discussion in its proper perspective, one has to remember that the "poor" boys mentioned in it and in the statutes were not usually the members of the very poorest class of the population, but the children of farmers and tradesmen and "poor relations" of gentlemen "destitute of the help of their friends." Leach has pointed out that this had been the meaning of the term in medieval school foundations, which provided for the education of "poor" scholars,[30] and that still is the meaning of the term in our sixteenth-century discussion. Furthermore, some "gentlemen's sons" had undoubtedly been going to grammar schools for a long time, despite the aristocratic disdain of book learning; the Grammar School at Macclesfield, for instance, was established in 1502 to teach "gentlemen's sons and other good men's children of the town and country thereabouts."[31] What was new was the idea that schools should accommodate only gentlemen's sons to the exclusion of others, coupled with the conviction that "the knowledge of government and rule in the commonwealth" could be, and indeed had to be, acquired in a school.

The teaching of the humanists and, more effectively, the demand of the government for "learned men," served to convince a reluctant aristocracy that it was necessary to send their childern to schools and universities. They promptly took up the challenge, and it has been said that they did this so vigorously as to start "a stampede toward bookish education."[32] Hexter, who coined this colorful statement, has gathered some interesting data to support it. Thus, his investigation of the limited evidence contained in the registers of Eton College establishes that, by the middle of the century, "the social complexion of Eton has begun to change,"[33] and partly substantiates William Harrison's contemporary charge that the sons of the rich were pushing the poor out of the great grammar schools and the universities to the extent of taking over even the scholarships meant for them. The same thing was happening at Winchester, where, from 1569 on, a number of scions of noble families found it convenient to discover that they were related to the founder, William of Wykeham, and to avail themselves of the privileges the founder had provided for them;[34] previously there had been little inclination on the part of their fathers and grandfathers to take advantage of his provisions. At Shrewsbury, which had close to four hundred pupils, the sons of the nobility and gentry of north Wales and northwest England outnumbered the boys from the town, but did not monopolize the school. The resulting "social mixture at school must have strengthened the fibre of the nation";[35] a similar mixture, though with a larger proportion of wealthy citizens' than of country gentlemen's children, existed at Westminster and Merchant Taylors', the latter providing for one hundred well-to-do children and one hundred and fifty poor ones.[36] (Edmund Spenser was one of the poor scholars there.)

Of the first hundred students who entered Caius College, Cambridge, in 1564 and after, one was a nobleman's and one a knight's son, twelve were sons of esquires, and seventeen were sons of gentlemen. These thirty-one, constituting slightly less than one-third of the group, were outnumbered by fifty-nine members of the middle class; the remaining ten were poor men's sons.[37] The lists of matriculations at Oxford between 1571 and 1622,[38] which A. Clark has analyzed statistically, do not give a complete picture of the composition of the student body, since not all students matriculated formally. There were sons of wealthy parents, for instance, who attended the universities "informally" and had their private tutors there. (The universities tried to stop this practice during Elizabeth's reign.) While for this and other reasons the available records do not provide the complete picture, Clark's analysis shows that the number of knights' and gentlemen's sons, listed as "filii equitis," "filii armigeri," and "filii generosi," with an occasional nobleman's son in addition, increased more rapidly than that of "filii plebei," and that the former began to outnumber the latter in the later 1580's. The following figures will serve to illustrate this development: in 1571, 35 men of aristocratic origin (including 2 members of the nobility) matriculated, as against 54 "plebei" and 22 men of unstated origin. In 1585, 131 members of the former group were still outnumbered by 217 of the latter. In that year, the origins of only 5 are not known; separately listed (like the occasional "filii doctoris") are 11 "filii clerici" and 1 "filius decani." Even if we count these professional groups among the "gentlemen," the "plebei" still prevail. Two years later, in 1587, 89 gentlemen outnumbered 77 plebeians, and, in 1588, the figure of 124 as against 99 is still more convincing evidence of the fact that the proportions were being reversed. In 1594, the figures were 225 and 170; in 1600, 142 and 110. (The small numbers in such categories as "clergymen's sons" are not included in these figures.)

Hexter thinks that in the third quarter of the sixteenth century, the proportion of "filii plebei" and gentlemen's sons had been about five to three, and that around 1600 it had changed to about five to six in favor of the latter.[39] Rowse, on the other hand, maintains that while "the gentry were sending their children increasingly to the university, . . . they remained a minority."[40] The matriculation figures would seem to contradict this assertion if they are taken to indicate the actual proportions of the student body. As we have noted, however, they are not necessarily complete; also, men may have been listed as gentlemen's sons even though they did not belong to the landed gentry; finally, the sons of gentlemen often did not stay at the university as long as others since they frequently found it unnecessary to take their degrees, and this fact alone shows that the matriculation figures cannot be taken to indicate the real proportions of the student population actually in residence at any given time.

While it thus may well be true that the sons of the aristocracy remained a minority at the universities, the significance of the figures lies in the fact that an "invasion of the universities and Inns of Court by the gentry"[41] was taking place on a large scale.

Fitzherbert tells us, in 1602, that it had come to be the accepted practice for boys to attend grammar schools, particularly the "public" schools, where they would learn "grammaticae, poeticae, latinaeque linguae praecepta," and to proceed to the universities from there.[42] Philip Sidney might be taken as a typical example of such a career: together with his friend Fulke Greville, he attended Shrewsbury School. He afterward went up to Oxford and became a member of Gray's Inn, while Greville went to Cambridge and to the Middle Temple. Robert Dudley, Earl of Leicester, more than twenty years older than Sidney (who was born in 1554), probably had still been educated privately. Many of those going to the universities and the Inns of Court did not bother to complete the formal requirements of these institutions: Fulke Greville, who may serve as an illustration for many similar careers, did not take a degree at Oxford, and was not called to the bar.[43] This phenomenon does not necessarily reflect on the intelligence or industry of these young gentlemen, but rather indicates their desire to retain amateur status and not to be considered professional scholars or lawyers; it also shows that a classical education and a "knowledge of the laws" as such rather than formal qualifications were considered important and sufficient as preparation for a public career.

The Inns of Court in London were "the third university of the realm" to which "the gentry and prosperous middle class were sending their sons in ever greater numbers to acquire a legal education in the Common Law."[44] The author of the above-mentioned memorandum for Parliament on educational reforms went so far as to propose "that none study the laws, temporal or civil, except he be immediately descended from a nobleman or gentleman, for they are the entries to rule and government, and generation is the chiefest foundation of inclination."[45] His radical proposal was not carried out, but it is a strong indication of the growing—though not new—tendency of members of the aristocracy to provide legal training for their children, and of the government to require such training. The constant increase in the number of fellows of the Inns of Court was in part due to the growth in the number of noblemen's and gentlemen's sons who went there.

Intellectual life at the Inns of Court was far from being confined to legal studies. Many plays, for instance, were written there or performed in their halls for the first time. Thus, the tragedy *Gorboduc* was written by Thomas Sackville and Thomas Norton, two members of the Inner Temple, and first produced there in 1561. A number of other plays, often translated from or modeled on Seneca, had members of the Inns of Court as their authors and producers. We shall note the important part played by students and members of the legal profession in the translation of these and other classical and contemporary works into English. A majority of the young men at the Inns of Court would still have elicited adverse comments from Elyot, had he been alive, because they went there without the benefit of that philosophical education which he considered prerequisite, and which they might have, but had not, acquired at the universities.[46] He would have been comforted, however, by the growing number of those who followed his precepts by going both to the universities and to the Inns of Court—men like Fulke Greville, or like Walter Raleigh, who prefaced his legal education at Lyons Inn and the Middle Temple by a sojourn at Oriel College, Oxford. We shall see presently that in the Parliaments of Elizabeth, the number of those members who had gone through both kinds of education increased steadily.

Hexter provides some interesting data which illustrate the growing popularity among the sons of the aristocracy of a course of studies which took them from a public school to a university and then to an Inn of Court. In his investigation of the careers of Etonians, he finds that fewer than ten future members of Parliament had been at Eton during the hundred years after 1440, whereas forty future M.P.'s went there during Elizabeth's reign.[47] Among these forty, eighteen were sons of knights or peers and six were sons of knights' or peers' daughters; twenty became knights themselves, six became peers, others married into nobility or gentry, and only six had no visible connection with titled families. All these forty men went to the universities from Eton, and more than two-thirds proceeded to the Inns of Court.

The social composition and education of the Elizabethan House of Commons has recently been investigated by J. E. Neale.[48] He amply demonstrates not only that country gentlemen were being increasingly attracted to parliamentary service, but that a growing number of those elected to Parliament had a higher education. In the Parliament of 1584, 240 out of 460 members were country gentlemen, i.e., more than one-half of the total membership; a good many of the 75 royal officials who also sat in this Parliament must have sprung from the same class. As to educational qualifications, Neale's figures for this Parliament are indeed remarkable. Where only 67 out of 420 members of the 1563 Parliament had gone to Oxford and Cambridge, in 1584, 145 out of 460 had attended the universities. If one adds those who had gone to the Inns of Court, the total numbers of those with a higher education are 139 in 1563, and 219 in 1584. The figures for 1593 further emphasize this "stark and staring" trend, as Neale calls it: 161 members had been to the universities, 252, or considerably more than one-half of the membership of the House, had had some higher education. One final group of Professor Neale's figures should be noted here: in 1563, only 36 members had had both a university and a legal education; in 1584, their number grew to 90, and in 1593 to 106, almost one-fourth of the total membership. The rapidly increasing number of those who had had the benefit of both types of education illustrates the widespread adoption of this combination.

Neale attributes the growing erudition of the House to the invasion of the institutions of higher learning by the gentry. It is significant that not more than roughly one-third of those members of Parliament who had attended the universities had taken a degree, and that approximately the same proportion of those who had gone to the Inns of Court had been called to the bar.[49] A majority of these gentlemen, then, did not find such distinctions necessary to qualify for election to the House. They are representative, in this respect, of their class: valuing education as such, they treated its professional aspects with the noble disdain which they felt their station demanded. Nevertheless, the legal profession, which often proved extremely profitable in the days of Elizabeth, did attract many of them, especially younger sons; and it offered a fine opportunity for sons of yeomen and others to advance socially and to style themselves "gentlemen."

If Parliament attracted educated men, or if a humanistic and legal education became a helpful qualification for a man desirous of being elected to Parliament, the same situation prevailed in the other spheres of public life. Thus, "among the great crown servants who surrounded Elizabeth . . . there is scarcely one without a university education."[50] The queen's "inner circle of ministers were all Cambridge men: Burghley and his son Robert, Lord Keeper Bacon and all his family, Sir Thomas Smith and Walsingham";[51] Sidney and Raleigh had been at Oxford. The queen herself had been taught by

William Grindal and Roger Ascham, both Cambridge men. She took considerable interest in the universities, to which she paid numerous visits. On these occasions, Elizabeth would listen to long orations and disputations in Latin, and herself reply to them learnedly. The questions discussed on such occasions, while academic, were not necessarily remote—two questions debated on her visit to Oxford in 1566 were "Princeps declarandus est electione, non successione," and "Praestat gubernari ab optima Lege, quam ab optimo Rege."[52] The queen took a keen interest in these disputations. She was always on the lookout for promising young talent. She demanded a high intellectual level of her courtiers, ministers, ambassadors, judges, and magistrates, and the example of the Court did not fail to have its effect on the country at large. It became fashionable to be well versed in the classics and to have some legal training, and this fashion extended from the courtier to the country gentleman.[53]

Learning, indeed, came to be the mark of a gentleman, a mark which had not distinguished his forebears, and if we are to believe Sir Thomas Smith, it became the major distinguishing attribute in an age in which the distinctions between the various estates had become blurred, in which many people had recently climbed up on the social ladder.

As for gentlemen [Smith says in *De Republica Anglorum*[54]], they be made good cheape in England. For whosoever studieth the lawes of the realme, who studieth in the universities, who professeth liberall sciences, and to be shorte, who can live idly and without manuall labour, and will beare the port, charge and countenaunce of a gentleman, he shall be called master . . . and shall be taken for a gentleman: . . . (and if neede be) a king of Heraulds shal also give him for mony, armes newly made and invented, the title whereof shall pretende to have beene found by the sayd Herauld in perusing and viewing of olde registers. . . .

This provides a neat summary of the situation, and it indicates that learning could be and was used to legitimize recent social advancement or to achieve such advancement. "England was never merry since the new learning came up,"[55] said the conservative old Duke of Norfolk, indicating his disapproval of the more flexible social order that was connected with this development. Some men did become "gentlemen," according to Smith's definition of the term, by their studies: Thomas Wilson, writing at the end of the century, complained about the typical rich yeoman's son who, dissatisfied with his social position,

must skipp into his velvett breches and silken dublett and, getting to be admitted into some Inn of Court or Chancery, must ever after thinke skorne to be called any other than gentleman.[56]

145

Such former yeomen, like younger sons of gentlemen, often turned their legal earnings into land, thus becoming country gentlemen in their own right. (Profits from trade, of course, were frequently employed for the same purpose by tradesmen and merchants.) Some judges and lawyers earned a great deal of money, £20,000 and £30,000 p.a.[57] The most remarkable example of such legal acquisitiveness is the great Sir Edward Coke, who in 1594 became Elizabeth's attorney-general; he left fifty-eight manors when he died in 1634.[58]

Study at the universities, like legal study, could pave the way to advancement under a learned queen. But what made gentlemen "good cheape" in England was not the new learning so much as the general redistribution of wealth and the resulting fluidity of social classes. Tawney has shown that "in the century and a half between the Reformation and the Restoration, . . . a redistribution [of land] took place on a scale not seen since the Conquest."[59] Although the Crown was still distributing lands one hundred years after the dissolution of the monasteries, the major impact of the Dissolution was felt in the twenty years after 1536, when about one-fifth of the available land came into the market.[60] By the time of Elizabeth, the great scramble was over, and the men, or their descendants, who had enriched themselves under Henry and Edward[61]—and had advanced on the social ladder in the process, now felt themselves secure in their "ancient" possessions and positions. If the "majority of the Elizabethan nobility were the second or third generation of *nouveaux riches*,"[62] they had not usually risen from the gutter but from the gentry, and the forbears of many great Elizabethans had been members of the lesser gentry or even yeomen. There was, then, a very close connection between gentry and nobility, and the barrier separating yeomen from gentlemen was not insuperable. "A glimpse into the background of the yeomen and the gentry largely dispels the doctrine of 'gentle blood' as a basis for distinction between them," Miss Campbell tells us,[63] and she illustrates the "rapidity with which members of the yeomanry could advance beyond the station to which they were born."[64] Rowse describes the rise of the Furse family of Devonshire—slow and steady in this instance—from the ranks of the yeomanry into the gentry, and similar developments in Leicestershire between 1540 and 1600.[65] One out of many examples will suffice to show the possibilities of social advancement under the Tudors and Stuarts: "a nondescript man-at-arms, follower of Henry VII in one generation . . . a knighthood in the next generation, a peerage in the next, with two earldoms at the hand of James"[66]—such

146

is the history of the Cecils, and while it is more spectacular than most such careers, it is nonetheless typical. Men from the towns, and of "obscure" origin, did sometimes rise very rapidly in the service of the government. Thomas Cromwell is a classic example of this. Merchants and tradesmen from the smaller towns moved to the country and into gentility, though this was exceptional. The social gap separating tradesmen from gentlemen could more easily, though even there rarely, be bridged by the money of the great London fortunes.[67] The lines between gentlemen, knights, and noblemen were much more fluid and easier to cross than the line between the urban middle class and the landed aristocracy.[68]

While the largest individual grants of monastic lands passed into the hands of peers, the largest aggregate share passed into those of the gentry,[69] with yeomen rounding out their holdings on a more modest scale and city merchants and tradesmen also entering the field.[70]

Tawney has established that in a particular area members of the gentry and their relatives acquired one-half to two-thirds of these lands.[71] As to the gentry's total holdings, he has shown that in ten counties it held 67 per cent of three thousand manors in 1561, and that it improved its relative position as against other groups, including the nobility, in the ensuing eighty years: by 1640, the figure had risen to 80 per cent.[72] These figures, one would assume, include those who had found it necessary to pay the King of Heralds for their new coats of arms[73]—the newly enriched yeomen, merchants, and others who had risen into the ranks of the gentry. It would be wrong to attribute this development exclusively to the distribution of the monastic lands: the gentry had been gaining ground since the thirteenth and particularly in the fifteenth century, and the assimilation of merchants and yeomen into that class had not been unkown then. But the culmination of these processes came with the Dissolution and the large spoils the gentry reaped from it. Favored and used by the early Tudor monarchs, that class expanded in size and power, gained a dominant social position, and further consolidated its gains under Elizabeth. Its sheer weight in numbers is impressive: Thomas Wilson, in 1600, estimates the number of knights at about five hundred, and that of esquires, among whom he includes all other country gentlemen, at approximately sixteen thousand, as against nineteen earls and marquesses, thirty-nine barons, and two viscounts; he evidently finds the aggregate wealth and power of the latter group less impressive than that of the former.[74]

The line between the lower ranks of the gentry and the yeomanry was somewhat elastic, while in its upper ranks this "nobilitas minor" was closely related to the "nobilitas maior." Many noble families had recently risen from the gentry, and there were close family ties. The separation between the various classes tended to become somewhat more rigid under Elizabeth,[75] a great believer in the hierarchy of "order and degree," than it had been under her predecessors when the major scramble for wealth and power took place. There continued to be formal, legal, and real distinctions between nobility and gentry, yet the decisive dividing line was not that which distinguished noblemen from gentlemen but that separating those who might call themselves knights, esquires, or gentlemen from those who could not add such designations to their names. Elyot's advice, addressed in the main to the gentry, proved equally useful to the nobility. The scions of both groups imbibed the wisdom of the ancients and of the common law to fit them for their stations, while men of lower birth used such learning to advance themselves or to legitimize their recently acquired possessions and dignities. Of all the social classes the gentry was the most energetic and powerful, the decisive element in Elizabethan society: in Rowse's words, "it was they essentially who changed things, who launched out along new paths . . . , who achieved what was achieved, who gave what all societies need—leadership. One may fairly say that most of the leading spirits of the age, those who gave it its character and did its work, were of this class. Many of them belonged to it, or were recruited from it; some of them passed on, like the Cecils and the Bacons, the Russells, Cavendishes and Sackvilles, into the new nobility; others—a more numerous regiment—were recruited into it from the ranks of merchants or yeomen, successful soldiers or sailors, or churchmen."[76]

Elyot, with his *Governour*, had set the tone for a whole flood of literature[77] that concerned itself with the education of those who would qualify for a position of importance in the state. This is not surprising in a situation in which the state was demanding new qualifications, in which the humanists were setting up a new scheme of education to supply these qualifications, in which old ideals were fading, and in which new men, anxious to establish themselves and their families as "gentlemen," were eager for guidance. Elyot's own work retained its popularity, being republished a number of times throughout the century,[78] and it found many rivals. Among these, we might mention as representative *The Institucion of a Gentleman*, published anonymously in 1555,[79] Lawrence Humphrey's *The Nobles or of Nobilitye*, published in 1563, and Sir Humphrey Gilbert's *Queene Elizabethes Achademy* (1562[?])—a scheme for the separate education of the aristocracy, reminiscent of Starkey. There was also Ascham's rather stern treatise, *The Scholemaster*, "specially purposed for the priuate brynging up of youth in Ientlemen and Noble mens houses,"[80] published posthumously in 1570. That the fashion was continued vigorously beyond Elizabeth's reign is attested by the appearance of works like Henry Peacham's *The Compleat Gentleman* in 1622. A very large number of similar works written by Englishmen throughout the seventeenth and into the eighteenth century could be added to this list,[81] as well as a number of books that appeared in English translations: Sir Thomas North was the translator of Guevara's *The Diall of Princes,* published in English in 1557; the most notable and influential translation was *The Courtyer of Count Baldesar Castilio* by Sir Thomas Hoby, which appeared in 1561. In the aggregate, works such as these formed the social ideal of Englishmen in the sixteenth century. They are all concerned with fashioning a gentleman in virtuous and gentle discipline, although there are, of course, differences in educational plans and emphasis between them. There is much imitation and repetition from one book to the next, but the greater ones have their individual quality. The most outstanding work among them is *The Courtier:* Elizabethans seem to have read it and carried it on their persons, like a later generation of Europeans carried, with comparable enthusiasm, Goethe's *Werther*. Apart from being an outstanding literary work which appealed to their artistic and aesthetic sense, *The Courtier* was for the Elizabethans a guide to manners and behavior at a Court more splendid, more at the center of things, more closely resembling the courts of the Italian Renaissance than that of any English sovereign before it. The elegant Italian work was more strictly a "courtesy" book than its more homespun English counterparts; in describing his "governour," Elyot had not thought specifically of the needs of courtiers. Their needs were met by Castiglione. The ethical idealism of both authors and of their imitators was closely related, and was based on the ideals of classical antiquity.

The English authors of such treatises were clearly concerned with some of the same problems that had worried Elyot. They believed in an aristocratic social order, but they were not ready to grant that high birth or great wealth or military prowess alone could make a gentleman. On the contrary, some authors minimized the importance of these traditional qualifications, and considered learning in itself sufficient to make a gentleman. Thus, Richard Pace, writing in 1517, had tried to stimulate the interest of the boys of St. Paul's in studies by stressing their usefulness: both in former ages and in the present day many low-born men had become most noble and illustrious through "doctrina." "And true nobility is that made by virtue rather than by a famous and long pedigree."[81a] Not only was the advancement of ordinary men through learning and virtue thus legitimized, but the accent was moved from the old to the new qualifications of gentility. If, on the one hand, boys of "ungentle" origin were admonished to pursue their studies diligently because they might gain high position through them, boys of "gentle" origin were urged to study letters because otherwise they might lose out to the industrious poor.

Most writers after Pace demanded a combination of the old and the new qualifications. Like Elyot, they generally tried to convince the aristocracy that it should defend its position against the onrush of "new men" by the acquisition of "learning," and that learning, combined with the qualifications of blood and wealth, made the best gentlemen. The *Institucion of a Gentleman* states that "a ryght gentleman ought to be a man fyt for the warres, and fyt for the peace, mete for the court and mete for the countrey."[82] A "royster," an uncouth and unlearned ruffian, hardly meets these qualifications, even if he is of gentle descent. He is "gentle ungentle," and as such not equal to the "ungentle gentle," the man of low birth, who "by his vertue, wyt, pollicie, industry, knowledge in lawes, valiency in armes, or such lyke honeste meanes becometh a welbeloved and hygh estemed man, preferred then to great office."[83] The author of the *Institucion* allows only "honest" means of social advancement, and strongly disapproves of those men who have recently helped themselves to the spoils of the monastic lands. Such men who have advanced "neyther by their learning nor worthynes," but "by certein darke augmentacion practices" (a reference to the Court of Augmentations) should be classified as "worshypful unworthie."[84] These upstarts "have chieflye florished since the puttinge downe of Abaies"[85] and, in contrast to the "honest" kind, are not considered to be gentlemen by the author of the *Institucion:* "Coppered chaynes gylded are noo pure golde."[86] But he thinks if low-born men have "worthely rysen to honour," they are worthy "to bee called nobles or gentlemen."[87] Lawrence Humphrey agrees with this feeling: "If by theyr owne vertue and commendacion of wisedome, they attaynde to this higher room, as many at this day both singulerly learned, and guyltles and sincere in life: then are they truly most honourable, and worthy a higher state."[88] Yet it is generally agreed that preferable to the "ungentle gentle," who is thus advanced by his virtue, is the "gentle gentle," the gentleman born, who is also learned and virtuous.[89] The ideal condition is achieved "when noble vertues in nobled race doe shyne," as Humphrey puts it, when the high-born use their "gotten goodes" and do not fall asleep over them.[90] Humphrey, who was president of Magdalen College, Oxford, admonished the nobility to "ever caste theyr eyes to . . . antiquytye, and hit propose theym selves for paterne."[91] (It is indicative of the growing number of men of aristocratic parentage at the universities that the president of an Oxford college should feel called upon to instruct them in their duties.) Humphrey, too, was unhappy about men who had risen through the dissolution of the monasteries; but although in his view they had lost sight of the interests of the community as a whole, seeking "not the commen but theyr private commoditye," he is ready to give in and to consider them gentlemen if they are good men in other respects.[92]

As we have tried to show in the preceding pages, humanistic concepts came to be an integral and effective part of English education during the half-century that separates the first years of the reigns of Henry VIII and of Elizabeth. The ideal of the learned, responsible gentleman who devotes himself to the tasks of government, as envisaged by Elyot and Starkey and further elaborated by others, became the model for an increasingly active and powerful gentry. By the middle of the sixteenth century, learning, formerly so despised by him, came to be a characteristic attribute of the English gentleman. In 1581 George Pettie, the translator of Stefano Guazzo's *La Civile Conversazione*, summed up the situation in these words, to his readers:

Alas you wyll be ungentle Gentlemen, yf you be no Schollers: you wyll doo your Prince but simple service, you wyll stande your Countrey but in slender steade, you wyll bryng your selves but to small preferment, yf you be no Schollers.[93]

It is clear from his further remarks that he felt many gentlemen were scholars though they refused to admit it. This constitutes a considerable change from the complete ignorance deplored by Elyot fifty years earlier. It is only fair to add, however, that in 1622 Henry Peacham was still voicing the old complaint, by this time with much less justification, that "there is nothing more deplorable, then the breeding in generall of our Gentlemen."[94] The principles and admonitions of the earlier humanists continued to be voiced by their successors, and they were in fact implemented with surprising speed. The demand of the state for learned officials and courtiers caused the prejudice of the hunting nobles against learned clerks and bookish learning not so much to vanish completely as to become obsolete. Learning came to be regarded as necessary equipment, but it was to remain unobtrusive, was not to be shown unnecessarily, and was not supposed to become an end in itself. A gentleman needed it to serve the state, and to that end his learning was subordinated. Alexander Barclay had said early in the century that "doing is the fruite and learning but the sede . . . the ende of learning is the dede,"[95] and this remained the guiding principle of those who acquired a humanistic education. Nobility and gentry had come to realize that they would bring themselves "but to small preferment" if they could not command a knowledge of letters, and so the courtiers and country gentlemen of the later part of Henry VIII's reign, and of the reigns of Edward VI, Mary, and Elizabeth, had their sons brought up in letters and the law in ever growing numbers. That development bore its fruit under Elizabeth, who, herself educated by humanists, appreciated and rewarded intellectual accomplishments on a scale hitherto unknown. The atmosphere of her reign was more favorable to the free growth of men and their thoughts than had been that of previous reigns: the middle course followed by Elizabeth in religious matters took much wind out of the sails of religious factionalism and fanaticism, which had proved major obstacles to such growth before her. More immediately than ever before, men adopted the examples of classical antiquity as their model.

One significant phenomenon which exemplifies this development is the extraordinary outcropping of translations of Greek, Latin, Italian, French, and Spanish works at the beginning of her reign. It has been shown that most of the translators were members of the Inns of Court, and that many of them had previously been at one of the universities.[96] They had had at least a good part of their education under Mary and even under Edward. Most of the humanistic lawyers who produced these translations came from the gentry; some of them were knights. G. H. Conley has examined the dedications prefixed to English translations of the classics in this period and has ascertained that, out of sixty-nine works, about two-thirds were dedicated to members of the privy council.[97] The translators frequently described the friendliness of their patrons and the interest they took in their work: it seems that in some cases patrons like Cecil caused these labors to be undertaken. Almost all the translators were young: most of them were born after 1535, and some were only sixteen years old when they produced their translations. In translating classical and other works, they had cultural and political aims, but they also had ulterior personal motives: on the one hand, they wished to strengthen the cause of humanism by making classical and humanistic writings available to anybody who could read English; on the other, they wanted to attract the attention of the great men at Court by displaying their abilities in these translations. This may be illustrated by a quotation from Nuce's translation of Seneca's *Octavia:*

> If the translating of Latine, or other Bookes of other languages, into our mother tong, doth eyther profite the commonwealth, or the wryter at all, do not then condemne the yong sprong writers, if that in all pointes they please not thee which may by the grace of God, through thy gentle and curteous accepting of a little toye, hereafter employ their labour to more serious and weighty matters, both to their owne commoditie and thy learning, and especially to the profit of our native countrie.[98]

Sir Thomas North may be taken as a representative example of this group of translators. He was born about 1535, may have gone to Peterhouse, Cambridge, and went to Lincoln's Inn in 1557. In that year, his translation of Guevara's *Diall of Princes* appeared, a book which its title-page proclaims to be "ryght necessary and pleasaunt, to all gentylmen and others whiche are lovers of virtue."[99] In 1579, the work which constitutes his major claim to fame appeared, his translation (from Amyot's French version) of *The Lives of the Noble Grecians and Romanes* by Plutarch, which was to be so magnificently exploited by Shakespeare in his Roman plays. If Englishmen will read these *Lives*, "what service is there in warre, what honor in peace, which they will not be ready to doe, for their worthy Queene?"[100] And he tells his readers, in a passage which is strongly reminiscent of Sidney's and Spenser's reasons for writing "heroic poems," that "all other learning is private, fitter for Universities then cities, fuller of contemplacion than experience, more commēdable in the students them selves, than profitable unto others. Whereas stories . . . teache the living, revive the dead, so farre excelling all other bookes, as it is better to see learning in noble mens lives, than to read it in Philosophers writings."[101] He told the queen that he hoped "the common sorte of your subiects, shall not onely profit them selves hereby, but also be animated to the better service of your Maiestie."[102]

Sir Thomas Hoby, the translator of the *Cortegiano*, is another typical representative of this group, an Elizabethan gentleman, courtier, official, and scholar. Born in 1530, he went to St. John's College, Cambridge, at the age of fifteen. After two years there, he proceeded to Strassburg, where he stayed with Martin Bucer and attended Sturm's lectures. We then find him on several embassies in Germany and France with his elder stepbrother Sir Philip Hoby, until, in 1554, under Mary, he retired to Padua with some English friends. Knighted in 1566, he succeeded Sir Thomas Smith as ambassador to France, where he died in the same year. He began to translate Castiglione's book in Paris in 1552 and apparently finished most of the work on it in Padua in the winter of 1554–55.[103] The translation was thus virtually completed before he was twenty-five. In Padua he was in the company of Cheke, who later gave the finished manuscript a critical reading.[104] It was published, after the accession of Elizabeth, in 1561, and republished in 1577, 1588,[105] and 1603. Hoby's career, combining political activity and intellectual achievements, was cast in the mold of Castiglione, and was to be followed by the similar careers of many other Elizabethan courtiers—most notably by that of Sir Philip Sidney.

The feeling of kinship with the states of antiquity, and the desire to emulate them, produced the great literary activity of the translators during the first twenty years of Elizabeth's reign. The young men whom their humanistic education had inflamed with an enthusiasm for Greece, Rome, and Renaissance Italy translated a large proportion of the known classical works, and a number of Italian and other humanistic books, into English. They rightly thought that their fellow-countrymen would be more apt to read them in English than in a foreign language, and they were motivated in their translations by the didactic aim of causing themselves and others to live up to the ideals which they found in this literature. Hoby, who defends the practice of translation in his dedicatory epistle, expresses this attitude as follows:

The translation of Latin or Greeke authours, doth not onely not hinder learning, but furthereth it, yea it is learning it selfe, and a great stay to youth, and the noble ende to which they ought to apply their wittes, that with diligence and studie have attained a perfect understanding, to open a gap for others to follow their steps, and a vertuous exercise for the unlatined to come by learning, and to fill their mind with the moral vertues, and their bodies with civill conditions. . . .[106]

The translations, then, are a manifestation of the widespread interest in the classics, and the elevated social origin of most of the translators indicates that humanistic education had made much headway among them. Another indication of the great importance that came to be attached to education is the educational journey to the Continent, particularly to Italy, the "grand tour," usually undertaken under the supervision of a tutor as the concluding stage in the proper training of a gentleman for future public service.[107] In the fifteenth and early sixteenth centuries, Italy had been the place where the new classical learning could be acquired; at that time, it had mainly attracted young scholars, most of them members of the church, who went there for the sake of scholarship. The interests of the group that had surrounded Reginald Pole in Padua in the 1520's and 1530's[108] had already assumed a political complexion, as exemplified by Starkey, and this shift in emphasis became further accentuated among those who went to Italy in the later part of the century. By this time, humanistic education was well established in England, and a knowledge of the works of classical and humanistic authors could be acquired at home. Young gentlemen went to Italy still conscious of the fact that humane letters had been reborn there, but the main purpose of their journeys now was to acquire a knowledge of the political conditions, of the government, manners, and language of Italy and other countries. Such practical experience was to add the practical touch to their education which up to that point had been largely theoretical.

This practice evoked many complaints which prove the popularity of these tours. Puritan authors saw Jesuits lurking at every street corner, trying to ensnare young Englishmen into popery, and they pointed to all kinds of unspeakable dangers to their morals. "These be the inchantementes of Circes, brought out of Italie, to marre mens maners in England," Ascham exclaimed,[109] pointing out that the Italians themselves had a fitting description of Italianate Englishmen:

> Englese Italianato
> e un diabolo incarnato.[110]

Ascham esteemed what he considered good in the Italian tradition, and recommended that young gentlemen read Hoby's translation of the *Cortegiano* in England: one year spent at home in reading and practicing its precepts would do them more good than three years in Italy![111]

In the second half of the sixteenth century, Italy appeared to many Englishmen like a school for learning atheism and treacherous ways of killing.[112] Italians were thought to be followers of Machiavelli, who had invented the most abominable crimes, and an Englishman traveling in Italy was likely to become infected by their Machiavellian ways. The name "Machiavelli" was even used as a synonym of "devil" in Elizabethan England.[113] A major factor that contributed to this negative attitude was Gentillet's anti-Machiavellian work, *Discours sur les moyens de bien gouverner*, published in Geneva in 1576, widely read in England and published in English in Simon Patericke's translation in 1602,[114] long before *The Prince* appeared in English in 1640. In the "Epistle dedicatorie," Patericke gives a good account of the Elizabethan attitude of moral indignation against Machiavelli: "by maintaining wholesome unitie amongst all degrees, [Queen Elizabeth] hath hitherto preserved the State of her realme, not onely safe but florishing not by Machiavelian artes, as Guile, Perfidie, and other Villanies practising: but by true vertues, as Clemencie, Iustice, Faith. . . . O how happy are yee . . . that the infectious Machiavelian doctrine, hath not breathed nor penetrated the intrails of most happy England."[115] This encomium brings out the contrast between the humanistic and what had come to be known as the Machiavellian approach to political ethics, and it states the English preference for the former. There were, of course, men who practiced Machiavellian *virtù* in England, and the queen's policy was not always guided by the true virtues ascribed to it by Patericke; but Castiglione, the representative of humanistic idealism, rather than Machiavelli, set the norm of life at the court of Elizabeth, and the virtues of the *Governour* established the standard for the country.

# VII

# Sir Philip Sidney

IN VARYING degrees of perfection, Elizabeth's statesmen, courtiers, adventurers, and soldiers embodied the humanistic ideal. In the orbit of the court, the influence of this conception of man was pervasive, and some of its manifestations could be demonstrated in such different characters as Burleigh, Essex, Raleigh, in Senecan tragedies like Norton and Sackville's *Gorboduc* and in Lyly's *Euphues*. Its purest crystallization was to be found, however, in the figure of Sir Philip Sidney, the period's "president of noblesse and of cheualree."[1] The early heroic death of this poet, courtier, diplomat, and soldier served to perpetuate his image in unblemished splendor as that of the gentleman par excellence.[2] In an age in which men strove for many-sided perfection, his universality was matched by few. He became the embodiment both of Elyot's "governour" and of Castiglione's courtier.[3]

The Elizabethan gentleman was more adaptable and urbane than his counterpart in the Henrician age: where Elyot was stiff and wooden and self-consciously assertive, Sidney was flexible and elegant and graciously secure. The framework of Elizabethan society was wider, its level higher than that of Henry's court. What often looks like theorizing scholarship in the Henrician generation of humanists became an essential part of life and experience in Sidney's generation, and lived in its thought and poetry. The philosophical foundations of the humanistic ideal had been laid by the preceding generation. In its main aspects, the conception remained valid, but instead of being presented in philosophical treatises it now fired the artistic imagination: it appeared in literary descriptions and in poetic creations. Novels and poems were inspired by the inseparable ideals of the good man and the perfect state. Their authors enthusiastically tried to stimulate their readers by the noble examples they set, and thereby to spur them to the realization of the humanistic dream.

The literary media and the artistic quality of presentation changed between the earlier and the later period. The underlying conceptions, however, although enriched by Italian thought, which was by then more easily accessible in English translations of many major works, remained essentially identical with those promulgated by the humanists of Henry's reign. The seeds planted at that time came to fruition in the later part of the century.[4] More perfect branches—more delicate southern variations—had been grafted on the original plant, but its root and stem remained and imparted their quality to the fruit. The humanistic tradition, partly hidden under the troubles of the middle of the century, continued unbroken in its impact on education and thereby on the generation that grew up with and surrounded Elizabeth.

Their classical education and their journeys to Italy made Sidney and his generation more conscious of aesthetic values than their predecessors had been. The appreciation for the literary aspects of classical and Renaissance literature displayed by many of Sidney's contemporaries had been exceptional in the preceding period. It is hardly necessary to mention that they modeled the products of their sudden and astounding literary creativity largely on Italian examples, such as Petrarch, Sannazaro, Castiglione, and Ariosto. They appropriated and developed classical and Italian models and cast their own creations in these forms. In their literary genius, in their mastery of form, the Elizabethans far surpassed the generations of their fathers and grandfathers to whose images of man and society they gave new life in heroic poems like the *Arcadia*[5] and the *Faerie Queene*. Sidney and his contemporaries burst out of the narrow framework of Elyot's conception into a new universality more akin to that postulated by Castiglione,[6] but their political thought still rested on the foundations laid by Elyot and his generation.

Philip Sidney was born into that class which was the principal target of humanistic exhortations, and he was proud of the fact:

> In all truth I mai justli affirm that I am by my fathers syde of ancient and allwaies well esteemed and welmatched gentry yet I do acknowledg I sai that my cheefest honor is to be a Dudlei and truli am glad to have caws to sett foorth the nobility of that blood whereof I am descended. . . .[7]

His family was typical of the Tudor gentry which managed to make capital out of the religious and political changes of the period. Henry Sidney, his father, was knighted on the same day as William Cecil[8] and received Penshurst, the family's castle, in 1552, after its former owner had been executed.[9] Despite the fact that some of his close relatives were involved in Jane Grey's unhappy venture, and despite his former identification with the Protestant party, Henry Sidney maintained his properties and position during Mary's reign and even prevailed upon King Philip to act as his son's godfather.[10] Like most members of his class, he seems to have had little compunction about conforming to or compromising with the dominant religion if that seemed necessary to protect himself, which does not preclude his preference for the religion of Elizabeth's reign over that of Mary's. Men like him were eminently practical, "profoundly secular,"[11] and not prone to make martyrs out of themselves if they could help it; their theological interests were not very marked,[12] their convictions were somewhat flexible and apt to be subordinated to patriotic and political motives as well as to personal interests. Sir Henry's administrative abilities were utilized by Mary and by Elizabeth; under the latter, he became the very able Lord Deputy of Ireland. Dealing with questions of state must have been his primary occupation. This may partly account for his son's similar interests.

Whatever Sir Henry's theology, the church—Anglican again—proved to be a good and probably lifelong source of income for his son Philip who at the tender age of nine[13] became the incumbent of the first of several parsonages; he never exercised the corresponding ecclesiastical functions. Philip undoubtedly developed strong Protestant convictions, especially after witnessing the horrors of St. Bartholomew's Night in France, and as a consequence of the influence which Hubert Languet, the French Protestant humanist, had on his thought during the most receptive period of his life.[14] By friendships and marriage,[15] Sidney became prominently associated with the Protestant party, and he favored a foreign policy designed to strengthen and advance the Protestant cause in Europe. Yet it would be wrong to lay too much emphasis on the importance of theological convictions in his thought.[16] His primary interest was the state, and for him, as for so many Elizabethans, Protestantism was virtually identical with English patriotism. His interests, like those of his father, were basically secular, despite his more serious occupation with religious questions.

His education shows the effect of the humanistic program. He was not instructed at home by a private tutor, as Elyot had insisted a young gentleman should be educated—a demand obviously impossible to carry out on any extensive scale—but when he was ten he was sent to Shrewsbury, a school in which the writings advocated by the chorus of humanists formed the backbone of the curriculum. He must have had to study such works as Cicero's *De Officiis*, Xenophon's *Cyropaedia*, Isocrates, Virgil, Caesar, Sallust, Livy, Horace, Ovid, i.e., predominantly Latin and almost exclusively classical authors.[17] When he was about fourteen, he went to the University of Oxford.[18] His uncle, Robert Dudley, Earl of Leicester, was chancellor of the university. There, Philip Sidney continued his humanistic studies for three or four years under good tutors[19] and found stimulating company among his contemporaries. His intellectual attitudes developed and took shape in the active and lively atmosphere of the university.[20] His education was completed in the "grand tour" of the European continent, a sojourn of three years in France, Germany, and Italy, which was later supplemented by journeys in a diplomatic capacity.

This course of study and travel was to become the standard curriculum of young English noblemen for centuries. Shrewsbury, Christ Church, and the grand tour would have been considered a good preparation for a gentleman's public career in the eighteenth as well as in the sixteenth century and would still be highly thought of in the twentieth, as would be the predominant concentration on the study of Roman and Greek literature, philosophy, rhetoric, and history. In the prolonged and serious occupation with humanistic subjects, Sidney, as a typical representative of his class and generation, carried out the program that Elyot had prescribed for one who wished to govern, a plan that in Elyot's day had only begun to be translated into practice. The form of Sidney's education differs from that prescribed by Elyot in so far as Elyot had not thought of public schools and universities as places of training for future governours. He mentioned private tutors and the Inns of Court. It seems likely that he would have approved of schools and universities if he could have seen how, through the efforts of two generations of humanists, they had been raised to a level where they could provide an adequate humanistic education. Furthermore, many young gentlemen had their private tutors at the universities and as traveling companions, so that even this requirement was generally met. Elyot's plan had thus developed into the curriculum that was fashionable in Sidney's day. The members of the aristocracy were expected to study the classics which were supposed to enable them to serve the state in whatever capacity their prince might need them.

Elyot had praised poetry because he felt that it could lead man toward the imitation of the virtues it portrays through its immediate appeal to his senses and emotions. In *The Defence of Poesie*,[21] Sid-

ney very extensively defends the same view of the didactic function
of poetry. His treatment of the question is much more elaborate
than Elyot's brief statements; it is well fortified with authorities and
extensively argued. His arguments represent his own poetic program and intentions: he is not, like Elyot, content with referring his
readers to the poets of antiquity, but tries to emulate them in his
own poetry, particularly in his "heroical poem" in prose, the
*Arcadia*. The *Defence*, Fulke Greville's testimony as to Sidney's
purposes, and the *Arcadia* itself clearly reveal Sidney's poetic intentions.

The *Arcadia* is the result of Sidney's ambition to write a modern
*Cyropaedia* (grouped by him with the "heroical poems") to compete with the works of Plato, Homer, and Virgil,[22] and to give new
life to the dry doctrines of the philosophers in his poetic images.
Sidney "would have shown how the poetical philosophers like Plato
and Sir Thomas More should be surpassed at their own trade. . . .
The *Arcadia* . . . was to be as moral, as didactic, as the *Republic* or
the *Utopia*, but vastly more effective"[23]—more effective, because
Sidney, in the *Defence*, places the poets above the philosophers, although he counts the best philosophers among the poets: where
philosophers only give instructions for right behavior, poets present
in their heroes lively examples of ideal actions in all possible circumstances; they captivate their readers' attention by interesting tales
and thus draw them toward the imitation of the virtues. Philosophers who do not merely teach dry doctrine but rather show in
their works the image of the perfect man and the perfect society
may thereby be raised into the ranks of the poets. If the didactic
purpose of poetry is satisfactorily achieved, its form is of relatively
minor importance. Thus, rhyme is not essential, being purely orna-
mental. Since "it is not ryming and versing that maketh *Poesie*,"[24]
since therefore the aim and not the form counts, the *Arcadia* and the
*Faerie Queene* belong to the same category of heroic epic as the
*Iliad* and the *Aeneid*, and even the *Republic* and the *Utopia* can
share this honor with them in so far as they "lead and draw us to as
high a perfection, as our degenerate soules . . . can be capable of."[25]

The epic poet combines and surpasses the teachings and examples
of philosophers and historians in his pleasing and perfect images;[26]
he delights in order "to move men to take that goodnesse in hand,
which without delight they would flie as from a stranger."[27] Sidney
shares the humanistic view that knowledge makes men good by guiding them to virtuous activity. Such activity alone justifies the acqui-

sition of knowledge: one should study "with the end of well doing, and not of well knowing onely . . . the ending end of all earthly learning, being verteous action."[28] Since such action is the desired result, poets are better teachers than historians and philosophers: such scholars are apt to teach mere book learning,[29] whereas the former, by inciting their readers to the imitation of their virtuous images and actions, move them to do that which they teach: "No learning is so good, as that which teacheth and moveth to vertue, and . . . none can both teach and move thereto so much as *Poesie*."[30] The poet thus takes precedence over the philosopher and the historian.[31] He inflames his readers with the virtues that take shape in his heroes, with their courtesy, justice, and courage. His epic shows how one has to behave in all situations, and gives examples of self-control and just rule, of the combination of "inward" and "outward government" on which Elyot had insisted. Plato's statement that he "who could see vertue, woulde bee woonderfullie ravished with the love of her bewtie"[32] is borne out by the effect of the heroic poem on its reader.[33]

Like his humanistic predecessors, Sidney feels compelled to defend "bookishnes,"[34] by which he means any kind of learning, and poetry in particular,[35] against ignorant attacks. His opponents preach the "doctrine of ignorance"[36] that it would be much better to accomplish deeds worth describing than to relate what ought to be done. He counters with the argument that great deeds can only be accomplished if they are guided by reason, and that reason is the result of knowledge which is to be found in its purest and most accessible form in the works of the poets. There are those who declare that Plato banished poetry from his ideal state; that, according to Sidney, is a misrepresentation of Plato's intention which was to prevent the abuse of poetry. Actually, Sidney says, Plato "attributeth unto *Poesie*, more then my selfe do; namely, to be a verie inspiring of a divine force, farre above mans wit."[37] If Plato had censured all poetry he would have condemned his own writings, which are poetical creations: "though the inside & strength [of Plato's work] were Philosophie, the skin as it were and beautie, depended most of Poetrie."[38]

The defense of poetry against Plato's censures in the *Republic* was more difficult than its defense against contemporary ignorance. Sidney debated against Plato with Platonic arguments and aims:[39] if Plato banished poesy from his republic, he did so because he feared it might be abused and have a bad moral effect, whereas Sidney

162

argued that the good poet through his work could accomplish better than anyone else exactly what Plato desired. The poet "sheweth himselfe a passionate lover of that unspeakable and everlasting bewtie, to be seene by the eyes of the mind,"[40] i.e., of Plato's perfect patterns, which he represents in his work. His heroes strive to realize or approximate the perfection of these patterns in their deeds, and the virtues which they thus illustrate in action become easily understandable and imitable for the reader. In painting the beauty of virtue, Sidney's poet achieves Plato's aim to move men to virtue.[41] Sidney's very struggle to make poetry compatible with Plato's doctrine, to make it serve Platonic ends, reveals his great indebtedness to and reverence for Plato's thought. Since the poet's office is higher than that of the philosopher, the work of his favorite philosopher, Plato, like that of Xenophon, has to be defined as poetry, and by his classification it fits into that category.

Sidney really saw poetry as a creative and directing force in history. It was through the example of Homer's epics that the Greeks were led to the greatest heights in their history; Achilles was Alexander's model and inspired him in his heroic enterprises. Such statements are not the empty expressions of humanistic exuberance. Sidney felt poetry to be such a force;[42] in the heroes of the *Arcadia*, he described his own ideals of life and conduct. His friend Greville gives an account of the intimate connection between his poetical creations and his life:

For that this representing of vertues, vices, humours, counsells, and actions of men in feigned, and unscandalous Images, is an inabling of freeborn spirits to the greatest affaires of States: he himself hath left such an instance in the too short scene of his life, as I fear many Ages will not draw a line out of any other mans sphere to parallel with it.[43]

Sidney as a poet took over the humanistic conception of the just ruler, of the good man and governor, and his own life became a symbol of that ideal for his contemporaries and for succeeding generations. In his opinion, the philosophers can portray the just state ruled by good men only imperfectly; he tries to surpass them in such representation with his poetic creations. That intention is made abundantly clear in *The Defence of Poesie*, and is carried out in the *Arcadia*. If he there attempts that highest literary form, the heroic poem, he creates his heroes, princes, ladies, and the catalogue of virtues they exemplify in all their actions, with the distinct purpose of spurring his readers to an imitation of their noble lives and deeds. This purpose underlies and, in so far as that is possible, holds together the maze of involved love stories, disguises, matters of state, wars, and adventures. It has not always been recognized under the infinite entanglements of the loving couples: Milton thought the work "a vain and amatorious poem,"[44] and it has taken the painstaking analysis of modern scholarship to rediscover the full significance and extent of its moral and political teachings. Thus, Brie[45] elaborately tried to prove that Sidney gives an allegorical representation of various philosophical systems in the *Arcadia:* Aristotle's *Politics,* he argued, provides the almost exclusive basis of Sidney's ideas on the state, whereas the "private" virtues can partly be traced to the *Nicomachean Ethics,* to Cicero and others, but also to Plato.[46] The "narrow systematizations"[47] and elaborate interpretations Brie had to put on Sidney's passages in order to prove the pure Aristotelianism of his political thought, and to distinguish it from the more Platonic qualities of his private ethics, have rightly been attacked,[48] while his emphasis on its importance as a political treatise[49] has served as a basis for further study and discussion. The intimate connection between the qualities of the individual and those of the state creates such a fusion of private and political virtues and values that this kind of distinction seems highly arbitrary. Neither Sidney in the *Arcadia* nor Spenser in the *Faerie Queene*[50] follows a purely Aristotelian scheme: both follow their humanistic predecessors in taking from a number of classical authorities, as well as from contemporary authorities dependent on these ancient sources, those ideas that can best serve to give depth and breadth to their own constructions.

Sidney's conceptions of man and state continue in the tradition of his humanistic predecessors. The state, when rightly ordered, is to be guided by the good man whose education, convictions, and behavior become the basic factors of its existence. "Sidney meant no less than to write a book in which would be exemplified the rules of conduct necessary to be known by anyone who was destined to take a part in the government of men."[51] Yet his book is more than an allegorically disguised guide to manners and politics; it is really the crystallization of the ideals that guided Sidney's own life and, as such, is expressive of his "singular unity . . . of thought, word, and deed."[52] Neither the poetic thought nor the literary product is conceived as an end in itself; both are supposed to spur the gentle reader to action. The *Arcadia* breathes Sidney's own "high passion for action";[53] in its imaginary world, the good wins over the bad in the victories of its heroes, fortitude triumphs over fate, nobility over vulgarity. Thus, the *Arcadia* constantly points to the duty of courageous, virtuous action guided by reason. It is by such activity that the good state becomes reality; one could almost say that for Sidney the state exists in this activity, since it has ever again to be vindicated and regained by heroic action. The sword of virtue is exercised constantly, and there seems to be no rest for him who wields it. There are always new tests in which the heroic individual proves his own worth and that of the state. Thus "chivalry and nationalism, the old spirit of adventure and the new learning"[54]—all these components of the English Renaissance are combined in the *Arcadia*. They are welded together in the delicate but powerful harmony of Sidney's life and work.

The central themes of the *Arcadia* are the deeds of the two friends, Pyrocles and Musidorus, and their love for two sisters of royal blood. Like the treatment of friendship in Lyly's *Euphues*, this is strongly reminiscent of Elyot's handling of a similar friendship theme in the story of Titus and Gysippus. Brie suggests Sidney's and Lyly's common dependence on Boccaccio's tale.[55] It seems possible that they may both have become acquainted with it through Elyot's work. In Elyot and in Sidney the Platonic element in the friendship of the heroic couple is much more prominent than in Boccaccio's version of the story. In Sidney's scheme of virtues, friendship between good and just men and love for noble women occupy a key position; they are emphasized even more than in Elyot's work.[56] A good state cannot exist without good men, and good men are enabled to go through the hardships and dangers necessary for the establishment and defense of such a state by the strength that comes from their friendship for each other and from their love for good women. Friendship and love are thus not merely private affairs but are intimately connected with the well-being of the community, and, therefore, they are of great political importance and consequence. Sidney follows the classical doctrine that real friendship is possible only between good men and can only produce good.[57] Friendship and love, in fact, are necessary for the attainment and realization of that virtue which cannot be arrived at by purely rational means,[58] but which ultimately can only be seen through the mystery of love: "Did ever mans eye looke thorough love upon the majesty of vertue, shining through beauty, but that he became . . . a captive?"[59] The "sweete mysteries" of philosophy are revealed to the lover; perfect virtue is seen in the example of the friend.[60] Poetry contains these mysteries, but in such a manner that it will not reveal to unworthy "prophane" wits what should only be accessible to noble minds.[61]

Through the virtuous images and actions of its heroes, the *Arcadia* depicts the application of divine wisdom in the world, particularly in the harmonious organization of the state. Pyrocles, Musidorus, Philisides, and other exemplary figures of the novel display all those qualities that had been demanded by Castiglione and Elyot: Sidney's hero is good, graceful, courageous, mild, just, liberal, "honorablie courteous, and wronglesly valiaunt, considerately pleasant in conversation, & an excellent courtier without unfaithfulnes."[62] These qualities prove their worth in countless situations where the good and just man finally wins over evil and base wickedness. Selflessly, the Arcadian heroes battle for the good. Pyrocles and Musidorus wander through the world, liberate badly governed countries from tyrants and put good rulers in their places,[63] just as they alleviate all sorts of other unjust situations. They employ their rare gifts for the benefit of mankind to find "exercises of their vertue."[64]

The wise, just, and noble king Euarchus, who combines all the virtues that a ruler should have, and who is thus Sidney's poetic image of the ideal ruler in action, behaves in a similar fashion. He not only rules his own country in an exemplary manner but, after vanquishing his enemies, introduces "good government in their countries."[65] Sidney may have derived this idea from the *Utopia:* the Utopians use their victories for the same purpose.[66] Euarchus is so absolutely just that he maintains death sentences even when he recognizes that he has pronounced them against his own son and his nephew. The idea of completely objective and perfect justice prevails over any personal or otherwise subjective considerations.[67]

Euarchus embodies Sidney's political ideal. He is the perfect representative of hereditary monarchy,[68] and is contrasted with the representatives of bad or inadequate states. Sidney concentrates his attention on the human element in the state, on the characters and actions of the rulers, rather than on the institutions and constitutions of the states he is describing. Good laws and institutions can be rendered inoperative by bad rulers; only the human quality of the ruler can guarantee a well-ordered, just commonwealth. "I might as easily sette downe the whole Arte of governement" as describe the character and actions of the good king,[69] Sidney remarks. The ruler's qualities and the art of government are thus considered to be virtually identical. Euarchus rules largely by the pattern he sets for everyone in his own life: the example the good prince gives is "more prevailing then direction"; his life is the law of the state.[70] He is the head of the organism of the commonwealth, the "father of people" who puts his own interests last and does everything with the common good in mind.[71] Constant control of the affairs of state is demanded of him; his responsibility never ceases. In the story of another king, Basilius, Sidney demonstrates the disorders that are likely to ensue if a ruler neglects attendance to his duties in favor of a private, pastoral mode of life.[72]

There can be no doubt that Sidney was a monarchist,[73] and that monarchy, as the head of an aristocratic structure, seemed to him to be the best form of rule. It has been argued by Briggs that Sidney was suspicious of absolute monarchy, and that he wanted to limit the powers of the monarch both by law and by sanctioning insurrection against tyranny. One part of this interpretation has recently been challenged by Ribner. While agreeing that Sidney believed in the "mixed state" of limited monarchy, Ribner denies that Sidney granted the people the right of rebellion against its legally constituted ruler.[74] Nevertheless, the belief that tyranny and unjust rule should be destroyed by some means is clearly reflected in his writings.

Sidney was evidently afraid that Elizabeth's possible marriage to the Duke of Anjou would lead to a subversion of the ancient English liberties, and to conditions similar to those prevailing in France. Greville may exaggerate Sidney's feelings on the subject and interpolate his own ideas, yet it seems from various passages in the *Arcadia*, in the *Defence*, and from Sidney's letter to the queen on the subject of her proposed marriage to the duke,[75] that his feelings were similar to what Greville later reported of them: the "ancient, and reverend pillars" of the French state, such as parliaments, laws, and customs, had become supplanted by the "narrowness of . . . Imperiall Mandates." The estates which have submitted to such arbitrary form of government "must justly be reputed voluntary slaves in the choice of that passive bondage."[76] If Elizabeth married the Frenchman, the danger existed that monarchy would rise "above her ancient legall Circles, by banishing all free spirits, and faithfull Patriots . . . till the *Ideas* of native freedom should be utterly forgotten";[77] the "moderate form of Monarchie" prevailing in England might easily be changed "into a precipitate absoluteness."[78]

In speaking about the absolutism of King Antiphilus in the *Arcadia*, Sidney, in his own somewhat less well defined words, gives vent to his feelings about that type of government: Antiphilus, who ruled "as everie winde of passions puffed him," i.e., with complete arbitrariness, "quickly made his kingdome a Teniscourt, where his subjects should be the balles." This behavior Sidney attributes to his having been "suddenly borne into an unknowne Ocean of absolute power," a fact which prevented him from realizing "that he was a king of reasonable creatures, who would quickly scorne follies, and repine at injuries."[79] In other words, Sidney felt arbitrary absolutism to be contrary to ordinary common sense, which demands that people be treated as reasonable human beings.

Sidney presumably was acquainted with such constitutional limitations on the powers of the monarch as had been advocated in the *Vindiciae contra Tyrannos,* in Hotman's *Francogallia,* and in Buchanan's *De Jure Regni.*[80] Even if he may not have supported that part of Huguenot doctrine which granted the subjects a formal right of armed insurrection against a ruler who had become a tyrant, Sidney frequently and with great detail described the overthrow of such a person who, as Greville puts it, is a living image "of the dark Prince, that sole author of dis-creation, and disorder."[81] A typical scene of that kind is the rebellion against the tyrannous king of Phrygia in the *Arcadia,* a rebellion in which his principal heroes actively participate:

Certaine yong men of the bravest minds, cried with lowde voice, Libertie; and encouraging the other Citizens to follow them, set upon the garde, and souldiers as chiefe instruments of Tyrannie: and quickly, aided by the Princes, they had left none of them alive.[82]

While this has almost the sound of a democratic tirade, Sidney is not a democrat. Freed from the yoke of tyranny,

some of the wisest (seeing that a popular licence is indeede the many-headed tyranny) prevailed with the rest to make *Musidorus* their chiefe: choosing one of them (because Princes) to defende them, and him because elder and most hated of the Tyrant, and by him to be ruled. . . . The whole estates of the country with one consent, gave the crowne and all other markes of soveraigntie to *Musidorus;* desiring nothing more, then to live under such a government, as they promised themselves of him.[83]

The people thus reveal their complete faith in the ability of a real prince to rule properly. This prince, in turn, moved by a strong feeling for legitimacy, turns the crown over to a worthy relative of the late tyrant. The fact remains, however, that the tyrant has meanwhile been killed by the prince, and that the latter has received the crown from the people. Sidney thus permits the tyrant to be killed by a person of royal blood,[84] and he sees the source of authority in the people, although he does not believe in the many-headed tyranny of popular license. "The mass of the people . . . are not to be trusted with power nor are they to have a direct share in the administration of public affairs, though government is to be carried on for their benefit and though they are the ultimate source of authority. Their duty is to obey."[85] The right kind of state is a constitutional or limited monarchy; such a form is indicated as the finale of the whole episode. The new ruler receives his power "with such conditions, & cautions of the conditions, as might assure the people . . . that not onely that governour, . . . but the nature of the government, should be no way apt to decline to Tyranny."[86]

There is another rebellion in the *Arcadia* in which one of the heroes participates: that of the conquered Helots against the regime of inequality under which they have to live.[87] Sidney betrays considerable sympathy with the lot of this subjugated people, which forms the lowest social group.[88] He lends the revolt the legitimacy that comes with the support of one of his princes, and in the end grants the Helots certain political rights which they had long been denied. While in this instance he countenances resistance against a tyrannous rule imposed by conquerors, he usually remains thoroughly suspicious of the lower classes and their aspirations and echoes the opinions of the leading circles in church and state when he describes in vivid detail the uprising of the Arcadians against the lawful hierarchical order.[89] The fickle multitude, the contradictory opinions and demands of different groups,[90] the shouting for liberty and the concomitant general lack of responsibility are described in highly deprecatory fashion. In his treatment of these scenes, Sidney evinces a deep distrust of the political instincts of the people, a general lack of faith in their political abilities when they are without legitimate leadership. A mob which deposes its "Prince, delivered unto [it] by so many roiall ancestors"[91]—in other words, its hereditary monarch—and intends to run its own affairs, is only too likely to become the victim of a demagogue who will turn into a tyrant as soon as he has been placed in power by his fellow-revolutionaries. Sidney warns them of "the tyrannous yoke of your fellow subject, in whom the innate meanes [meanness] will bring forth ravenous covetousnes, and the newnes of his estate, suspectfull cruelty."[92]

Sidney engages in the usual anti-Machiavellian tirades when he speaks of bad princes and tyrants. Such men never feel safe, they suspect everybody and subject many to unjust trials.[93] Under

169

tyranny or the equally damnable oligarchy,[94] corruption undermines the structure of the state, men of virtue are suppressed because their splendor would make the rottenness of the rulers dangerously obvious, and virtue itself is almost forgotten, for the tyrant's "minde [has] no eye to espie goodnesse."[95] Fear, based on cruelty, soon becomes the only connecting link between the tyrant and his people, whereas conversely, in the good state, "Vertu & justice are the onely bondes of the peoples love."[96] Fear is a weak tie between ruler and people: once it is "untied by a greater force,"[97] such as the victorious intervention of the *Arcadia*'s heroes, it dissolves completely. The people instantly desert the hated tyrant and are again ready to appreciate the advantages of a good monarchy. Trickery in foreign policy is another typical trait of tyranny: thus, the bad queen Cecropia sends wild animals to stir up trouble among her unsuspecting neighbors.[98] Fortunately the representatives of virtue in the *Arcadia* triumph over this attempt and over numerous other kinds of treachery and wickedness after passing courageously through many trials and perils.

Tyrannous and popular license are both bad, and both have to be vanquished by young men desirous of finding proper exercise for their virtues, anxious to still their hunger for high honor.[99] It is their task, after they have overcome evil rulers and evil forms of government, to establish the kind of moderate, limited monarchy that is exemplified in the realm of King Euarchus. Sidney places a certain emphasis on the maintenance of popular liberties within the framework of a balanced state of this type. Euarchus is beloved by his people because he "vertuouslie and wisely" acknowledged "that he with his people made all but one politike bodie, whereof himselfe was the head."[100] He never restrained the people's liberty "without it stretched to licenciousnes" and showed "a delight to their welfare."[101] Sidney proffered similar advice to Elizabeth in a practical situation: "Lett some suche particular actions be found out . . . by which you may gratify all the hartes of your people."[102] If Euarchus "loved greatnesse, it was, because therein he might exercise his goodnes."[103] Power, that is, carries with it the responsibility that its bearer employ it in the best interests of the community, guided by his superior knowledge. Power that is not balanced by such goodness destroys the balance of the world: "infinitenes of power, & knowledge, without like measure of goodnesse, must necessarily bring foorth destruction and ruine."[104]

There are, as we have seen, indications that Sidney wants more than benevolent paternalism. Not only does he advocate constitutional checks on the power of the monarch—although he does not define these checks in detail—but he sometimes urges active participation by the people in the functions of government. When the Helots are liberated, they are "capable both to give and receive voice in election of Magistrates."[105] We are justified in deducing from this statement that Sidney was in favor of some form of representative government. This impression is strengthened by his treatment of another scene, where the people are described as being helpless after the loss of their monarch, not so much because they are politically incapable but because they have no experience in political matters. The scene is

a notable example, how great dissipations, Monarchall governement are subject unto. For nowe theyr Prince and guide had lefte them, they had not experience to rule, and *had not whome to obaye. Publicke matters had ever bene privately governed*, so that they had no lively taste what was good for themselves.[106]

The salient point is that the monarch had not divided his power with anyone else, had not given political responsibility to any person or group that could take over the leadership in this emergency. Such a group would be the magistrates,[107] whom Sidney evidently wanted as a powerful middle group standing between the monarch and the people:

There could be no government without a Magistrate, and no Magistrate without obedience, and no obedience where every one upon his owne private passion, may interpret the doings of the rulers.[108]

The actual "magistrates" or, as Elyot would have said, the "governours," in Sidney's day were mostly members of the nobility and gentry in the country, and merchants in the cities. It can be safely assumed that Sidney was not much interested in a really democratic process of election for public office, even if, in the *Arcadia*, the people occasionally are entitled to vote and to elect officers from among themselves. On the whole, Sidney was an ardent partisan of the status quo. His occasional sympathy with the people and their aspirations does not go so far as to make it necessary for him to offer a serious counter-argument to such popular complaints as that voiced in the great rebellion in the *Arcadia*. To the question, "why none but great men & gentlemen could be admitted into counsel . . . but yet [the commons'] blood & sweat must maintain all . . . ,"[109] Sidney would answer that the people must obey if they have a good monarch and a worthy aristocracy. Popular gov-

171

ernment, which may look very good in theory, or even a pure aristocracy probably would not function well, "being a matter more in imaginacion then practise."[110] His ideal remains a mixed government, based on carefully circumscribed rights and obligations of the various estates and administered jointly by a beneficent, patriarchal monarch and a virtuous aristocracy. One of the principal obligations of such a government is to preserve as much liberty for the various estates—including the lowest—as is compatible with the well-being and good order of the state. Sidney shows rebellions and princely interventions against tyrannous governments, and the downfall and death of tyrants; but he certainly provides no justification for rebellion against the hierarchical order as long as monarch and magistrates fulfil their functions adequately.

Sidney would probably have subscribed to the opinion of his friend Fulke Greville, whose statements on questions of political theory are more explicit and direct than his own. Greville indicates that Sidney's ideal had largely been realized in Elizabeth's England, in contrast to contemporary France. Elizabeth preserved the rights of yeomen and gentlemen instead of making "conquered Out-Laws," slaves and boors of them.[111] The central position in the social structure, according to Greville, was held by the gentry: "their number and wealth was moderate, and their spirits and powers counterpoised with her Majesty, from being Authors of any new Barons Wars, and yet reserved as brave halfe paces between a Throne and a people."[112]

The Aristotelian influence in this conception of balance, of the importance of the mean between extremes, is obvious. Sidney was mainly concerned with this mean, with his own social group that constituted the "brave halfe paces between a Throne and a people." His *Arcadia*, ostensibly describing the deeds of young princes, was meant as an inspiration for the gentry and nobility of England in the manner which had been postulated by *The Defence of Poesie*. Its heroes are educated in such a way "that all the sparkes of vertue, which nature had kindled in them, were so blowne to give forth their uttermost heate."[113] Pyrocles, "the onely yong Prince in the world, formed by nature, and framed by education, to the true exercise of vertue"[114] is to have the same effect on readers that Sidney himself had on his contemporaries. Fulke Greville tells us that

this one man's example, and personall respect, did not onely encourage Learning, and Honour in the Schooles, but brought the affection, and

172

true use thereof both into the Court, and Camp. Nay more, even many Gentlemen excellently learned amongst us, will not deny, but that they affected to row, and steer their course in his wake.[115]

Some of the characters—young princes and old rulers—whom Sidney presents in his heroic poem display all the virtues, others lack certain specific ones, and yet others are embodiments of wickedness. He paints his characters not only in black and white, but realizes that there are intermediate shades. Thus, Euarchus is the perfect king: he "measured his greatnesse by his goodnesse" and was "a Prince of a goodly aspect, and the more goodly by a grave majestie, wherewith his mind did decke his outward graces."[116] Basilius, on the other hand, although not an evil ruler, is a very weak one: he lacks certain royal attitudes and attributes and should therefore only partly be imitated; his weakness is to be shunned.

In the zealous love of his people . . . he doth . . . passe al the princes living. Wherof the cause is, that though he exceed not in the vertues which get admiration; as depth of wisdome, height of courage and largenesse of magnificence, yet is hee notable in those which stirre affection, as trueth of worde, meekenesse, courtesie, mercifulnesse, and liberalitie.[117]

Antiphilus, the king who made a tennis court of his kingdom, is one of Sidney's major examples of a bad ruler: vain, subject to flattery, arbitrary toward his subjects, "obscurely borne,"[118] and stupid enough to presume "that what he did was liked of every bodie,"[119] to think that he was "the wysest, the woorthyest, and best beloved, that ever gave honour to a royall tytle."[120] Similar examples of badness—like the evil Plexirtus[121]—abound in the *Arcadia;* only one other need be mentioned as being the direct antithesis of Sidney's heroes. He is Timantus, who fits perfectly into the Elizabethan conception of a Machiavellian. Real virtue does not mean anything to him, "hee counted it but a schoole name."[122] All his values are determined by the advantage they may give him, not by any absolute standards. Thus, he measures "both revenge, and rewarde, as the partye might eyther helpe or hurt him." To this complete relativist, nothing means anything except in so far as it affects his own advancement and success, "thinking small difference by what meanes he came by it."[123] In every respect, he is opposed to Sidney's ideal code: "Servile (though envious) to his betters: and no lesse tirannycallie minded to them hee had advauntage of. . . . In summe, a man that could be as evill as he listed, and listed as much, as any advancement might thereby be gotten."[124] By thus depicting the "rather shamelesse then bolde"[125] Timantus as the perfect and more than obvious villain, Sidney achieves his pedagogic purpose as well as by the opposite process of showing the catalogue of virtues embodied in Euarchus.

The *Arcadia*, then, is meant to cause the reader to imitate the examples of virtue and to shun those of vice and wickedness that are portrayed in it. By the example of his heroes, Sidney's readers are to be inspired to do their part toward establishing on earth that "unexpressable harmonie" that God has created in the cosmos at large, and that He wants man to imitate in his microcosm. It is not surprising that the divine order of the world and the organization of human society should be closely compared by Sidney: "Perfect order, perfect beautie, perfect constancie" are neither the results of chance, nor are they brought about by "many natures conspiring together, as in a popular governement." Sidney believes in the divinely ordained, hierarchical order of nature and, by analogy, of the state. It cannot be that "the Elementishe and ethereall partes should in their towne-house set downe the boundes of each ones office." These different parts would rather "have sought each others ruine, then have served as well consorted partes to such an unexpressable harmonie" if it had not been for "a wisedome which made them concurre."[126] "A right heavenly Nature,"[127] a deity, "an all-knowing God"[128] orders the world with this His wisdom. Similarly, the rule of such wisdom must be enforced in the state if concord is to prevail: "if there be not a superiour power and wisedome," the "under ones" among the citizens "cannot by nature regarde to any preservation but of themselves,"[129] and then there is discord, as there would be among the elements. The ruler who partakes of reason, whose knowledge serves the good, whose power is employed in the pursuit of justice reflects God's infinite wisdom, power, goodness, and justice. Monarchy, then, is the earthly reflection and realization of the divine world order:

One mans sufficiencie is more available then ten thousands multitude. So evill ballanced be the extremities of popular mindes: and so much naturall imperiousnes there rests in a well formed spirit. . . . *Neptune* had no more force to appease the rebellious winde, then the admiration of an extraordinary vertue hath, to temper a disordered multitude.[130]

For Sidney, then, monarchy, but not absolute monarchy as in France, was the desirable polity, with the prince supported by a free and loyal gentry, by a people protected in its rights and liberties. The examples of knights and princes portrayed by Sidney in the *Arcadia* were meant to appeal to his countrymen and, more specifically, to his own class. The great model, indeed, was both what he depicted with his pen, and his own life and death: he was considered the perfect courtier and governour, knight and scholar. Elyot might have found him lacking in self-control, might have found fault with his daring rashness, but the Elizabethans saw in "the noble and vertvous Gentleman most worthy of all titles both of learning and cheualrie M. Philip Sidney"[131] the embodiment of their ideal. His early death in the battle of Zutphen enhanced this reputation and made him their hero.

# VIII

# Edmund Spenser

EDMUND SPENSER[1] was greatly moved by the example of Sidney's life and death, by his poetic aims and achievements. We do not know the exact nature of Spenser's connection with Sidney and the true degree of his indebtedness to the heroic author of the *Arcadia*. It can safely be said, however, that "Spenser's love for Sidney was probably the deepest formative influence upon his life and character" and served to "vitalize some of his most beautiful conceptions in *The Faerie Queene*."[2]

In Sidney, the ideal of the age had been embodied: he was virtuous, courteous, valiant, and liberal.[3] The death of this perfect courtier, knight, and gentleman had occasioned an unusual number of elegies and eulogies of which the little volume in which Spenser's *Astrophel*[4] appeared is representative.[5] More important than this poetic monument to Sidney's glory is the symbolic knight of courtesy in the sixth book of *The Faerie Queene*, Sir Calidore. While this imaginary figure cannot be fully identified with an actual person such as Sidney, with whom it has been customarily associated, or with Essex, who has been more recently suggested as its prototype, there can be no doubt that many of the courtly accomplishments which had been personified by Sidney are depicted in that poetic image of ideal courtesy.[6] It is thus not surprising that the sixth book of *The Faerie Queene*, in which Sir Calidore exemplifies courtesy, the virtue for which Sidney was particularly renowned, should show the influence of Sidney's *Arcadia* both in plot[7] and in purpose. The similarity of Spenser's and Sidney's poetry is perhaps more easily demonstrable in this than in other parts of *The Faerie Queene*, but the close affinity of their aims and methods is evident throughout their main works. Both poets are agreed on the didactic purpose and justification of poetry in general.[8] The fact that the *Arcadia* was written in prose and *The Faerie Queene* in verse[9] did not in their eyes put the two into different categories. Both Sidney and Spenser thought of their works as heroic poems, and they both felt that the main purpose of such poems was to teach a certain pattern of life by the examples they presented. Their ethical, political, and social ideas are largely identical, and their agreement thus went beyond an identity of views concerning the aim and form of poetry. It is apparent in their whole conception of life as presented in these works.

There are external similarities, such as the use of idealized past periods as settings for the respective actions. In both cases, the heroes, whether in classical or in medieval costume, are to provide examples for present and future generations. It must be admitted that the pseudo-medieval knights, whom Spenser provides as the carriers of his ideas, often seem unconvincing, even melodramatic, in their actions: the modern reader cannot accept without question the ever recurring victories of these heroes in unlikely situations, or indeed maintain his interest through the superabundance of battles for fair ladies and good causes against evil knights, the rabble, or monsters.

Spenser's philosophy is often hidden under the wealth of his story material, but, nevertheless, what we have called the humanistic conception of man, society, and the state will be found to provide the woof of Spenser's colorful tapestry. The threads that go into this tapestry are largely drawn from the stores of such predecessors as Castiglione, Elyot, and Sidney.[10] Spenser himself made this very plain. When he published the first three books of *The Faerie Queene*, he added his explanatory letter to Sir Walter Raleigh, in which he stated that "the generall end . . . of all the booke is to fashion a gentleman or noble person in vertuous and gentle discipline."[11] That very clear and concise statement needs no further comment to place his work into the category of such prose predecessors as the *Cortegiano,* the *Governour*, or the *Arcadia*. Since it was Spenser's intention, like Sidney's, to teach moral and social philosophy by the vivid portrayal of examples in poetry, we may try to rediscover the former in the latter, and to establish its relationship to the type of thought we have been considering.

Spenser, feeling that most men are not much interested in reading purely didactic works, presented his doctrine in the shape of entertaining and exciting "historicall fiction."[12] The reader of his poem will often lose sight of the didactic purpose which, according to the poet's own testimony, guided him through the entire work, and he will be much more impressed by the rich flowering of Spenser's imagination, by the pleasure which he took in colorful descriptions, by the boyish fun he had in relating the incredible and fantastic adventures of his heroes. Yet Spenser felt that these lyrical and epic elements of his poetry—the features on which his fame mainly rests today—were merely accessory to the didactic purpose which he claimed to be the *raison d'être* for *The Faerie Queene*. In fact, he sounds almost apologetic about having put his teaching into the form of a poem, and seems to feel the need of immediately justifying his enterprise by pointing to famous predecessors such as Homer and Virgil, Ariosto and Tasso, whom he considers to have employed the same form for the same purpose. Spenser is of the opinion that their great poems have been written primarily so that their heroes might serve as guides to other men. If we adopt Spenser's criterion, we shall not be surprised to learn that the main importance of Homer's poetry, for instance, lies in the fact that "in the Persons of Agamemnon and Vlysses [he] hath ensampled a good gouernour and a vertuous man.[13] Spenser considered this to be its primary merit. He claimed that Virgil pursued the same aim in portraying Aeneas,[14] and that Ariosto's and Tasso's motives were similarly inspired. So Spenser set out to imitate his illustrious predecessors by creating equally exemplary heroes, in the persons of Arthur[15] and twelve other knights.[16] It may seem strange that a man who was himself a great epic poet should thus have relegated the aesthetic and narrative elements of his own and of his precursors' epic poems to an almost insignificant background behind a primary didactic purpose which is not always easily discernible in his actual poem. Yet there can be no doubt that "it was Spenser's understanding, as it was that of his age, that the inculcation of morality was the chief purpose and justification of poetry."[17]

Spenser stated in his letter to Raleigh, and indicated in the subtitle of *The Faerie Queene* itself,[18] that he was trying to demonstrate in his work twelve moral virtues according to Aristotle.[19] That scheme would seem to put Spenser into a category apart from the other authors whose works we have been considering. Their ideas had also been influenced by Aristotle's philosophy, but they showed no less evident traces of Plato and the Stoics or of Neoplatonic and Christian thought. Their intellectual pedigree was thus very mixed, whereas Spenser here speaks of the pure and direct descent of his scheme from Aristotle and no one else.[20] This claim

178

need not be taken too seriously, for "not one of Spenser's virtues can be fitted into Aristotle's list without Procrustean operations."[21]

Evidently the commonplace system of medieval and Renaissance morality, which was based on the four "cardinal virtues" of wisdom, temperance, justice, and courage, was well known to Spenser. He worked with this vague and general conception, in which different classical philosophies and Christian thought were combined, rather than with the complexities of the purely Aristotelian system. Spenser's own protestations and the ingenious constructions of some of his interpreters to the contrary notwithstanding, neither holiness nor chastity nor courtesy—the themes of the first, third, and sixth books of *The Faerie Queene* respectively—can be considered pure Aristotelian virtues.[22] Despite the "Aristotelian" appearance which Spenser creates in a formal (and only half-completed) scheme of twelve books, the actual ideological content of his poem permits us to class Spenser with Castiglione, Elyot, and Sidney: his opinions and values are no more derived from one single source than are theirs. Plato and Cicero, the chivalrous tradition and humanistic doctrine, left their imprint on his work as they did on theirs. He uses the ideas of his contemporaries, of his immediate and medieval predecessors as well as those of the classical authorities and the Bible as they serve his purposes.[23] Spenser as a philosopher does not display the same creativeness that distinguishes him as a poet. He is not an original thinker, but he shows a wide knowledge of different philosophical systems and the ability to choose from and combine them.[24]

*The Faerie Queene*, then, is held together not so much by a distinct philosophical system as by its main purpose: "to fashion a gentleman or noble person in vertuous and gentle discipline."[25] In each of the projected books, Spenser had proposed to have a particular knight go forth on a series of quests to demonstrate some special virtue, while Arthur was intended to embody all these virtues at once. In this way, the several qualities that a knight ought to have were to be demonstrated and taught separately through the heroes of the different books and in complete integration through Arthur. Inculcation of his doctrine is Spenser's main purpose, and it matters little that in his actual work his scheme is not carried out in all particulars. His knights and other figures symbolize virtues or vices. Holiness, temperance, chastity, friendship, justice, and courtesy are the subjects of the six existing books. To this number, constancy might be added as the fragment of another book. Most of these virtues are familiar from previous sixteenth-century writers, but "Holinesse" and "Chastitie" as the themes of the first and third books of *The Faerie Queene* gain a new prominence in Spenser's work. The legend of chastity, of course, had a contemporary *raison d'être* in Spenser's sovereign, the "virgin queen." Apart from these two virtues, *The Faerie Queene* follows more or less the beaten path: temperance, friendship, justice, courtesy, and constancy had long been considered desirable attributes of a gentleman, and Spenser repeats and elaborates these themes.

Spenser's ideal, then, is very closely related to that of the Renaissance gentleman formulated by a writer like Castiglione[26] and adopted by many of Spenser's own contemporaries. It is evident, however, that Spenser's conception is not entirely derived from Renaissance sources, since it shows strong traces also of the ideals of both medieval Christian chivalry[27] and of the Protestant Reformation.[28] These Christian ideals find a stronger echo and a more conscious representation in his work than in that of most of his predecessors. The virtues of holiness[29] and chastity are indicative of this trend in Spenser's thought. Courtesy, it has been argued, is a matter of the heart for Spenser rather than a matter of expediency—spontaneous Christian benevolence in contrast to the reasoned code of manners elaborated by the Renaissance writers.[30] I cannot see such a sharp distinction between Spenser's ideal and that of earlier authors, but I agree that Spenser is more conscious of certain aspects of medieval and Reformation Christianity and puts greater emphasis on them in his work.

Special mention should be made of the fact that a whole book is devoted by Spenser to the theme of friendship.[31] It may seem surprising to find "The Legend of Artegall or of Iustice" immediately preceded by "The Legend of Cambel and Telamond, or of Friendship," since justice and friendship are apt to be put into two entirely different categories by the twentieth-century reader—the one into a public sphere, the other into a private one. For Spenser, however, the capacity of good men and women[32] for true friendship, based on virtue and absolute devotion to the friend, is on the same level as their capacity for knowing and administering true justice. In this respect, he follows, and enlarges on, Elyot and Sidney, both of whom had included more than the conventional descriptions of true friendship in their main works; he also follows the classical doctrines of Plato, Aristotle, and Cicero.[33]

Friendship for Spenser is the manifestation of cosmic love in the world of man. The world is held together in universal harmony by love. In the human sphere, friendship similarly works as "a harmonizing and unifying force":[34] it not only creates, but actually is, concord,[35] and banishes discord. Thus conceived, it is very closely related to that highest of all virtues—justice, which maintains and enforces harmony among men.[36] Hence it becomes quite logical for Spenser's treatment of justice to follow immediately upon that of friendship.

Spenser usually stresses the "gentle birth" of his virtuous knights and courtiers and the base and lowly origin of his villains,[37] but while he greatly favors those born of "gentle blood," he does not entirely exclude the possibility that those not blessed with the prerogative of noble birth may also become courteous knights. It is, he says,

> seldome seene, that one in basenesse set
> Doth noble courage shew, with curteous manners met.[38]

Seldom, Spenser says, not never. Presumably, then, it is not entirely impossible that noble deeds may be done and noble manners shown by one who comes of lowly ancestry. Thus, Sir Calepine states that brave and noble knights of unknown lineage have gained international fame. They may even have a better chance to attain to greatness than children who have been "dandled in the lap."[39] However, Spenser generally follows the fairy-tale tradition in finally revealing the noble origins of great persons whose lineage was originally obscure to themselves and to those with whom they came in contact. Spenser would have conceded that a man of undistinguished origins could become a true knight. That, at least, is how I interpret his statement that

> the bloosme of comely courtesie,
> Which though it on a lowly stalke doe bowre
> Yet brancheth forth in braue nobilitie
> And spreds it selfe through all civilitie.[40]

The lowly stalk from which a man may spring is not an absolute impediment to the achievement of courtesy and thereby of nobility. Spenser emphasizes that somewhere in the past even the noblest families must have been elevated from a lower social position into the more distinguished ranks, that the origin of all nobility is ultimately and inevitably the virtuous deed or character of some ancestor.[41] He fails to draw the explicit conclusion that not only noble deeds performed in the past by some ancestor but also deeds done in the present can ennoble a person of common origin, but such a conclusion seems implicit in his reasoning. On the other hand, Spenser assumes as axiomatic

> that gentle bloud will gentle manners breed[42]

without offering much in support of this questionable generalization, which is merely a repetition of the standard argument of his time. If he had to choose between one who adds his chivalrous and courtly accomplishments to the virtuous disposition resulting from noble birth and one who lacks such birth, he would choose the former.

Spenser would have been extremely unrealistic if he had not left some loophole for commoners, since numerous people in his day, including himself, had been and still were able to climb up the social ladder. The writers on courtesy could make deprecatory remarks about this phenomenon; they might even condemn it outright and insist on unadulterated blue blood, but to do this was certainly a sign of blind snobbishness. In general, one has the impression that most of them would have liked to see an aristocracy of the blood as well as of the brain and of the heart, but that they felt it was useless to insist rigorously on this combination. So somewhere, as a grudging concession to the current that carried so many of their contemporaries from the bottom or the middle levels to the top, they usually left an opening for the ungentle to slip into gentility via learning and the resulting virtue. That there were other less desirable ways by which the same thing could be and frequently was accomplished was known to them. These "go-getting" ways, which often involved unscrupulous methods, did not, however, receive their sanction. The authors of courtesy books, of the *Arcadia* and of *The Faerie Queene*, whether they insisted on blue blood or not, must have realized that their books would be read both by those whose veins pulsed with it as well as by those who lacked that precious substance and tried to make up for it in other ways. The latters' need for guidance in the ways of gentility was undoubtedly greater, and they were thus probably the more avid readers of the doctrines of courtesy.[43] Whatever the writers might say in their books about the undesirability of "base blood" in a gentleman, such blood had not constituted and did not in their day constitute an insuperable bar to a man's becoming a gentleman.[44] The difference, then, between those advocates of gentility who insisted on "blood and virtue" and those who placed their primary emphasis on virtue and were less concerned with the desirability of noble descent should not be overrated.

Of all the attempts to fashion "a good gouernour and a vertuous man"[45] so as to teach the youth of England by his example, Spenser's is the most ambitious: no one in his country had tried to portray the virtues of the ruling class in an epic poem conceived on the overwhelming scale of *The Faerie Queene*.[46] Sidney's *Arcadia*, for instance, was a less difficult undertaking in that the author did not contend with rhyme and meter. Despite this difference in form, the *Arcadia* and *The Faerie Queene* are strikingly similar in their general setting and their purpose. There is the same quest for honor, fair ladies, high achievement, justice, and glory in the imaginary settings of bygone ages; largely the same virtues are extolled, the same vices condemned. Spenser's avowed purpose—to teach morals by example—is perhaps more obscured and encumbered by the luxurious growth of his imagination than is Sidney's. From the almost archaic simplicity and directness of Elyot, from Castiglione's lucid, precise, and graceful description of his ideal courtier, it is a long way to the maze of quests through which Spenser's knights have to pass to prove their valor and show their virtues.

Where Elyot, with the same general aim in mind as Spenser, writes in a rather homespun manner, where he addresses himself to his contemporaries in their conversational language, Spenser, as we have pointed out, seems almost to hide his purpose under highly elaborate costumes, to obscure it behind intricate allegories. He combined medieval armor and monsters with a conscious archaism of language into the reconstruction of a chivalrous world that had long since been dead.[47] If we discount the literary qualities of the respective works and consider only their avowed purposes, it appears that the *Governour* and *The Faerie Queene* have almost identical aims, but take different roads to reach them. While Elyot's purpose, the education of a "governour," is evident everywhere, and while his advice is to the point and practical, Spenser conveys his advice by colorful "historicall fiction." Elyot's gentleman excels mainly by his skill in governing, by the justice which he administers equally among those intrusted to his care. The "governour" is primarily a "civilian," even if his prowess in physical exercise and war is held desirable and essential. He belongs to a nonmedieval social structure and represents an antecedent of the modern "civil servant." Spenser's exemplars of "vertuous and gentle discipline" in *The Faerie Queene* are knights, not civilians. They live in a restored feudal world, but are created as examples for men who constitute the upper class in a state that is much closer to absolutism than to feudalism. Sword in hand, Spenser's heroes enforce justice and seek out injustice to destroy it. Spenser apparently feels the need to point his moral by showing a chain of victories in which good wins over evil. Homer, his model, and Shakespeare, his contemporary, are greater poets partly because their heroes do not continually demonstrate high moral principles and do not inevitably win, i.e., because the events these poets portray are in accord with man's actual experience.

Spenser's romantic revival of an Arthurian past reflects the age and place in which he was living: "into the adventures of the knights he introduces a new kind, almost a direct transcript, from the life and warfare of the English army in Ireland."[48] The fighting in Ireland, buccaneering, high adventure in overseas exploration and in the struggle against Spain had placed a new value on a man's military qualities. There was a crusading spirit among the great soldiers, adventurers, and patriotic pirates of the Elizabethan era which lent itself to symbolization in terms of a glorious trail of knightly battles in pursuit of foul beasts or in the defense of fair ladies. There was prevalent an uninhibited conviction concerning the justice of the causes of England and of Protestantism that was matched by the self-assurance of Spenser's knights: without the slightest hesitation, these knights identify their motives and deeds with true honor, justice, and courtesy.[49] It was not accidental, then, that Spenser should have portrayed Elizabeth's courtiers and heroes in medieval armor. His knights were crusaders; his age was more heroically reckless than Elyot's had been. His contemporaries were not satisfied with sitting in their manors[50] and administering justice among the surrounding farmers, with catching and hanging cattle-thieves. They sailed the oceans, explored strange lands, fought and robbed the Spaniards, subdued the Irish, and saved their Protestant brethren from Catholic oppression.

Spenser's work, then, despite its medieval costume, was more appropriate for his day than may appear at first glance. His purpose was to educate his contemporaries, and he thought he would achieve

184

that best by telling "historical" tales. Quite apart from the didactic purpose, he evidently took great delight in telling his tales for their own sake: so much so, in fact, that he sometimes seems to have used his avowed didactic aim as an "excuse" for telling his stories. He cloaked both his moral doctrines and his allusions to contemporary events in topical and moral allegories. These allegories are often so elaborate and intricate that the meaning of many of them continues to be hotly debated to this day, especially where there is a question of identifying certain knights or events in *The Faerie Queene* with definite persons or happenings.[51] The "moral" allegory is usually more easily identifiable, and more important for our discussion. It is the vehicle which Spenser finds best suited to his purpose of fashioning a gentleman.

Despite his avowed purpose in *The Faerie Queene*, and despite his personal interest in political activity, Spenser is less of a political theorist than any of the other writers we have been considering. What he does say about his social ideals, however, and the manner in which he presents them, is so important that he must be included in an account of the most significant representatives of humanistic political thought in sixteenth-century England. Education and the political system are as interdependent and complementary in Spenser's thought as they are in that of the other humanists with whom we have been concerned.[52] Like his predecessors, Spenser believed that the character of society and state was determined exclusively by its leaders, by the kind of education these leaders had received, and the kind of moral code they had adopted as the result of that education. Like them, he proclaimed the almost unlimited educability of man.[53]

Spenser, like Elyot, believed in beginning the right training at a very early stage of childhood, when man is still soft and pliable.

> This litle babe, of sweete and louely face,
> And spotlesse spirit, in which ye may enchace
> What euer formes ye list thereto apply,
> Being now soft and fit them to embrace;
> Whether ye list him traine in cheualry,
> Or noursle vp in lore of learn'd Philosophy.[54]

As far as detailed suggestions for an educational curriculum are concerned, Spenser was not very explicit. It was not his purpose to educate by advising the schoolmasters what they should teach: others had done that before him. He meant to inspire the young directly by his own words and images. He tried to make his enormous pedagogical work, *The Faerie Queene*, so interesting that the noble youth of his country would read it, would emulate its great examples and shun the imitation of the wicked ones.[55] In the passage just quoted, Spenser seemingly makes a distinction between training in "cheualry" and in "learn'd philosophy," between training in arms and in the liberal arts. It is true that, in *The Faerie Queene*, he is concerned primarily with "cheualry," and addresses himself to Elizabeth's soldiers rather than to her statesmen. Nevertheless, I do not think that he makes a sharp distinction between the two types of education: the soldiers of his epic poem and the courtiers of *Mother Hubberds Tale* serve the same ideal, and their education therefore has to be guided by identical standards.[56] The various aspects of this ideal are expressed in his different works, which should be read together to provide the complete picture. "Cheualry" and "learn'd philosophy," in his conception, are ultimately inseparable. Thus he states, in *The Teares of the Muses*, that it behooves the mighty peers

> learnd themselues . . . to bee;
> That is the girlond of Nobilitie.[57]

He elaborates on this theme in the traditional humanistic manner by asserting that learning and the resulting wisdom approximate man to God.[58] To the studies of the spirit[59] are joined the exercises of the body, like training in the use of arms, in riding, swimming, wrestling, dancing, and hunting.[60] Physical training is somewhat more important for Spenser than it is for our other writers because he is apt to think of his gentleman as a soldier rather than as a civilian.[61] Basically, as J. L. Shanley has demonstrated, his "education would be very much like that well-rounded one proposed by Elyot, Ascham, and Mulcaster, in fact by every writer on the gentleman from Vittorino da Feltre to Milton."[62]

This similarity comes out most strikingly in the description of the good courtier in *Mother Hubberds Tale*, with which we shall be concerned in a different context.[63] Spenser does not go into such details as the drawing up of lists of "required reading" or educational curricula. The most important account of education given in *The Faerie Queene* is the passage describing Artegall's upbringing by Astraea.[64] In conformity with the theme of the fifth book, in which it occurs, its leitmotiv is justice:

> For Artegall in iustice was vpbrought
> Euen from the cradle of his infancie
> And all the depth of rightfull doome was taught
> By faire Astraea, with great industrie.[65]

Artegall's preparation for his future function in society begins while he is still an infant, and is continued systematically until he has reached his maturity. The details are not elaborated. Having learned to "weigh both right and wrong . . . and equitie to measure out along,"[66] Artegall is presented with the sword "Chrysaor that all other swords excelled."[67] His teacher, Astraea, departs from this world after thus crowning his education, and on that occasion also leaves her groom, Talus, "made of yron mould,"[68] to her pupil. This strange creature of Spenser's imagination, Talus, holds an iron flail in his hand

With which he thresht out falshood, and did truth vnfould.[69]

He does this in a very efficient manner by flailing those who oppose his master. In this occupation he has the definite advantage of being unbeatable. Thus endowed with Chrysaor and Talus, Artegall immediately proceeds to enforce justice. The same aim guides Artegall's actions and those of Elyot's governour: they both want to establish the rule of "justice." Their conceptions of justice[70] are very similar, but they differ greatly in the ways in which they carry it out in practice. The governour acts as a justice of the peace, administering the laws of the realm and upholding the proper social order. Artegall goes forth, sword in hand and Talus at his heel, and fights injustice of any kind, wherever he can find it. He does not so much enforce the letter of the law as what he considers to be a universal code of justice. When the allegorical figures and causes, for and against which he does battle, are translated into the real persons and issues they represent, it becomes apparent that Artegall's fight is that of Elizabethan England; that what he considers to be absolute justice is essentially the cause of Spenser's queen. It is a questionable undertaking to identify the not always lofty motives of national policies with principles of universal justice, but Spenser does so with uninhibited patriotic self-assurance.[71] Since we are concerned here with the principles themselves rather than with the way in which Spenser applied them in the political situation of his time, we shall not go into an analysis of the scenes of *The Faerie Queene* in the light of contemporary events, but shall proceed to investigate what kind of social philosophy lies behind this conception of justice, and what kind of society its champions were to defend against all opponents.

Having learned "the depth of rightfull doome" and gone through many adventures, Artegall finally comes face to face with the perfect administration of justice at Mercilla's court.[72] In Spenser's archaic representation of the process of jurisdiction, that merciful queen sits enthroned in the court and herself judges all issues. She holds a scepter, "the sacred pledge of peace and clemencie,"[73] but can also use the sword if necessary. Mercilla is surrounded by "iust *Dice*, wise *Eunomie*, myld *Eirene* . . . , goodly *Temperance* . . . and sacred *Reuerence*."[74] By their symbolic names, these figures indicate that Spenser wants firm and impartial courts,[75] the decisions of which are tempered with mercy and mildness and moved by the aim of maintaining social peace. He makes a special point of the fact that the queen, who sits "high in dreaded souerayntie,"[76] hears the "pleas of people meane and base"[77] as well as cases of the highest political importance. These cases are all decided without outside interference, such as bribery or intimidation.[78] "Guyle, and malice, and despight,"[79] that often do so much harm in princes' courts, are not admitted to Mercilla's presence. As a result of this ideal administration of justice, war is completely unknown in Mercilla's utopian land, "but ioyous peace and quietnesse alway"[80] prevail. The people realize that they can expect true justice from their queen.

Those who crowd the court to plead their causes or watch the proceedings are kept in order by a marshal appropriately named "Order."[81] While, in its immediate context, this name signifies only that its bearer keeps the parties and spectators at court in order,[82] it is also connected with Spenser's wider conception of an orderly society. When "Order" commands peace, the crowds become silent and well behaved. As we shall see, when the crowds, in another environment, refuse to heed a call to order, when they become insurgents and wage civil war, the sternest measures against them are permissible in the name of justice. This, however, does not happen in Mercilla's country, since she maintains peace at all times, justifying her strict rule by dispensing true justice tempered with mercy.

At her court, Artegall encounters the ideal hierarchical, peaceful society under authoritarian rule. It is his task, as it is the task of every other true knight, to approximate the world at large to this ideal state. Since the conditions found in Mercilla's country are not easily or frequently achieved, Artegall and with him all knights have to do everything in their power to create that divinely balanced, just, and harmonious order in all societies. That means putting down unjust usurpation of powers by a tyrant or by the people with all the means at the knight's disposal.

In his zeal, Spenser sometimes seems to confuse the rigid enforcement of justice with cruelty, and defends the latter when it is applied in what he considers to be a good cause.[83] He is right, of course, in pointing out that the rigid enforcement of justice backed by power is essential: justice is to be administered

> with dreadlesse might
> For powre is the right hand of Iustice truely hight.[84]

There can be no objection to this maxim; to illustrate it, however, Spenser, among other themes, chooses the description of Grantorto's defeat at the hands of Artegall and the restoration of Irena's rule.[85] In this thinly veiled allegory, Spenser treats recent events in Ireland and defends the very questionable methods employed by Lord Grey in the suppression of the Irish rebellion, in the course of which the Smerwick massacre occurred. Artegall—here the allegorical figure representing Grey— "sorely punished with heauie payne"[86] the adherents of the late tyranny, and Spenser defends him against accusations that in this process he had stained the sword of justice "with reprochfull crueltie,"[87] by arguing that he simply proceeded on the "right course":[88]

> His studie was true Iustice how to deale,
> And day and night employ'd his busie payne
> How to reforme that ragged common-weale.[89]

Spenser also emphasizes the need for stern punishment of rebels as a prerequisite for the reformation of a rotten commonwealth: Talus searches out and inflicts "most grieuous punishment" on those

> that vsd to rob and steale,
> Or did rebell gainst lawfull gouernment.[90]

No doubt, Spenser did believe in extremely stern measures for the sake of restoring and maintaining "justice." Faced with a practical political situation, he himself advocated extreme policies against the rebellious Irish in his *View of the Present State of Ireland*.[91] He would probably have advocated similar measures against any other disturbers of what he considered to be the just order.[92] It is difficult to understand how Spenser, the "poets' poet," can both preach the ideal of peace, "milde humanity, and perfect gentle mynd,"[93] and not only defend but go so far as to advocate actions that were considered cruel even by his none too tender contemporaries.[94] This contradiction seems to present a psychological problem[95] which, however, need not concern us here.

Whatever the means, the ideal condition to be achieved is the state of affairs that prevails under Mercilla's rule. That rule is an approximation of the fabulous period "during *Saturnes* ancient raigne" when

> all the world with goodnesse did abound:
> All loued vertue, no man was affrayd
> Of force, ne fraud in wight was to be found:
> No warre was knowne . . .
>
> . . . . . . . . . . . . . . . . . . .
>
> Iustice sate high ador'd with solemne feasts
>
> . . . . . . . . . . . . . . . .
>
> Most sacred vertue she of all the rest,
> Resembling God in his imperiall might . . .[96]

The administration of justice, originally God's own domain, has been lent by God to the princes who are, therefore, his lieutenants on earth. He makes the princes

> like himselfe in glorious sight,
> To sit in his owne seate, his cause to end,
> And rule his people right, as he doth recommend.[97]

Under these circumstances, where the absolute ruler acts as God's lieutenant, and his rule is sanctioned by divine right, any rebellion against him or his appointed officers and servants is virtually sacrilegious. In return, rulers and their subordinates must follow God's injunctions in the administration of justice, and Spenser gives his own version of these injunctions in the descriptions of Mercilla's court and of Artegall's deeds. His interpretations make it evident that by the term "justice" Spenser means political theory rather than abstract principles of jurisprudence. While some fine points of law do come up and are settled in the fifth book of *The Faerie Queene*, "justice" to Spenser means mainly the right order of state and society.[98] This order can be easily identified as an idealized version of the status quo in England, an authoritarian, hierarchically organized polity. That order will be maintained by the readers of *The Faerie Queene* if they follow the example of Artegall. Like him, they will then be defenders of justice, which is to say that they will be protagonists of a hierarchical social order, of the Tudor monarchy and its ruling class. At the same time, however, they will

190

be chivalrous protectors of the poor and the weak, in the tradition of medieval knighthood.

Spenser's conception of justice, like all systems of law, reflects the social and political order which it is intended to maintain. If its defenders have a privileged position, they are also charged with the corresponding responsibilities, and the highest intellectual, moral, and practical accomplishments are demanded of them. The true knight subordinates his personal interests to the supreme task of enforcing justice. The prestige, worthiness, and ability of the readers of *The Faerie Queene* will be enhanced if they imitate not only Artegall's justice—the supreme political virtue—but such other virtues as Calidore's courtesy, Guyon's temperance, and the examples of true friendship between good men. Not only the fifth book of *The Faerie Queene*, "Of Iustice," but also and in particular the second, fourth, and sixth books, with their respective themes of temperance, friendship, and courtesy, represent Spenser's restatements of the humanistic doctrine. Of these virtues, courtesy is the most comprehensive.[99]

The inner perfection of Spenser's gentleman, like that of Castiglione's *cortegiano*, finds its outward expression in courtesy.[100] True knights

> beare themselues aright
> To all of each degree, as doth behoue.[101]

The three graces bestow the art of perfect courtesy on them:

> They teach vs, how to each degree and kynde
> We should our selues demeane, to low, to hie;
> To friends, to foes, which skill men call Ciuility.[102]

Spenser's gentleman is taught how to act in accordance with the exigencies of his station and situation: he exhibits the right measure of respect, affability, or firmness, whichever may be needed. A breach of the courtly code by another knight who is bound by it arouses him to violent action, because

> they that breake bands of ciuilitie,
> And wicked customes make, those doe defame
> Both noble armes and gentle curtesie.[103]

The possibility that the noble code might be violated by unworthy knights was evidently much on Spenser's mind[104] since this frequently happens in his poem. Severe action against the sinners is indicated because general defamation of the whole class is likely to result from flagrant disregard of its standards. Any exclusive social body is likely to adopt such an attitude; the strict codes of officers' corps, castes of priests, and similar "elite" groups carry on traditions closely related to those described here. Spenser's true knight enforces his moral code againt recalcitrant, law-breaking members of his own class by battling them. He also fights others who might threaten the position and existence of this class, and with it that of "justice": ruthless tyrants are attacked until they tumble down; the common people are relentlessly pursued if they try to arrogate to themselves the functions of government. The knight, then, has to combat both internal and external enemies of his rule, both those fellow-knights who are misguided enough to violate the ethical code,[105] and those men who are blind enough not to see that the aristocratic organization of society is divinely ordained, and who oppose it in their malicious ignorance. Spenser's ideal knight—gentleman, courtier, soldier, administrator—does battle against both dangers, actuated by his absolute faith in the supremacy of his set of values, and aided by his confidence that God is on his side.

Thus conceived, courtesy is anything but an easy and superficial code of behavior. It requires tact but also dauntless courage and a strong sense of justice:

> For seldome yet did liuing creature see,
> That curtesie and manhood euer disagree.[106]

Courage, however, is not to be identified with wild foolhardiness:[107] it is to be tempered by wise self-control. Thus, Spenser repeats the contention of his predecessors that self-control is one of the principal virtues needed by a man who wants to rule others:

> In vaine he seeketh others to suppresse,
> Who hath not learned him selfe first to subdew.[108]

Like his spiritual predecessors, then, Spenser's gentleman should bridle his courage and vigor with reason and prudence so as not to become foolhardy or cruel.[109]

In various contexts, Spenser indicates the type of society his knight or courtier is to serve. Apart from the image, already mentioned, of the perfect administration of justice at the court of Mercilla, one of the clearest descriptions of the ideal state and its ruler occurs in *Mother Hubberds Tale*. There, it is presented in the shape of a negative definition: the ape, with the cunning advice of the fox, has seized the reins of government in the animal kingdom.[110] The rule of these two adventurers over their fellow-animals is described in considerable detail. In the emerging picture, just

monarchy and its perversion, cruel tyranny, are vividly contrasted
The ape began to

> rule and tyrannize at will,
> Like as the Foxe did guide his graceles skill,
> And all wylde beasts made vassals of his pleasures,
> And with their spoyles enlarg'd his priuate treasures.
> No care of iustice, nor no rule of reason,
> No temperance, nor no regard of season
> Did thenceforth euer enter in his minde,
> But crueltie, the signe of currish kinde,
> And sdeignfull pride, and wilfull arrogaunce.[111]

It can be deduced from this description of the tyrannous state that
Spenser considered unselfishness, justice, the rule of reason, moderation, and affability to be essential attributes of the good ruler as
well as of the knight, and that he condemned the practices inevitably associated with the opposite qualities.

In a similar passage, the fox, who is the tyrannous ape's clever
adviser, claims the throne for himself with the argument that he
deserves it for his "slie wyles and subtill craftinesse"[112]—the
qualities which, in Elizabethan opinion, were the distinguishing
attributes of the Machiavellian ruler. This craftiness consists in
certain methods of action which had become associated with
Machiavelli's name. Thus the fox follows Machiavelli's advice by
impoverishing the great nobles of the realm, for "he no count
made of Nobilitie."[113] He even does away with them by con-
cocting false accusations against them, or else he makes them
"dwell in darknes of disgrace."[114] Like the Florentine, the fox is
afraid that they may otherwise become too powerful and endanger
his rule. Furthermore, "of men of armes he had but small regard",[115]
he does not bestow the usual honors on his own knights and soldiers,
but rather employs "forreine beasts, not in the forest bred,"[116] just
as the typical Renaissance prince relied on foreign *condottieri* rather
than on his own armed nobility and citizenry: "For tyrannie is with
strange ayde supported."[117] It is with the aid of "monstrous beasts"
of all kinds that the tyrant keeps himself in power. At the same
time, he vitiates any "desire of honor, or braue thought of armes"[118]
that might arise in the hearts of the "yong lustie gallants"[119] at
his court, but keeps them busy "with fruitles follies, and vnsound
delights."[120] First and last, the tyrant is concerned with his own
interests. The people over whom he rules are nothing but objects
of exploitation which he can use to enrich himself. Not only
does he disdain nobles and soldiers, but "for the rascall Commons

least he cared."[121] He reveals his *sacro egoismo* when he blandly declares:

> Let God . . . care for the manie
> I for my selfe must care before els anie,[122]

and he practices this selfishness very successfully by plundering his own subjects. With what one might call his "terror organization" he manages to keep them subdued and quiet, so that "none durst speake, ne none durst of him plaine."[123]

The test of tyranny is the ruler's attitude toward knowledge and scholars:

> For men of learning little he esteemed;
> His wisedome he aboue their learning deemed.[124]

In other words, the tyrant naturally prefers his own shrewd cleverness to real learning or his *virtù* to *virtus* bred of true knowledge; such knowledge is dangerous for him and has to be discouraged or suppressed. Only that knowledge which he can twist to his own use can be permitted to exist in his kingdom. Thus, the tyrannous ape has no use for a "rightfull courtier" who might "descrie his lewd conditions,"[125] and therefore ridicules any "loue of letters,"[126] any real search for truth,[127] among his entourage. Erasmus and Elyot had indicated the contempt in which letters and learning were habitually held in their day by some of the more boisterous members of the nobility, but they had not necessarily attached any particular political significance to such an attitude. Spenser portrays and castigates the same ignorant attitude; however, since it is the tyrant who expresses his contempt for learning, such contempt becomes indicative of a tyrannous disposition. Since tyranny cannot suffer the quest for truth, the tyrant must banish the able, honest, and learned courtier from his court and country. The men around him must be servile and pliable instruments of his perverted will, and to keep them in this condition he has to prevent them from acquiring true knowledge. One way to accomplish this is to ridicule learning in their eyes. That is the way in which the ape, that classical image of the typical usurper, behaves when confronted with the aspiration for knowledge among his courtiers:

> And whenso loue of letters did inspire
> Their gentle wits, and kindly wise desire,
> That chieflie doth each noble minde adorne,
> Then he would scoffe at learning, and eke scorne
> The Sectaries thereof, as people base
> And simple men, which neuer came in place

Of worlds affaires, but in darke corners mewd,
Muttred of matters, as their bookes them shewed,
Ne other knowledge euer did attaine,
But with their gownes their grauitie maintaine.[128]

This is much the usual argument against "clerks and scholars," but with a different emphasis: for Spenser the attack on learning becomes a symptom of tyranny. This connection had not been so definitely established by his predecessors.

Against this negative background of usurpation, tyranny, suppression of virtues, and elevation of the vices, Spenser portrays the "braue Courtier." While the tyrant will have nothing to do with him, such a courtier ought to be the mainstay of a sound kingdom. Traits of Castiglione's *cortegiano* are readily apparent in his bearing, his entertainments, his functions, his convictions, as apparent indeed as they were in the real Elizabethan courtier. Hoby's translation[129] had done its part to spur people to an imitation of this ideal; Spenser, in his passage on the courtier in *Mother Hubberds Tale*,[130] re-creates it in his own image. A few lines of the poem will suffice to give its outline, and to establish its close dependence on the Italian conception. The courtier

will not creepe, nor crouche with fained face
But walkes vpright with comely stedfast pace,
And vnto all doth yeeld due curtesie.[131]

The *cortegiano*'s *grazia* is unmistakable in his "comely stedfast pace," and the "due curtesie" stems from Castiglione's demand that the courtier should always show due respect or affability, the proper kind of courtesy, toward people of different social stations.[132]

Very similar points are made by Spenser, as previously indicated,[133] with regard to the knight. This emphasizes the fact that his conceptions of the knight and the courtier are identical in their essential features. The courtier in *Mother Hubberds Tale* hates idleness and entertains himself with "knightly feates," with "warlike deedes," with hunting, running, wrestling, and shooting with the bow.[134] These recommended activities largely coincide with the advice on physical exercise given by Elyot and Ascham; the suggestion that the "courtly gentleman" revive his tired spirit "with sweete delight / Of Musicks skill"[135] is also familiar from the *Cortegiano* and the *Governour*. Like the *cortegiano*, Spenser's courtier finds comfort in the company and love of ladies. Finally, he withdraws to the realm of the Muses. With them, he "confers" not so much on literary and artistic subjects—as one might well expect—but rather on practical, even predominantly political themes:

> Of Natures workes, of heauens continuall course,
> Of *forreine lands,* of *people different,*
> Of *kingdomes change,* of *diuers gouernment,*
> Of *dreadfull battailes* of renowmed Knights;
> With which he kindleth his ambitious sprights
> To like desire and praise of noble fame.[136]

The Muses, then, instruct him in natural science, geography, history, political science, and in the arts of war. Other, more purely literary or artistic themes on which the courtly gentleman might be expected to converse with them are not mentioned in this context. This predominantly political orientation of his mind is explained by the fact that he is desirous of nothing but honor "to which he leuels all his purposis,"[137] and honor is to be gained in the prince's political or military service. Like Elyot's governour, he is not out to gain material rewards.[138] In order to be assigned to an honorable task in which he can distinguish himself, he must win the prince's favor.[139] Among the accomplishments which recommend him, the knowledge "of forreine lands . . . of diuers gouernment" obviously ranks very high. When he has thus trained himself in political and military skills, he becomes

> fit to vse in all assayes,
> Whether for Armes and warlike amenaunce,
> Or else for wise and ciuill gouernaunce.[140]

His "courting" thus culminates in practical political activity, in participation in the affairs of state. He never ceases to learn, but daily enriches "the storehouse of his powerfull wit,"[141] both in the performance of his practical tasks and in his discourses with the Muses.

Spenser and Castiglione hold very similar opinions as to what constitutes a good courtier. Elyot's governour, on the other hand, does not, like the courtier, live at court, does not have to gain influence on political affairs via the prince's person, and does not, therefore, have to put as much emphasis on the attributes of "courtesy" as Castiglione's and Spenser's courtiers are obliged to do. Both Elyot's governour and Spenser's courtier had their place in Elizabethan England. If the courtier was the more striking social type, the kind of country gentleman postulated by Elyot continued to exercise his important functions. These functions gradually became more complex and demanding: thus Lambard's

*Eirenarcha*, which was prepared for the country gentleman's use and published in the middle of Elizabeth's reign, far surpassed earlier manuals for justices of the peace in the number of legal duties and technicalities it enumerated.[142] In a later and more liberal period, when English society again became less centralized than it was under Elizabeth and her successors, the country gentleman returned to his earlier pre-eminence: the country squire is the most prominent social type of eighteenth-century England. Under Elizabeth, the brilliance of the court outshone the more rustic virtues, and the social ideal of the time in consequence was the "courtier" rather than the "governour." Yet not too great a distinction should be made between the two conceptions: they are but variations on the same theme. Both types existed side by side, and neither in theory nor in practice was there any sharp line dividing them. Spenser wrote for both: the knights of *The Faerie Queene* and the courtiers of *Mother Hubberds Tale* were meant to be examples for all the gentry and nobility of the realm, whatever their function and position.

We have been considering the outline which Spenser gives of his ideal gentleman in *Mother Hubberds Tale*, and have found that *The Faerie Queene* fills in that design with many details. It becomes apparent that Spenser, like Sidney, combines classical and medieval, Italian and English conceptions on the just state and its ruling class. The ideas which guide the conduct of their "good men," the system of justice which these men enforce in court and in battle are derived from the identical conviction that that state which is organized hierarchically, according to the value of its parts, is the best state; all other forms of society are wrong. In *Mother Hubberds Tale*, we have found a description and condemnation of tyranny; in *The Faerie Queene*, too, Spenser decries tyranny,[143] and he also relates an attempt to set up what may be described as an equalitarian democracy.[144] That attempt is condemned in equally scathing terms. Under neither form of government can the virtues flourish or justice prevail. Neither will let good men rule. Plato had condemned tyranny as the opposite of justice. He had also described its origin: the lovers of extreme liberty in a democracy become ardent followers of the demagogue who, as soon as these willing tools of his ambition have carried him into power, becomes a tyrant. Like Plato, Spenser sees in unbridled democracy and in the ensuing tyranny the opposites of the just state, and he accordingly portrays both as such in his treatment of justice.[145]

The ideal government for Spenser is that which he knew from actual experience: a strong monarchy directing the affairs of state through the medium of a powerful but pliant aristocracy. The Elizabethan system found a stout defender in the poet who set out to glorify it.[146] To uphold it, he violently denounced both the abuse of monarchical power in tyranny and the idea of popular democracy. Men are unequal because, just as God has created hills and dales, he has made kings and subjects, governors and the governed. Both have their functions, and both owe respect to each other:

> The hils doe not the lowly dales disdaine;
> The dales doe not the lofty hils enuy.
> He maketh Kings to sit in souerainty;
> He maketh subiects to their powre obay.[147]

Into this simple analogy with nature Spenser puts the essence of his political thought. He voices the same sentiments that had been expressed by men like Elyot and Sidney as well as by Anglican bishops and other exponents of the official doctrine of the English state and church. The dangerous doctrines of the Anabaptists and similar democratic groups, and the few revolts that were actually attempted, provoked a continuous stream of condemnations and counterarguments. These arguments are summed up and put into dramatic form by Spenser in his story of the wicked giant "who all things would reduce vnto equality."[148]

The giant promises to redistribute wealth and power, to create an equalitarian, democratic order, and thus induces a great crowd of common—"vulgar"—people to gather around him,

> Like foolish flies about an hony crocke,
> In hope by him great benefite to gaine,
> And vncontrolled freedome to obtaine.[149]

This desire upsets the God-made balance of the world. The redistribution of power and wealth is beyond the capacity of human beings, for it involves weighing the world anew,[150] a complete re-evaluation of values, which no mortal should be so rash as to think he could accomplish. Artegall, the defender of justice, takes the giant vigorously to task for his wicked demagogic equalitarianism: "In stead of right me seemes great wrong doest shew."[151] He brings in the familiar comparison of human society with the divine order of the world: since God has weighed all parts of matter in the universe to the last dram, and since He has arranged them in such a way that they all balance each other exactly, it is evident that He has set up an equally balanced hierarchical order among men.[152] He does not want "uncontrolled freedom" but a definite place, a closely circumscribed function for each component part of the universe, each member of human society:

> Such heauenly iustice doth among them raine,
> That euery one doe know their certaine bound.[153]

The giant is not at all convinced that this is true. To Artegall's pragmatic statement—which may be taken to represent Spenser's own opinion on the subject—that

> All change is perillous, and all chaunce vnsound[154]

he replies that things are in rather bad shape at the moment: "each estate quite out of order goth."[155] There is much injustice in the world, which the giant proposes to eradicate: he is going to level the hills with the plains and to throw the high mountains into the sea. His suggestion,

> Were it not good that wrong were then surceast,
> And from the most, that some were giuen to the least?[156]

applies both to nature and to mankind. He proposes to overthrow the great in the world just as he plans to topple the mountains into the sea:

> Tyrants that make men subiect to their law,
> I will suppresse, that they no more may raine;
> And Lordings curbe, that commons ouer-aw;
> And all the wealth of rich men to the poore will draw.[157]

This argument, which articulates a type of social protest that was widespread among the lower classes of Tudor society,[158] is brushed away by Spenser's Artegall in summary fashion: he points out to the giant that he misunderstands nature, and that therefore his analogy is wrong:

> Of things vnseene how canst thou deeme aright
> . . . . . . . . . . . . . . . . . . .
> Sith thou misdeem'st so much of things in sight?[159]

The order of society, then, is revealed in its true nature to the wise and righteous but not to the unjust—revealed to Artegall but not to the giant.[160] We cannot but wonder at the absolute certainty of Artegall's "knowledge" as to how God wanted to see society ordered.

It was all very well for Spenser to proclaim the existing order, with its rigorous distinctions of class and wealth, as God-given, to leave to Him all changes in positon and wealth,[161] since he—Spenser—happened to be sitting on top. To be sure, he was not surveying the world from one of the high mountains, but from a comfortable hill in the shape of his good Irish estate of Kilcolman.[162] Having started out with nothing, it was undoubtedly gratifying for Spenser to have been rewarded, for his secretarial and other services to the English crown in Ireland, by these conquered Irish lands[163] and by the elevated social position that came with them. A man who has risen from a position of inferiority to one of superiority in a social system in which inequality of power and wealth prevails is always prone to become a vociferous defender of the status quo.[164] Spenser was surely not an exception, nor were many of his contemporaries. The Tudors themselves still were a "new" family, and Elizabeth was always on her guard against anyone who might challenge her position. Most of the great families and many of the gentry owed their rise to the new dynasty, or were at least newly enriched and advanced under it. The Henrician parvenus, typical social climbers anxious to legalize their own rise and maintain their newly acquired privileges, became fervent advocates of the system of "order" and "degree."[165]

It is not mere chance that Spenser's philosophical tenets and his personal and material interests coincide, yet one would be wrong in assuming that his philosophy is based mainly on expediency and self-interest. Spenser was not one of the major beneficiaries of the regime, and he had had setbacks which might well have caused him to be bitter and disappointed with it. He did express his disappointment on a number of occasions but nevertheless felt that the status quo, despite its imperfections, was to be maintained. He believed that if people followed his poetic teachings, conditions would improve, but that nobody had the right to question the basic validity of the Elizabethan order, or to attack its physical structure. Whoever did so deserved to be treated as mercilessly as the giant and his followers are eventually treated by Artegall and Talus.

The Tudor gentry and nobility liked the notion that God should wish them to occupy the favorable position which in many cases they or their fathers had recently acquired, a notion which made any attempt to deprive them of their privileges virtually sacrilegious! Again, it does not follow that the idealistic arguments they advanced in defense of an aristocratic social order were nothing but a sham set up to hide their naked, materialistic egoism. Such an interpretation of their social philosophy would not do them justice, for they were honestly, if perhaps somewhat naïvely, convinced of the absolute superiority of a society organized according to "the discrepance of degrees, wherof procedeth ordre"[166] over any other form of social organization. They were equally convinced that they themselves were the best part of that society. With never ceasing insistence, writers and poets addressed themselves to this class, to point out the accomplishments of its good members and the vices and shortcomings of those unworthy of their position. Gentry and nobility had to be taught that, in order to be worthy of their privileges, perhaps even to retain them, they had to adopt a definite set of values from which certain practical virtues were to be derived. Behind the constant emphasis on what constitutes a good man and what a bad one stood the conviction that the "organic order" of society had to be implemented by the practice of those virtues which ought to distinguish the ἄριστοι, the "best" in society, from the "rabble."

While Spenser's arguments may sound rather naïve, there can be little doubt that he argued from sincere conviction, if perhaps overzealously. Like a true zealot, he does not mind the sternest measures against those opposed to his views, and like the inquisitors he probably felt that even to kill such people was a praiseworthy deed since it was for society's and ultimately their own good. The giant, who is opposed to Spenser's political philosophy as proclaimed by Artegall, is utterly destroyed by Talus. The iron man throws him into the sea,[167] where he is drowned. The justification for this action is that the giant is "lewdly minded,"[168] i.e., that he holds base, wicked social ideas. Spenser is evidently pleased when he describes his "bones all broken rudely" and draws the moral:

So was the high aspyring with huge ruine humbled.[169]

This was the just end which fate held in store for all potential demagogues. The fate that was to befall any "rascall crew"[170] which might be ready to follow such demagoguery was equally unpleasant if less spectacular. After the giant has been disposed of, in Spenser's episode, his followers

gan to gather in tumultuous rout
And mutining, to stirre vp ciuill faction.[171]

They had hoped to derive many advantages and riches from the giant's leadership: when they are frustrated by his death, they rise

201

in armed revolt to avenge it. The scene is reminiscent of a similar popular uprising in Sidney's *Arcadia:*[172] both authors evidently regarded such a movement as loathsome in the extreme and the crowd that participates in it as beneath contempt. It is a "lawlesse" multitude: that epithet implies both that it is violent and that it violates the divine will and law. The noble Artegall, whom the insurgent crowd attacks, considers it to be so much beyond the pale that

> loth he was his noble hands t'embrew
> In the base blood of such a rascall crew.[173]

And, indeed, he does not have to stain his hands with their unworthy blood, since his iron man, Talus, disposes of the rebels for him:

> But when at them he with his flaile gan lay,
> He like a swarme of flyes them ouerthrew[174]

so that they all run and hide in holes and bushes. That is the inglorious end of the attempted revolution.

The dangers, and the actual experience, of a popular uprising such as the one described here were undoubtedly very much on Spenser's mind, because, in addition to the scene just described, two other similar actions occur in the fifth book of *The Faerie Queene*. In each instance, Spenser takes much satisfaction in describing the final and triumphant dispersal of the riot by Talus. These two episodes center in the somewhat inadequate knight, Burbon, and follow one another in almost direct sequence. Here, as in the scene just considered, the crowd is described as being "lawless," which necessitates Talus' stern action against it. A "rude rout" is trying to oppress Burbon with "lawlesse powre" and to bring him "in bondage of their brutishnesse."[175] The action develops on lines parallel to the other riot scene; the knight-baiting becomes intolerable when good Sir Sergis, the "truest Knight aliue,"[176] and Artegall are attacked and forced to fall back. This is the signal for Talus' intervention; he again wields his flail with the result that the mob is dispersed "like scattred chaffe, the which the wind away doth fan."[177] The comparisons Spenser uses strikingly illustrate his opinions about the constancy of the mob. Like flies and chaff, it is blown hither and thither by the changing winds.

Hardly is the first mob dispersed when a crowd of rebellious peasants clusters around the noble knights like "a swarme of flyes vpon a birchen bough,"[178] which provides Spenser with another occasion to let Talus disperse them. The German Peasants' War, the

Pilgrimage of Grace, the Irish uprisings come to life in his vivid verses. We hear and see how the peasants

> Did them assault with terrible allarme
> And ouer all the fields themselues did muster,
> With bils and glayues making a dreadfull luster.[179]

The sight of this "base crew" draws Artegall and Burbon together: Artegall had been berating Burbon for conduct unbecoming a knight, but their quarrel is ended when the latter invokes the former's help "against these peasants, which haue me opprest."[180] After a moment of hesitation, Artegall agrees to help Burbon combat the latter's own subjects: the solidarity of knighthood prevails over a quarrel caused by an infraction of the chivalrous code. When the hierarchical balance of society is threatened, the cohesion of the upper class prevails over personal squabbles. This solidarity extends beyond national boundaries and is truly international in scope. Rulers unite in a "holy alliance" when the mob rises against one of them. Strangely enough, Burbon appeals for Artegall's assistance by claiming it as a matter of "courtesie."[181] Courtesy, then, even involves mutual assistance against one's own subjects, if they attempt to overthrow the social order.

After an initial setback, the knights begin to hunt the peasants "like squirrels" about the fields.[182] Talus with his iron flail insures the inevitable victory and makes "cruell hauocke of the baser crew."[183] While he overthrows the "raskall manie," he very properly leaves the "captains" of the uprising to the tender ministrations of the two knights who promptly subdue them. (Presumably the blood of these captains is not quite as base and, therefore, does not soil the victors quite as much as would that of the multitude.) Talus is merciless. He drives the scattered enemy into the sea, from that soil "which they troubled had with great turmoyle,"[184] until finally Artegall commands him to desist from his cruel deed and to stop the slaughter. That is evidently Spenser's conception of justice tempered with mercy. The advice for the treatment of the Irish in the *View* is based on a very similar conception.

Spenser's repeated disposal of such "raskall routs"[185] is typical of the Elizabethans. It reminds one of Shakespeare's treatment of revolutionary mobs,[186] as for instance in *Coriolanus:* the people with their tribunes become a ludicrous collection of loudmouthed cowards when they try to upset the existing hierarchy. Spenser sounds more violent and arrogant in his contempt than his fellow-poets: he lacked Shakespeare's greatness and the security and "gentleness" that came with Sidney's inherited social position. Spenser refuses to consider seriously that the revolting crowd may be impelled to act by some real and justified grievance, and he is unconcerned with the effects of economic problems on the living conditions of the poorer classes.[187] The neglect of such vital matters is frequently encountered among contemporary advocates of the established order. They were firmly convinced that any disturbance of that balanced order was due to a wilful disregard for the just proportions of the universe and of the body politic. Such wickedness led the lower classes to overstep the boundaries assigned to them in the social hierarchy.

It seems strange that Spenser, while envisaging a possible failure of the ruling class to live up to its standards, does not even consider that the ensuing misrule might justify popular action against it. "Tyrants that make men subiect to their law," "Lordings . . . that commons ouer-aw"[188] apparently are to be considered, by those who suffer from them, as necessary evils in an otherwise perfect system. The authority of the ruling class as such is not to be questioned. If its rule degenerates into vicious tyranny, a virtuous knight may come to the rescue and overthrow it, but the people must not take matters into their own hands. Spenser's example of such an action is the overthrow of the "cruell tyranny" of the "Souldan" and his wicked wife, Adicia, by Artegall.[189] This tyrannous couple had been breaking "all bonds of law, and rules of right,"[190] that is to say, it had been "lawless" like the mob in the riot scenes we have been considering.

> But the braue Prince [Artegall] for honour and for right,
> Gainst tortious powre and lawlesse regiment,
> In the behalfe of wronged weake did fight.[191]

It takes a knight to fight in the good cause, to deliver the "weak," in this case an unjustly oppressed people, from wicked power. The people have no right to take the initiative, but must find such a champion. We may assume that in the absence of such a champion the people are not entitled to throw off even a lawless yoke. Governours, Spenser and his predecessors insisted, should be good and just men. If they did not live up to established standards and properly discharge their duties, it became the task of more virtuous members of their class to overthrow them and by this action to maintain and strengthen the social order in its right proportions. If there is injustice and unrest in a state, it is due to the badness of the rulers rather than to economic or social factors: find a good ruler, surround him with wise and virtuous courtiers, give him brave and chivalrous knights and just magistrates, and all will be well.[192]

While Spenser is right in emphasizing the human quality of those who rule, he takes an oversimplified view when he follows the prejudices of his day and virtually disregards other factors. It is strange that the insight into certain aspects of society that had been displayed by More in the *Utopia* should have been lost by succeeding generations of humanists, and that it should have had no apparent effect on Spenser's thought. With their antagonism to the communism of *Utopia*,[193] the Elizabethan advocates of the established order tended to combine a disregard for social and economic problems of which More had been vividly aware. Spenser's limitations in this respect can hardly be explained by the argument that he was a poet and not a political theorist; he wrote the poetry we have analyzed with definite political aims.

Equalitarian aspirations of the common people had been condemned before Spenser by other exponents of the aristocratic doctrine. They had been described as "Anabaptist" or otherwise contrary to the laws of God and man. Spenser's views, then, are not new, but they are more vehemently expressed, a fact which may be ascribed to his experiences in Ireland. While he thus stresses the privileges of the ruling class more fervently than do his predecessors, his main emphasis continues to be on its duties. The performance of these duties is vividly portrayed in his great epic poem, where the knightly and courtly virtues come to life in the deeds of the Fairy Queen's heroes. Many streams of thought that had contributed to the ideal of the "good gouernour and . . . vertuous man" are fused, in this work, into Spenser's own poetic images.

# Epilogue

W E HAVE seen how humanistic doctrine developed into the attitude represented by Spenser. If he stressed the right of monarchs and gentlemen to rule, humanism also emerged on the other side as "classical republicanism." In this shape, important aspects of classical thought that had been increasingly disregarded by sixteenth-century authors came to the fore again. The defenders of Parliament in the seventeenth-century struggle could justifiably argue that they were the true heirs of Greece and Rome in fighting for the rights of free men against absolutist oppression. Had not men like Demosthenes and Cicero done the same? Royalist writers complained that the reading of the books of the ancient Greeks and Romans made men republicans.[1]

An important section of the parliamentary party in the Civil War favored a "mixed state" in which the balance between the monarchical and popular elements rested with an aristocracy exercising its power through Parliament. These men, mostly members of the gentry, were influenced in their thoughts and actions by the examples to be found in classical antiquity. In one of his early writings, Milton expressed this conception when he described as his ideal a commonwealth of England "where under a free and untutored monarch, the noblest, worthiest, and most prudent men, with full approbation and suffrage of the people, have in their power the supreme and final determination of highest affairs."[2] These "noblest, worthiest, and most prudent men" are surely descended from the "governour" of one hundred years earlier; Milton might stress their godliness more and their illustrious lineage less than Elyot, but he would expect them to become worthy and prudent through the study of the classics and of the Bible. Milton later turned against the monarchy and was disappointed with Parliament, "but the principle of the mixed state with a preponderant aristocratic element did not change."[3] Harrington, also a champion of the mixed state, wished to see in it an aristocratic element securely established on the basis of wealth and virtue. Again this involves, as a matter of course, the humanistic training of the aristocracy. Such doctrines could not be shared, and were in fact fought, by the more radical religious and political groups. Yet it is important to realize that some of the most prominent thinkers and leaders of the revolution upheld the aristocratic principle, probably in a more truly classical form than their royalist opponents, and that their ideas were in large part based on the precepts of republican Athens and Rome. Their political theory was thus strongly influenced by their humanistic education.

Leadership on both sides in the Civil War rested mostly in the hands of gentlemen who had received such an education.[4] If they differed in the interpretation and use of the classical authorities in their historical situation, there was nevertheless widespread agreement between many of them on the need for a humanistically trained aristocracy; this aristocracy might be seen as the loyal support of the Crown or as the dominant element in a powerful Parliament. In the later seventeenth and in the eighteenth centuries, the latter view came to prevail with the Whig ascendancy. Burke, the great defender of Whig principles, often expresses ideas similar to those found in our sixteenth-century authors, to whom he is related through a continuing intellectual tradition.

In the sixteenth century, humanism became the mark of the English ruling classes. From that time to the present, a humanistic education has been considered prerequisite in a gentleman. The actual form of this education has passed through changes, as has the ideal of the "governour" which it was from the beginning intended to serve. Both, however, have proved very tenacious and adaptable, and have vitally contributed to the development of the English art of government.

We have tried to show the effect humanism had on the ideals and social order of sixteenth-century England. This was the formative age. In the ensuing centuries, and on an expanding scene, its effects were not, perhaps, more intense, but they were more varied and almost incalculably widespread. Much of what has proved of value, both to herself and to others, in the thought, institutions, and life of Britain and her empire has its roots in the humanistic tradition.

# Notes

## CHAPTER I

1. Thus, Paul Joachimsen has defined humanism as "an intellectual movement which had its roots in an urge for the revival of classical antiquity." ("Humanismus soll eine geistige Bewegung sein, die in einem Drang nach Wiederbelebung des klassischen Altertums wurzelt.") "Der Humanismus und die Entwicklung des deutschen Geistes," in *Deutsche Vierteljahrsschrift für Literaturwissenschaft und Geistesgeschichte*, VIII (1930), 419.

2. R. Weiss, *Humanism in England during the Fifteenth Century* (Oxford, 1941), p. 182, stresses the "utilitarian conception of the humanities" as the "main feature of humanism in England during the fifteenth century"; he feels that "it consisted in drawing from Italy those elements which were of value in theology, philosophy or diplomacy," such as good Latin style. "Whereas in Italy the cult of the antique had completely transformed cultural values, in England we find neo-classicism . . . used for the furtherance of scholastic ends" during that period, Weiss states (*op. cit.*, p. 179). "Because humanism was hardly considered more than a medium this was also a decisive factor against the setting up of a humanistic society" (*ibid.*, p. 183).

3. Cf. Douglas Bush, *The Renaissance and English Humanism* (Toronto, 1939), p. 78.

4. There is a considerable body of scholarly literature that deals with the character and development of the ideal of the English gentleman from the sixteenth century on. Among the basic works are: Ruth Kelso, *The Doctrine of the English Gentleman in the Sixteenth Century* (Urbana, 1929); J. E. Mason, *Gentlefolk in the Making* (Philadelphia, 1935); V. B. Heltzel, *Chesterfield and the Tradition of the Ideal Gentleman* (unpublished dissertation in University of Chicago Library, 1925); August Hoyler, *Gentleman-Ideal und Gentleman-Erziehung mit besonderer Berücksichtigung der englischen Renaissance* (dissertation, Leipzig, 1933). These and other studies will be referred to later in the present work.

5. Cf. R. R. Reid, *The King's Council in the North* (London, 1921), pp. 102–3: at one time "there was in it not one man above the degree of knight"; it was composed of knights and lawyers.

6. For the social status of his ancestors, see R. W. Chambers, *Thomas More* (London, 1935), pp. 51–52.

7. E. P. Cheyney, *A History of England from the Defeat of the Armada to the Death of Elizabeth* (New York, 1926), II, 387. Part VIII of this work gives an excellent account of Elizabethan local government. On the organization of government in the early sixteenth century, see K. W. M. Pickthorn, *Early Tudor Government* (Cambridge, 1934).

8. There were frequent new editions of this manual: thus, up to 1600, it appeared again in 1582, 1588, 1591, 1592, 1594, 1599. It was evidently much needed. For other similar works, cf. B. H. Putnam, *Early Treatises on the Practice of the Justices of the Peace in the 15th and 16th Centuries* (Oxford, 1924).

9. Lambard, *op. cit.*, p. 10.

10. J. E. Neale, *The Elizabethan House of Commons* (London, 1949), p. 147, points out that in Elizabeth's later years there ought to have been in Parliament 90 country gentlemen, to represent the counties, and 372 citizens and burgesses, to represent cities and boroughs. In fact, however, an analysis of the social composition of the 1584–85 Parliament, which covers 447 out of a total of 460 members, produces the surprising figure of only 53 merchants and borough officials, with the remainder belonging to the gentry and the professional classes. Even if various allowances are made, the proportion of "gentlemen" and others is the opposite of what it should be in theory. Neale, who is primarily concerned with the Elizabethan period, points out that "this invasion of the boroughs by the country gentlemen reaches back a long way," and that one may speak of "infiltration" before the Reformation, of "invasion" after it (*ibid.*, p. 148).

11. *Loc. cit.*

12. Cf. Neale, *op. cit.*, pp. 77 ff., for some lively accounts of sheriffs' activities.

13. Sir Fulke Greville (Lord Brooke), *Life of Sir Philip Sidney* [1652], ed. N. Smith (Oxford, 1907), p. 189.

14. Thus Richard Pace, in *De Fructu qui ex doctrina percipitur liber* (Basel, 1517), p. 70, tells young men that in the old days, when government was better and wiser than now, the power was in the hands of the orators, of Demosthenes in Athens and of Cicero in Rome. He restates the classical doctrine that orators must be good men: "Quorum non solum eloquentia admirabilis, sed etiam praestantissimum ingenium, doctrina excellens, vita honestissima, mores denique laudatissimi fuerunt. Et cui unum ex his deest, hunc ego in oratorem non admitto." (Christ and St. Paul are praised for their oratorical skills: *ibid.*, p. 72.)

15. The use of this principle in Shakespeare's work, and part of its history, is well presented by J. E. Phillips, Jr., in *The State in Shakespeare's Greek and Roman Plays* (New York, 1940).

16. See W. G. Zeeveld's discussion of these problems in "Social Equalitarianism in a Tudor Crisis," *Journal of the History of Ideas*, VII (1946), 35–55; reprinted in his *Foundations of Tudor Policy* (Cambridge, Mass., 1948), pp. 190–225. Zeeveld here analyzes the theories and arguments advanced on both sides in the Pilgrimage of Grace of 1536, and demonstrates that "paradoxically, principles of social equality were voiced . . . not by the Pilgrims but by Henry VIII's own apologists."

17. In Book I of the *Utopia*.

18. Investigated, for instance, by S. B. Liljegren, *The Fall of the Monasteries and the Social Changes in England Leading up to the Great Revolution* (Lund, 1924). See also chap. vi, below.

19. P. O. Kristeller, *The Philosophy of Marsilio Ficino* (New York, 1943), p. 16.

20. That work was completed in 1468 (Kristeller, *op. cit.*, p. 17).

21. Pier Candido Decembrio's translation of the *Republic,* based on that of Chrysoloras, probably reached Humphrey in 1443, a draft of the first five books having preceded this by three years (Weiss, *op. cit.,* pp. 54–57).

22. The term is used and defined in *The Institucion of a Gentleman,* published anonymously in 1555. (C. Whittingham's reprint [London, 1839] of the 2d ed. of 1568, sig. cVIIIʳ.)

23. *Of the Knowledge Which Maketh a Wise Man. A Disputacion Platonike* (1st ed.; London, 1533). Cf. chap. iv, note 26, for a brief bibliographical discussion of this work.

24. *The Courtyer of Count Baldessar Castilio done into Englyshe by Thomas Hoby* (London, 1561).

25. These translations will be discussed more fully in the last part of chap. vi.

26. W. F. Schirmer, *Der englische Frühhumanismus* (Leipzig, 1931).

27. *Op. cit.*, p. 182. Cf. note 2, above.

28. *Op. cit.*, p. 136.

29. Weiss, *op. cit.*, pp. 51, 54–57. For the translation of the *Republic,* and the history of this translation from Chrysoloras to Pier Candido Decembrio, see E. Ditt, "Pier Candido Decembrio," in *Memorie del R. Istituto Lombardo di Scienze e Lettere. Classe di Lettere ...*, XXIV² (Milan, 1931), 30–33. "La traduzione di Candido è più fedele di quella del padre, il quale si concede spesso ripetute omissioni, che Candido poi completa"; also, it is much more intelligible and polished (*ibid.*, p. 32).

30. In 1438. See Weiss, *op. cit.*, p. 48.

31. Weiss, *op. cit.*, pp. 66–67, lists gifts of 265 books during Duke Humphrey's lifetime; Humphrey left all his Latin books to the university, but it is "extremely doubtful" whether they reached it.

32. *Ibid.*, p. 115.

33. For a full account, see Weiss, *op. cit.*, chaps. vi–vii.

34. *Ibid.*, pp. 145, 148, 174.

35. *Ibid.*, pp. 153–56.

36. *Ibid.*, p. 159, note 2.

37. *The Castell of Helth* (London, 1541), "Proheme."

38. "Das ist die grundlegende Tatsache des englischen Humanismus im 16. Jahrhundert, dass er zum Ausgangspunkt der puritanisch-reformatorischen Bestrebungen wird" (*Geschichte der englischen Literatur* [Halle, 1937], p. 194). The emphasis on the "pedagogic-theological" side is seen as a step toward Puritanism, and the major significance of humanism is to be found in its character as a transitional stage on the way to Puritanism. The thesis was first fully stated in Schirmer's *Antike, Renaissance und Puritanismus* (Munich, 1924). Schirmer there argues that Elyot's "governour" is much more Christian and "bourgeois" than Castiglione's courtier, and that the two authors' attitudes are opposed to each other (pp. 86 ff.); and he speaks of an unmistakable "Verbürgerlichung" in Elyot, Ascham, and Milton (p. 113). Elyot, as we shall note, does not particularly stress the Christian religion in his major works, and

he certainly is no Puritan. If his mode of expression is less elegant than Castiglione's, his ideas are hardly "bourgeois." Castiglione, *Il Cortegiano*, ed. V. Cian (Florence, 1929), p. 444, advocates the practice of the "vera religione."

39. 3d ed.; London, 1887.

40. J. Leland, *Commentarii de Scriptoribus Britannicis* (Oxford, 1709), II, 483.

41. Cited by J. N. Johnson, *The Life of Thomas Linacre* (London, 1835), p. 324.

42. See V. Flynn in *Times Literary Supplement* for September 12, 1935, on this assumption.

43. See P. S. Allen, "Linacre and Latimer in Italy," *The English Historical Review*, XVIII (1903), 514–17.

44. R. J. Mitchell, *The English Historical Review*, L (1935), 696–98.

45. Richard Pace, a younger contemporary of Linacre, praises this universality (*op. cit.*, p. 76): Linacre is a great grammarian, orator, physician, editor, disputant: "Est enim is summus medicus, et par orator, ut tum experientia, tum libris felicissime editis, manifestum fecit omnibus. . . ."

46. E. F. Rogers, *The Correspondence of Sir Thomas More* (Princeton, 1947), letter 3, pp. 8–9.

47. *The Life of John Picus Erle of Myrandula . . . Translated . . . by maister Thomas More*. Chambers, *op. cit.*, p. 94, thinks it was translated about 1505.

48. On Grocyn's life, see M. Burrows, . . . *Memoir of William Grocyn* (Oxf. Hist. Soc. Collectanea, 2d series, Oxford, 1890), pp. 334 ff.: 1463, in Winchester; 1467–1481, Fellow of New College. Then at Magdalen until 1488; journey to Italy; Exeter College, Oxford, in 1491; vicar of St. Lawrence Jewry, London, in 1503.

49. Weiss, *op. cit.*, p. 174.

50. Cf. C. W. Boase, . . . *Register of . . . Exeter College, Oxford* (Oxford, 1894), p. lxxii. Boase claims that Grocyn lectured in the Hall of Exeter College. Grocyn paid rent for his room in 1492.

51. On his written work, see Chambers, *op. cit.*, p. 82.

52. W. Schenk, *Reginald Pole, Cardinal of England* (London, 1950), p. 3.

53. Cf. chap. ii, notes 6, 7, 15.

54. R. Weiss, *Times Literary Supplement* for September 26, 1935, thinks that he was already in Rome in 1493.

55. J. H. Lupton, *The Life of John Colet, D.D.* (London, 1887), p. 51, assumes this. Actually, very little is known about Colet's sojourn in Italy, about the places he visited and the people he met. See D. Weinstein, *The Place of John Colet in the Development of English Humanism* (Master's thesis in University of Chicago Library, 1950), pp. 24–31.

56. *Two Treatises on the Hierarchies of Dionysius*, trans. J. H. Lupton (London, 1869).

57. Cf. Lupton, *Life*, p. 52.

58. *Ibid.*, p. 86.

59. Rogers, *op. cit.*, letter 3.

60. Lupton, *op. cit.*, p. 76, quotes this dictum: "Those books in which Christ is not found are but a table of devils."

61. Pace, *op. cit.*, pp. 13–14.

62. A. Hyma, "The Continental Origins of English Humanism," *Huntington Library Quarterly*, IV (1940), 17.

## CHAPTER II

1. It is now generally assumed that Erasmus was born on October 27 or 28, 1469, and not, as he usually claimed, in 1466. Cf. Preserved Smith, *Erasmus, a Study of His Life, Ideals and Place in History* (New York, 1923), pp. 7–8, 445–46; J. Huizinga, *Erasmus*, ed. W. Kaegi (3d German ed.; Basel, 1941), p. 11; Margaret Mann Phillips, *Erasmus and the Northern Renaissance* (New York, 1950), p. 6.

2. For a summary of these visits, see P. Smith, *op. cit.*, p. 59.

3. *Ibid.*, pp. 69–70.

4. P. S. and H. M. Allen, *Opus Epistolarum Des. Erasmi Roterodami, denuo recognitum et auctum.* (11 vols.; Oxford, 1906–47.) (This will hereafter be cited as *Op. Ep.*)

5. The standard but no longer adequate account of this group is F. Seebohm's *The Oxford Reformers* (3d ed.; London, 1887). More recent descriptions of Erasmus' relations with the English humanists are to be found in the biographies already mentioned, in R. W. Chambers, *Thomas More* (London, 1935); in W. F. Schirmer, *Antike, Renaissance und Puritanismus* (Munich, 1924), pp. 77–85; and in such articles as Albert Hyma's "Erasmus and the Oxford Reformers," *Nederlandsch Archief voor Kerkgeschiedenis*, n.s., XXV (1932), 69–92, 97–136; "Erasmus and the Oxford Reformers (1503–1519)," *op. cit.*, n.s., XXXVIII (1951), 65–85; and "The Continental Origins of English Humanism," *Huntington Library Quarterly*, IV (1940), 1–25; J. A. K. Thomson's "Erasmus in England," in *England und die Antike* (Leipzig, 1932); and A. L. Rowse's "Erasmus and England" in his *The English Spirit* (New York, 1945), pp. 75–87.

6. Cf. Karl Bauer, "John Colet und Erasmus von Rotterdam," *Archiv für Reformationsgeschichte*, Ergänzungsband V (1929), 155–87.

7. Erasmus describes the life of Colet in a long letter to Jodocus Jonas, written in 1521: *Op. Ep.* IV, ep. 1211, pp. 514–27; translated by J. H. Lupton, in *The Lives of Jehan Vitrier and John Colet* (London, 1883), pp. 19–46. The account of More is contained in a letter to Ulrich von Hutten, written in 1519: *Op. Ep.* IV, ep. 999.

8. Cf. H. Exner, *Der Einfluss des Erasmus auf die englische Bildungsidee* (Breslau dissertation; Berlin, 1939); J. F. Larkin, *Erasmus' De Ratione Studii; Its Relationship to Sixteenth Century English Literature* (abstract of dissertation; Urbana, 1942); H. de Vocht, *De Invloed van Erasmus op de Engelsche Tooneelliteratuur der XVI° en XVII° Eeuwen* (Ghent, 1908).

9. For these dates, cf. P. Smith, *op. cit.*, pp. 59, 64.

10. *Ibid.*, p. 305.

11. Chambers, *op. cit.*, p. 49, establishes "with fair certainty" that More was born on February 6, 1478.

12. *Ibid.*, pp. 70–71. Erasmus' description of his visit is found in *Op. Ep.* I, ep. 1, p. 6. English translation in F. M. Nichols, *The Epistles of Erasmus* (3 vols.; London, 1901–18), I, 201–2.

13. *Op. Ep.* I, ep. 114, of October 28, 1499.—Twenty-six letters from Erasmus to More, twenty-four from More to Erasmus, and a number of letters exchanged between Erasmus and More's family are known. Cf. the tabulation in E. F. Rogers, *The Correspondence of Sir Thomas More* (Princeton, 1947), pp. xv–xxii.

14. In *Op. Ep.* IV, ep. 1211, p. 515, Erasmus states that when they met, Colet "was about thirty years old, two or three months younger than I."

15. *Loc. cit.*—Colet's lectures and other works have been published by J. H. Lupton, who is also the author of the standard biography, *The Life of John Colet, D.D.* (London, 1887).

16. Huizinga, *Erasmus* (New York, 1924), p. 37, finds that the friendship with Colet "definitely decided the bent of Erasmus' many-sided mind," but later modifies this statement. Chambers, *op. cit.*, p. 72, states even more emphatically: "There is little trace of Erasmus having at this date influenced Colet. But the influence of Colet upon Erasmus was enormous." This one-sided interpretation has been disputed by Hyma, "Erasmus and the Oxford Reformers," *op. cit.*, pp. 118–26, and the extent of their friendship as such has been questioned by the same author, "Erasmus and the Oxford Reformers (1503–1519)," *op. cit.*; see also D. Weinstein, *The Place of John Colet in the Development of English Humanism* (unpublished Master's thesis, University of Chicago, 1950), pp. 64–67.

17. Cf. P. Mestwerdt, *Die Anfänge des Erasmus: Humanismus und Devotio Moderna* (Tübingen, 1917), and A. Hyma, *The Youth of Erasmus* (Ann Arbor, 1930).

18. Cf. Lupton, *The Life of John Colet*, pp. 52, 67, 79, 86.

19. *Op. Ep.* I, ep. 116 (November, 1499).

20. *Op. Ep.* I, ep. 118 (December 5, 1499). Translation adapted from F. M. Nichols, *op. cit.*, I, ep. 110.

21. Chambers, *op. cit.*, p. 97. The result was published in Paris in November, 1506, as *Luciani . . . opuscula . . . ab Erasmo Roterodamo et Thoma Moro . . . traducta*.

22. *Ibid.*, p. 94.

23. E. F. Rogers, *op. cit.*, letter 3, pp. 8–9.

24. Chambers, *op. cit.*, p. 89; V. J. Flynn, *The Life and Works of William Lily, the Grammarian* (unpublished Ph.D. dissertation; Chicago, 1939), pp. 68–69. Their translations were published by Froben as *Progymnasmata* (Basel, 1518). See also C. R. Thompson, *Translations of Lucian by Erasmus and St. Thomas More* (Ithaca, 1940); but see L. Bradner and C. A. Lynch, *The Latin Epigrams of Thomas More* (Chicago, 1953), pp. xii–xiii, for a different, later dating.

25. *Op. Ep.* I, ep. 215; Chambers, *op. cit.*, p. 100.

26. *Op. Ep.* I, ep. 214.

27. *Op. Ep.* I, ep. 191; quoted from Nichols, *op. cit.*, I, ep. 191.

28. P. Smith, *op. cit.*, p. 66.

29. The pension amounted to twenty pounds annually. *Ibid.*, pp. 69–70.

30. *Ibid.*, pp. 70–72.
31. *Ibid.*, p. 75.
32. In a letter written in 1532 (*Op. Ep.* X, ep. 2750). Erasmus "corrects" himself by calling it, rather, "scholam ac gymnasium Christiane religionis."
33. Cf. Chambers, *op. cit.*, pp. 118–20, for his mission to Flanders.
34. P. Smith, *op. cit.*, pp. 87–88; *Op. Ep.* II, ep. 461.
35. It was printed by June 17 and had been dedicated to the later Charles V in March. (*Op. Ep.* II, ep. 393.)
36. Chambers, *op. cit.*, p. 121.
37. Erasmus' latest biographer, Mrs. Phillips, remarks on this point: "The *Utopia* indeed, contained a great deal of Erasmian thought; it was rumoured that Erasmus was the author of the first part of the book. . . . He and More were so closely linked by thought and temperament, that the interpenetration of their ideas is a matter of course. . . . It is as if the two friends . . . had pooled their ideas during those years culminating in 1516. . . . There is no doubt that they had shared their opinions and interchanged ideas in discussion for a long time past" (*op. cit.*, p. 124).
38. Cf. P. Smith, *op. cit.*, p. 65.
39. *Op. Ep.* III, ep. 968; cf. Chambers, *op. cit.*, pp. 168–69.
40. For Erasmus' part in the revision of *Libellus de constructione octo partium orationis*, see Flynn, *op. cit.*, pp. 118, 131. For the statutes, see Lupton, *The Life of John Colet, D.D.*, pp. 279–80.
41. Arthur F. Leach, *Educational Charters and Documents, 598 to 1909* (Cambridge, 1911), pp. 468, 510.
41a. Exner, *op. cit.*, pp. 117 ff., investigates this influence in some detail, and shows it, among others, in Elyot, Starkey, Ascham, Humphrey.
42. Begun in 1501, published 1503. (*Op. Ep.* I, ep. 164, and Phillips, *op. cit.*, p. 46.) In the standard edition of Erasmus' works (*Opera Omnia emendatiora et auctiora . . . studio et opera Joannis Clerici* [10 vols.; Lugduni Batavorum, 1703–6], hereafter abbreviated *LB*), the *Enchiridion* is printed in Vol. V, cols. 1–66, the *Institutio* in Vol. IV, cols. 559–612. English citations from the *Institutio* follow L. K. Born's translation, *The Education of a Christian Prince* (New York, 1936).
43. On this point, cf. Pierre Mesnard's chapter on "Érasme ou l'évangélisme politique" in his *L'Essor de la Philosophie Politique au XVIᵉ Siècle* (Paris, 1936), particularly pp. 118–19, 137–38.
44. The biographies by P. Smith, Huizinga, Phillips, K. A. Meissinger (*Erasmus von Rotterdam* [Zurich, 1942]), and others contain much useful material on and critical evaluation of this aspect of Erasmus' thought. Among the more specialized studies, the following are particularly valuable for our purposes: Rudolf Pfeiffer, *Humanitas Erasmiana* (Leipzig, 1931); and "Die Einheit im geistigen Werk des Erasmus," *Deutsche Vierteljahrsschrift für Literaturwissenschaft und Geistesgeschichte*, XV (1937), 473–87; J. Huizinga, "Erasmus über Vaterland und Nationen," in *Gedenkschrift zum 400. Todestage des Erasmus von Rotterdam* (Basel, 1936); Rudolf Liechtenhan, "Die politische Hoffnung des Erasmus und ihr Zusammenbruch," *ibid*. Erasmus' political theories are examined by F. Geldner, *Staatsauffassung und Fürstenlehre des Erasmus von Rotterdam* (Ber-

lin, 1930); Mesnard, *op. cit.*; L. K. Born, in the introduction to his translation of the *Institutio;* A. Renaudet, in the chapter "La Critique du Gouvernement et de la Société" of his *Études Érasmiennes, 1521–1529* (Paris, 1939); R. P. Adams, "Designs by More and Erasmus for a New Social Order," *Studies in Philology*, XLIV (1945), 131–45. For a critical interpretation of Erasmus' attitude to Christianity, cf. Hyma's studies. For my interpretation, cf. also "Erasmus: Leistung und Forderung," in *Deutsche Beiträge*, ed. A. Bergstraesser (Chicago, 1947), pp. 73–93. The major part of the present chapter is an abbreviated and revised version of my article, "Erasmus on the Social Functions of Christian Humanism," *Journal of the History of Ideas*, VIII (1947), 78–106.

45. Quoted from W. H. Woodward, *Studies in Education during the Age of the Renaissance* (Cambridge, 1906), p. 116.

46. *Loc. cit.*: "Educatio superat omnia." See also *ibid.*: "Efficax res est natura sed hanc vincit efficacior institutio."

47. He does not always hold this opinion, however, and even takes the opposite point of view. Cf. a passage in *De Pueris . . . Instituendis, LB* I, 508: "If then you ask: 'What is to be done to boys who respond to no other spur [than flogging]?' My answer is: 'What would you do if an ox or an ass strayed into your schoolroom?' Turn him out to the plough or the pack-saddle, no doubt. Well, so there are boys good only for the farm and manual toil: send your dunces there for their own good." (Translation quoted from W. H. Woodward's rather free rendering in: *Desiderius Erasmus concerning the Aim and Method of Education* [Cambridge, 1904], p. 209.)

48. *LB* IV, 578: "Deus ipse, ne coactis imperaret, et Angelis et hominibus liberum dedit arbitrium, quo splendidius et augustius redderet imperium suum."

49. Huizinga, *Erasmus* (New York, 1924), p. 193.

50. *Ibid.*, p. 244. Cf. also Hyma, "Continental Origins of English Humanism," *op. cit.* in note 5, p. 17, where Erasmus' rationalism is compared to that of Voltaire. Pfeiffer, in "Die Einheit im geisten Werk des Erasmus" (*op. cit.* in note 44), strongly attacks these attempts to class Erasmus with the eighteenth-century rationalists, and argues for his Christianity instead. His argument seems to me to go too far. Mrs. Phillips (*op. cit.*, pp. 83–84) also finds that "Erasmus cannot fairly be called a rationalist" since he distrusted intellectual subtlety and abstract argument. She finds that "both the rational method and the more direct spiritual grasp are necessary" for Erasmus, and that "faith completes the work of reason, just as Christ's teaching lets in a flood of light on the groping of the classical moralists." Mrs. Phillips assigns to him a middle position between the mystics and the rationalists.

51. Opinion on Machiavelli's political thought as a whole remains divided. I cannot here enter into the discussion of what motives Machiavelli had in writing *The Prince*, or try to demonstrate the relationship of the ideas expressed in that work to those found in his other writings. Suffice it to say that I consider *The Prince* the antithesis to Erasmus' teaching in the political field, notwithstanding the fact that Machiavelli

on the whole seems to hold ideas different from the doctrine he advocates in that work.

52. L. K. Born, "Erasmus on Political Ethics: The Institutio Principis Christiani," *Political Science Quarterly*, XLIII (1928), 539 n.: "There is no evidence that Erasmus knew of Machiavelli's *Il Principe*, but his own treatise forms a perfect antithesis to it." L. Gautier Vignal, *Érasme* (Paris, 1936), p. 172, claims that both books were presented to their respective recipients in the same year. The first draft of *The Prince* had been completed in December, 1513; Machiavelli first intended to dedicate it to Giuliano Medici, but changed the dedication, probably after Giuliano's death, to his nephew Lorenzo. The first printed edition appeared in Rome in 1532. Cf. also L. Enthoven, "Über die Institutio Principis Christiani . . . ," *Neue Jahrbücher für das klassische Altertum*, XXIV (1909), 312–29.

53. In his *Humanitas Erasmiana*. See also A. Gwynn, *Roman Education . . .* (Oxford, 1926), pp. 57 f.

54. On the *Philosophia Christi*, cf. Pfeiffer, *Humanitas Erasmiana*, and Mrs. Phillips' chapter, "The Philosophy of Christ" (*op. cit.*, pp. 40–85), particularly the discussion (pp. 77–83) of Erasmus' description of this philosophy in the preface to the first edition of his New Testament, the *Paraclesis*.

55. Cf. Otto Schottenloher, *Erasmus im Ringen um die humanistische Bildungsform* (Münster, 1933).

56. *LB* X, 1742: "Prometheus nobis est imitandus. . . ."

57. *LB* I, 683.

58. *LB* IV, 578: Christ "solus est totus imitandus . . . in hoc absolutum est omnis virtutis ac sapientiae exemplar."—Other biblical figures may sometimes be imitated, but in certain instances that would be decidedly wrong. Thus, princes should not try to excuse their promiscuous lives by pointing to the example of Solomon and his concubines (*LB* V, 49). Christ is the only reliable guide.

59. "Christus est totius eruditionis et eloquentiae scopus." (Quoted from Exner, *op. cit.*, p. 79.)

60. *LB* V, 47: "Si claro genere es, non obscurabunt, sed decorabunt nobilitatem generis, mores Christo digni."

61. *LB* IV, 598: "Nam olim patriciis otium datum est a sordidioribus opificiis non ad nugandum, sed discendas eas disciplinas, quae ad Rempublicam administrandam faciunt."

62. *LB* IV, 588. The Academic and Stoic schools exerted the principal influence on his views. In the *Institutio*, Erasmus, according to an analysis of his borrowings from other writers, "was indebted most of all to Plato, . . . in close position for second place [are] Cicero, Seneca, and Plutarch." (L. K. Born, introduction to his translation, p. 98. *Ibid.*, p. 97, he notes that more than seventy passages drawn from Plato are in the *Institutio*.)

63. *LB* I, 523: "Sed in primis ad fontes ipsos properandum, id est, Graecos et antiquos. Philosophiam optime docebit Plato, et Aristoteles. . . ."

64. *LB* V, 45: "Neque quisquam proprie sibi studeat, sed pro sua virili quisque quod accepit a Deo in commune conferat. . . ."

65. *LB* V, 39: ". . . animus ad Christum anhelantis, a vulgo tum factis, tum opinionibus quam maxime dissentiat, nec aliunde quam ab uno Christo, pietatis exemplum petatur." *Ibid.*, 40: "Exemplum nostrum Christus est, in quo uno omnes insunt beate vivendi rationes: Hunc sine exceptione licebit imitari." *Ibid.*, 41: "Vera nobilitas est, inanem contemnere nobilitatem: vera nobilitas est, servum esse Christi."

66. *LB* V, 47. Cf. also *Op. Ep.* V, ep. 1333, where Erasmus feels it necessary to defend his dedication of a biblical text to a prince against more popular competition: "Quasi vero soli omnium principibus apta munera deferant, qui de venatu, de alendis canibus, de habendis equis, de machinis bellicis, aut fortasse de lusu aleae libellos barbarica quapiam lingua elucubratos offerunt." Evidently he does not find princes and nobility as readily disposed to read his pious injunctions as they are to amuse themselves with sporting books. We shall see that other sixteenth-century authors of pedagogical treatises voice similar complaints.

67. Cf. Mesnard's discussion, *op. cit.*, pp. 91–92.

68. Huizinga, *Erasmus* (New York, 1924), p. 130, claims that "the warp of his mind is Christian; his classicism only serves him as a form, and from Antiquity he only chooses those elements which in ethical tendency are in conformity with his Christian ideal." I do not think that this is quite accurate, or that it is possible to stretch the term "conformity" to such a degree. Hyma, on the other hand, argues that Erasmus was a great admirer of Valla, and that Valla cannot be termed a "Christian" humanist, since he was indifferent to the teachings of Jesus and refused to follow them. (See his "Continental Origins . . . ," *op. cit.*, note 5, p. 213.) Erasmus himself, according to Hyma, "was not moved by feelings of profound guilt and remorse for his misdemeanors," and is thus on the side of pagan rationalists like Valla and Voltaire rather than on that of the Christians. Since the feelings of sin, guilt, and remorse gained in importance as the attributes of a Christian through the efforts of the Reformers, Erasmus' comparative lack of them would seem to be shared by many pre-Reformation Christians who are not *ipso facto* pagans. Erasmus was a Christian in that, for instance, he advocated the imitation of Christ and the practice of brotherly love in all human relations, and in that he devoted a major part of his life to the elucidation of Christian doctrine by the writing of theological works. Ultimately, he was somewhere between the pagan and Christian positions. His position is well summed up by Mrs. Phillips (*op. cit.*, p. 82): His "emphasis on the powers and potentialities of mankind is essentially humanistic, but Erasmus manages to hold it and remain a Christian, thus maintaining his central position between the pagan humanists rejoicing in their confidence in man's native powers and goodness, and the Lutheran and Calvinist denying to man any virtues of his own at all. Erasmus did not work out this position either. . . ." Cf. also R. McKeon, "Renaissance and Method in Philosophy," *Studies in the History of Ideas*, III (New York, 1935), 72 ff. Pfeiffer, *Humanitas Erasmiana*, p. 24, indicates the problem as follows: ". . . inwiefern einer eindringenden

systematischen Betrachtung diese Verbindung von pietas und humanitas, von pistis und paideia standhält, inwiefern es eben ein System eines solchen christlichen Humanismus überhaupt geben kann, das bleibe hier ungefragt." See also E. F. Rice, Jr., "Erasmus and the Religious Tradition, 1495–1499," *Journal of the History of Ideas*, XI (1950), 387–411.

69. Quoted from Woodward's translation of *De Ratione Studii* (*Erasmus concerning ... Education*, p. 164).

70. This touches on the question, recently asked by Douglas Bush (*The Renaissance and English Humanism* [Toronto, 1939]) and others, whether humanism was in any essential respect different from scholasticism, whether there was such a chasm between the Middle Ages and the Renaissance as Jakob Burckhardt (*Die Cultur der Renaissance in Italien* [Basel, 1860]) originally claimed. I am of the opinion that the Renaissance and humanism distinctly represent a new scheme of life and thought. Erasmus certainly felt dissatisfied with scholasticism, broke with it, and tried, in his humanism, to forge a new unity of classicism and Christianity on a plane different from scholasticism.

71. Pfeiffer, in "Die Einheit im geistigen Werk des Erasmus" (*op. cit.*, note 44), argued that such unity had been achieved by Erasmus on a predominantly Christian basis, but I cannot agree with his conclusion.

72. Notwithstanding the fact that he advised Colet in the foundation of St. Paul's School, and that he lectured in various universities, such as Cambridge and Louvain. Cf. Gautier Vignal, *op. cit.*, p. 133: "L'enseignement parlé ne l'a jamais intéressé. ..."

73. Cf. Larkin, *op. cit.*

74. "Laurentium Vallam tibi censeo diligenter evolvendum, qui de Latini sermonis elegantia scripsit elegantissime" (*LB* I, 522).

75. Huizinga, *op. cit.*, p. 243, says: "He was the only one of the humanists who really wrote for all the world, that is to say, for all educated people."

76. Thus, Budé may have borrowed very extensively from Erasmus' *Institutio* when composing his *De l'Institution du Prince*. (Cf. L. K. Born, *The Education of a Christian Prince*, Introduction, p. 28.)

77. L. K. Born, *ibid.*, p. 20.

78. Cf. *LB* V, 49: "... Christianus non exercet potestatem in suos, sed caritatem, et qui maximus est omnium, ministrum se cogitet esse, non dominum."

79. *LB* II, 957: "... quid aliud est Pax, quam multorum inter ipsos amicitia?"

80. *LB* IV, 577: "Cogitato semper, dominium, imperium, regnum, majestatem, potentiam, Ethnicorum esse vocabula, non Christianorum. Christianum imperium nihil aliud esse quam administrationem, quam beneficentiam, quam custodiam."

81. Cf. *LB* II, 1202, Adage *Civitas non civitas*: No body politic, no "civitas" exists, "ubi summa rerum penes unum hominem est." "At Respublica non est, ubi unius arbitratu aguntur, ferunturque omnia. ... Regnum est imperare liberis, neque quicquam absque civium consensu tentare."

82. *LB* V, 354 (*De bello Turcis inferendo*): ". . . non oportet rem omnium periculosissimam suscipere, sine civitatum et patriae consensu."

83. Cf. Geldner's observation (*op. cit.*, p. 88) that in his theory Erasmus was a democrat; L. K. Born, *op. cit.*, p. 23, note 104; and Renaudet, *op. cit.*, p. 79.

84. Note Erasmus' interesting complaint about the weakened power of the citizenry and the growing despotic absolutism in his treatise on the Turkish War, *LB* V, 365: ". . . incredibile dictu, quantum decesserit libertati populi, civitatum auctoritati, majestati Senatuum, ordinis Ecclesiastici reverentiae. Contra, quantum accreverit Principum potentiae, quantum exactionibus, in summa, quantum additum illi nimium jactato, quod Principi placuit lex est." Or his emphasis on freedom of speech in the *Adagia*, *LB* II, 634: "Neque vero mirum aut magnum, si Principes permittant populo, quae velint dicere: cum ipsis liberum sit, quae velint facere."

85. Cf. the passages from the *Adagia* quoted by P. Smith (*op. cit.*, p. 200) which certainly justify his remark that Erasmus at times expresses "a bitter hatred of monarchy." However, Mesnard (*op. cit.*, pp. 124–25) rightly observes that Erasmus does not advocate the sovereignty of the people, and that, despite his criticisms, he does on the whole support the monarchical form of government. Cf. also Phillips, *op. cit.*, p. 148, in support of this view.

86. Phillips, *op. cit.*, p. 128.

87. *LB* V, 40: "Vulgus sunt, quicumque in specu illo Platonico vincti suis affectibus inanes rerum imagines pro verissimis rebus admirantur." He expresses the same judgment in *LB* IV, 565.

88. *LB* V, 40.

89. In the Adage *Scarabaeus*, *LB* II, 871 ff. Quoted from P. Smith, *op. cit.*, p. 201.

90. Cf. also *Enchiridion*, *LB* V, 13: There may be revolt "ni penes unum sit imperii summa." The ruler should distrust the wishes of the people and presumably act contrary to them: "Immo hoc tibi suspectum quid esse oportet, quod plurimis placet" (*LB* V, 40).

91. Cf. Huizinga, *Erasmus* (New York, 1924), p. 195.

92. L. K. Born, *op. cit.*, p. 6, quotes Erasmus as actually saying that flattery is the best way of influencing princes.

93. In the Adage *Aut Regem*, *LB* II, 109; similarly, *LB* V, 366: "Optima quidem est Monarchia, si Princeps detur Deo similis."

94. Cf. Renaudet, *op. cit.*, p. 106. L. K. Born, *op. cit.*, p. 33, thinks that Erasmus either wants this absolutism, or else that he is in favor of a monarchy limited by aristocracy and democracy if the prince does not rise above the average.

95. *LB* V, 48–49: "Quid enim absurdius, quam Principem Christianum Hannibalem, Alexandrum Magnum, Caesarem aut Pompejum sibi proponere? . . . Nihil tam decorum, tam magnificum, tam gloriosum Regibus, quam ad summi Regis Jesu similitudinem quam proxime accedere, qui ut erat maximus, ita & optimus erat." Cf. Mesnard (*op. cit.*, pp. 122–24), on the difference between Christian and pagan rulers.

96. Erasmus mentions this in *LB* V, 49, but does not solve the prob-

lem: Christ "negavit regnum suum de hoc mundo esse, cum esset coeli terraeque Dominus."

97. Cf. the following phrase (*LB* V, 13): "Porro Rex ipse nulli paret nisi legi, lex respondet honestatis ideae." This "honestatis idea" would seem to be a rather vague basis for a legal system! Similarly, *ibid.*, 48: "Non protinus jus esse putato, quod vis, sed id tantum velis quod jus est." (According to classical definitions, he would be a tyrant if he declared his will to be the law.)

98. *LB* IV, 595: "Bonus sapiens et incorruptus Princeps nihil aliud est quam viva quaedam lex." The origins of this conception have been investigated by E. R. Goodenough, "The Political Philosophy of Hellenistic Kingship," *Yale Classical Studies*, I (New Haven, 1928), 55–102. See also L. K. Born, *op. cit.*, and M. Rostovtzeff, *Social and Economic History of the Hellenistic World*, I (Oxford, 1941), 298, and the references to other treatises περὶ βασιλείας, *ibid.*, III, 1594. Goodenough quotes and analyzes passages attributed to Diotogenes and Ecphantus, investigates their relationship to Pythagorean, Platonic, and oriental thought, and indicates their influence. The Erasmian statement quoted here, as well as a number of others, is clearly derived from sources such as these, presumably through intermediary authors like Plutarch.

99. *LB* IV, 566: "Ne putaris temere dictum a Platone, et a laudatissimis laudatum viris, ita demum beatam fore Rempublicam, si aut philosophentur Principes, aut Philosophi capessant Principatum."

100. *LB* IV, 583: "Regem agere non potes, nisi te ratio rexerit. . . ." Cf. Goodenough, *op. cit.*, p. 95, for Plutarch's identification of λόγος— *ratio*—with the "living law."

101. *LB* IV, 570: "Deus ut pulcerrimum sui simulacrum in coelo constituit solem, ita inter homines evidentem ac vivam sui collocavit imaginem, Regem." Also *LB* II, 109: "Quod sol in coelo, id Princeps in populo. Sol oculus mundi, Princeps oculus multitudinis." The comparison with the sun, later to be embodied by the *Roi Soleil*, clearly goes back to the Orient, via Rome and the Hellenistic monarchies. Goodenough (*op. cit.*, p. 82) thinks that the Persian conceptions are most important in this connection. He quotes a passage from Ecphantus (*ibid.*, pp. 76–78) in which the "admixture to a Pythagorean-Platonic base of oriental or Egyptian sun symbolism" can be clearly seen.

102. In *LB* IV, 576, Erasmus states the prince's duty: ". . . sapientia bonitateque omnibus antecellat, et nullius indigens, nihil aliud studeat quam prodesse Reipublicae." Also *ibid.*, 584: "Qui ad commodum publicum spectat, Rex est: qui ad suum, Tyrannus." For an example of a passage which similarly stresses the correspondence between king and God, see the Ecphantus fragment in Goodenough, *op. cit.*, pp. 67–68.

103. One of the most typical passages of this kind occurs in the Adage *Aut Regem* . . . , *LB* II, 108–9: "Proinde primum omnium, Principis animus omnibus erroribus liberandus est, ut perspiciat, quid vere honestum, quid vere gloriosum, quid vere magnificum. Deinde instillandum turpitudinis odium, et amor honesti, quo videlicet perspiciat, quid Principem deceat, et nihil appetat, nisi quod sit bono ac salutari Principe dignum. Ut honestum ubi sit videat, et hoc uno metiatur omnia, nec un-

quam ab hoc aberret scopo. Atque hanc vocant sapientiam, qua necesse est, ut Princeps tanto caeteros antecellat mortales, quanto dignitate, opibus, ornatu, potentiaque antecedit."

104. *LB* II, 941: "Indiligens paedagogus corrumpit puerum, malus praeceptor vitiat discipulum, Rex improbus populum item corrumpit."

105. *LB* II, 107: "Siquidem Princeps, aut magno orbis totius malo stultus est, aut magno omnium bono sapit: tametsi proclivius est laedere quam prodesse. . . ."

106. *LB* II, 109: The tyrant "aut non sapit, aut si sapit, in publicam perniciem sapit. Quod habet potentiae, in reipublicae pestem abutitur. . . . At nulla belua nocentior tyranno."

107. *LB* IV, 574: "Bonus Princeps non alio animo debet esse in suos cives, quam bonus paterfamilias in suos domesticos. Quid enim aliud est regnum quam magna familia? Quid Rex nisi plurimorum pater?"

108. After a comparison of the classical and medieval sources of the *Institutio*, L. K. Born (*op. cit.*, p. 128) comes to the conclusion that Erasmus, while not borrowing directly from medieval "mirrors of princes," did follow the medieval pattern (*ibid.*, p. 126). He mentions such points as Erasmus' emphasis on the prince's moral and personal qualities, and his use of the organic analogy of the state. As to direct sources, Born concludes that on the whole Erasmus followed classical rather than medieval writers (*ibid.*, p. 95). It seems to me that Erasmus was familiar with medieval thought on the subject, but that he preferred classical sources. When he did incorporate medieval notions into his own work, he chose those which were closest to Greek and Roman ideas, both in origin and content. In his own use and interpretation of such ideas, he emphasized their classical rather than their medieval context.

109. *Op. Ep.* III, ep. 858: "Quaeso te, quid aliud est civitas quam magnum monasterium? Monachi abbati suo parent aut praepositis; cives episcopo ac pastoribus suis obsequuntur. . . ."

110. In *LB* IV, 577, he refers to the pagan philosophers who said that "non alius modi esse imperium Principis in populum, quam quale est animi in corpus"; *ibid.*, 579: ". . . Respublica corpus quoddam . . . ex variis membris compactum. . . ."

111. *LB* IV, 602: "Ut animi partes non omnes perinde valent, sed quaedam imperant, aliae parent, et tamen corpus tantum paret: Ita Principem summam Reipublicae partem plurimum sapere, et ab omnibus crassis affectibus alienissimum esse oportet. Ad hunc, proxime accedent magistratus, qui partim parent, partim imperant: parent Principi, imperant plebi." Similarly *LB* IV, 577: "Ut in homine quod praestantius est imperat, nimirum, animus, rursum in animo quae pars est optima, ea praesidet, nempe, ratio. . . . Ita quisquis in Republica tamquam in magno corpore imperandi partes occupavit, eum oportet bonitate, sapientia, vigilantiaque caeteros anteire." Cf. also *LB* V, 14.

112. I cannot agree with Born, who thinks that Erasmus "ardently supported Plato's doctrine of the philosopher-king, yet he could not adopt his scheme for the rule of an aristocracy" (*op. cit.*, p. 98). Erasmus indeed did not adopt, but he tried to adapt, this scheme to his Christian

humanism and to contemporary conditions, as he adapted the philosopher-king; and he was strongly in favor of nobility and civic patriarchate.

113. *LB* V, 13: "Quare necesse est, ut plus in ea valeat, qui plus sapit, pareat, qui minus."

114. *LB* V, 48: "Hoc Principatum esse puta, non opibus praecedere, sed quam plurimum omnibus prodesse"; and *LB* II, 108: ". . . hinc maximam reipublicae pestem nasci, quod ad gerendos magistratus adsciscuntur, non qui prudentia, rerum usu, vitae integritate, plurimum prodesse reipublicae possint, sed qui maxima pecuniae summa licitentur. . . ."

115. *LB* V, 13: "Qui vero Optimates sunt, aut natu majores, audiendi sunt illi quidem in consultationibus, at ita si statuendi arbitrium penes unum maneat Regem, quem admoneri quidem oportet nonnumquam[,] cogi vero aut praeire non convenit."

116. F. Geldner, *op. cit.*, p. 88: "Erasmus ist in der Theorie Demokrat, Aristokrat aus Neigung, und der Wirklichkeit gegenüber Monarchist."

117. It has been criticized by Mesnard (*op. cit.*, p. 127), who does not find in Erasmus' work "aucune thèse réellement démocratique," and who argues that "c'est à l'intérieur de la notion de royauté que se développe toute la politique érasmienne." He summarizes his interpretation in the clause: "Érasme, théoricien et censeur de la monarchie." Similarly, Phillips, *op. cit.*, p. 148.

118. Cf. Phillips, *op. cit.*, p. 148: ". . . all his respect goes to an aristocracy of education and intellect, all his pity to the common people. He does not credit the people with the wisdom to govern themselves."

## CHAPTER III

1. The reprint of Ralph Robynson's first English translation of *Utopia* (London, 1551) in Everyman's Library (London, 1935) will be cited in this chapter. This is the most readily available text; *Utopia* has become a kind of English classic in its sixteenth-century style. It has been compared for accuracy with the critical edition of the Latin text by Marie Delcourt: *L'Utopie* (Paris, 1936); some passages are reproduced from that edition. Her text is based on the three earliest editions: Louvain, 1516; Paris, 1517; and Basel, 1518. The Basel text, published by Froben and decorated with Holbein's title-page, was edited by Erasmus and probably incorporates More's corrections (cf. Delcourt, *op. cit.*, p. 25).

2. The best modern biography is *Thomas More* by R. W. Chambers (London, 1935).

3. Cf. the account of More's life given by Erasmus in his letter to Ulrich von Hutten (Allen, *Op. Ep.* IV, letter 999, pp. 12–23, dated Antwerp, 23 July, 1519; trans. F. M. Nichols in *The Epistles of Erasmus* [London, 1918], III, letter 585*b*, pp. 387–403). Marie Delcourt, in "Recherches sur Thomas More: La tradition continentale et la tradition anglaise," *Humanisme et Renaissance*, III (1936), 22–42, draws attention to the fact that the period from 1510 to 1520 in More's life has generally been slighted by his English biographers—both by sixteenth-century

authors and modern scholars, including Chambers. She argues, and I agree, that More the humanist, "frère d'armes d'Erasme," Latin author, and reformer—the More of that period—has been overshadowed by More the English author, religious controversialist, and traditionalist of the later period. (Thus, More's son-in-law Roper, in his biography, does not even mention the *Utopia*.) She sees an "étroite parenté" between the political ideals of More in *Utopia* and those of Erasmus in the *Institutio*. The recent critical edition of *The Correspondence of Sir Thomas More* by E. F. Rogers (Princeton, 1947) has done much to redress the balance and provides a valuable instrument for the study of More the humanist. D. Nisard had already pointed to the importance of More's friendship with Erasmus during this period of literary creativity. He also pointed to the later change in More's attitude and interests. (*Études sur la Renaissance: Érasme, Thomas Morus, Melanchthon* [Paris, 1855], pp. 185–86.)

4. Cf. Karl Kautsky, *Thomas More und seine Utopie* (2d ed.; Stuttgart, 1907), for an interpretation from a Marxian point of view. Kautsky argues that More's communism is the result of, and reaction to, the rise of capitalism (p. 317). Russell Ames, in *Citizen Thomas More and His Utopia* (Princeton, 1949), follows Kautsky in accepting the economic interpretation of history, but argues that the materialistic dialectic is at a different, earlier stage and sees *Utopia* as "a product of capitalism's attack on feudalism, a part of middle-class and humanist criticism of a decaying social order" (p. 6). I do not agree with either thesis.

5. Most interpreters of *Utopia*, including the socialist ones, seem to agree with this view. Thus, Kautsky (*op. cit.*, p. 304) says that socialism for More is a question of culture rather than one of the stomach; Ames, too, may have a similar interpretation in mind when he says that the central aspect of *Utopia*—with which essentially his book is not concerned—is its aim "to promote humanistic, Erasmian social reform" (*op. cit.*, p. 14). Cf. *Utopia*, p. 81: While the Utopians are capable and willing to do much physical labor, they keep it within the limits of necessity; "but in the exercise and studie of the mind they be never wery."

6. Quoted from *Utopia*, translated into English by G. C. Richards (Oxford, 1923), p. 132. The Latin text is to be found in the Basel, 1518, edition of *Utopia*, following the text; it is reproduced in Rogers, *Correspondence*, letter 27, pp. 81–84. Busleyden appears to have written this letter at Erasmus' request. Cf. Rogers, *loc. cit.*, and Allen, *Op. Ep.* II, letter 384, p. 375.

7. The question arises mainly from the fact that, in *Utopia*, it is the traveler Hythlodaye who describes the Utopian economic system approvingly, whereas More describes himself as asking a number of skeptical questions about it. Kautsky evidently thinks Hythlodaye represents More's own views; Ames also regards Hythlodaye as More's mouthpiece, and sees in "More's brief disagreements . . . an interlocutory device . . . for the purpose of technical 'legal' self-protection" (p. 37). W. E. Campbell, in *Erasmus, Tyndale and More* (London, 1949), pp. 92–93, takes the opposite view: he thinks More's objections to Hythlo-

daye in the dialogue represent the author's actual views, i.e., that he is in favor of private property and of social distinctions based on economic inequality. Campbell had argued along the same lines in *More's Utopia and His Social Teaching* (London, 1930), p. 47. H. W. Donner, in *Introduction to Utopia* (London, 1945), pp. 70–71, also argues that More remains skeptical about the communistic scheme presented by Hythlodaye, and does not accept it. Generally, writers who give a socialist interpretation of *Utopia* take the first attitude; those inclining to a Catholic interpretation take the second. In his "Thomas More and Communism," *PMLA*, LXIV (1949), 558, note 45, Edward L. Surtz, S.J., suggests an interesting explanation: If he "regards communism abstractly or academically . . . , More favors communism. If he looks at it as a practical statesman who knows what is in man . . . , he defends private property. . . . Hythloday represents More's ideal views; he himself voices his practical judgments in his own person." In any case, More is honored by Soviet Russia as a precursor of Marx and by the Catholic church as a saint.

8. *Utopia* was not published in England during More's lifetime, and the first English translation appeared sixteen years after his death. In the introduction to her Latin edition of the work (*L'Utopie*, p. 14), Marie Delcourt claims that "Henry VIII ... paraît avoir totalement ignoré l'Utopie"; More presumably did not urge the king to acquaint himself with its dangerously revolutionary doctrines.

9. A useful, brief compilation of the dates and events of More's life is appended by P. E. Hallett to his translation of the life of Thomas More from Thomas Stapleton's *Tres Thomae* (Douai, 1588), *The Life and Illustrious Martyrdom of Sir Thomas More* (London, 1928), pp. 229–32. While More, in contrast to a country squire like Elyot, was essentially a citizen of London, he did have some connections with local county government: in 1514, he was reappointed justice of the peace for Hampshire (Ames, *op. cit.*, p. 46); in 1532, when he was chancellor, he is found on fifteen commissions of the peace (*ibid.*, p. 63). As he rose in the royal service, he received the grants of several manors in Kent and Oxfordshire in 1522 and 1525 (for details, *ibid.*, pp. 58–60 and Appendix F), which he gradually lost again after resigning the chancellorship on May 16, 1532. The acquisition of these properties must have served partly to identify his interests with those of the landed gentry. Besides, More obviously was handsomely rewarded for his services by these grants as well as fees and pension payments, and certainly did not follow Utopian principles in this respect. William Roper, *The Lyfe of Sir Thomas Moore, knighte*, ed. E. V. Hitchcock (London, 1935), pp. 52–55; N. Harpsfield, *The Life and death of Sᵣ Thomas Moore, knight* . . . , ed. E. V. Hitchcock (London, 1932), p. 109; Stapleton, *op. cit.*, pp. 88–89; and some modern interpreters emphasize More's poverty. They are, however, mainly concerned with the state of affairs after, not before, his resignation, when, as Ames notes, More again lost his acquisitions. The manor of South, Kent, had belonged to the Duke of Buckingham; More accepted it after his attainder and execution (Ames, *op. cit.*, p. 58), described by Chambers (*op. cit.*, p. 191) as judicial murder.

10. N. Harpsfield, *op. cit.*, p. 22, says that at this time "the king was in hande with Cardinall Woolsey, then Lorde Chauncellour, to winne him and to procure him to his graces service." Harpsfield claims that at that time More refused a pension, but Ames, *op. cit.*, p. 52, points out that More seems to have become definitely committed to the Crown in 1516, because in the *Calendar of Letters and Papers of the Reign of Henry VIII*, ed. J. S. Brewer and J. Gairdner (London, 1862–1910), II, 875, under the heading of "New fees and annuities," there appears the entry: "Th. More, councillor, for life, 100 *l.*" This entry refers to *payments* made in 1516. See *ibid.*, p. 1317, where in June, 1518, this sum is provided again, but also *ibid.*, p. 1363, where the Venetian ambassador describes More as "newly made counsellor" in September, 1518. J. H. Hexter, *More's Utopia, the Biography of an Idea* (Princeton, 1952), pp. 107–9, quotes the letter More wrote to Erasmus in 1516 in which he stated that he declined the pension. Hexter concludes that "More held back for fully two years before he made his final commitment," i.e., until 1518. I agree with Ames that More probably entered royal service in 1516 after much hesitation, and consider the listing of the pension in 1516 a strong point in support of this view, despite the letter to Erasmus —More may have changed his mind—and the ambassador's statement.

11. Cf. Erasmus' letter to Hutten, in Nichols, *op. cit.*, III, 398; Hexter, *op. cit.*, pp. 15–27, provides a cogent analysis of the stages in the composition of *Utopia* which qualifies Erasmus' brief statement on this subject.

12. Cf. Harpsfield, *op. cit.*, p. 20: he was sent "at the sute and instance of the englishe merchauntes, and by the kinges consent." Cf. also Roper, *op. cit.*, p. 9.

13. *Utopia*, p. 13.

14. *Ibid.*, p. 15.

15. Cf. Chambers, *op. cit.*, p. 156, where an identification of Erasmus' and Hythlodaye's attitudes with regard to this question is implied. Hexter, on the other hand (*op. cit.*, pp. 113–14), tries to identify Hythlodaye's argument with the views supposedly held by More in 1516. This latter interpretation does not seem very plausible to me.

16. *Utopia*, p. 34: "Plato judgeth that weale publiques shall by this meanes atteyne perfecte felicitie, eyther if philosophers be kynges, or elles if kynges geve themselves to the studie of philosophie. . . ."

17. *Loc. cit.* More says to Hythlodaye: "There is nothynge more apperteining to youre dewty, that is to saye, to the dewtie of a good man," than to enter a prince's service as adviser.

18. *Loc. cit.*

19. *Utopia*, p. 35.

20. *Loc. cit.*

21. Unless kings are brought up to be philosophers, "they woulde never thoroughlye allowe the counsell of Philosophers, beynge themselves before even from their tender age infected, and corrupt with perverse, and evill opinions" (*Utopia*, pp. 34–35).

22. *Ibid.*, p. 42.

23. *Ibid.,* p. 43. Hythlodaye adds that a philosopher in that position is worse than a spy and almost as bad as a traitor.

24. *Ibid.,* p. 41.

25. *Loc. cit.*

26. *Ibid.,* p. 42. More argues that it is useless to attempt to re-educate the prince. The adviser must be crafty, subtle, and witty if he is to succeed in achieving even the limited objectives he describes. Hythlodaye's "absolute" position seems hopeless to him, "for it is not possible for al thinges to be well, onles all men were good" (*loc. cit.*). It is precisely at this point that Hythlodaye turns to the description of Utopia, where the condition which More thinks can hardly exist at all is achieved because the Utopians are all good men and philosophers.

27. Roper, *op. cit.,* pp. 56–57.

28. Harpsfield, *op. cit.,* pp. 147–48. It does not seem to occur to Harpsfield that by this last remark he destroys his own argument: More, who Harpsfield thought gave good advice, was not saved from utter ruin and destruction any more by this course of action than Cromwell, who gave "bad" advice!

29. More resigned the chancellorship on May 16, 1532, for reasons of ill-health. Almost two years later, on April 17, 1534, he was sent to the Tower after refusing to swear to the Act of Succession, which involved the repudiation of papal supremacy. (Cf. Chambers, *op. cit.,* p. 304; A. F. Pollard, *Henry VIII* [London, 1902], pp. 220 ff.; and the very detailed discussion in G. Constant, *The Reformation in England* [London, 1934], I, 129, 216, 241–49.)

30. On July 6, 1535, after being convicted of treason on apparently perjured testimony to the effect that he had denied that Parliament had the right to make Henry the Supreme Head of the Church in England (Chambers, *op. cit.,* pp. 337–39).

31. Cf. the following statement made by Hythlodaye: "Yf you had bene with me in Utopia and had presentelye sene theire fasshions and lawes, as I dyd, whyche lived there v. years and moore, and wolde never have commen thence, but onlye to make that newe lande knowen here: Then doubtles you wolde graunt, that you never sawe people wel ordered, but onlye there" (*Utopia,* p. 45).

32. *Ibid.,* p. 114.

33. *Ibid.,* p. 43.

34. *Ibid.,* p. 34. He approves of the Platonic notion of the philosopher-king but turns against More's argument in favor of the philosophical adviser to an unphilosophical king.

35. Thus *ibid.,* p. 45: "Me thinketh that men shal never there live wealthelye, where all thinges be commen"; and p. 114, where he argues that "all nobilitie, magnificence, wourshippe, honour, and majestie, the true ornamentes and honoures . . . of a common wealth" would be destroyed under such a system.

36. *Ibid.,* p. 114.

37. Marie Delcourt does not think that Henry VIII ever read More's criticism of his social policy. Cf. "Le pouvoir du roi dans l'Utopie," *Mélanges Abel Lefranc* (Paris, 1936), p. 109.

38. See the remark with which More concludes *Utopia* (p. 115): "Many thinges be in the Utopian weale publique, which in our cities [civitatibus] I maye rather wishe for, then hope after." Similarly, Hythlodaye doubts whether Europeans, like Utopians, are ready to adopt good institutions found in other lands (*ibid.*, p. 46).

39. "They beleve that by mans reason [no system of virtues and pleasures] can be found trewer than [theirs], onles any godlyer be inspired into man from heven" (*ibid.*, p. 80). There is such similarity between the views of the Utopians and the precepts of Christ that Hythlodaye has persuaded a number of them to embrace the Christian faith. Only the presence of a priest who can administer the sacraments is still needed to make Christians of them (*ibid.*, pp. 100–101).

40. *Ibid.*, p. 15. However, in his letter to Peter Giles, More admits that they forgot to ask Hythlodaye "in what part of the newe world Utopia is situate . . . in what sea that ylande standeth . . ." (*ibid.*, p. 9).

41. A. E. Morgan, *Nowhere Was Somewhere* (Chapel Hill, 1946), p. 34. H. S. Jevons had pointed out some similarities between More's account and the practices of the Incas some years before. Cf. his "Contemporary Models of Sir Thomas More. Utopia and the Socialized Inca Empire," in *Times Literary Supplement*, November 2, 1935, p. 692. Harpsfield (*op. cit.*, pp. 102–3) says that More has placed Utopia in one "of the newe founde landes," and claims that many people thought it really existed.

42. Cf. Morgan's Appendix "Concerning Voyages to South America before and Shortly after Columbus, and Trips from the Atlantic Coast to Peru before Pizarro." Both Morgan and Jevons find considerable agreement in the incidental details of the habits and dress of the Incas and the Utopians, apart from the more important similarities in social and economic matters. One difference not stressed by Morgan is the fact that the Inca empire was ruled by an autocratic government, whereas in Utopia all offices are elective. Chambers (*op. cit.*, p. 143) does not think that More used the Inca empire as a pattern.

43. Donner, *op. cit.*, pp. 27–28. Cf. also J. H. Lupton, *Utopia* (Oxford, 1895), p. xxxviii, who, like Donner, thinks that More used the account of Vespucci's travels in Martin Waldseemüller's *Cosmographiae introductio . . . Insuper quattuor Americi Vespucij nauigationes* (St. Dié, 1507). The first decade of Pietro Martire d'Anghiera's *De Orbe Novo* had been published in his *Opera. Legatio babilonica. Occeanea decas. Poemata* (Hispali [Sevilla], 1511). English trans. F. A. MacNutt (New York, 1912): cf. the description of the common ownership of land and the lack of private property, "that source of all evils" (p. 103). There are a number of similarities between the descriptions in this first decade and *Utopia*, such as the similarity of religious attitudes.

44. Donner, *op. cit.*, p. 29. Cf. also W. H. Fyfe, "Tacitus' Germania and More's Utopia," *Proceedings and Transactions of the Royal Society of Canada*, XXX (1936), Sec. II, 57–59, who notes a strong resemblance in style, subject matter, and details between *Utopia*, Book II, and *Germania*.

45. Donner, *op. cit.*, p. 28.

46. *Utopia*, p. 15.

47. *Ibid.*, p. 42.

48. *Ibid.*, p. 119: "A Meter of IIII. Verses in the Utopian Tongue." These verses first appear in what is purported to be the Utopian language, then in their "rudely englished" form. In the third edition—*De optimo reip. statv deqve noua insula Vtopia libellus uere aureus . . . Thomae Mori . . .* (Basel, 1518)—the poem appears on p. 13 in "Utopian" characters, followed by the Latin. The relevant lines are:

> "Una ego terrarum omnium absque philosophia
> Civitatem philosophicam expressi mortalibus."

49. *Utopia* (London, 1935), p. 119. This "hexastichon" is the first poem in the 1518 edition, and appears there on p. 11. The Latin, which follows in full, is much more concise than the English translation:

> "Utopia priscis dicta, ob infrequentiam,
> Nunc civitatis aemula Platonicae,
> Fortasse victrix, (nam quod illa literis
> Deliniavit, hoc ego une praestiti,
> Viris et opibus, optimisque legibus)
> Eutopia merito sum vocanda nomine."

50. Cf. Machiavelli, *The Prince and Other Works*, trans. Allan H. Gilbert (New York, 1946), p. 141, chap. xv: "I think it more effective to go back to the practical truth of the subject than to depend on my fancies about it. And many have imagined republics and principalities that never have been seen or known to exist in reality."

51. *Utopia*, pp. 39–40. (These are Hythlodaye's words.)

52. Chambers, *op. cit.*, p. 132.

53. "The History of King Richard the Thirde," in *The Workes* (London, 1557), pp. 35–71 (reproduced in *The English Works*, ed. W. E. Campbell [London, 1931], Vol. I); and "Historia Richardi Regis . . . Tertii," in *Latina Opera* (Louvain, 1565), ff. 44ᵛ–56ᵛ.

54. Cf. H. A. Glunz, *Shakespeare und Morus* (Bochum-Langendreer, 1938), p. 24. It was begun in 1513/14 and finished in 1516/17. Glunz carefully discusses both the English and the Latin versions of Richard III, and the relationship of their political ethic to that of *Utopia*.

55. Chambers, *op. cit.*, p. 117.

56. Glunz, *op. cit.*, p. 26, contrasts Richard III with King Utopus of the *Utopia*, and carefully analyzes the juxtaposition of Richard and Edward. More's description of the two kings leaves no doubt as to their characters: Edward is "of hearte couragious, politique in counsaile, in adversitie nothynge abashed, in prosperitie, rather ioyfull then prowde, in peace iuste and mercifull, in warre, sharpe and fyerce . . ." (*op. cit.*, p. 35), whereas Richard is a real villain, "ill fetured of limmes, croke backed . . . malicious, wrathfull, envious"; he is "a deepe dissimuler . . . arrogant of heart . . . dispitious and cruell" (*ibid.*, p. 37). Later, he describes the bad sleep of the tyrant (*ibid.*, p. 69).

57. *Epigrammata* (Basel, 1518; published together with *Utopia* in the same volume). Typical, "De bono rege et populo" (p. 214):

"Totum est unus homo regnum, idque cohaeret amore.
Rex caput est, populus caetera membra facit."

. . . . . . . . . . . . . . .

or "De Principe bono et malo" (p. 215):

"Quid bonus est princeps [?] canis est custos gregis inde
Qui fugat ore lupos. quid malus? ipse lupus."

. . . . . . . . . . . . . . .

Other interesting titles are (p. 214): "Bonum principem esse patrem non dominum"; "Quid inter tyrannum et principem." One epigram states that the king rules by popular consent (p. 217): "Populus consentiens regnum dat et aufert"; "Quis optimus reipub[licae] status" (pp. 247–48) debates the best form of government; "De cupiditate regnandi" (pp. 262–63) deals with the cupidity and badness of kings. There is a long *Declamatio* by More in response to Lucian's *Pro Tyrannicida* (in *Luciani . . . Dialogi . . .* [Paris, 1514], ff. 126–35) which shows his interest in the problem of tyrannicide. (He debates whether he who caused the tyrant to commit suicide instead of killing him should be rewarded.) See Glunz, *op. cit.*, pp. 41–42, and Chambers, *op. cit.*, p. 89, for discussions of the political and ethical content of the epigrams. "In his own epigrams, More expresses his passionate hatred of royal tyranny, in a way he never permitted to himself later, when he was a servant to the King" (Chambers, *loc. cit.*). For a critical text and translations, see L. Bradner and C. A. Lynch, *The Latin Epigrams of Thomas More* (Chicago, 1953).

58. The distinction, as made in practice, is vigorously attacked (*Utopia*, p. 90). Cf. Delcourt, "Le pouvoir du roi dans l'Utopie" (*op. cit.*, p. 102): "L'éthique politique de l'*Utopie* rejette précisément toute distinction entre la morale privée et la morale publique."

59. The discussion was started by Hermann Oncken's paper, "Die Utopia des Thomas Morus und das Machtproblem in der Staatslehre," *Sitzungsberichte der Heidelberger Akademie der Wissenschaften, Philosophisch-Historische Klasse* (1922), 2. Abhandlung. It was taken up by Oswald Bendemann, *Studie zur Staats- und Sozialauffassung des Thomas Morus* (Berlin, 1929); H. W. Donner, *op. cit.*; Gerhard Ritter, *Die Dämonie der Macht* (6th ed.; Munich, 1948); and others.

60. "Sir Thomas More and *Justum Bellum*," *Ethics*, LVI (1946), 303–8.

61. Robert P. Adams, "The Philosophic Unity of More's *Utopia*," *Studies in Philology*, XXXVIII (1941), 50.

62. *Ibid.*, pp. 58–60.

63. *Utopia*, pp. 61–62.

64. *Ibid.*, p. 55.

65. *Ibid.*, p. 60.

66. *Loc. cit.*

67. *Utopia*, p. 50. "Out of every one of these families or fermes commeth everye yeare into the citie XX. persones which have continewed II. yeres before in the countrye. In theire place so manye freshe be sent thether oute of the citie. . . ." The city magistrates send out labor contingents to help with the harvesting (*ibid.*, p. 51).

68. *Ibid.*, p. 56. If there is no need for this amount of work, "an open proclamation is made, that they shall bestowe fewer houres in worke" (*ibid.*, p. 59).

69. For journeys to other cities, permission of the higher authorities is needed; without it, a citizen is punished as a fugitive, and with bondage for a second offense. If he wants to walk in the fields near his own city, a man needs "the good wil of his father, and the consente of his wife"! (*ibid.*, p. 65).

70. ". . . there is nothinge within the houses that is private, or anie mans owne. And every tenth yeare they chaunge their houses by lot" (*ibid.*, p. 53).

71. Cf. Delcourt, "Le pouvoir du roi dans l'Utopie," *op. cit.*, p. 101: "Morus pense que le communisme peut se concevoir, non seulement pour une élite, comme c'est le cas dans la *République* de Platon, mais pour toute la masse d'un peuple."

72. *Utopia*, p. 49.

73. There are three groups of such "bondemen" or "servi" (*Utopia*, pp. 83–84): the largest group are men who have been condemned to death in other countries, and whom the Utopians obtain cheaply; the group most harshly treated consists of Utopians who misbehaved but should have known better, "being so godlye broughte up to vertue in soo excelente a common wealth"; the third group consists of poor foreign laborers who come of their own free will, work harder than Utopians, are treated well, and may depart when they please.

74. *Ibid.*, p. 91: "They do daylie practise and exercise themselves in the discipline of warre, and not onelie the men, but also the women upon certen appointed daies. . . ."

75. *Utopia*, pp. 95–96.

76. *Ibid.*, pp. 49, 53. Cf. Delcourt, "Le pouvoir du roi dans l'Utopie," p. 101.

77. Cf. Machiavelli, *Discourses on Livy*, Vol. I, chap. ix (in *The Prince and Other Works* [New York, 1496], pp. 273–75)—particularly the discussion of Romulus.

78. *Utopia*, p. 66.

79. R. P. Adams, *op. cit.*, p. 48.

80. *Utopia*, p. 50.

81. *Ibid.*, p. 60; cf. the Latin text in *L'Utopie*, ed. Delcourt, pp. 120–21, which has here been used to correct the English translation.

82. *Loc. cit.*

83. *Utopia*, p. 50.

84. *Ibid.*, p. 54.

85. *Ibid.*, p. 56: "The chiefe and almooste the onelye offyce of the Syphograuntes is, to see and take hede, that no manne sit idle: but that everye one applye hys owne craft with earnest diligence."

86. He lives there (*ibid.*, p. 62). "The Siphograunte and his wife sitte in the myddes of the high table, forasmuch as that is counted the honorablest place, and because from thence all the whole companie is in their sight" (*ibid.*, p. 63).

87. "The eldeste . . . rulethe the familye. The wyfes bee ministers to

theire husbandes, the children to theire parentes, and . . . the yonger to theire elders" (*ibid.*, p. 61). Children stand or serve at table (p. 63); husbands and parents have authority to punish (p. 86); magistrates are called "fathers" (p. 88). Note also the way in which discipline is enforced in church (p. 109).

88. *Ibid.*, p. 54.

89. In addition, there is an indeterminate number of children and bondmen.

90. For this and the following details, cf. *Utopia*, p. 54; Delcourt, "Le pouvoir du roi dans L'Utopie," p. 103, calls him a "préfet de la ville."

91. The Latin term is "protophylarchus."

92. "Comitia" is More's term (*L'Utopie*, ed. Delcourt, p. 111); this suggests the more popular character of that body, in contrast to the senate of the chief philarchs.

93. *Utopia*, p. 54. The restriction of political discussions to senate and council meetings clearly applies to the *princeps* and magistrates, and is designed to prevent them from conspiring. Chambers' contention (*op. cit.*, pp. 131, 137) that this regulation is directed against the people and intended to limit popular liberty cannot be maintained. The Latin text of the relevant passage (*L'Utopie*, p. 111) is clearer than the English: "Extra senatum aut comitia publica de rebus communibus inire consilia capitale habetur."

94. *Utopia*, p. 54.

95. *Ibid.*, p. 105.

96. *Ibid.*, p. 51.

97. *Ibid.*, p. 49.

98. *Ibid.*, p. 54.

99. *Ibid.*, p. 66.

100. *Ibid.*, p. 68.

101. *Ibid.*, p. 54.

102. Marie Delcourt investigates this problem in "Le pouvoir du roi dans l'Utopie," *op. cit.* She finds that there is "aucune précision sur la désignation du roi ..." (p. 103), thinks that More forgot to elaborate this point, and suggests that his election takes place in a manner similar to that of the local *princeps*.

103. In the introduction to his English-Latin edition of *Utopia* (Oxford, 1895), p. xlv, J. H. Lupton argued that there has been no king in Utopia since Utopus, and that More's use of the term "princeps" denotes only local mayors. Ames agrees with this view and thinks the island is a republican city league (*op. cit.*, pp. 18, 87).

104. The passage is in Allen, *Op Ep.* II, letter 499, pp. 412–14, translated in F. M. Nichols, *The Epistles of Erasmus* (London, 1904), II, letter 486, pp. 442–44. More's letter is dated by Allen *circa* 4 December, 1516, i.e., shortly after *Utopia* had been finished. More writes to Erasmus: "You have no idea how I jump for joy, how tall I have grown, how I hold up my head, when a vision comes before my eyes, that my Utopians have made me their perpetual sovereign [. . . perpetuum destinari mihi principatum ab Utopianis meis]. I seem already to be marching along, crowned with a diadem of wheat, conspicuous in a

Greyfriar's cloak, and carrying for a sceptre a few ears of corn, surrounded by a noble company of Amaurotians; and with this numerous attendance meeting the ambassadors and princes of other nations [. . . stipatus insigni Amaurotorum comitatu atque ita celebri pompa legatis atque principibus aliarum gentium occurrere]. . . . I will effectually provide that all the mortals who are subject to our clemency, shall show you that honour, which they owe to those whom they know to be dearest to their sovereign [. . . ut mortales omnes quos clementiae nostrae regit imperium, id honoris exhibeant vobis quem debent eis quos intelligunt ipsorum principi esse charissimos]." In this passage More seems to think of himself as the *princeps* of all the Utopians, over whom he has *imperium;* as a merely local mayor he would not receive foreign ambassadors and princes. One final possibility is vaguely suggested by this passage, however: perhaps the *princeps* of the capital city, Amaurote, is ex officio sovereign of the whole island!

105. *Utopia*, p. 105: "occultis . . . suffragiis."

106. *Loc. cit.* The meaning of More's text is not entirely clear as to the numbers of churches and priests; it seems logical to assume that he thinks of twelve churches or temples—three for each part of the city—and one cathedral, i.e., twelve ordinary priests and one pontifex for thirteen churches, plus the latter's seven *comites*, the total number adding up to twenty. Cf. *L'Utopie*, pp. 192–93.

107. *Utopia*, p. 105.

108. *Ibid.*, p. 106. This is followed by the typical statement indicating the purpose of this education: "Nor they be not more diligente to instructe them in learning, then in vertue and good maners" ("Nec prior literarum cura quam morum ac virtutis habetur").

109. Chambers, *op. cit.*, p. 137.

110. Cf. the epigrams referred to above, note 57.

111. *Utopia*, p. 58 (". . . in literatorum classem . . ."); and *ibid.*, p. 81 (". . . e numero scholasticorum . . .").

112. *Utopia*, p. 58 (". . . literatorum ordine . . ."). Cf. also *ibid.*, p. 56: "they . . . that be namelye chosen and appoynted to learninge" ("qui ad literas nominatim selecti sunt").

113. *Ibid.*, p. 58 ("Ex hoc literatorum ordine legati, sacerdotes, tranibori, ac ipse denique deligitur princeps . . .") (*L' Utopie*, p. 117).

114. *Loc. cit.*

115. *Loc. cit.* ("ad perdiscendas disciplinas perpetuam vacationem . . ."). The prince, bishop, chief philarchs, and ambassadors also get the best food! (*Utopia*, p. 62).

116. The small number of persons who do not perform physical labor is favorably contrasted with the large number of idle persons, such as gentlemen, and their unproductive retinues, in contemporary society (*Utopia*, pp. 57–58).

117. *Ibid.*, p. 91.

118. *Ibid.*, p. 71: "For though there be not many in every citie, which be exempte and discharged of all other laboures, and appointed only to learning . . . yet all in their childhode be instructe in learninge. And the better parte of the people, bothe men and women throughe oute all their

whole lyffe doo bestowe in learninge those spare houres, which we sayde they have vacante from bodelye laboures." Cf. also *ibid.*, p. 56: There are special lectures for the selected scholars in the morning; but these lectures are open to everyone who is interested.

119. See above, note 113. Hexter, *op. cit.*, p. 40, argues that "gradations of rank . . . were entirely based on election to office by popular vote," but later (*ibid.*, p. 57, note 2) modifies this view when he states that "the highest offices in Utopia go only to a specially educated intellectual élite."

120. *Ibid.*, p. 56.

121. Pierre Mesnard, *L'Essor de la philosophie politique au XVI<sup>e</sup> siècle* (Paris, 1936), p. 163.

122. *Utopia*, p. 58: "the people persuaded by the commendation of the priestes, and secrete election of the Siphograuntes. . . ."

123. *Ibid.*, p. 71.

124. *Ibid.*, p. 58: "Often it chaunceth that a handicraftes man ['mechanicus quispiam'] doth so earnestly bestowe his vacaunte and spare houres in learninge, and throughe diligence so profyteth therin, that he is taken from his handy occupation, and promoted to the company of the learned."

125. *Loc. cit.* ("ad opifices retruditur").

126. Cf. *Utopia*, pp. 81, 83, 100–101.

127. On toleration in Utopia, cf. *ibid.*, pp. 101–3. While there is wide toleration, there are some points of dogma which all Utopian citizens must believe in (pp. 102 ff.): "No man should conceave so vile and baase an opinion of the dignitie of mans nature, as to think that the soules do die and perishe with the bodye; or that the world runneth at al aventures governed by no divine providence. And therfore thei beleve that after this life vices be extreamelye punished and vertues bountifully rewarded." (This point closely resembles Peter Martyr's account [*De Orbe Novo*, trans. F. A. MacNutt, I, 102–3] of an old native who states his belief in the immortality of the soul and the two courses it can follow, much to the astonishment of Columbus, who did not think that a man who lived in a state of nature could have such knowledge. This account may well have suggested to More his interpretation of natural religion.) "Hym that is of a contrary opinion they counte not in the numbre of men . . . muche lesse in the numbre of their citizien. . . . Wherfore he that is thus minded is deprived of all honours, excluded from all offices . . . in the weale publique. . . . Howbeit they put him to no punishment. . . ."

128. *Utopia*, p. 46.

129. *Utopia*, p. 81. They learned Greek in less than three years; Hythlodaye discovers similarities between their language and Greek and Persian, and therefore thinks "that this nation tooke their beginninge of the Grekes" (*loc. cit.*), which partly explains their predisposition toward Greek language and literature.

130. *Utopia*, p. 71.

131. *Loc. cit.*

132. An interesting literary link with Florentine Platonism is the work

of his youth (according to Chambers, *op. cit.*, p. 94, written about 1505), "The life of John Picus Erle of Myrandula . . . with diuers epistles and other workes of . . . John Picus . . . Translated out of latin into Englishe by maister Thomas More," in *The Workes* (London, 1557), pp. 1–34.

133. *Utopia*, p. 71.

134. *Ibid.*, p. 81 ("Habent ex me . . . Platonis opera pleraque, Aristotelis plura") (*L'Utopie*, p. 156).

135. *Utopia*, p. 82.

136. *Luciani Erasmo interprete Dialogi . . . quaedam etiam a Thoma Moro latina facta . . .* (Paris, 1514).

137. *Utopia*, p. 82.

138. *Ibid.*, p. 81. Hythlodaye says that "in latin there was nothing that I thought they would greatly alow, besides historiens and Poetes."

139. Cf. J. F. Larkin, *Erasmus' De Ratione Studii: Its Relationship to Sixteenth Century English Literature* (abstract of thesis, Urbana, 1942), pp. 2, 10; and V. J. Flynn, "The Life and Works of William Lily, the Grammarian" (unpublished dissertation, University of Chicago, 1939), pp. 119 ff.

140. Cf. Ames, *op. cit.*, pp. 184–86; J. H. Lupton, *A Life of John Colet, D.D.* (London, 1887), pp. 280–81.

141. For his practical interests in education, in the study of grammar and rhetoric, see W. Nelson, "Thomas More, Grammarian and Orator," *PMLA,* LVIII (1943), 337–52. Nelson argues that More was a professional grammarian in his early years, and that his humanistic rather than his legal qualifications made his career.

142. Cf. Harpsfield, *op. cit.*, pp. 19, 77–78; Erasmus' letter to Budé, *Op. Ep.* IV, letter 1233, p. 577 (*circa* September, 1521); Stapleton, *op. cit.*, pp. 98–111; Foster Watson, *Vives and the Renascence Education of Women* (London, 1912), chap. v, pp. 175–94, which reproduces the account of education in More's house given by Cresacre More in *The Life and Death of Sir Thomas More* (1631); Chambers, *op. cit.*, pp. 178 ff.

143. In Rogers, *op. cit.*, letter 60, pp. 111–20, dated Abingdon, 29 March [1518]; Stapleton, *op. cit.*, pp. 41–42.

144. Rogers, *op. cit.*, letter 15, pp. 28–74, dated Bruges, 21 October [1515]. Like the letter to Oxford University, this letter is a defense of humanistic methods against scholastic attacks, of Greek from its detractors. Thus, the emendation of Latin texts with the aid of their Greek originals is vigorously defended and advocated (cf. pp. 57–61). It grew out of Erasmus' controversy with Dorp over the *Encomium Moriae* and the Greek New Testament.

145. Harpsfield, *op. cit.*, p. 93.

146. Rogers, *op cit.*, p. 249, note; cf. Stapleton, *op. cit.*, p. 44.

147. For an account of the group around More, see A. W. Reed, *Early Tudor Drama: Medwall, the Rastells, Heywood, and the More Circle* (London, 1926).

148. Letter cited in note 142 above.

149. Harpsfield, *op. cit.*, p. 19.

150. *Ibid.*, pp. 78–79; cf. Stapleton, *op. cit.*, pp. 112–19, for an extensive

account of Margaret's erudition and such details as her emendation of a passage in St. Cyprian (p. 113).

151. Harpsfield, *op. cit.*, p. 83.

152. *Ibid.*, p. 97.

153. Cf. Hyrde's "Dedicatory Letter or Introduction to Erasmus' Treatise on the Lord's Supper, as Translated by Margaret Roper" (London, 1524), in Watson, *op. cit.*, pp. 159–73, which is concerned with the education of women.

154. Stapleton, *op. cit.*, p. 99. Cf. also Rogers, *op. cit.*, p. 120; Chambers, *op. cit.*, p. 182.

155. Cf. Campbell, *op. cit.*, p. 60: "Another student [at Cambridge] for whom Erasmus entertained real regard was William Gunnell, sometime of Wolsey's household, and later a tutor in the family of Sir Thomas More." In September, 1513, in order to escape the plague, Erasmus went to his house at Landbeach, near Cambridge (*ibid.*, p. 61). Nichols, *op. cit.*, II, 614–18, Appendix I, discusses, and prints there and elsewhere, several letters which were presumably sent by Erasmus to Gunnell.

156. Stapleton, *op. cit.*

157. *Ibid.*, p. 102; Latin text in Rogers, *op. cit.*, p. 121. Rogers dates the letter May 22, [1518?]; his name is here spelled "Gonell."

158. *Utopia*, p. 106.

159. See note 143, above. Here quoted from translation in Stapleton, *op. cit.*, p. 41.

160. Hallett translates "liberales artes" in the last clause by "natural arts"; I have changed this to "liberal arts."

161. "Nam in philosophia, exceptis duntaxat his, quae Cicero reliquit et Seneca, nihil habent Latinorum scholae, nisi vel Graecum, vel quod e Graeca lingua traductum est" (Rogers, *op. cit.*, p. 117). At the beginning of *Utopia*, More attributes the same opinion to Hythlodaye, who knew that in philosophy "nihil quod alicuius momenti sit, praeter Senecae quaedam ac Ciceronis extare latine" (*L'Utopie*, p. 47). Richard Pace, in *De Fructu* (Basel, 1517), p. 102, expresses similar views on Greek and Roman philosophy; his opinion of the latter is even lower than More's.

162. *Ibid.*, p. 118.

163. In his letter to Hutten (*op. cit.*, p. 4) Erasmus indicates the closeness of their friendship and claims that it was More who made him write the *Praise of Folly*. Erasmus evinced great interest in the publication of *Utopia*, asked More to revise the text, and supervised Froben's publication of the 1518 edition (*L'Utopie*, ed. Delcourt, pp. 24–25).

164. *Utopia*, p. 101.

165. R. P. Adams, *op. cit.*, p. 65. Cf. *Utopia*, pp. 42, 100.

166. Cf. R. P. Adams, "Designs by More and Erasmus for a New Social Order," *Studies in Philology*, XLII (1945), 142: "In effect . . . More invited his readers to contemplate the . . . superb civilization which men could build when the powers of pure reason in everyday life were completed by a true Christian renaissance." In this article, Adams mainly investigates the Stoic origins of More's and Erasmus' thought. The Utopians, he thinks, are simultaneously Stoics and Epicureans (p. 144).

167. *Utopia*, pp. 72 and 102–3. See also note 127, above.

168. *Utopia*, p. 73. In Latin: "Vitam ergo iucundam, inquiunt, id est voluptatem, tanquam operationum omnium finem, ipsa nobis natura praescribit; ex cuius praescripto vivere virtutem definiunt" (*L'Utopie*, pp. 142–43).

169. *Utopia*, p. 72.

170. They believe that the immortal soul is "by the bountiful goodnes of God ordeined to felicitie" (*ibid.*, p. 72).

171. *Ibid.*, p. 73.

172. More lists the pleasures (*ibid.*, pp. 77–80). For a discussion of their criteria, see Adams, "The Philosophic Unity of More's Utopia," *op. cit.*, pp. 60–64. In the introduction to his translation of *Utopia*, p. xvii, G. C. Richards derives these pleasures from Plato's *Republic*, Book IX, and Cicero, *De Finibus*.

173. Adams, "The Philosophic Unity of More's Utopia," *op. cit.*, p. 60.

174. *Utopia*, p. 73.

175. *Ibid.*, p. 74.

176. *Ibid.*, p. 79.

177. *Loc. cit.*

178. *Utopia*, p. 77.

179. *Loc. cit.*

180. *Utopia*, pp. 79–80.

181. A man who holds false religious opinions is not permitted to disseminate them among the people (*Utopia*, p. 103).

182. Chambers is particularly concerned in *Thomas More*, in *The Saga and Myth of Sir Thomas More* (London, 1927), and in *The Place of St. Thomas More in English Literature and History* (London, 1937), to prove that More's views with regard to religion, and especially with regard to religious toleration, remained consistent throughout, and to defend him from the charges that his theoretical views on the latter subject, as expressed in *Utopia*, are very much at variance with his practical attitudes and activities as chancellor. Cf. *The Place of St. Thomas More . . .* , pp. 44–45. The argument about this point began in More's own days, with Tyndale's accusations against him. I do not think that Chambers (and others who plead the same cause) have proved their point, which needs further investigation.

183. In his review of Chambers' *Thomas More*, *American Historical Review*, XLI (1936), 528–30.

# CHAPTER IV

1. H. H. S. Croft, in Vol. I of his edition of *The boke named the Gouernour* (2 vols.; London, 1883)—hereafter referred to as *Governour* —gives the most comprehensive account of the "Life of Elyot," and much documentary material. Croft's edition of the *Governour* is based on the first edition (London, 1531).

2. *Governour*, I, 94. Cf. *infra*, p. 20.

3. James Wortham, in "Sir Thomas Elyot and the Translation of Prose," *Huntington Library Quarterly*, XI (1948), 219–40, shows a close correspondence between Elyot's and Erasmus' theories and methods of

translation. He sees this similarity in the translation of the sense rather than of words, in the striving for brevity, and in other points, and finds that Elyot's translation of Isocrates' *Doctrinal of Princes* (London, 1534) incorporates "almost all the principles stated by Erasmus and Elyot" (p. 239).

4. Thomas Stapleton, *The Life and Illustrious Martyrdom of Sir Thomas More*, trans. P. E. Hallett (London, 1928), p. 44. Croft's interpretation (*op. cit.*, I, lxii) that Elyot went to More's "school" is not borne out by the text of the passage.

5. Quoted by Croft, *op. cit.*, p. cxxx. Croft speaks of "Elyot's friendship and intimacy with Sir Thomas More" (p. cxxxi).

6. *Ibid.*, p. cxxx. As a bribe, Elyot offered Cromwell the first year's fruits from any lands that Elyot might obtain through his intercession.

7. *Ibid.*, pp. cxxxii–cxxxiii.

8. William Roper, *The Lyfe of Sir Thomas Moore, knighte*, ed. E. V. Hitchcock (London, 1935), pp. 103–4.

9. *Times Literary Supplement* (July 7, 1930), p. 592.

10. His "Historical Notes" appended to Nicholas Harpsfield, *The life and death of S$^r$ Thomas Moore, knight* . . . , ed. E. V. Hitchcock (London, 1932), pp. 353–55.

11. Harpsfield, *op. cit.*, pp. 205–6; Stapleton, *op. cit.*, p. 226.

12. *Op. cit.*, p. 104.

13. Even a book devoted to More's friends (E. M. G. Routh, *Sir Thomas More and His Friends* [London, 1934]) does not investigate this particular friendship.

14. Croft, *op. cit.*, p. lxix.

15. Leslie C. Warren, in "Humanistic Doctrines of the Prince from Petrarch to Sir Thomas Elyot: A Study of the Principal Analogues and Sources of *The boke named the Gouernour*" (unpublished dissertation [except for chap. v, published separately, Chicago, 1939], University of Chicago, 1937), p. 122, argues that "Elyot differed widely in political belief with More . . . , Erasmus, and Vives," and that "Elyot's political doctrines were in the Italian humanistic tradition of Petrarch, Palmieri, and Patrizi rather than in the tradition of . . . More, Vives, and Erasmus" (p. 124). Warren's argument is concerned with their attitudes toward monarchy and absolutism, and he contrasts Elyot, the "apologist for the Tudor ideal of secular absolutism" (p. 130), with the others, going so far as to state that "in his monarchical doctrines Elyot far exceeds even the Italian writers . . . and with . . . Erasmus, Vives, More, and Starkey, he had little in common. He welcomed despotism as the one safeguard against chaos" (p. 134). Warren seems to me to exaggerate the difference between Elyot and the others, and to overemphasize one aspect of Elyot's thought at the expense of another. Elyot's concern was both to stress the superiority of the monarchical principle and to show the aristocracy its proper education and standards. With respect to the latter, he was indebted to More and Erasmus as well as to the Italians, and his thought represents a further development of ideas current in More's circle.

16. Francesco Patrizi, *De Regno et Regis Institutione* (Paris, 1519). I have used the edition published in Paris in 1531.

17. Matteo Palmieri, *Libro della vita civile* (Florence, 1529).

18. *Il libro del cortegiano del conte Baldesar Castiglione* (Venice, 1528).

19. On Italian humanism and its influence, in so far as they concern us here, see: L. Einstein, *The Italian Renaissance in England* (New York, 1916); W. H. Woodward, *Vittorino da Feltre and Other Humanist Educators* (Cambridge, 1897) and *Studies in Education during the Age of the Renaissance* (Cambridge, 1906); G. Saitta, *L'educazione dell' umanesimo in Italia* (Venice, 1928); F. Battaglia, "F. Patrizi, politico senese del quattrocento," *Annuario dell' Università di Siena* (1933–34), 25–79, and *Enea Silvio Piccolomini e Francesco Patrizi: due politici senesi del quattrocento* (Florence, 1936); Francesco Sarri, "Il pensiero pedagogico ed economico del senese Francesco Patrizi," *Rinascita*, I (1938), 98–138; Piero Rebora, "Aspetti dell' umanesimo in Inghilterra," *Rinascita*, II, (1939), 366–414 (particularly pp. 390 ff.), and "Echi di Urbino nella cultura inglese," *Studi urbinati*, XII (1939), 3–25; Napoleone Orsini, *Studii sul rinascimento italiano in Inghilterra* (Florence, 1937); W. Schrinner, *Castiglione und die englische Renaissance* ([dissertation, Breslau] Berlin, 1939).

20. Cf. Warren, *op. cit.*, Born's introduction to his translation of Erasmus' *Education of the Christian Prince*, and T. F. Crane, *Italian Social Customs of the Sixteenth Century and Their Influence on the Literatures of Europe* (New Haven, 1920). Crane describes the Provençal origins of this pattern, its migration into Italy, and its diffusion and literary representation in the different countries of Europe.

21. Cf. Albert D. Menut, "Castiglione and the Nicomachean Ethics," *PMLA*, LVIII (1943), 308–21.

22. Cf. *Il Cortegiano del Conte Baldesar Castiglione*, ed. V. Cian (3d ed.; Florence, 1929), p. 417: The courtier should lead the prince "per la austera strade della virtú," he should "a poco a poco infondergli nell' animo la bontà, ed insegnargli la continenzia, la fortezza, la giustizia, la temperanzia." *Ibid.*, p. 432: If the prince is "aiutato dagli ammaestramenti e dalla educazione ed arte del Cortegiano, ... sarà giustissimo, continentissimo, temperatissimo, fortissimo e sapientissimo, pien di liberalità, magnificenzia, religione e clemenzia...." Cf. also *ibid.*, pp. 411–12.

23. Cf. B. H. Putnam, *Early Treatises on the Practice of the Justices of the Peace in the Fifteenth and Sixteenth Centuries* (Oxford, 1924).

24. *The Courtyer of Count Baldessar Castilio done into Englyshe by Thomas Hoby* was published in London in 1561; the original, in 1528.

25. *The Image of Governance, compiled of the actes and sentences notable, of the moste noble Emperour Alexander Seuerus, late translated out of Greeke into Englyshe* . . . (London, 1541 [1540]). (The title-page of this work gives 1541 as the date, but the colophon is dated 1540.) Croft (*op. cit.*, I, cxlvii) thinks the materials for this work were probably gathered, together with those for the *Governour*, in 1529/30, and finds that it is a compilation rather than the translation of one Greek work (p. cliv). It was reprinted in 1544, 1549, and 1556 (p. clxiv).

26. The first edition, published by Thomas Berthelet (London, 1533), is entitled *Of the Knowledeg* [!] *whiche maketh a wise man.* The second edition has the subtitle *A disputacion Platonike.* Copies of the original editions are very rare; I use the reprint of the 1533 edition, edited by E. J. Howard: *Of the Knowledge Which Maketh a Wise Man* (Oxford, Ohio: Anchor Press, 1946). This is not the first modern edition of the work. Kurt Schroeder had made it available in his *Platonismus in der englischen Renaissance vor und bei Thomas Eliot* (Berlin, 1920), where it appears as follows: *Of the knowledg which maketh a wise man. A disputacion Platonike.* Schroeder (*ibid.*, p. i) claimed that he was reproducing "buchstäblich getreu" the first edition in the British Museum, but his inclusion of the subtitle, and other variations in the title and text, would seem to indicate that the edition used by him differs slightly from the two editions described by Howard.

27. Thus, in November, 1527, Elyot was sheriff for Oxfordshire and Berkshire and also clerk of assize of the western circuit. (Croft, *op. cit.*, I, liv–lvi.) As late as 1545, the year before he died, Elyot was sheriff of Cambridgeshire and Huntingdonshire. Cf. *ibid.*, p. clxvii, and Elyot's remark in *A preservative agaynste deth* (London, 1545), p. 3 (of photostat reproduction in Huntington Library): ". . . for as muche as I am a sheriffe."

28. Croft suggests this, *op. cit.*, I, lxviii.

29. *Ibid.*, p. l.

30. Elyot's own words, quoted *ibid.*, p. lx.

31. In 1542, for the borough of Cambridge. This is not absolutely certain, however (*ibid.*, p. clxvi).

32. *Governour*, I, 25–26.

33. In the extensive introduction and footnotes to his edition of the *Governour*, Croft has assembled a great body of materials. Among more recent contributions, the following should be mentioned: Pearl Hogrefe, "Elyot and the boke called Cortegiano in Ytalion," *Modern Philology*, XXVII (1929–30), 303–11; Leslie C. Warren, *op. cit.*; and Joseph Schlotter, *Thomas Elyots "Governour" in seinem Verhältnis zu Francesco Patrizi* (dissertation, Freiburg i.B., 1938). References to other studies will be found below.

34. Schlotter, *ibid.*, p. 19.

35. *Ibid.*, p. 25.

36. *Ibid.*, p. 29. This dissertation, although well reasoned in parts, serves a very distinct political purpose and therefore gives a distorted picture of Elyot's thought. Schlotter tries to present the "governour" as something like a neo-Nordic *Führer.* That is obvious nonsense.

37. *Op. cit.*, p. 107. Schlotter (*op. cit.*, p. 22), on the other hand, claims that only one out of the twenty-seven chapters of Book I of the *Governour* can be at all compared with two out of thirteen chapters of Patrizi's Book I! Most of Warren's parallel passages, however, are not taken from Patrizi's first book, but rather from Books II and III. On the whole, Warren's claims with regard to Patrizi's influence are better substantiated than Schlotter's thesis that there was very little, if any, such influence.

38. Warren, *op. cit.*, pp. 108 n., 120 n.

39. *Ibid.*, p. 109.

40. Warren, *op. cit.*, pp. 110–11.

41. *Ibid.*, p. 115.

42. *Ibid.*, pp. 116–19. Warren refers to the treatise written for Frances-co di Carrara in 1373. See also in J. H. Whitfield, *Petrarch and the Renascence* (Oxford, 1943), the chapter: "The Successors of Petrarch: Humanist Education" (pp. 94–115).

43. Warren, *op. cit.*, pp. 120–21.

44. Cf. Hogrefe, *op. cit.*, and Warren's criticism of this article (*op. cit.*, pp. 112–13 n.). Warren thinks that Miss Hogrefe exaggerates Castiglione's influence, but is "convinced that Elyot read this book," a conviction which the present author shares.

45. Sir Henry Ellis, *Original Letters*, 3d series II (London, 1846), 177–78, letter from Bonner to Cromwell, written in 1530: "I hartely pray you at this tyme by this beyrer . . . to sende me . . . especially, if it please you, the boke called Cortigiano in Ytalion. . . ." This letter makes it apparent that Cromwell then owned the *Cortegiano* and had talked or written about it. Cf. also a passage in a letter from Elyot to Cromwell written in 1536, printed by Croft, in the *Governour*, I, cxxv: ". . . you whome I have allway accompted one of my chosen frendes for the similitude of our studies. . . . Sir, as ye knowe, I have ben ever desyrouse to reade many bookes specially concerning humanitie and morall philosophy. . . ." This passage makes it evident that both Cromwell and Elyot not only liked to read a certain type of books, but that they were also in the habit of discussing them. The conclusion is almost inevitable that they should have talked about the *Cortegiano*, which Cromwell had in his possession, and which concerns "humanitie and morall philosophy."

46. Paul Van Dyke, *Renascence Portraits* (New York, 1905), chap. iii (pp. 138–258) on Thomas Cromwell, and the Appendix, "Reginald Pole and Thomas Cromwell: An Examination of the *Apologia ad Carolum Quintum*" (pp. 377–418). Van Dyke attacks Pole's report, repeated by R. B. Merriman (*Life and Letters of Thomas Cromwell* [Oxford, 1902], I, 85 ff.), that Cromwell read Machiavelli at the beginning of his political career and used him as a guide to his future actions. Van Dyke (*op. cit.*, p. 394) thinks that the book on statecraft which Pole reports Cromwell offered to lend him in or after 1528 was the *Cortegiano*, not the *Principe*; he argues that the latter was not available in print before 1532, and that the conversation as reported by Pole was concerned with the attitude of the prudent counselor toward his prince, which is Castiglione's, not Machiavelli's, theme. If Cromwell discussed the *Cortegiano* with Pole, whom he saw only once in his life, he is certain to have discussed it with closer friends, such as Elyot. Warren (*op. cit.*, pp. 102–3) and Franklin L. Baumer (*The Early Tudor Theory of Kingship* [New Haven, 1940], 170 n.) expressly agree with Van Dyke's interpretation. It furnishes additional proof that Cromwell owned and discussed the *Cortegiano* and makes it very likely that Elyot read it. W. G. Zeeveld (*Foundations of Tudor Policy* [Cambridge, Mass., 1948], pp. 77, 158, 184–89) attacks Van

Dyke's thesis, but does not disprove it. He proves that Richard Morison, writing in Cromwell's employ, cited from Machiavelli's works (not *The Prince*) probably in 1535 and certainly in 1536, but he does not prove that Cromwell read *The Prince* at or before this time.

47. Warren (*op. cit.*, pp. 100 and 105–6) argues that the circumstances attendant upon the publication of the *Governour* point to the conclusion that Cromwell saw the "propaganda value" of Elyot's humanistic political views and induced him to publish them at this crucial time. Baumer is not specific on this point, but demonstrates the clever use which the government made of the printing press. (See particularly *op. cit.*, Appendix A, "Henry VIII's Propagandist Campaign," pp. 211–24.) It is probably not a mere coincidence, then, that Berthelet, the royal printer, should have published Elyot's *Governour* at this particular time. Yet Elyot's work cannot simply be explained as a piece of propaganda for the secular, absolute state, written at Cromwell's behest—as Warren's remarks seem to imply.

48. Warren, *op. cit.*, p. 112.

49. On this point cf. also Schrinner, *op. cit.*, pp. 40 ff.

50. *Governour*, I, 26: ". . . for as moche as . . . I intende to write of theyr education and vertue in maners, whiche they have in commune with princes, in as moche as therby they shall, as well by example as by authoritie, ordre well them, whiche by theyr capitall governour shall be to theyr rule committed, I may . . . name them governours. . . ."

51. *Image of Governance*, f. 104ᵛ (last page).

52. *Ibid.*, Preface: "And this present boke . . . shall be to all them which will reade it sincerely, a very true paterne, wherby they may shape all their procedinges."

53. *Governour*, I, 24.

54. *Ibid.*, I, 28.

55. *Loc. cit.*: ". . . noble mennes children . . . from the wombes of their mother, shal be made propise or apte to the governaunce of a publike weale." For his suggestions on the education of small children, Elyot is indebted to Plutarch, *De liberorum institutione*, and to Patrizi, *op. cit.* The *De liberorum institutione*, also known as *De educatione puerorum*—the latter being the more exact rendering of the Greek title—was translated by Elyot and published by Berthelet in London in 1535(?) under the title: *The education or bringinge up of children*. . . .

56. *Governour*, I, 29. Cf. Patrizi, *op. cit.*, II, title 6, p. 66: "Omnis prima educatio muliebris est. . . ."

57. *Governour*, I, 30.

58. *Ibid.*, I, 31. Cf. Patrizi, *op. cit.*, II, title 7, p. 67: "Maternae igitur curae erit, . . . ut nihil turpe aut indecorum audiat, cernat aut suspicari possit."

59. *Governour*, I, 31.

60. *Ibid.*, I, 32. This is "accordynge to the counsaile of Quintilian."

61. *Ibid.*, I, 35. Elyot seems to have been doubtful himself, because he immediately changes his tune and demands only clean and elegant English if the nurses do not meet his Latin standards.

62. *Ibid.*, I, 33: ". . . hit shal be no reproche to a noble man to instruct his owne children. . . ."

63. *Ibid.*, I, 34.

64. *Ibid.*, I, 36: He should have "gentilnes, mixte with gravitie. . . ." There follows a remark which, since it is made about a teacher, sounds rather strange: "And if he be also lerned, he is the more commendable"!

65. *Ibid.*, I, 38.

66. *Ibid.*, I, 43. Patrizi has an extensive chapter on music (*op. cit.*, II, title 15, pp. 83 ff.) but does not give this particular reason for learning it.

67. Warren (*op. cit.*, p. 112) thinks that the similarity of Elyot's and Castiglione's arguments in favor of the study of these arts makes it almost certain that Elyot read the *Cortegiano*. Patrizi also mentions them (for instance, *op. cit.*, pp. 81, 85), but his treatment bears little similarity to Elyot's—certainly much less than does Castiglione's.

68. *Governour*, I, 48.

69. *Loc. cit.*

70. Cf. Theodore Stenberg, *Sir Thomas Elyot's Defense of the Poets* ("University of Texas Studies in English," Vol. VI [1926]), pp. 121–45. Stenberg argues that "Elyot appears to be the first English writer who attempts to distinguish between the function of poetry and that of rhetoric" (p. 126); he "is the first English prose writer who attempts a defense of poetry" (p. 134). In contrast to the prevailing humanistic Ciceronianism which makes rhetoric the central discipline, "Elyot gives to poetry a basic place in his system of education" (p. 131) and recommends that the first seven years of systematic study be devoted to the classical poets.

71. *Governour*, I, 58–59. Croft points to Quintilian as the source of part of this quotation. Elyot shows a certain amount of originality in extolling Homer above Virgil. This judgment, which was contrary to the medieval evaluation, was not shared by all his humanistic contemporaries.

72. *Governour*, I, 76. We have already noted (chap. i, note 3) that the need for polished, humanistic Latin oratory in diplomatic intercourse had been one of the main incentives for the rise of humanistic studies in the fifteenth century. The knowledge of good rhetorical Latin style led to employment and advancement in the diplomatic service. The rather superficial veneer of humanism that was thus engendered seemed unsatisfactory to later humanists such as Elyot, and caused their attacks against this kind of formal Ciceronianism. Still, Elyot, who was an ambassador himself for a while, could certainly appreciate the need for fluent oratory, and demanded its mastery from his governours.

73. *Governour*, I, 84. Elyot mentions that the great Scipio always carried Xenophon's *Cyropaedia* with him on account of the practical benefits to be derived from its perusal.

74. *Ibid.*, I, 82–83.

75. On this point, cf. Emil Wolff, "England und die Antike," in *Britannica*, XIII (Hamburg, 1936), 253–318. Professor Wolff's remarks on Lord Cromer's *Ancient and Modern Imperialism* are particularly relevant.

76. *Governour*, I, 91, 141.

77. *Ibid.*, I, 92.

78. *Ibid.*, I, 93.

79. *Ibid.*, II, 294. Croft points out that Cicero called Plato "Deum philosophorum" (in *De Natura Deorum* ii. 12), and that Quintilian compared him to the Delphic oracle (*De Institutione Oratoria* x. 1). The humanists occasionally thought of the great pagans as being divine and placed them on the same level as the Christian saints. Thus Erasmus' "Sancte Socrate, ora pro nobis" (*LB* I, 683).

80. *Governour*, I, 94.

81. *Ibid.*, I, 95.

82. *Ibid.*, I, 94.

83. I believe that Elyot did not greatly change in his attitude. His main interests were secular, not religious. As far as the latter were concerned, he did not go over to the reformers; he stayed as close to Catholicism as he safely could while remaining a loyal subject of Henry VIII. This produced some ambiguity in his actions and attitudes. He approved of the reform of "abuses," aided in the abolition of the monasteries, and denounced the "Bishop of Rome." In 1535 he was appointed one of the commissioners for the visitation of religious houses, being rewarded in 1539 with former church lands (Warren, *op. cit.*, pp. 94–95). In 1536, when it was highly advisable to do so, he wrote to Cromwell: "the bostars and advauntars of the pompouse authoritie of the Busshop of Rome I never esteemyd" (quoted by Croft, *op. cit.*, I, cxxvi); it was in the same year that he besought his lordship "to lay apart the remembraunce of the amity betwene me and Sir Thomas More . . ." (see above). These statements prove mainly that Elyot was content to be a nationalist in matters ecclesiastical as well as secular, and that he preferred to keep his head on his shoulders rather than to share the fate of his great friend More whose friendship had become so dangerous. There are comparatively few references in his works to religion. In the *Governour*, II, 366, "our catholyke fayeth" is mentioned as agreeing with Plato on a certain point. More interesting on account of its date (1541), on p. 4 of his Introduction to *The Image of Governance* he declares: "In none of these warkes I dare undertake, a man shall finde any sentence against the commandments of god, the trewe catholyke faythe. . . ." It might be taken as an indication of Protestantism that in his last work, *A preservative agaynste deth* (London, 1545), he quotes the Bible more frequently than usual; yet he talks of mass as a matter of course (p. 3), thinks that the devil perverts holy scripture to keep men from fasting, praying, and almsgiving (pp. 9 ff.), attacks the theory of predestination as devilish (p. 27), and defends good works (p. 28). All these points strongly indicate Catholic convictions. When he came through Nürnberg as ambassador, in 1531, he walked out of a Protestant service (Croft, *op. cit.*, I, lxxix); five years later, he uttered the above-mentioned and other antipapal sentiments when he was under pressure to do so, but still seemed reluctant to hand over certain Catholic treatises as ordered: he minimized their number, claimed he virtually never read them, and declared they were scattered in "sondry houses of myne own" (Croft, *op. cit.*, I, cxxvii). His attitude toward religion, and his relative evaluation of *sacrae* and *humanae litterae*, is

probably honestly expressed by another statement in the same letter to Cromwell: "Sir, as ye knowe, I have ben ever desyrouse to reade many bookes specially concerning humanitie and morall philosophy, and therefore of such studies I have a competent numbre. But concerning holy scripture I have very fewe, for in questionistes I never delyted, unsavery gloses and commentes I ever abhorred . . ." (*ibid.*, I, cxxvi). (It would be interesting to know what books "concerning humanitie and morall philosophy" he had on his shelves!) Elyot's attitude toward the Catholic church, in the few respects in which it did change, changed for political and economic rather than for religious reasons. His is the typical compromise that a man of his position had to make if he wanted to avoid prison, death, or exile. Like the overwhelming majority of his countrymen, Elyot chose the compromise rather than exile or martyrdom.

84. *Governour*, I, 169.

85. *Ibid.*, I, 170.

86. Published in Paris in 1517.

87. For this particular injunction, Elyot gives a reason which anybody who has ever been on horseback can appreciate: he should learn to ride "whiles he is tender and the brawnes and sinewes of his thighes nat fully consolidate" (*Governour*, I, 185–86).

88. *Ibid.*, I, 181–82.

89. He devotes seven chapters (Vol. I, chaps. xix–xxv, pp. 203–69) to the subject of dancing.

90. *Ibid.*, I, 228. Socrates appears as Elyot's authority on this point, "the wysest of all the grekes . . . from whom all the sectes of philosophers, as from a fountaine, were derivied." Elyot compares dancing to the movement of the celestial bodies, and declares that according to Plato the former becomes more perfect as it becomes more similar to the latter (p. 218).

91. *Ibid.*, I, 241. T. S. Eliot closely follows his namesake's discourse on the subject in his poem "East Coker" (*Four Quartets* [New York, 1943], p. 12):

> "The association of man and woman
> In daunsinge, signifying matrimonie—
> A dignified and commodious sacrament.
> Two and two, necessarye coniunction,
> Holding eche other by the hand or the arm
> Whiche betokeneth concorde."

Lines 1–4 closely resemble *Governour*, I, 233–34; lines 5–6 are quoted verbatim from p. 235.

92. *Governour*, I, 305.

93. *Ibid.*, I, 141.

94. *Ibid.*, I, 144–45.

95. *Ibid.*, I, 161.

96. *Ibid.*, I, 141–44, 160.

97. *Ibid.*, I, 132.

98. *Ibid.*, I, 98. Elyot complains that gentlemen are much more interested in cooks and falconers than in teachers, and that they are very

stingy toward the latter. His remarks are illuminating about the contempt in which "clerks" and their learning were still held in Elyot's day. Elyot's censure sounds justified: not being a teacher himself, he did not have to plead his own cause, but was able to survey the situation objectively.

99. *Ibid.*, I, 99. For other examples of this attitude, see J. H. Hexter, "The Education of the Aristocracy in the Renaissance," *Journal of Modern History*, XXII (1950), 1–4, 9. Hexter rightly points out that this attitude underwent a radical change in the course of the sixteenth century.

100. *Ibid.*, I, 104.

101. *Ibid.*, I, 112.

102. *Ibid.*, I, 116.

103. *Ibid.*, I, 122. In support of this statement, Elyot invokes Plato.

104. *Ibid.*, I, 123.

105. Written about 1583, published in 1595. Cf. Stenberg, *op. cit.*, for details of Sidney's dependence on Elyot. William Webbe's *A Discourse of English Poetrie* (1586) is also very heavily indebted to Elyot, according to Stenberg. Croft, in his footnotes, mentions Sidney and Puttenham's *The Arte of English Poesie* (1589) as arguing in a vein similar to Elyot's.

106. *Governour*, I, 131.

107. *Ibid.*, I, 120–21.

108. *Ibid.*, I, 132.

109. *Ibid.*, I, 136.

110. *Ibid.*, I, 136–37.

111. *Ibid.*, I, 143–44.

112. *Ibid.*, I, 161.

113. Elyot's own words deserve to be quoted (*Governour*, I, 161–62): properly educated young men "have wonne such a treasure, wherby they shall alway be able to serve honourably theyr prince, and the publike weale of theyr countrary, principally if they conferre al their doctrines to the moste noble studie of morall philosophie, whiche teacheth both vertues, maners, and civile policie: wherby at the laste we shulde have in this realme sufficiencie of worshypfull lawyars, and also a publike weale equivalent to the grekes or Romanes."

114. As expressed, for instance, in Bembo's famous oration at the end of the *Cortegiano* (pp. 490–98). If he did use the *Cortegiano*, as seems most likely, Elyot was familiar with that passage. Elyot's interest in the Italian Neoplatonists is evinced by his translation of *The rules of a Christian lyfe made by Picus erle of Mirandula* (London, 1534, published together with *A . . . Sermon of Holy saynt Ciprian*) where he says that Pico's picture should be in all noble men's chambers, and his grace and virtues in their souls and manners.

115. Cf. note 26 above.

116. *Of the Knowledge*, pp. 93–94.

117. *Governour*, II, 364.

118. *Ibid.*, I, 28.

119. *Of the Knowledge*, pp. 189–90.

120. *Governour*, II, 366.

121. *Ibid.*, II, 122.

122. *Ibid.*, II, 121 ff. Most of Elyot's passages on the subject are translated from Cicero's *De Amicitia*, some from his *De Officiis* and from Aristotle's *Ethics*. (Cf. Croft's notes.) Concerning his friendship with More, see the beginning of this chapter. In the letter to Cromwell (cited in note 5, above) Elyot addresses Cromwell as follows: "you whome I have allway accompted one of my chosen frendes for the similitude of our studies, which undoubtidly is the moste perfeict fundacion of amitie" (Croft, *op. cit.*, p. cxxv).

123. *Governour*, II, 132–66 (i.e., Book II, chap. xii).

124. *Ibid.*, II, 133.

125. By F. Dannenberg, *Das Erbe Platons in England bis zur Bildung Lylys* (Berlin, 1932), pp. 212 ff.

126. *Image of Governance*, f. 86$^r$.

127. *Governour*, II, 184–85.

128. The same applies to purely practical knowledge, of which Elyot gives a very clear definition in *Of the Knowledge*, pp. 51–52: ". . . it is agreed by us bothe, that neyther the knowynge of good catell from bad, nor howe to plante well and to make a fayre orchard, ne the devisynge of fayre houses, and buyldinges, nor the increasinge of goodes or possessions, or the optayninge of great offices or dignities, or the sharpe witte and quickenes in raisoninge: is that knowlege, wherin is wisedome?" (The reply, of course, is negative.)

129. Elyot explains this in the *Governour*, I, 131, and II, 373.

130. *Ibid.*, I, 5.

131. *Of the Knowledge*, p. 80.

132. *Ibid.*, p. 98: ". . . durynge the tyme that hit is conserved by contemplacyon of the divine maiestie, hit is perfecte and makethe mannes soule lyke unto god."

133. *Ibid.*, pp. 99, 102.

134. Thus *Governour*, II, 378.

135. *Image of Governance*, f. 86$^r$.

136. Thus on the verso of the title-page of *The Image of Governance* (London, 1541 [1540]); on the same page in *The Bankette of Sapience* (London, 1542); and in *The Defence of good Women* (London, 1540). This motto, according to C. N. Elvin (*A Handbook of Mottoes* [London, 1860], p. 58), is the motto of the Veel rather than that of the Elyot family. The coat-of-arms is the Elyot coat quartered with a three-tower design which was thought by Croft (*Governour*, I, xlix) to indicate some connection with the ancient royal Portuguese family. According to J. W. Papworth and Alfred W. Morant ( . . . *Ordinary of British Armorials* [London, 1874]), this, like the motto, seems to belong to the Veel (Wyle, Vile, Vclley) family. Since part of this family, like Sir Thomas Elyot's ancestors (*Governour*, I, xxvii), came from Somersetshire and Devonshire, it seems likely that there was a connection between the two families which gave Sir Thomas Elyot the right to this particular coat-of-arms.

137. *Governour*, II, 369.

138. *Ibid.*, I, 5.

139. *Ibid.*, I, 4.

140. Act III, scene 1, particularly lines 141–59.

141. Act I, scene 3, lines 78–134. J. H. Hanford ("A Platonic Passage in *Troilus and Cressida*," *Studies in Philology*, XIII [1916], 100–109), shows its connection with the *Republic.*

142. D. T. Starnes, *Shakespeare and Elyot's "Governour"* ("University of Texas Studies in English," Vol. VII [1927]), pp. 112–35. Starnes shows Shakespeare's dependence convincingly.

143. J. E. Phillips, Jr., *The State in Shakespeare's Greek and Roman Plays* (New York, 1940). Apart from showing the influence of Elyot's thought, Phillips gives a valuable description of the type of political theory which Elyot represents.

144. *Governour*, I, 3–5. There are other similar passages scattered through Elyot's works, of which I quote only one: "Order in everye thinge is perceyved to be, whiche order lyke a streyghte lyne issueth oute of provydence, and passethe directely throughe al thynges that be created. And therin be degrees, wherin those thynges being sette, one hathe preemynence over a nother in goodnes" (*Of the Knowledge*, p. 103).

145. *Governour*, I, 11–12.

146. *Ibid.*, I, 15 ff.

147. Act I, scene 3, lines 81–110, 124–26.

148. *Governour*, I, 42–43.

149. *Ibid.*, I, 5–6.

150. *Ibid.*, I, 6.

151. *Loc. cit.*

152. *Governour*, I, 12: "The capitayne hym selfe laboureth nat for his sustinance, but all the other for hym."

153. I am here only referring to the *Utopia.*

154. *Governour*, II, 187. Many similar passages in the first six chapters of Book III (II, 186–246). Thus II, 214: "Justyce onely bereth the name of good, and like a capitayne or leader precedeth all vertues in every commendation."

155. *Ibid.*, II, 212; cf. also *Of the Knowledge*, pp. 69 ff.

156. *Ibid.*, II, 258: ". . . faithe is the fundation of Justyce, whiche is the chiefe constitutour and maker of a publike weale . . ." as well as its conservator. *Ibid.*, II, 226: Elyot declares that he translates the Latin *fides* as "faith," "credence," "trust," "fidelity," or "loyalty," and distinguishes between the meanings of these terms. (He occasionally confuses his terms, however, which makes his reasoning rather involved.)

157. *Ibid.*, II, 209.

158. *Ibid.*, II, 205: ". . . of no better claye is a gentilman made than a carter, and of libertie of wille as moche is gyven of god to the poore herdeman, as to the great and mighty emperour." And *ibid.*, II, 206: ". . . knowe thy selfe, that is to saye, knowe that thou arte verely a man compacte of soule and body, and in that all other men be equall unto the."

159. *Ibid.*, II, 212.

160. *Ibid.*, II, 210–11: ". . . howe farre out of reason shall we iudge them to be that wolde exterminate all superioritie, extincte all governaunce and lawes, and under the coloure of holy scripture, whiche they do violently wraste to their purpose, do endevour them selfes to bryng the life of man in to a confusion inevitable . . ." which will arise unless they can compel God to change men into angels.

161. *Ibid.*, II, 202–3.

162. See above.

163. *Governour*, I, 3.

164. Warren (*op. cit.*, p. 98) argues that Elyot and More were "poles apart" politically because More wanted a "commune weale" and Elyot a "publike weale." While More's *Utopia* is indeed a more democratic society than that envisaged by Elyot, Warren's sharp juxtaposition assumes that More is in complete agreement with the social structure described in *Utopia*, which seems unlikely, and it overlooks their basic agreement with regard to the functions of a humanistic aristocracy.

165. *Governour*, I, 2. The advocates of such an order "be thereto moved more by sensualite than by any good reason or inclination to humanite."

166. Warren, *op. cit.*, p. 107, thinks that in making this distinction Elyot follows Patrizi's differentiation between "populus" and "plebs."

167. Thus *ibid.*, I, 24. Cf. also Baumer, *op. cit.*, pp. 105, 205.

168. *Governour*, I, 25: ". . . it is expedient and also nedefull that under the capitall governour be sondry meane authorities, as it were aydyng hym in the distribution of iustice in sondry partes of a huge multitude."

169. P. 2 of the Preface.

170. *Governour*, I, 26–27. They should not be "inferiour to other in vertue," however, i.e., as between two equally good men, Elyot would choose the wealthier one.

171. *Ibid.*, I, 27.

172. Rich men "wyll nat be so desirous of lucre (wherof may be engendred corruption), as they whiche have very litle . . ." (*loc. cit.*). Elyot's argument can easily be criticized, but undoubtedly has a certain validity where no provision is made for the payment of civil servants.

173. *The Castell of Helth* (London, 1541), p. 1 of "Proheme." Similar to *Governour*, I, 27, and other passages.

174. *Image of Governance*, p. 2 of the Preface. (*Commodity* here means *wealth*.) Elyot made much of his supposed poverty when asking Cromwell to be rewarded for his services in 1536 (cf. Croft, *op cit.*, I, cxxxi), but did not mention in *The Image of Governance* which appeared in 1541 that meanwhile he had received one or two grants of manors. (Cf. Warren, *op. cit.*, p. 95, and S. B. Liljegren, *The Fall of the Monasteries* . . . [Lund, 1924], pp. 43, 51, where he appears as grantee in 1539 and 1540.) Even in 1536 he reported to Cromwell that his books were scattered "in sondry houses of myne own" and therefore not readily accessible (Croft, *op. cit.*, I, cxxvii); the statement about his "sondry houses" does not sound as if he had been suffering extreme penury! Elyot was not exactly impoverished, but, as he says in the *Image of Governance* (*loc.*

*cit.*), he might have been wealthier if he had "employed his study about the increase of his wealth" rather than in the writing of books, where "I sette the trees, but the printer eateth the fruites."

175. *Governour*, I, 27: ". . . where vertue is in a gentyll man, it is commenly mixte with more sufferance, more affabilitie, and myldenes, than . . . it is in a persone rural, or of very base linage." See the discussion of the ascendancy of "virtue" over "high birth" in the ensuing century in V. B. Heltzel, "Chesterfield and the Tradition of the Ideal Gentleman" (unpublished dissertation, University of Chicago, 1925), pp. 24–34.

176. Cardinal Pole, who tried to represent Cromwell as a complete "Machiavellian," undoubtedly went too far, for obvious polemical reasons. Cf. Van Dyke, *op. cit.*, Appendix, pp. 377–418, and note 46, above. Warren, *op. cit.*, p. 102, makes a good case for the assumption that Cromwell did not read *The Prince* before 1539.

177. Elyot thinks such social rise is due to good fortune (*Of the Knowledge*, p. 47).

178. *Governour*, I, 27: ". . . where the persone is worshypfull, his governaunce, though it be sharpe, is to the people more tollerable, and they therwith the lasse grutch."

179. *Loc. cit.*

180. The following passage is typical of this attitude: "And excepte excellent vertue and lernynge do inhabile a man of the base astate of the communaltie, to be thought of all men worthy to be so moche avaunced: els suche governours wolde be chosen out of that astate of men whiche be called worshipfull, if amonge them may be founden a sufficient nombre, ornate with vertue and wisedome, mete for suche purpose . . ." (*Governour*, I, 26). M. Campbell, in *The English Yeoman under Elizabeth and the Early Stuarts* (New Haven, 1942), pp. 33 ff., describes the rather fluid line of demarcation between yeomen and gentlemen at a later period, and (p. 49) speaks of the "rapidity with which members of the yeomanry could advance beyond the station to which they were born." If one investigated the same problem in Elyot's period one would probably arrive at similar conclusions.

181. Cf. *Of the Knowledge*, p. 47: Real wisdom is not in him who "findeth the menes to gather great sommes of money, offices, or greatte possessions with littel labour."

182. *Governour*, II, 4. As Croft points out, Elyot in his passage on this theme follows Erasmus (*Institutio Principis Christiani*) verbatim.

183. *Governour*, II, 6.

184. *Ibid.*, II, 1.

185. *Ibid.*, II, 6.

186. *Ibid.*, II, 12. Like the sun, it casts on the beholders "a pleasaunt and terrible reverence."

187. E.g., *Cortegiano*, pp. 63 ff.

188. *Governour*, II, 45.

189. *Ibid.*, II, 40.

190. *Ibid.*, II, 55–92. In the *Governour*, Elyot demands Roman *liberalitas* (II, 113): A man should give "accordyng to his substance, and where it is expedient . . . he ought to consider to whom he shulde gyve,

howe moche, and whan." In *A preservative agaynste deth,* his last and most Christian work, Elyot completely reverses his attitude and insists on *caritas:* "It is not the person to whome it is given that maketh the acte thankfull to God."

191. *Governour,* II, 262–63.

192. *Ibid.,* II, 272.

193. *Ibid.,* II, 443: ". . . the generall and universall astate of the publike weale wolde be preferred in consultation before any particular commoditie. . . ."

194. *Ibid.,* I, 27.

## CHAPTER V

1. J. M. Cowper (ed.), *England in the Reign of King Henry the Eighth: A Dialogue between Cardinal Pole and Thomas Lupset, Lecturer in Rhetoric at Oxford.* Part II (London, 1871). ("E.E.T.S., Extra Series," Vol. XII.)

2. S. J. Herrtage (ed.), *England in the Reign of King Henry the Eighth: Starkey's Life and Letters.* Part I (London, 1878). ("E.E.T.S., Extra Series," Vol. XXXII.)

3. Thus, J. W. Allen, *A History of Political Thought in the Sixteenth Century* (London, 1928), pp. 142–53; R. W. and A. J. Carlyle, *A History of Medieval Political Theory in the West* (London, 1936), VI, 259–63. Allen calls the *Dialogue* "by far the most remarkable piece of writing concerned with politics that was produced in England under Henry VIII, with the exception of More's *Utopia*" (Allen, *op. cit.,* p. 143).

4. E.g., F. L. Baumer, "Thomas Starkey and Marsilius of Padua," *Politica,* II (1936), 188–205, and *The Early Tudor Theory of Kingship* (New Haven, 1940); J. A. Gee, *The Life and Works of Thomas Lupset* (New Haven, 1928), pp. 147–56; W. G. Zeeveld, *Foundations of Tudor Policy* (Cambridge, Mass., 1948); W. Schenk, *Reginald Pole, Cardinal of England* (London, 1950), pp. 36–45.

5. K. M. Burton (ed.), *A Dialogue between Reginald Pole and Thomas Lupset* (London: Chatto & Windus, 1948). Miss Burton has changed the title given to the *Dialogue* by its first editor, Cowper, because Pole was not yet a cardinal when the work was completed (cf. her edition, p. 196); her text, which is based on the manuscript (*ibid.,* p. 19) and partly modernizes Starkey's spelling, is used here because in its original form (as printed by Cowper) the text presents an obstacle to easy reading. All citations of the *Dialogue* in this chapter will refer to Miss Burton's edition.

6. Cf. Burton, *op. cit.,* pp. 197–201. (Appendix B, "The Life of Thomas Starkey.")

7. Cf. Zeeveld, *op. cit.,* p. 128.

8. See description of this manuscript, *ibid.,* pp. 143–44, and Burton, *op. cit.,* pp. 195–96.

9. A number of letters are printed by Herrtage, *op. cit.;* the letters and works are discussed particularly by Zeeveld, *op. cit., passim.*

10. Cf. Herrtage, *op. cit.,* p. viii, note 4.

11. June 30, 1516, according to the *DNB.*

12. Gee, *op. cit.,* p. 147.

13. Herrtage, *op. cit.,* p. vii.

14. Herrtage, *op. cit.,* p. x, prints a letter from Starkey to Cromwell in which he outlines his qualifications and states: "Fyrst, here in oxforth a grete parte of my youthe I occupyd my selfe in the study of phylosophy, joynyng therto the knolege of both tongys bothe latyn & greke, and so aftur passyd over in to Italy, whereas I so delytyd in the contemplacyon of natural knowlege . . . that many tymys I was purposyd to have spend the rest of my lyfe holly therin . . . tyl at the last, movyd by chrystyan charyte, phylosophy set apart, I applyd my selfe to the redyng of holy scrypture. . . ." After studying "holy letturys certayn yerys" he turned to the civil law. Cetrainly this was a very comprehensive education, and it shows Starkey as a typical man of his age in his quest for universality.

15. This is assumed by Zeeveld, *op. cit.,* p. 57.

16. Pole had been at Magdalen, where he and Starkey must have been contemporaries (Schenk, *op. cit.,* p. 3). For his education and his relations with such humanists as Linacre, Latimer, and More, see *ibid.,* pp. 3–7. Pole had first gone to Padua on a visit in 1519, and he again went there in 1521 for his prolonged residence, with an annual allowance of £100 from the king (Zeeveld, *op. cit.,* pp. 40–41, and Schenk, *op. cit.,* p. 7).

17. Cf. the genealogical tables in Schenk, *op. cit.,* p. 172.

18. For a description of this circle, see Zeeveld, *op. cit.,* pp. 39–81 (chap. iii, "Padua, Paris, and the Divorce"); also Schenk, *op. cit.,* pp. 7–17; Gee, *op. cit.,* pp. 105–20 (chap. ix).

19. Cf. Zeeveld, *op. cit.,* pp. 67 ff., 75, 79 ff., 85 ff.

20. *Ibid.,* p. 91.

21. Herrtage, *op. cit.,* p. viii. He received the living of Great Mongeham, Kent, from which Thomas Lupset had resigned, on July 31, 1530. It is interesting that he should have succeeded his friend.

22. Starkey's letter to Cromwell, printed in Herrtage, *op. cit.,* p. x; cf. note 14, above.

23. Zeeveld, *op. cit.,* p. 90.

24. Herrtage, *op. cit.,* p. lxviii. Starkey tells Cromwell that he had always hoped he might "have some occasyon & tyme wherin I myght apply such lernyng as I attaynyd un to, at the last to some use & profyt of my cuntrey; thys hathe byn I testyfye god the end of my studys, thys hathe byn ever before my yees, and to thys now I loke un to wythe gretur desyre then ever I dyd hytherto to any other thyng in my lyfe" (*ibid.,* pp. lxvii–lxviii).

25. Discussed by Zeeveld, *op. cit.,* pp. 143–44, and by Burton, *op. cit.,* pp. 195–96.

26. Herrtage, *op. cit.,* pp. xiii–xvii, prints Starkey's letter of that date to Pole in which he states that he has entered "the kyngys servyce."

27. Herrtage, *op. cit.,* p. lxxiii, assumed that the *Dialogue* was not finished until June, 1538. Gee (*op. cit.,* p. 151) argues, however, that the *Dialogue* must have been finished before the manuscript of Pole's

*Pro Ecclesiasticae Unitatis Defensione* reached the king in June, 1536. Gee concludes that the *Dialogue* was probably finished before February 15, 1535, when Starkey reported his recent court appointment to Pole, and Zeeveld states that "we know" that this appointment "was a reward for the *Dialogue*," concluding that "Starkey must . . . have set to work on the *Dialogue* soon after his arrival in England in late December and must have concluded it before February 15" (*op. cit.*, p. 144, note 48). Miss Burton's view (*op. cit.*, p. 195) that the *Dialogue* was composed between 1533 and 1535 "and presented to Henry VIII after Starkey became his chaplain, early in 1535, but before June, 1536," is correct in that it places the completion of the work after February 15, 1535; but the earliest date by which it could have been completed is considerably later than that. (Starkey may have received his appointment on the strength of "What ys pollycy aftur the setece of Arystotyl" which he sent to Cromwell when applying to him for a position [Zeeveld, *op. cit.*, pp. 142–43].) Actually, the *Dialogue* was completed later, while Starkey was engaged in his correspondence with Pole on the king's behalf. (Cf. the letters printed by Herrtage, *op. cit.*, pp. xiii–xxxi.) Near the end of the *Dialogue* (p. 187), Starkey refers to Erasmus' "Book of the Preacher" as having come out "a late." He obviously means the *Ecclesiastes*. Now the first edition of that work, *Ecclesiastae libri IV siue de ratione concionandi*, came off the Froben press in Basel in August, 1535. The editors of Erasmus' letters (*Op. Ep.* XI, pp. 189–90, letter 3036) argue convincingly that the *Ecclesiastes* came off the press after August 24 and probably was ready by August 31. They find that "the rumor of the Preface reached England early in October"; Starkey cannot have read it before that date, and we may therefore date the completion of the *Dialogue* between October, 1535, and June, 1536, with a probability in favor of its completion in the last months of 1535.

28. Herrtage, *op. cit.*, p. lxxv.

29. Zeeveld believes that Starkey was quite ignorant of Pole's real attitude until his fateful book arrived (*op. cit.*, pp. 104–5, 160–63). Starkey almost certainly had a "clear record" in this matter since otherwise he could hardly have cleared himself of the suspicion of collusion with Pole which naturally fell on him. Nevertheless, one wonders what would have happened to him if he had not died when he did. Starkey died between August 25 (Herrtage, *op. cit.*, p. viii, note 4) and September 1, 1538 (Burton, *op. cit.*, p. 201), and it was at just this time that Henry began to wreak his terrible vengeance upon Pole by arresting and executing his relatives. The first arrest was that of Sir Geoffrey Pole, Reginald's younger brother, on August 29, 1538. (Schenk, *op. cit.*, p. 82.) It seems very doubtful whether Starkey, Pole's former friend, would have escaped the fate of Lord Montague, Pole's eldest brother, and of Lady Salisbury, his mother, whose chaplain he had been. They were beheaded, and others shared the same fate. (*Ibid.*, pp. 83–85.)

30. The book was sent from Venice on May 27, 1536, with a covering letter to the king. In the first sentence of this letter, Pole states that he was motivated "furst by Master Sterkeys letters, chapleyn to your grace," to write the book. (Herrtage, *op. cit.*, p. xxxi.)

31. For his activities during the last two years of his life, cf. Zeeveld, *op. cit.*, pp. 226–27, and Burton, *op. cit.*, p. 201.

32. After examining the views held by the Lupset of the *Dialogue*, Gee (*op. cit.*, p. 155) concludes that Starkey very probably did not misrepresent him. Not one of the views attributed to Lupset is "at variance with any thought Lupset expressed in his extant works," although it cannot be definitely stated "whether or not all of these opinions were held by him." With regard to Pole, Schenk (*op. cit.*, p. 36) states that "we cannot be quite certain that every one of Pole's alleged opinions was actually held by him. . . . In most cases, however, there seems to be no reason why Starkey should have distorted Pole's views. We can, at any rate, regard this work as evidence that questions of this kind were discussed in Pole's circle." It seems doubtful to me that Pole held all the views attributed to him, particularly those with regard to the reform of religious institutions (cf. Burton, *op. cit.*, p. 5, on this point), but on the whole these statements describe the situation accurately.

33. Gee, *op. cit.*, pp. 38–39.

34. *Ibid.*, pp. 43–51.

35. *Ibid.*, p. 153.

36. Herrtage, *op. cit.*, p. viii.

37. *Ibid.*, p. lxxiv.

38. *Ibid.*, p. lxxv.

39. *Ibid.*, pp. lxxiv–lxxv. The same order of investigation is also described, somewhat more briefly, in the *Dialogue* itself (Burton edition), pp. 39–40.

40. Cf. Burton, *op. cit.*, pp. 16–17, where "The Realisation of Starkey's Reforms" is discussed. Miss Burton shows that some of Starkey's "suggestions corresponded in the main with reforms actually effected by Henry VIII," but she finds it "impossible to say how far this coincidence of ideas was due to chance." We may safely assume that Starkey's suggestions received serious consideration from Henry and Cromwell.

41. Notably in Baumer's and Zeeveld's specialized works; more general accounts are given by Allen and Carlyle. (Cf. notes 3 and 4, above.) Starkey's *Exhortation to Unity and Obedience*, which was printed in 1536, has been fully analyzed by Zeeveld (*op. cit.*, pp. 145–56), who considers it the basis of the Anglican *via media* (*ibid.*, p. 128).

42. "Thomas Starkey and Marsilius of Padua," *op. cit.*, pp. 191–92.

43. *Ibid.*, p. 195.

44. Kurt Schroeder, *Platonismus in der englischen Renaissance vor und bei Thomas Eliot* (Berlin, 1920), pp. 75–84; Friedrich Dannenberg, *Das Erbe Platons in England bis zur Bildung Lylys* (Berlin, 1932), pp. 83–116.

45. Cf. Burton, *op. cit.*, p. 15; Baumer, "Thomas Starkey and Marsilius of Padua," *op. cit.*, p. 191, note 1.

46. Cf. Schenk, *op. cit.*, p. 5; Zeeveld, *op. cit.*, p. 127.

47. Herrtage, *op. cit.*, p. lxxiv.

48. E. M. W. Tillyard, Preface to Miss Burton's edition of the *Dialogue*, p. v.

49. *Op. cit.*, p. 134. (Part II, chap. iii.) Baumer's view is similar. (*Early Tudor Theory of Kingship*, p. 208.)

50. Zeeveld, *op. cit.*, pp. 114–15.

51. Zeeveld, *ibid.*, pp. 113–14, rightly defends the "government apologists," including Starkey, against Janelle's charges of Machiavellianism and dishonesty, and against Baumer's charges that they carried out a deliberate policy of deception. (He excepts only Richard Morison from this vindication of their intellectual honesty.) Miss Burton (*op. cit.*, p. 3) also defends Starkey from charges of insincerity and sycophancy.

52. Quoted by Zeeveld, *op. cit.*, p. 115. The letter was written in 1531 (*ibid.*, p. 75). On Harvel, cf. *ibid.*, p. 102. Cf. also Burton, *op. cit.*, p. 198.

53. *Op. cit.*, p. 112.

54. *Dialogue* (ed. Burton), p. 69; similar passages *ibid.*, pp. 26, 29, 31, 33, 35, 50, 62, 105, 152.

55. *Ibid.*, p. 51.

56. *Ibid.*, p. 54.

57. *Ibid.*

58. *Dialogue*, p. 185.

59. *Ibid.*, p. 186.

60. *Ibid.*, pp. 185–87.

61. *Ibid.*, p. 39.

62. *Ibid.*, p. 22.

63. *Ibid.*, p. 23.

64. *Ibid.*, p. 24.

65. "Socrates ever was wont to say: if the mind of man were instruct with sure knowledge and stable opinion, it should never err nor decline from the straight line of virtuous living." Starkey here engages in a discussion of the differences between Plato's and Aristotle's views on the relationship of knowledge and virtue, but his conclusion is that both would agree that "if man had certain and sure knowledge of the good, he would never leave it and follow the ill." (As is usual with many humanists, Starkey derives his ideas from both authors, does not make rigid distinctions between their views, and minimizes their differences: "Howbeit betwix them I think this discord that appeareth is but in words only and nothing in deed, as it is in many things mo [=more] wherein they seem greatly to dissent.") While Starkey thus believes that knowledge and virtue are intimately connected, he points out that man has free will and may choose not to act according to his knowledge of the good; however, when man "leaveth the best and taketh the worst" he is blinded "by pleasure or profit," by "ignorance . . . and by corrupt judgment," and his will "is thus drowned with affects." Out of such captivity, the will must be freed by "diligent instruction and wise counsel" which restores the rule of true knowledge, and thus virtue. (*Ibid.*, pp. 42–44.)

66. *Ibid.*, p. 26.

67. *Ibid.*, p. 29. Similarly, *ibid.*, p. 30: "man by nature in excellence and dignity even so excelleth all other creatures here upon earth as God exceedeth the nature of man."

68. *Ibid.*, p. 26.
69. *Loc. cit.*
70. *Op. cit.*, p. 36.
71. *Ibid.*, p. 26.
72. *Ibid.*, p. 31.
73. *Loc. cit.*
74. *Op. cit.*, p. 29.
75. *Ibid.*, p. 31.
76. ". . . the law of nature is ever one, in all countries, firm and stable, and never for the time varieth," whereas the civil law is "diverse and variable" in every country. (*Ibid.*, p. 32.)
77. *Ibid.*, p. 34.
78. *Ibid.*, p. 36.
79. *Loc. cit.*
80. *Op. cit.*, p. 37.
81. *Ibid.*, p. 38.
82. *Loc. cit.*
83. *Loc. cit.*
84. *Op. cit.*, p. 40.
85. *Ibid.*, p. 47.
86. *Ibid.*, p. 56.
87. *Ibid.*, p. 57.
88. *Ibid.*, p. 58.
89. Schroeder, *op. cit.*, p. 83; similarly, Dannenberg, *op. cit.*, p. 99, who points out that Starkey's view is more Platonic than More's because he insists on the beauty of the state.
90. *Dialogue*, p. 64.
91. *Ibid.*, p. 84. Similarly, *ibid.*, p. 103, where it is stated that "civil war, sedition and discords" have "destroyed all common weals," and p. 145, where discord is described as "the ground of all ruin of policy, whereof the country of Italy is in our days most manifest example." "Seditious persons that openly despise this order, unity and concord" must "be cut off" by "perpetual banishment or rather, death," because otherwise they might "infect the rest" of the body, "corrupting the whole." (*Ibid.*, p. 146.)
92. *Ibid.*, p. 55.
93. *Ibid.*, p. 48.
94. *Ibid.*, p. 136.
95. *Ibid.*, p. 152.
96. *Ibid.*, p. 55.
97. *Ibid.*, p. 150.
98. *Loc. cit.*
99. *Op. cit.*, p. 151.
100. *Ibid.*, p. 165.
101. "It is not man that can make a wise prince of him that lacketh wit by nature, nor make him just that is a tyran for pleasure. But this is in man's power: to elect and choose him that is both wise and just, and make him a prince; and him that is a tyran, so to depose." (*Ibid.*, p. 153.)

102. "For some people there be to whom the rule of a prince more agreeth than a common counsel. . . . To other, contrary, is more convenience the rule of a common counsel. . . ." (*Ibid.*, pp 60–61.)

103. *Ibid.*, p. 165. Starkey advocates a system of checks and balances on the power of the king. He wants a kind of standing committee of fourteen members whose duty it would be to watch jealously over "the liberty of the whole body of the ream" and to counteract any tyrannical tendencies the ruler might develop. This "little parliament" has the right not only to call the real parliament, but it elects the king's own council which, in turn, has considerable powers. (*Ibid.*, p. 166.) This latter council bears a distinct, though somewhat remote, resemblance to the modern cabinet. Cf. also *ibid.*, p. 155, and the discussion in Carlyle, *op. cit.*, pp. 261–63.

104. *Dialogue*, p. 61.

105. *Loc. cit.*

106. *Op. cit.*, p. 65.

107. *Ibid.*, p. 64.

108. Thus *ibid.*, pp. 79, 93–94, 142–46, 156–60.

109. *Ibid.*, p. 59.

110. *Ibid.*, p. 55.

111. *Ibid.*, p. 152.

112. *Ibid.*, p. 62.

113. *Ibid.*, pp. 63–64.

114. *Ibid.*, p. 172.

115. *Ibid.*, p. 156.

116. *Ibid.*, p. 106.

117. *Ibid.*, p. 173. Too many lawyers are "hungry advocates and cormorants of the court." (*Ibid.*, p. 113.)

118. Cf. *ibid.*, pp. 79, 123–24, 171.

119. *Ibid.*, p. 161. Similarly, *ibid.*, p. 92.

120. *Ibid.*, p. 178.

121. *Ibid.*, p. 142.

122. *Ibid.*, p. 147.

123. *Ibid.*, pp. 144, 147, 183.

124. *Ibid.*, p. 144. Starkey declares that this subject is "the chief key whereby the rest of our song must be governed and ruled," i.e., that it is the principal theme of the last part of the *Dialogue*.

125. *Ibid.*, p. 44.

126. *Ibid.*, p. 123.

127. *Ibid.*, p. 171.

128. *Ibid.*, pp. 169–70.

129. "If the nobility were brought up in [the civil law], undoubtedly our country would shortly be restored to as good civility as there is in any other nation; yea, and peraventure much better also." (*Ibid.*, p. 175.)

130. *Ibid.*, p. 182. He there discusses the problems in the "order of studies in universities" and "in the education of the nobility," and declares that "*each one of these two matters* require a whole book." (Italics mine.)

257

131. He seems to have come from the lower gentry; his maternal grandfather was a knight. Cf. *DNB*.

132. *Ibid.*, p. 184.

133. *Ibid.*, p. 147.

134. *Ibid.*, p. 175.

135. *Ibid.*, p. 155.

136. *Ibid.*, p. 166.

137. *Ibid.*, p. 107.

138. *Ibid.*, p. 182.

139. "Among these, of late days, the Bishop of Carpenteras—one of the wisest men of our time—hath put forth a book." (*Loc. cit.*) Jacopo Sadoleto was the Bishop of Carpentras. His *De Liberis Recte Instituendis* had been published in Venice in 1533. He and Pole were friends, and he knew Starkey. Pole took the manuscript of the book to Venice, where it was printed. (Zeeveld, *op. cit.*, pp. 48–49, 80–81, 85; Burton, *op. cit.*, p. 194.)

140. *Dialogue*, p. 188. Miss Burton identifies this as the *Enchiridion Militis Christiani*. If we take Starkey literally, however, he would appear to refer to the *Christiani Hominis Institutum* (first published in London, 1514; printed in *LB* V, cols. 357–60). This, however, is hardly a "book," as Starkey describes it, but only a rather brief, though frequently reprinted "carmen." While Starkey might have meant to refer to this work, he probably confused the title with that of the *Institutio Principis Christiani*. Starkey would then have translated "Institutio" by "Instruction" and substituted "man" for "prince."

141. *Dialogue*, p. 182.

142. *Ibid.*, p. 150.

143. *Ibid.*, p. 151.

144. *Ibid.*, p. 191.

145. *Ibid.*, pp. 31–32.

146. *Ibid.*, p. 184. Cf. also *ibid.*, p. 44.

147. *Ibid.*, p. 185.

148. *Ibid.*, p. 186.

149. *Ibid.*, p. 190.

150. *Ibid.*, p. 171. It is interesting that Starkey in this sentence first describes "Plato's common weal" as his goal, and that then, as an afterthought, he corrects himself to change it to "or else, rather" the institution of Christian doctrine.

151. *Loc. cit.*

152. *Op. cit.*, pp. 62–63.

## CHAPTER VI

1. R. W. Chambers, *Thomas More* (London, 1935), p. 379. Chambers is indebted to J. S. Phillimore's views, stated in "Blessed Thomas More and the Arrest of Humanism in England," *Dublin Review*, CLIII (1913), 1–26.

2. Chambers' terms, *loc. cit.*

3. Douglas Bush, "Tudor Humanism and Henry VIII," *University of Toronto Quarterly,* VII (1938), 162–77; and *The Renaissance and English Humanism* (Toronto, 1939), pp. 73–79.

4. "Tudor Humanism and Henry VIII," p. 165.

5. *Ibid.,* p. 173. Cf. A. F. Pollard, *The History of England from the Accession of Edward VI to the Death of Elizabeth (1547–1603)* (London, 1910), p. 322: "At no period has the quickening of national intelligence been so marked as during the alleged decay of university education."

6. Bush, "Tudor Humanism and Henry VIII," p. 170.

7. *Ibid.,* p. 167. (This evaluation is based on A. F. Leach's studies in the history of English education.)

8. Cf. A. F. Leach, *English Schools at the Reformation, 1546–8* (Westminster, 1896), where the problem is fully documented and dealt with.

9. A. L. Rowse, *The England of Elizabeth* (New York, 1951), p. 497.

10. For these and similar foundations, cf. Rowse, *op cit.,* pp. 489–503.

11. *Ibid.,* p. 496.

12. Leach, *op. cit.,* p. 107.

13. A. F. Leach, *Educational Charters and Documents, 598 to 1909* (Cambridge, 1911), pp. 448–51.

14. *Ibid.,* pp. 508–13.

15. Cf. A. L. Rowse, *op. cit.,* pp. 513, 517.

16. On the intellectual life at the Cardinal's College during the 1520's, see W. G. Zeeveld, *Foundations of Tudor Policy* (Cambridge, Mass., 1948), chap. ii (pp. 17–38).

17. Bush, "Tudor Humanism and Henry VIII," p. 175. Bush illustrates the point: "William Cecil might have remained a college don and crowned his life with an edition of Aristotle's *Politics;* instead he applied ancient wisdom (not without help from Machiavelli) to practical statesmanship" (*The Renaissance and English Humanism,* p. 79). On this and other points dealt with here, see also Paul N. Siegel, "English Humanism and the New Tudor Aristocracy," *Journal of the History of Ideas,* XIII (1952), 450–68. (This interesting article, which appeared after the completion of the present work, on the whole agrees with my conclusions.)

18. Printed in "E.E.T.S., Extra Series," Vol. VIII (1869), pp. 1–12. Written in 1562 or later (*ibid.,* p. xi).

19. Cf. R. Kelso, *The Doctrine of the English Gentleman in the Sixteenth Century* (Urbana, 1929), p. 121.

20. In his "Description of England," *The First and Second Volumes of Chronicles . . . First Collected . . . by Raphaell Holinshed, William Harrison, and others* (London, 1587), pp. 149–50, Harrison states: "It is in my time an hard matter for a poore mans child to come by a felowship (though he be never so good a scholer & worthie of that roome.)." He complains that elections of scholars are apt to be "packed" in favor of gentlemen's sons, and that bribery causes grammar schools to send the sons of the rich rather than those of the poor to the universities. Colleges were "erected by their founders at the first, onelie for poore mens sons . . . but now they have the least benefit of them, by reason the

rich doo so incroch upon them." And Gilbert, *Queene Elizabethes Achademy*, p. 11, states that, if his scheme for a separate academy for the aristocracy is adopted, "the other universities shall then better suffize to releive poore schollers, where now the youth of nobility and gentlemen, taking up their schollarshippes and fellowshippes, do disapoincte the poore of their livinges and avauncementes." These specific charges and statements indicate the very considerable change that was taking place in the social composition of the undergraduate population at Oxford and Cambridge, and, as we shall see, they are corroborated by other evidence; yet Rowse (*op. cit.*, pp. 520–21) is right in cautioning against exaggerating these changes.

21. On this point, cf. J. H. Hexter, "The Education of the Aristocracy in the Renaissance," *Journal of Modern History*, XXII (1950), 4; G. R. Potter, "Education in the Fourteenth and Fifteenth Centuries," *The Cambridge Medieval History*, VIII, 700; and A. F. Leach, *English Schools at the Reformation, 1546–8*, p. 109, who states that "it was the middle classes, whether country or town, the younger sons of the nobility and farmers, the lesser landholders, the prosperous tradesmen, who created a demand for education, and furnished the occupants of Grammar Schools." See Sylvia L. Thrupp, *The Merchant Class of Medieval London, 1300–1500* (Chicago, 1948), pp. 155–63, for a description of the education of merchants in late medieval London.

22. Richard Pace, *De Fructu qui ex doctrina percipitur liber* (Basel, 1517), p. 15. (Author's translation.) William Camden tells his abbreviated version in *Remaines . . . Concerning Britaine* (London, 1605), p. 220.

23. Historical Manuscripts Commission, *Calendar of the Manuscripts of the . . . Marquis of Salisbury*, Part I (London, 1883), "Considerations Delivered to the Parliament, 1559," p. 163. The editor of this lengthy memorandum refrains from suggesting who the author might have been (cf. *ibid.*, pp. ix and 165); J. E. Neale, in *The Elizabethan House of Commons* (London, 1949), p. 303, attributes it to an "anonymous planner"; Rowse, *op. cit.*, pp. 259–60, connects it with William Cecil. If Cecil was the author, as seems very possible, the proposal is particularly significant.

24. Historical Manuscripts Commission, *loc cit.*

25. Cf. Ronald S. Crane, "The Vogue of Medieval Chivalric Romance during the English Renaissance" (abstract of thesis, Menasha, Wis., 1919), pp. 21–22, 24, 28–29.

26. The account of the meeting is reprinted by Leach, *Educational Charters* pp. 470–71, from John Strype, *Memorials of Thomas Cranmer.*

27. Leach, *Educational Charters*, p. 457.

28. *Ibid.*, p. 459.

29. Sir Ernest Barker, *Traditions of Civility* (Cambridge, 1948), pp. 156–57.

30. Leach, *English Schools at the Reformation*, pp. 108–9.

31. Quoted by Leach, *loc. cit.*

32. Hexter, *op. cit.*, p. ¯

33. *Ibid.*, p. 6.

34. *Ibid.*, p. 7. Cf. also William Harrison's remark (*op. cit.*, p. 149):

"Some gentlemen also, whose friends have beene in times past benefactors to certeine of those houses, doo intrude into the disposition of their estates . . . onelie thereby to place whome they thinke good. . . ."

35. Rowse, *op. cit.*, pp. 503–4.

36. *Ibid.*, pp. 505–6.

37. *Ibid.*, p. 521.

38. A. Clark, *Register of the University of Oxford, 1571–1622* (Oxford, 1887), Vol. II, Part II, p. 414 (Table C).

39. Hexter, *op. cit.*, p. 8.

40. Rowse, *op. cit.*, p. 521.

41. Neale, *op. cit.*, p. 303.

42. Nicholas Fitzherbert, *Oxoniensis . . . Academiae Descriptio* (Rome, 1602), reprinted in Charles Plummer, *Elizabethan Oxford, Reprints of Rare Tracts* (Oxford, 1887), p. 17: "Ad Academiam non accedunt, nisi qui in gymnasiis, scholisque publicis per omnes Angliae provincias . . . disseminatis (inter quas habentur insigniores Vuintoniensis, Etonensis, Dunelmensis, Londinensis) grammaticae, poeticae, latinaeque linguae praecepta imbiberint."

43. Neale, *op. cit.*, p. 305. Neale gives other examples of this practice.

44. Rowse, *op. cit.*, p. 522.

45. Historical Manuscripts Commission, *op. cit.*, I, 163.

46. Rowse, *op. cit.*, p. 522.

47. Hexter, *op. cit.*, p. 6. Cf. also A. F. Pollard's statement (in the *Times* of October 1, 1932, quoted from Chambers, *More*, p. 67) that only three or four of the Commons of Henry's great Reformation Parliament are known to have received a university education.

48. Neale, *op. cit.*, pp. 302–3. (The figures are approximate, particularly those for the Parliament of 1563.)

49. *Ibid.*, pp. 304–5.

50. Hexter, *op. cit.*, p. 5.

51. Rowse, *op. cit.*, p. 515. Cf. J. E. Neale, *Queen Elizabeth* (London, 1935), pp. 22–23, 62, for the importance of the "Cambridge group" in the government.

52. Plummer, *op. cit.*, p. 201.

53. Neale, *The Elizabethan House of Commons*, p. 308, finds that "fully half the country gentlemen in the Parliament of 1584 held county office, and another thirty odd . . . were later to hold office." While those country gentlemen who became members of Parliament were presumably somewhat above the intellectual level of their fellow justices of the peace, the educational developments noted in the membership of the House undoubtedly reflect a similar development in the entire gentry and, therefore, among county officials.

54. Sir Thomas Smith, *De Republica Anglorum* (1583; ed. L. Alston [Cambridge, 1906], pp. 39–40).

55. Quoted from Rowse, *op. cit.*, p. 244.

56. Thomas Wilson, *The State of England Anno Dom. 1600*, ed. F. J. Fisher ("Camden Miscellany," Vol. XVI [London, 1936]), p. 19. Attorneys had begun to be recognized as gentlemen in the later part of the fifteenth century (Thrupp, *op. cit.*, p. 242).

57. Wilson, *op. cit.*, pp. 24–25. Cf. also R. H. Tawney, "The Rise of the Gentry, 1558–1640," *The Economic History Review*, XI (1941), 18.

58. Rowse, *op. cit.*, p. 238. (Tawney, *loc. cit.*, counts only fifty.) They did not all come out of legal fees—marriages and politics helped.

59. Tawney, *op. cit.*, p. 23.

60. Rowse, *op. cit.*, p. 235.

61. Lawrence Stone, "The Anatomy of the Elizabethan Aristocracy," *The Economic History Review*, XVIII (1948), 2, divides the distribution of the spoils into two major periods, the first lasting from 1538 to 1547, and the second and even more extensive distribution taking place in the reign of Edward VI.

62. Stone, *op. cit.*, p. 3.

63. M. Campbell, *The English Yeoman under Elizabeth and the Early Stuarts* (New Haven, 1942), p. 33.

64. Campbell, *op. cit.*, p. 49.

65. Rowse, *op. cit.*, pp. 226, 232.

66. *Ibid.*, p. 226.

67. *Ibid.*, pp. 249–50. Sylvia L. Thrupp, *op. cit.*, pp. 279–87, investigates the movement of London merchants into the landed gentry and comes to similar conclusions for the fifteenth century.

68. I agree with Hexter's argument (*op. cit.*, p. 5 n.) that the gentry, titled and untitled, should not be lumped with the middle class: "a view that separates the gentry from the titled nobility and binds them to merchants and tradesmen finds little justification in Tudor habits of thought." Thomas Wilson groups nobility and gentry together as "nobilitas maior" and "nobilitas minor"; among the latter, apart from knights, esquires, and gentlemen, he lists lawyers, professors, and members of the clergy, but not merchants or other mercantile groups. He counts around five hundred knights and finds that "many of them equall the best Barons and come not much behind many Erles" in income and wealth (*op. cit.*, p. 23).

69. Tawney, *op. cit.*, p. 26.

70. S. B. Liljegren, *The Fall of the Monasteries and the Social Changes in England Leading up to the Great Revolution* (Lund, 1924), pp. 123–24. Liljegren shows that in 1544, for instance, estates were purchased by groups of London tradesmen. Up to seventy-seven buyers pooled their resources to purchase an estate; they presumably put their money into land for investment purposes.

71. Tawney, *op. cit.*, p. 27.

72. *Ibid.*, p. 35. In his attack on "The Anatomy of the Elizabethan Aristocracy" by L. Stone, H. R. Trevor-Roper has questioned the validity of some of Tawney's figures ("The Elizabethan Aristocracy: An Anatomy Anatomized," *The Economic History Review*, III, Ser. 2 [1950–51], 279–98). While Tawney finds that in this group of manors the nobility lost 47.1 per cent of their holdings and the gentry increased theirs by 17.8 per cent between 1561 and 1640, Trevor-Roper considers these figures "somewhat artificial" because he does not agree

with the methods by which Tawney determines membership in the respective groups, and on which his comparison rests. "The over-simplified assumption that the nobility, as a class, were in decline, while the gentry, as a class, were rising should perhaps be restated: perhaps both classes were being transformed at an unequal rate" (*op. cit.*, pp. 294–95). In his reply ("The Elizabethan Aristocracy—A Restatement," *The Economic History Review*, IV, Ser. 2 [1952], 302–21), Stone, after examining the Victoria County Histories of twelve and a half counties, supports Tawney's view and finds that the drop between 1558 and 1642 in the number of manors held by the peerage was even more marked than Tawney had suggested (*op. cit.*, pp. 309–11 and Appendix A). Trevor-Roper and Stone agree that the aristocracy passed through financial difficulties in Elizabeth's later years; they disagree on the seriousness of these difficulties, which Stone now admits were originally exaggerated by him.

73. On the activities of the College of Arms, cf. Rowse, *op. cit.*, pp. 247–48. One Clarenceux king granted five hundred coats of arms, others did almost as well; on the other hand, claims to gentility were not infrequently disallowed.

74. Wilson, *op. cit.*, pp. 22–23. It seems useful to quote here part of Stone's redefinition of the concept of "the rise of the gentry" (*The Economic History Review*, IV, Ser. 2, 320): it was "a shift in the distribution of the national income in favour of the group of middle landowners recruited partly from the older gentry but more especially from new stock, a shift which was at the expense both of the very large landowners and of the peasantry; . . . this shift, coupled with the growth of higher education, of administrative experience in the shires and in political experience at Westminster, led to the emergence of the House of Commons as the most powerful organ in the state. . . ."

75. Rowse, *op. cit.*, pp. 247, 275.

76. *Ibid.*, pp. 235–36.

77. Kelso (*op. cit.*) discusses this literature fully, and provides an extensive bibliography of treatises on the gentleman published in Europe up to 1625. J. E. Mason, *Gentlefolk in the Making: Studies in the History of English Courtesy Literature and Related Topics from 1531 to 1774* (Philadelphia, 1935), is also valuable. *A Check List of Courtesy Books in the Newberry Library*, compiled by Virgil B. Heltzel (Chicago, 1942), lists most of the relevant English works among its roughly fifteen hundred entries. A summary of W. L. Ustick's dissertation, "The English Gentleman in the Sixteenth and Early Seventeenth Century . . ." has appeared in *Harvard University . . . Summaries of Theses, 1932* (Cambridge, Mass., 1933), pp. 289–92.

78. The *STC* lists eight editions: 1531, 1537, 1544, 1546, 1553, 1557, 1565, 1580.

79. C. Whittingham's reprint (London, 1839) of the second edition (London, 1568) is used here.

80. From the title-page of the first edition (London, 1570); repro-

duced in E. Arber's edition ("English Reprints," London, 1935), p. 13.

81. Cf. Virgil B. Heltzel, "Chesterfield and the Tradition of the Ideal Gentleman" (unpublished dissertation, University of Chicago, 1925), pp. 471–88.

81*a.* Pace, *op. cit.*, p. 98: "Et illa demum vera est nobilitas, quam virtus facit, magis quam clara longaque generis series."

82. 1839 reprint, sig. c V[r].

83. *Ibid.*, sig. c VIII[r].

84. *Ibid.*, sig d IV[r].

85. *Ibid.*, sig. d IV[v].

86. *Loc. cit.*

87. *Op. cit.*, sig. d III[v].

88. L. Humphrey, *The Nobles or of Nobilitye* (London, 1563), sig. h I[r].

89. *Institucion*, sig. c IV[v].

90. Humphrey, *op. cit.*, sig. i II[v].

91. *Ibid.*, sig. i III[v].

92. *Ibid.*, sig. h II[v].

93. *The Civile Conuersation of M. Steeuen Guazzo* (London, 1581), f. I[v]. Pettie translated Books I–III; Book IV was translated by B. Young in 1586. On the importance of learning for a gentleman and the change in its character between the sixteenth and eighteenth centuries, cf. Heltzel, *op. cit.*, pp. 75–121.

94. Henry Peacham, *The Compleat Gentleman* (London, 1622), "To the Reader."

95. A. Barclay, *The Myrrour of Good Manners* (*ca.* 1520); quoted from Kelso, *op. cit.*, p. 112.

96. Cf. M. A. Scott, *Elizabethan Translations from the Italian* (New York, 1895), p. 156; C. H. Conley, *The First English Translators of the Classics* (New Haven, 1927), pp. 26 ff.; F. O. Matthiessen, *Translation: An Elizabethan Art* (Cambridge, Mass., 1931).

97. Conley, *op. cit.*, pp. 39–40.

98. Quoted from Conley, *op. cit.*, p. 35.

99. Antonio de Guevara, *The Diall of Princes . . . Englysshed oute of the Frenche by Thomas North* (London, 1557), title-page.

100. Plutarch, *The Lives of the Noble Grecians and Romanes*, trans. Thomas North (London, 1579), f. ii[v]. Matthiessen, *op. cit.*, p. 54, points out that Plutarch had not been on the list of authors prescribed by Elyot.

101. *Op. cit.*, f. iii[r].

102. *Ibid.*, f. ii[r].

103. Matthiessen, *op. cit.*, p. 23. For Hoby's life, cf. also the Introduction to Walter Raleigh's edition of *The Courtier* (London, 1900).

104. Cf. Cheke's letter, reprinted .in "Everyman" edition of *The Courtier* (London, n.d.), pp. 7–8.

105. *The Courtier of Count Baldessar Castilio* (London, 1588), has Italian, French, and English texts in parallel columns; it was presumably intended to help teach the languages as well as courtesy.

106. 1588 edition, f. 3.

107. The grand tour could be very expensive; that of the Earl of Oxford, in 1576, cost £3,761. (Stone, *The Economic History Review*, XVIII [1948], 10.) (The present-day equivalent would, of course, be a multiple of that sum.)

108. Cf. Zeeveld, *op. cit.*, chap. iii.

109. *Scholemaster* (Arber ed.), p. 78.

110. *Loc. cit.*

111. *Op. cit.*, p. 66.

112. Cf. Mario Praz, *Machiavelli and the Elizabethans* (London, [1928]), pp. 34–37.

113. *Ibid.*, p. 37.

114. Innocent Gentillet, *A Discourse upon the Meanes of well Governing . . . Against Nicholas Machiavell, the Florentine* (London, 1602). Cf. also E. Meyer, *The Source of Machiavellianism in the Elizabethan Drama* (Heidelberg, 1895).

115. Gentillet, *op. cit.*, sig. [iv$^r$].

## CHAPTER VII

1. Edmund Spenser, *The Shepheardes Calender* (London, 1579), dedicatory poem "To his booke," lines 3–4.

2. Anthony à Wood says of him: "Certain it is, he was a noble and matchless gentleman" (*Athenae Oxonienses* [London, 1813], I, 520). And Sir Henry Sidney, Philip's father, writes to Robert, Philip's brother, on March 25, 1578: "Imitate hys [Philip's] Vertues, Exercyses, Studyes, and Accyons; he ys a rare Ornament of thys Age, the very Formular, that all well dysposed young Gentylmen of ouer Court, do form allsoe thear Maners and Lyfe by. In Troth I speak yt wythout Flatery of hym, or of my self, he hathe the most rare Vertues that ever I found in any Man" (*Letters and Memorials of State in the Reigns of Queen Mary, Queen Elizabeth, King James . . .*, ed. Arthur Collins [London, 1746], I, 246—usually called "Sidney Papers"). Sidney's life is presented as "the very formular" by Thomas Moffet to the young William Herbert (who seems to have been in need of such a formular) in *Nobilis, or A View of the Life and Death of a Sidney*, ed. and trans. V. B. Heltzel and H. H. Hudson (San Marino, 1940). Berta Siebeck, in *Das Bild Sir Philip Sidneys in der englischen Renaissance* (Weimar, 1939), has collected many passages in prose and verse testifying to the high esteem in which Sidney was held by his contemporaries as a "matchless gentleman," and showing how he embodied and exemplified the ideal of his age.

3. M. S. Goldman (*Sir Philip Sidney and the Arcadia* [Urbana, 1934], p. 149) thinks it "very nearly impossible" that Sidney should not have been acquainted with the *Cortegiano*, which in his day was the "secular breviary" of the court circles.

4. Piero Rebora's description of this slow growth and eventual flowering agrees with my interpretation: "I primi tre quarti del secolo decimosesto, aspri ed aridi di poesia, sono il periodo dell' Umanesimo inglese che

vien preparando una base spirituale alla fioritura d'arte, di pensiero e di prassi religiosa e politica dell' età di Shakespeare.... Le lettere e le arti.... eromperanno in piena maturità d'espressione solo quando le basi politiche ed educative, ormai ben solide, lo permetteranno" ("Aspetti dell' Umanesimo in Inghilterra," *Rinascita*, II [1939], 367–68).

5. The *Arcadia* will here be quoted from A. Feuillerat's edition of *The Countesse of Pembrokes Arcadia* in *The Complete Works of Sir Philip Sidney* (Cambridge, 1922). (The Roman numerals after *Arcadia* will designate the volumes of this edition of the *Works*.)

6. "His intent, and scope was, to turn the barren Philosophy precepts into pregnant Images of Life," says his friend and biographer, Sir Fulke Greville (Lord Brooke) (*Life of Sir Philip Sidney* [1652], ed. N. Smith [Oxford, 1907], p. 15). Gabriel Harvey, in the fourth book of *Gratulationum Valdinensium Libri IV* (London, 1578), describes Sidney as the exemplary "aulicus" in the "Castilionaeo choro," i.e., as the living representative of Castiglione's ideal. Cf. Siebeck, *op. cit.*, pp. 46–47.

7. *Defence of the Earl of Leicester*, in *Complete Works*, III, 65–66.

8. On October 11, 1551. (M. W. Wallace, *The Life of Sir Philip Sidney* [Cambridge, 1915], p. 7.)

9. Wallace, *op. cit.*, p. 18. Wilton House, where Philip Sidney later was a frequent guest of his sister Mary, Countess of Pembroke, had come into the possession of her husband's family after the convent formerly located there had been dissolved (cf. Goldman, *op. cit.*, p. 109, note 21); the property of this family—the Herbert family—was thus also typical new Tudor wealth. Their title, incidentally, was granted in 1551.

10. Wallace, *op. cit.*, p. 12.

11. L. Strachey originally made this apt remark about Elizabeth; Goldman, *op. cit.*, p. 60, applies it to the Sidneys.

12. Cf. Goldman, *op. cit.*, pp. 54–57.

13. Wallace, *op. cit.*, pp. 28–29; Goldman, *op. cit.*, p. 59.

14. Cf. *The Correspondence of Sir Philip Sidney and Hubert Languet*, ed. and trans. S. A. Pears (London, 1845); Sidney's part of the correspondence is available, together with his other letters, in Vol. III of the *Complete Works*, ed. Feuillerat (Cambridge, 1923). For their relationship and its importance, cf. Wallace, *op. cit.*, pp. 144–45; Goldman, *op. cit.*, pp. 82 ff.; also W. Platzhoff, "Die Gesandtschaftsberichte Hubert Languets als historische Quelle und als Spiegel seiner Persönlichkeit," *Historische Zeitschrift*, CXIII (1914), 505–39.

15. To Frances Walsingham, the daughter of Sir Francis.

16. Goldman (*op. cit.*, p. 57) finds it "practically impossible to determine his exact theological position, to decide just how Protestant he really was."

17. Wallace, *op. cit.*, p. 42. In a letter to his brother Robert, Philip suggests to him a "reading list" in history on a somewhat more advanced level. Thucydides, Herodotus, and Xenophon, as well as the Roman historians, are included; while traveling, Robert is to pay particular attention to "the establishments or ruines of great Estates. . . ." These instructions are followed by the typical advice to "take a delight to keepe

and increase your musick" and to practice horsemanship (*Complete Works*, III, 130–33, letter XLII of October 18, 1580).

18. *Ibid.*, p. 88.

19. *Ibid.*, pp. 101–2: Thomas Thornton and Dr. Thomas Cooper—the latter, in Wallace's opinion, "probably the most distinguished man of his day at Oxford." Cooper was vice-chancellor of the university while Sidney was there.

20. Wallace emphasizes that "the usual condemnation of the Universities at this time is too sweeping" (*op. cit.*, p. 97).

21. *The Defence of Poesie* (London, 1595), in *Complete Works*, III, 1–46. (Hereafter designated as *Defence*.)

22. *Defence*, p. 15. Xenophon, in giving us "the pourtraiture of a just Empyre under the name of *Cyrus*, . . . made therein an absolute heroicall Poeme" (*ibid.*, p. 10).

23. Goldman, *op. cit.*, p. 155.

24. *Defence*, p. 27. Sidney likes verse for many reasons, and defends it; he merely argues that there can be poetry without verse. A similar statement, *ibid.*, p. 10: "The greatest part of Poets have apparelled their poeticall inventions in . . . *vers*. Indeed but apparelled verse: being but an ornament and no cause to Poetrie . . ." (E. Arber's edition of the *Apologie for Poetrie* [1595] [London, 1869], p. 28, punctuates more sensibly: "apparelled, verse being but an ornament . . ."). C. M. Dowlin claims that Sidney was original in this part of his theory: "In reaching his conclusion that edifying prose romances were heroic poems, Sidney anticipated an attitude toward prose narrative that did not appear in print until after Tasso, and by doing so he revealed a commendable originality." ("Sidney and Other Men's Thought," *Review of English Studies*, XX [1944], 271.)

25. *Defence*, p. 11.

26. *Ibid.*, p. 14.

27. *Ibid.*, p. 10.

28. *Ibid.*, pp. 11–12.

29. Sidney sees the "moral *Philosophers* . . . coming towards me, with a sullain gravitie," whereas the historians are "loaden with old Mouse-eaten Records" (*Defence*, p. 12).

30. *Ibid.*, p. 28.

31. *Ibid.*, pp. 18–19: "Moving to well doing, indeed setteth the Lawrell Crowne upon the *Poets* as victorious, not onely of the *Historian*, but over the *Philosopher*. . . ." Similarly, *ibid.*, p. 26, where Sidney points out that even the Bible "hath whole parts in it Poeticall."

32. *Ibid.*, p. 25.

33. *Loc. cit.*: "The Heroicall . . . is . . . the best and most accomplished kindes [!] of Poetrie." (Later editions read "kinde" instead of "kindes"— cf. *ibid.*, p. 382.)

34. *Ibid.*, p. 31. Cf. also *Arcadia*, I, 152, where Dametas expresses the prejudice against learning: "They might talke of booke-learning what they would; but for his part, he never saw more unfeatlie fellowes, then great clearks were."

35. *Defence*, p. 4: "poore Poetrie . . . from almost the highest estimation of learning, is falne to be the laughing stocke of children. . . ."

36. *Ibid.*, p. 31.

37. *Ibid.*, p. 34.

38. *Ibid.*, p. 5.

39. See Irene Samuel, "The Influence of Plato on Sir Philip Sidney's *Defense of Poesy*," *Modern Language Quarterly*, I (1940), 383–91. Miss Samuel claims that Sidney certainly knew the *Republic*, the *Phaedrus*, and the *Symposium*; almost certainly the *Apology*, *Phaedo*, and *Ion*; perhaps the *Epistles* and *Critias*. Plato's ideas, she argues, were the main source of the *Defence*.

40. *Defence*, p. 7.

41. C. M. Dowlin, "Sidney's Two Definitions of Poetry," *Modern Language Quarterly*, III (1942), 573–81, sees the tenth book of the *Republic* as the main basis for Sidney's advocacy and practice of feigning notable images of virtues and vices in poesy.

42. His simple statement that "*Poetrie* is the Companion of Camps" (*Defence*, p. 32) intimates the close interconnection between poetry and action in his own life.

43. Greville, *Life*, p. 2.

44. *Eikonoklastes*, in *Prose Works* (London: Bohn, 1848), I, 327–28. Milton felt that it should not "be read at any time without good caution." T. S. Eliot, incidentally, considers it "a monument of dulness" ("Apology for the Countess of Pembroke," *Harvard Graduates' Magazine*, XLI [1932], 74).

45. Friedrich Brie, *Sidneys Arcadia: Eine Studie zur englischen Renaissance* (Strassburg, 1918).

46. Brie, *op. cit.*, pp. 71, 121. Brie cannot find a trace of Plato's *Republic* anywhere in the *Arcadia;* he thinks Sidney must have disapproved of that work on account of its communism, the community of women, and its Utopian character in general (p. 71, note 1). When one considers Sidney's praise in the *Apologie*, for instance, this thesis remains hardly tenable. There have been many persons who did not accept every single one of Plato's tenets and yet were strongly influenced by his thought, Sidney among them.

47. A. Feuillerat, in *Modern Language Notes*, XLVI (1931), 190.

48. For instance by R. W. Zandvoort (*Sidney's Arcadia: A Comparison between the Two Versions* [Amsterdam, 1929]), who states that "Brie often puts a more 'allegorical' construction on a phrase or passage than the words will carry" (p. 133). Brie's work had been preceded by E. Greenlaw's brief study, "Sidney's *Arcadia* as an Example of Elizabethan Allegory," *Anniversary Papers by Colleagues . . . of G. L. Kittredge* (Boston, 1913), pp. 327–37. Greenlaw pointed out that Sidney meant to illustrate certain political and moral theories, that his book sprang out of his interest in problems of government, and that the *Arcadia*, conceived as a heroic poem, is a prose counterpart of the *Faerie Queene*.

49. It was Sidney's purpose to write "in erster Linie einen politischen Roman, in zweiter ein heroisches Epos in Prosa." (Brie, *op. cit.*, p. 255.)

Zandvoort (*op. cit.*, p. 158) denies that the *Arcadia* is primarily a political *allegory;* he agrees, however, that political questions play an important part in it, and points to the revisions Sidney made in his work as proof that political problems became more predominant in his thought as he grew older. Greville (*op. cit.*, p. 15) had emphasized the function of the *Arcadia* as a medium through which Sidney expressed his political thought: his aim was "lively to represent the growth, state, and declination of Princes, change of Government, and lawes: vicissitudes of sedition, faction, succession, confederacies, plantations, with all other errors, or alterations in publique affaires."

50. See discussion in chapter viii, below. It is Brie's contention (*op. cit.*, pp. 113–15) that Sidney's supposed illustration of the Aristotelian virtues in the *Arcadia* suggested the scheme of the *Faerie Queene* to Spenser. He sees Aristotle as the main connecting link between these works, but exaggerates not so much their similarity as the importance of Aristotle in both instances. Cf. Zandvoort, *op. cit.*, p. 131.

51. A. Feuillerat, in *Modern Language Notes*, XLVI (1931), 191. Feuillerat there agrees with Zandvoort—whose book he is reviewing—that the *Arcadia* is not an allegory. He considers it as Sidney's attempt to present a "heroical poem."

52. Goldman, *op. cit.*, p. 14.

53. *Ibid.*, p. 215.

54. *Loc. cit.*

55. Brie, *op. cit.*, p. 183.

56. Cf. *Arcadia* (original version), in *Complete Works* (Cambridge, 1926), IV, 163: Friendship is "the very foundacyon whereuppon my Lyfe ys buylt," says Dorus.

57. *Arcadia*, I, 82: "If we love vertue, in whom shal we love it but in a vertuous creature?" *Ibid.*, II, 197: "That sweete and heavenly uniting of the mindes, which properly is called love, hath no other knot but vertue, and therefore if it be a right love, it can never slide into any action that is not vertuous."

58. *Ibid.*, I, 56: "Knowledges . . . are . . . not all the minde may stretch it selfe unto. . . . I see [their] bounds . . . but the workings of the minde I finde much more infinite, then can be led unto by the eye." *Ibid*, p. 80: "Notable men" have claimed that love is "the highest power of the mind."

59. *Ibid.*, pp. 451–52. For a similar passage, see *ibid.*, p. 190.

60. *Ibid.*, II, 163. Pyrocles to Musidorus: "There did I learne the sweete mysteries of Phylosophy; there had I your lively example, to confirme that which I learned; there lastly had I your friendship."

61. *Defence*, p. 45: "There are many misteries contained in *Poetrie*, which of purpose were written darkly, least by prophane wits it should be abused."

62. *Arcadia*, I, 97. Cf. *ibid.*, p. 16: "a mind of most excellent composition (a pearcing witte quite void of ostentation, high erected thoughts seated in a harte of courtesie, an eloquence as sweete in the uttering, as slowe to come to the uttering, a behaviour so noble . . . and all in a man . . . not

... above one & twenty yeares.).'' See also *ibid.*, pp. 190, 206, 446, for the right attitude, qualities, and virtues.

63. *Ibid.*, p. 206: "Therefore having well established those kingdomes, under good governours, . . . they determined . . . to see more of the world, & to imploy those gifts esteemed rare in them, to the good of mankinde."

64. *Loc. cit.* "True exercise of vertue" is mentioned also in *Arcadia*, I, 77: Pyrocles is "formed by nature, and framed by education" for it.

65. *Ibid.*, I, 338.

66. On the problems connected with this simple justification of war, and on the derivation of the idea of such a just war, see my discussion, "Sir Thomas More and *Justum Bellum*," *Ethics*, XLVI (1946), 303–8.

67. *Arcadia*, II, 204: "*Euarchus* . . . loved goodnesse more then himselfe." Fortunately, the death sentences against the virtuous heroes are not carried out: a rather absurd dramatic climax reveals at the last moment that they are innocent. (*Ibid.*, II, 204–5.)

68. See his description in *Arcadia*, I, 185 ff.

69. *Ibid.*, p. 187.

70. *Ibid.*, pp. 186, 502.

71. *Ibid.*, p. 468: The ideal prince is "a father of people, who ought with the eye of wisdome, the hand of fortitude, and the hart of justice to set downe all private conceits, in comparison of what for the publike is profitable."

72. Cf. E. Greenlaw, "Sidney's *Arcadia* as an Example of Elizabethan Allegory," *op. cit.*, pp. 336–37.

73. Goldman (*op. cit.*, p. 184, note 42) points to the probable influence of Bodin's thought on Sidney's monarchist statements: "Again and again, in the *Arcadia* one encounters references to monarchical government which seem echoes of the ideas of Bodin." On the other hand, Sidney also echoes the native monarchist tradition as, for instance, Elyot represents it. Cf. F. L. Baumer, *The Early Tudor Theory of Kingship* (New Haven, 1940), for a comprehensive treatment of this tradition in the half-century before Sidney.

74. W. D. Briggs, "Political Ideas in Sidney's *Arcadia*," *Studies in Philology*, XXVIII (1931), 137–61, and "Sidney's Political Ideas," *ibid.*, XXIX (1932), 534–42; Irving Ribner, "Sir Philip Sidney on Civil Insurrection," *Journal of the History of Ideas*, XIII (1952), 257–65.

75. *A Discourse of Syr Ph. S. to the Queenes Majesty touching hir Mariage with Monsieur*, in *Complete Works*, III, 51–60.

76. Greville, *op. cit.*, p. 98.

77. *Ibid.*, p. 53.

78. *Ibid.*, p. 54.

79. *Arcadia*, I, 330.

80. See the articles by Briggs and Ribner cited in note 74, above.

81. Greville, *op. cit.*, p. 116. Machiavelli and the devil were often practically synonymous in Elizabethan usage. Cf. Mario Praz, "Machiavelli and the Elizabethans," *Proceedings of the British Academy*, XIV (1928), 49–97.

82. *Arcadia*, I, 200–201.

83. *Ibid.*, p. 201.

84. Briggs (*op. cit.*, XXVIII [1931], 144) refers to Sidney's *Defence*, III, 15, where Sidney says tyrants "Occidentos esse" (in Arber's edition of the *Apologie* [*op. cit.*, p. 39], this passage reads, correctly, "occidendos esse"). According to Briggs's interpretation, Sidney feels that rebellions should be led by duly qualified persons, such as princes or magistrates, who would act in the interests of the people against misrule. In this, Briggs argues, Sidney agrees with the *Vindiciae*. See also W. G. Zeeveld, "The Uprising of the Commons in Sidney's *Arcadia*," *Modern Language Notes*, XLVIII (1933), 209–17, particularly p. 214, note 8. Ribner, *op. cit.*, pp. 262–63, argues against the assumption that Sidney grants anybody, even the nobles, the right of armed insurrection, and claims that Sidney specifically disagrees with Huguenot doctrine in this respect. This may be correct as far as ordinary nobles are concerned, but Sidney's view seems to me to be that at least princes of royal blood either have the right, or are used by God, to do away with tyrants.

85. Briggs, *op. cit.*, XXVIII, 153. Brie, *op. cit.*, pp. 67–68, overemphasizes Sidney's royalism, as does Zandvoort, *op. cit.*, pp. 154–57, who also exaggerates Sidney's "unmitigated contempt" for the lower and middle classes. Briggs's statement, which I quote in my text, seems like a more accurate definition of Sidney's creed than Zandvoort's interpretation (*op. cit.*, p. 156): "A wise and strong monarch, who knows how to keep the great nobles in their places, and acknowledges that he with his people makes all but one body politic; lords and gentlemen admitted into counsel; the commons to abstain from prying into matters of government." Such variations in interpretation arise because Sidney offers his political theory not in a treatise but in the veiled form of his "heroical poem." The problem is further complicated because he frequently wrote with practical situations rather than political theory in mind; he was often "turning into a didactic fiction his reactions to the affairs of his native land." (Goldman, *op. cit.*, p. 184.) Such varied theories as those of the *Vindiciae* and of Bodin's *République* may have come to his mind as he was contemplating different political situations.

86. *Arcadia*, I, 202.

87. *Ibid.*, pp. 37–47. See Briggs, *op. cit.*, XXVIII, 140–41, for a brief analysis. Ribner, *op cit.*, p. 259, questions the validity of Briggs's analysis since this is a revolt of a formerly free people against foreign conquerors, similar to that of the Dutch, and as such is different from ordinary civil insurrection. (See also his "Machiavelli and Sidney: the Arcadia of 1590," *Studies in Philology*, XLVII [1950], 152–72.)

88. A note of sympathy for the poor is also struck in *A Discourse on Irish Affairs*, where he complains about the tyrannous rule of Irishmen over their fellow-countrymen: "Privileged persons be all the riche men of the pale, the burdne only lyinge uppon the poore, who may grone, for theyr cry can not be hearde" (*Complete Works*, III, 46).

89. *Arcadia*, I, 315 ff.

90. Unity prevails only so long as no positive measures have to be taken. Then each social and economic group voices its own particular

demands so that nothing is achieved. Typical: "The peasants would have the Gentlemen destroied, the Citizens . . . would but have them refourmed" (*ibid.*, p. 315). Then follows the exclamation: "O weak trust of the many-headed multitude . . . who can set confidence there . . . ?" (*ibid.*, pp. 318–19). Cf. Goldman, *op. cit.*, p. 154.

91. *Arcadia*, I, 317.

92. *Loc. cit.*

93. *Ibid.*, I, 196–97. Obviously, Sidney here had the distorted contemporary picture of the Machiavellian prince in mind. Cf. Praz, *op. cit.*, and E. Meyer, *Machiavelli and the Elizabethan Drama* (Weimar, 1897): the Elizabethans knew Machiavelli's doctrines largely from I. Gentillet's anti-Machiavellian treatise, *Discours sur les moyens de bien gouverner ... contre N. Machiavel* (n.p., 1576). Some of Machiavelli's doctrines, according to Greville, *op. cit.*, p. 133, ought to be "cryed down, and banished, to reign among barbarous heathen spirits."

94. "*Oligarchie;* that is, when men are governed in deede by a fewe, and yet are not taught to know what those fewe be. . . ." The oligarchs make "the Kinges sworde strike whom they hated, the Kings purse reward whom they loved." Corruption, high taxation, etc., create a "very dissolution of all estates, while the great men . . . grew factious among themselves." This state of affairs can be remedied only by a monarch who holds the aristocracy in check (*Arcadia*, I, 185–86).

95. *Ibid.*, p. 196.

96. *A Discourse . . . to the Queenes Majesty . . .* , in *Complete Works*, III, 58.

97. *Arcadia*, I, 212.

98. *Ibid.*, pp. 119–25, 365. Cecropia, incidentally, is an atheist, an attitude thought to be typical of a Machiavellian ruler.

99. *Ibid.*, p. 205.

100. *Ibid.*, p. 187. "While by force he tooke nothing, by their love he had all."

101. *Loc. cit.*

102. *A Discourse . . .* , in *Complete Works*, III, 60.

103. *Arcadia*, I, 185.

104. *Ibid.*, p. 410.

105. *Ibid.*, pp. 46–47. The Helots are "to bee hereafter fellowes, and no longer servaunts."

106. *Ibid.*, II, 130–31 (italics mine).

107. Cf. Briggs, *op. cit.*, XXVIII, 154: "Sidney recognizes the value . . . of a training in the administration of public affairs on the part of the upper classes, which a monarchy 'privately' administered is incapable of providing."

108. *Arcadia*, I, 317. In this context, Sidney might mean "monarch" when saying "magistrate"; however, I believe he means "authorities" in general, for there can obviously be government without a monarch, but not without any kind of authorities.

109. *Ibid.*, pp. 322–23.

110. *Ibid.*, II, 131. Sidney, while not approving of these other forms of government, does not condemn them explicitly, but only makes the cited

statement. This may indicate that he thought aristocracy and democracy possible but not desirable in his time and country. They are advocated by "the discoursing sorte of men" rather than by "the active" (*loc. cit.*).

111. Greville, *op. cit.*, pp. 190–92. In this very preservation of free and strong social groups, the "differences between Monarchs, and Tyrants" are "published . . . clearly to the world" (*ibid.*, p. 98).

112. *Ibid.*, p. 189.

113. *Arcadia*, I, 189.

114. *Ibid.*, p. 77.

115. Greville, *op. cit.*, pp. 34–35.

116. *Arcadia*, I, 185.

117. *Ibid.*, p. 19. Greenlaw (*op. cit.*, p. 335) considers "the contrast between Evarchus, the wise prince, and Basilius, king in name only" as the "central theme in Sidney's treatment of the Prince." While it is true that from Basilius' weakness anarchy results, and that this is contrasted with the conditions in Euarchus' kingdom, it seems to me that the central theme is the contrast between good and evil princes, just monarchs and Machiavellian tyrants. Basilius deviates from the pattern set for the perfect prince, but is not its antithesis, like Plexirtus and Antiphilus. The weakness of his character and the lack of responsibility in his behavior cause the turmoil that breaks out in his kingdom: it is weakness, however, not wickedness, as in the case of the other rulers.

118. *Arcadia*, I, 331. Perhaps this obscure, base origin is the cause of his wickedness; however that may be, he feels it necessary to fake his pedigree so as to prove his royal blood.

119. *Ibid.*, p. 330.

120. *Ibid.*, p. 331.

121. "Plexirtus stands for the Machiavellian tyrant: he secured the crown by unjust means; kept it by the aid of foreign mercenaries who were established in citadels, the nests of tyrants and murderers of liberty; he disarmed his countrymen . . . blinded his father . . . sought the death of his brother . . ., following the precept that all who have any claim to the throne must be destroyed; he was crafty enough to hide his faults" (Greenlaw's summary, *op. cit.*, p. 334). Greenlaw observes that "every one of the characteristics of Plexirtus is a concrete illustration of principles taken from Machiavelli or from the hostile summary of the theory by Gentillet." (*Loc. cit.*)

122. *Arcadia*, II, 133.

123. *Ibid.*, p. 132.

124. *Ibid.*, pp. 132–33.

125. *Ibid.*, p. 132.

126. This and previous quotations in this paragraph are taken from *Arcadia*, I, 408.

127. *Ibid.*, p. 409.

128. *Ibid.*, p. 410.

129. *Ibid.*, p. 409.

130. *Ibid.*, II, 157.

131. From Spenser's dedication to Sidney in *The Shepheardes Calender*.

## CHAPTER VIII

1. Only some of the numerous books and articles dealing with Spenser's social and political views can be mentioned in this chapter. Other works can readily be found in F. I. Carpenter, *A Reference Guide to Edmund Spenser* (Chicago, 1923), in Dorothy F. Atkinson's *Edmund Spenser: A Bibliographical Supplement* (Baltimore, 1937), and in the annual bibliographies in the spring issues of *Studies in Philology*. Most of the results of scholarly investigation and interpretation are now combined in the notes and commentaries of *The Works of Edmund Spenser: A Variorum Edition*, ed. E. Greenlaw, C. G. Osgood, F. M. Padelford, R. Heffner (Baltimore, 1932–49) (hereafter referred to as *Variorum*). H. S. V. Jones, *A Spenser Handbook* (New York, 1930), is a useful reference work. J. C. Smith and E. de Selincourt, *The Poetical Works of Edmund Spenser* (London, 1937), has a good introduction by de Selincourt. W. L. Renwick's *Edmund Spenser: An Essay on Renaissance Poetry* (London, 1925) and Leicester Bradner's *Edmund Spenser and "The Faerie Queene"* (Chicago, 1948) should also be mentioned. The best biography is A. C. Judson, *The Life of Edmund Spenser* (Baltimore, 1945).

2. De Selincourt, *op. cit.*, Introduction, p. xiii.

3. These epithets are used in L. Bryskett's *A pastorall Aeglogue vpon the death of Sir Phillip Sidney Knight*, which, like Spenser's *Astrophel* and other elegies commemorating Sidney, appeared together with *Colin Clouts come home againe* (London, 1595).

4. *Astrophel. A Pastorall Elegie vpon the death of the most Noble and valorous Knight, Sir Philip Sidney*. On the significance of this poem, and on the relationship between Spenser and Sidney, see the commentaries in *Variorum, The Minor Poems*, I (1943), 483–90. In *Colin Clouts come home againe* (lines 450–51) Spenser states that, while "Astrofell" was living, there "was none his Paragone."

5. Berta Siebeck gives a comprehensive account of this literature in *Das Bild Sir Philip Sidneys in der englischen Renaissance* (Weimar, 1939).

6. Cf. Josephine W. Bennett, *The Evolution of "The Faerie Queene"* (Chicago, 1942), pp. 212–15. The voluminous earlier discussion relative to Sir Calidore's identity is abridged in *Variorum, FQ* VI (1938), Appendix II, 349–64, "The Prototype of Sir Calidore."

7. Cf. Bennett, *op. cit.*, p. 213.

8. Thus *Prosopopoia: or Mother Hubberds Tale*, in J. C. Smith and E. de Selincourt, *The Poetical Works of Edmund Spenser*, pp. 495–508, lines 811–12:

> "Poets . . . onely pride
> Is vertue to aduaunce, and vice deride."

9. C. B. Millican (*Spenser and the Table Round* [Cambridge, 1932], p. 115) makes the point that in Spenser's day no clear distinction was drawn between epic and romance, that "Spenser combines the form of epic and romance." "Spenser's conception of himself as an epic poet . . .

did not conflict with his conception of *The Faerie Queene* as a romance of chivalry on the pattern of the *Orlando Furioso.*" Cf. Bennett, *op. cit.,* p. 105.

10. B. E. C. Davis (*Edmund Spenser: A Critical Study* [Cambridge, 1933], p. 68) states that "ideal humanity, the concrete imitation drawn from accepted ethical theories, becomes the hero of *The Faerie Queene* which, from this aspect, belongs to the same order of literature as *The Boke of the Governour, The Courtier* and *Euphues.* . . . The faerie knight is first and last the complete gentleman. . . . His moral virtue is tempered by the social graces of courtesy, friendliness, and urbanity."

11. *A Letter of the Authors expounding his whole intention in the course of this worke . . . to . . . Sir Walter Raleigh . . .* (in *Variorum, FQ* I. 167).

12. *Letter to Raleigh, loc. cit.*

13. *Ibid.*

14. *Ibid.*: His "like intention was to doe in the person of Aeneas."

15. Arthur, according to the letter, is portrayed "before he was king" as "the image of a braue knight." He embodies "magnificence" in which all the other virtues are contained in perfection.

16. *Ibid.*: "Of the XII. other vertues, I make XII. other knights the patrones, for the more variety of the history."

17. Bennett, *op. cit.,* p. 216. Renwick, *op. cit.,* p. 180, calls *The Faerie Queene* "a political tract as well as a fine story."

18. "Disposed into twelue bookes, Fashioning XII. Morall vertues." He seems to have thirteen virtues in mind, according to the *Letter to Raleigh,* "magnificence" and the twelve "other vertues."

19. The debate whether Spenser's virtues are or are not Aristotelian is presented in *Variorum, FQ* I, Appendix I, 314–62, "Plan and Conduct." J. J. Jusserand ("Spenser's 'Twelve private Morall Vertues as Aristotle hath devised,'" *Modern Philology,* III [1906], 373–83) pointed to a number of discrepancies between the Spenserian and the Aristotelian schemes. W. F. De Moss (*The Influence of Aristotle's "Politics" and "Ethics" on Spenser* [Chicago, 1918]) tried to vindicate the Aristotelian character of Spenser's work by interpreting such conceptions as "holiness" and "courtesy" into Aristotle's system of virtues. H. S. V. Jones ("*The Faerie Queene* and the Mediaeval Aristotelian Tradition," *Journal of English and Germanic Philology,* XXV [1926], 283–98) modified De Moss's interpretation by suggesting that Spenser's Aristotelianism is that of the scholastic philosophers and of Melanchthon, i.e., that his system is only very indirectly derived from Aristotle. See also Viola B. Hulbert, "Spenser's Twelve Moral Virtues 'According to Aristotle and the Rest,'" *University of Chicago Abstracts of Theses* ("Humanistic Series," Vol. V [1928]), pp. 479–85. Platonism, on the other hand, pervades Spenser's thought. W. Riedner (*Spensers Belesenheit. 1. Teil. Die Bibel und das klassische Altertum* [Leipzig, 1908]) and M. Bhattacherje (*Studies in Spenser* [Calcutta, 1929] and *Platonic Ideas in Spenser* [London, 1935]) have demonstrated many similarities in Spenser's and Plato's thought, and believe that Spenser was well acquainted with some of Plato's works. But the question whether Spenser read Plato in the

original (and, if so, which works) has not been definitely settled. A. E. Taylor ("Spenser's Knowledge of Plato," *Modern Language Review*, XIX [1924], 208–10) does not think that he knew any Platonic works at first hand, and Davis (*op. cit.*, p. 59) holds that his Platonism is derived "mainly, if not wholly" through Italian channels. Apart from this thorny question of derivation, however, the great importance of Platonism in Spenser's thought cannot be doubted. "Whilst . . . the formal scheme of *The Faerie Queene* is Aristotelian, the life and soul of the allegory lies in Renaissance neo-Platonism" (Davis, *op. cit.*, p. 213). Like Plato rather than like Aristotle, Spenser always "presupposes the absolute type, the perfect lover, warrior, courtier as measure to the scale of values" (*ibid.*, p. 65). In conclusion, it should be mentioned that Renwick (*op. cit.*, p. 175) thinks that Cicero is Spenser's greatest inspiration, and describes *FQ* as "the *de Officiis* and the *de Finibus* of the Renaissance," as "an exposition of the general consensus of the best ethical doctrine" (p. 158). Spenser chose from his authorities, either directly or through secondary works, whatever ideas seemed to suit his purpose best. It seems to me that the *synthesis* he produced has too often been obscured by the tendency of modern scholarship to dissect it in an *analysis* of its infinitely variegated origins. It has been noted that his poetic imagery resembles a rich mosaic; so does his philosophy.

20. Bryskett quotes Spenser as having made another statement concerning the purpose and scheme of *The Faerie Queene*. Bryskett's report of Spenser's words is probably not accurate. (It occurs in his description of a conversation which, according to Judson [*op. cit.*, p. 107], probably took place in the spring of 1582.) However, it is interesting that in the passage ascribed to him by Bryskett, Spenser makes no specific mention of Aristotle, whereas he does refer to L. Bryskett's translation of G. B. Giraldi Cintio's *Dialoghi della Vita Civile* as "comprehending all" the "Ethicke part of Morall Philosophie" in an easily comprehensible manner. Spenser's reference to *The Faerie Queene*, as given by Bryskett in *A Discourse of Civill Life* (London, 1606), pp. 26–27, is as follows:

"I haue already vndertaken a work . . . in *heroical verse*, under the title of a *Faerie Queene* to represent all the moral vertues, assigning to euery vertue, a Knight to be the patrone and defender of the same: in whose actions and feates of armes and chiualry, the operations of that vertue . . . are to be expressed, and the vices and vnruly appetites that oppose themselues against the same, to be beaten downe and ouercome." Bryskett himself points out that Cintio gathered his ideas from Plato, Aristotle, and from "other excellent writers besides" (*ibid.*, p. 32).

21. Bennett, *op. cit.*, p. 219. Cf. her whole chaper on "The Illustration of the Virtues," *ibid.*, pp. 216–30. Mrs. Bennett (*ibid.*, p. 227) advances the hypothesis that Spenser had originally planned to illustrate the scheme of four cardinal virtues, and only later expanded their number to twelve.

22. *Ibid.*, p. 217. Neither does Spenser's temperance in Book II fit into an Aristotelian scheme, according to J. L. Shanley, "Spenser's Temperance and Aristotle," *Modern Philology*, XLIII (1946), 170–74.

23. É. Legouis (*Edmund Spenser* [Paris, 1923], p. 216) speaks of an "égalité presque absolue de doctrines entre lesquelles il ne choisit pas. Il s'inspire de Platon sans cesser d'être le disciple respectueux d'Aristote ... ne paraît avoir aucune conscience de ses disparates." Davis (*op. cit.*, p. 211) attacks Legouis's deprecatory remarks and insists on Spenser's capacity for independent thought.

24. It is evident from the *Fowre Hymnes*, for instance, that he was aware of the differences between various philosophical systems: the first two, supposedly written in his younger years, evince strongly Platonic leanings, whereas the last two, products of his more mature years, in obvious contrast proclaim a Christian ethic. Paul N. Siegel ("Spenser and the Calvinist View of Life," *Studies in Philology*, XLI [1944], 201–22) argues that Spenser's views are always consistent with the Calvinist ethic, that he is primarily a disciple of Calvin, and that he is also an avowed adherent of Platonism. He claims that Spenser reconciled these two elements, and that he could be an apostle of beauty and a lover of the good things of life without ceasing to be a Calvinist. I can neither accept the definition of Calvinism which this view entails, nor can I follow Mr. Siegel in virtually identifying Spenser's gentleman with Calvin's elect. While Spenser shows the influence of Calvinism, I do not think that his thought can be called predominantly Calvinist.

25. *Letter to Raleigh.*

26. And, of course, a great many other writers on courtesy. The subject is dealt with fully in *Variorum, FQ* VI, Appendix I, 336–48. For a list of other works which Spenser may have known and used, see also A. C. Judson, "Spenser's Theory of Courtesy," *PMLA*, XLVII (1932), 122. For the similarity of Spenser's and Castiglione's conceptions, cf. *ibid.*, p. 126, and Jones, *A Spenser Handbook*, pp. 291–93. See also W. Schrinner, *Castiglione und die englische Renaissance* (Berlin, 1939), pp. 92–97, 117, 125–27; and *Variorum, FQ* VI, 329.

27. Cf. Judson, "Spenser's Theory of Courtesy," *op. cit.*, p. 135; also Schrinner, *op. cit.*, p. 93. Schrinner's distinction between Castiglione's "Renaissance" and Spenser's "Christian" conceptions of self-control and temperance, between Castiglione's "aestheticism" and Spenser's "moralism" seems to me to be too sharply drawn.

28. Siegel (*op. cit.*) claims that Calvinism prevails in the shaping of Spenser's gentleman. Generally, I think, Spenser's "Christianity" should not be overemphasized in contradistinction to the "paganism" of other predecessors and contemporaries. Davis (*op. cit.*, p. 67) remarks that Spenser's Christianity is overlaid with Renaissance paganism, and that it is difficult to make a Puritan out of him: "He never displays the Puritan sense of man's utter worthlessness and self-contempt in the presence of his Maker" (*ibid.*, p. 242).

29. The book of Holiness does not seem to me to have the central importance in *FQ* that Siegel (*op. cit.*, p. 204) claims for it.

30. Judson, "Spenser's Theory of Courtesy," *op. cit.*, pp. 134–36. In Judson's interpretation, Renaissance courtesy is motivated by calculating self-interest, whereas the motivation of the Christian-medieval ideal is spontaneous warmheartedness and uninterested benevolence. Spenser

places his "emphasis on the chivalric ideal," but the two conceptions "at certain points . . . no doubt merge" (*ibid.*, p. 136). In its ideal form —as distinguished from its later degradation—the Renaissance ideal of courtesy does not proclaim the perfection of the individual as an ultimate end in itself: the harmonious development of the individual and its outward expression in courteous manners are supposed to enable the courtier to render better service to his prince and thus to aid the community at large. His own perfection is subordinated and conducive to that of the state. While this is a more calculated and secular conception than the Christian ideal of courtesy, its ultimate aim is the perfection and advantage of the community rather than merely that of the individual.

31. Cf. John Erskine, "The Virtue of Friendship in the *Faerie Queene*," *PMLA*, XXX (1915), 831–50, and Charles G. Smith, *Spenser's Theory of Friendship* (Baltimore, 1935), also "The Virtue of Friendship and the Plan of Book IV," in *Variorum*, FQ IV, Appendix I, 281–313. Bennett (*op. cit.*, pp. 167–68) considers the story of Amyas and Placidas (*FQ* IV. VII–IX) as Spenser's best treatment of friendship.

32. The friendship of women is illustrated in the same book of *FQ*, in the story of Britomart and Amoret.

33. C. G. Smith (*Spenser's Theory of Friendship*, pp. 29 ff.) refers to many outstanding formulations of the classical doctrine that friendship can exist only between good men and must be based on virtue. He lists Plato, Aristotle, Cicero, Elyot, Montaigne, and others. This is followed by lists of authorities on the themes that friendship is possible only between equals, that it is impossible between the wicked, and on similar points. Many of these statements were proverbial in Spenser's day.

34. *Variorum*, FQ IV. 308. C. G. Smith there quotes in support of this point *An Hymne in Honour of Love*, lines 75–91; *An Hymne in Honour of Beautie*, lines 194–98; and *Colin Clouts come home againe*, lines 841–52.

35. Cf. *Variorum*, FQ IV, 282–83.

36. Cf. *ibid.*, p. 291.

37. Cf. J. L. Shanley, *A Study of Spenser's Gentleman* (Evanston, 1940), pp. 7–8.

38. *FQ* VI. III. 1.

39. *FQ* VI. IV. 36.

40. *FQ* VI. 4. Cf. commentary on this and related passages in *Variorum*, FQ VI, 337. Judson ("Spenser's Theory of Courtesy," p. 124) interprets these lines differently. Bradner (*op. cit.*, pp. 151–52) is also of the opinion that for Spenser, courtesy "comes from noble or gentle birth," and that "Spenser means to say [in Book VI] that courtesy in its full flower . . . is found only in those of gentle birth. . . . Nowhere in Spenser do we find the opinion . . . that courtesy or gentility is a gift of God which may crop up in any person." However, Bradner modifies his position by stating that we cannot be sure what Spenser means by gentle birth, and that Spenser probably only meant that one must be a "gentleman."

41. *The Teares of the Muses* in *Variorum*, *The Minor Poems* Vol. II (Baltimore, 1947), lines 91–96. A similar note is struck in the sonnet

Spenser wrote for W. Jones's translation of G. B. Nenna's *Il Nennio* (*Nennio, or a Treatise of Nobility: Wherein is discoursed what true Nobilitie is, with such qualities as are required in a perfect gentleman* [London, 1595]). These are Spenser's words:

> "Who so wil seeke by right deserts t'attaine,
> Vnto the type of true Nobility,
> And not by painted shewes and titles vaine,
> Deriued farre from famous Auncestrie,
> Behold them both in their right visnomy
> Here truly pourtray'd, as they ought to be,
> And striuing both for termes of dignitie,
> To be aduanced highest in degree.
> And, when thou doost with equall insight see
> The ods twixt both, of both then deem aright
> And chuse the better of them both to thee. . . ."

The *Nennio* takes the side of virtue against blood in the current controversy, i.e., it voices the more democratic doctrine. It concludes that "the nobilitie of the minde, is farre more true, and farre more perfect, then the nobility of blood conioyned with riches." He is "worthy of far more greater glorie who of himselfe becommeth noble, than hee who is simplie borne noble" (f. 96ᵛ). Spenser himself probably would not have gone so far, but it seems unlikely that he would have written a sonnet to recommend this work if he had disapproved of its contents. I do not think that he absolutely insisted on the noble birth of the courtier, as for instance Bhattacherje, *Studies in Spenser*, p. 83, claims.

42. Vice versa, in *FQ* VI. III. 1, he assumes that gentle deeds and manners show "of what degree and what race" a man "is growne." He indicates "that good Poet," probably Chaucer, as his authority for this statement; as Judson ("Spenser's Theory of Courtesy," pp. 123–24) points out, however, he twists Chaucer's meaning, which was that one who does gentle deeds is a gentleman—i.e., Chaucer's doctrine is more democratic than Spenser's. Legouis (*op. cit.*, p. 206) thus describes Spenser's attitude: "Il se plut à proclamer l'excellence du sang noble avec ... un air de foi que déjà le XIVᵉ siècle n'avait plus."

43. Louis B. Wright ("Handbook Learning of the Renaissance Middle Class," *Studies in Philology*, XXVIII [1931], 58–59) stresses the appeal of such books as the *Courtier* to the middle class, and points out that social climbers (such as well-to-do merchants) would be avid readers of aristocratic conduct books. It would be interesting to determine to what social group in the United States today most readers of Emily Post's writings on etiquette belong—probably to the lower strata of society and not to those for which Mrs. Post ostensibly writes. Molière's *Bourgeois gentilhomme* reveals the existence of a similar situation in seventeenth-century France.

44. Such social advancement, however, must have been more difficult in the second half of the sixteenth century than it had been in the first when what became the "Tudor gentry" was still in the process of active formation and consolidation.

45. *Letter to Raleigh.*

46. Even in its known incomplete state, the poem is longer than *Paradise Lost,* the *Aeneid,* and *Gerusalemme Liberata* combined (Bennett, *op. cit.,* p. 228).

47. Bradner (*op. cit.,* p. 7) finds that "the setting of *The Faerie Queene* was just as unreal to the Elizabethans as it is to us." Spenser was, of course, imitating the manner of Ariosto and Tasso in this form of literature; he was more specifically concerned with moral and didactic aims than these Italian authors.

48. M. M. Gray, "The Influence of Spenser's Irish Experiences on *The Faerie Queene," Review of English Studies,* VI (1930), 413–28. Gray proves his point by introducing a number of close parallels between scenes described in *FQ* and scenes that actually took place in Ireland.

49. In his *View of the Present State of Ireland,* in *Variorum,* ed. R. Gottfried (Baltimore, 1949); or in the allegorical defense of Lord Grey in *FQ* V, this attitude is very evident. Spenser not only defends and advocates very cruel measures but takes them for granted because they serve to further the right cause. Legouis (*op. cit.,* p. 217) defines this attitude as follows: Spenser "se crut parfait chrétien en pratiquant la politique de Machiavel." E. Greenlaw (*Studies in Spenser's Historical Allegory* [Baltimore, 1932], p. 139) bears out this judgment when he describes the theme of the fifth book of *FQ* as "the necessity for the exercise of imperial power to the utmost in putting down rebellion . . . , the right of a strong nation to aid an oppressed and suffering people, and . . . the right of England to establish an Empire beyond the seas."

50. Spenser himself from time to time grew restless over his quiet country life in Ireland (cf. de Selincourt, *op. cit.,* p. xxx).

51. The historical allegory of *FQ* has no particular bearing on the present investigation and is therefore almost entirely disregarded. Bradner (*op. cit.,* p. 124) distinguishes three levels of meaning in *FQ:* (1) the "moral or religious meaning"; (2) the "national allegory"; (3) the "personal allegory." Our principal concern here must be with (1).

52. Greenlaw (*Studies in Spenser's Historical Allegory,* p. 146) points out that the *Utopia* and the *Governour,* the *Arcadia* and the fifth book of *The Faerie Queene* can all be grouped together as political treatises.

53. As we shall see, however, he was very conscious of differences of rank and birth, and certainly never advocated an aristocracy selected solely on the basis of intellectual ability.

54. *FQ* VI. IV. 35.

55. Cf. the *Letter to Raleigh* and Bryskett's report, quoted in note 20, above.

56. Cf. *Mother Hubberds Tale,* lines 780–82, where this identity is expressly stated.

57. Lines 83–84.

58. "Men to God thereby are nighest raised": *Teares . . . , op. cit.,* line 90; cf. also *ibid.,* lines 487–534.

59. Cf. Shanley, *A Study of Spenser's Gentleman,* pp. 13–14.

60. Shanley, *ibid.,* p. 14.

61. As Shanley points out, another innovation in Spenser's thought is the fact that he lays greater stress on religious education than most of his predecessors had done. This is in keeping with his more Christian scheme of virtues.

62. Shanley, *ibid.*, p. 14.

63. See below, pp. 192–96.

64. *FQ* V. I. 5–8.

65. *FQ* V. I. 5.

66. *FQ* V. I. 7.

67. *FQ* V. I. 9.

68. *FQ* V. I. 12. The relation of this figure to Greek mythology is analyzed in *Variorum*, *FQ* V. 165–67. Talus' functions and actions are summarized by F. M. Padelford, "Talus: The Law," *Studies in Philology*, XV (1918), 97–104.

69. *FQ* V. I. 12.

70. For Spenser's conception, cf. *Variorum*, *FQ* V, 269–98, Appendix I, "The Virtue of Justice and the Plan of Book V."

71. Alfred B. Gough, in his edition of *The Faerie Queene, Book V* (Oxford, 1918), p. 271, finds "an unconscious irony in the selection of the most atrocious chapter in English history as an example of the virtue of justice." He is referring to Spenser's allegorical defense of Lord Grey's activities in Ireland.

72. *FQ* V. IX. 21 f.

73. *FQ* V. IX. 30.

74. *FQ* V. IX. 32.

75. *FQ* V. IX. 36: "Dealing of Iustice with indifferent grace."

76. *FQ* V. IX. 34.

77. *FQ* V. IX. 36. Similarly, *FQ* V. II. 1:

> "Nought is more honorable to a knight
>
> .  .  .  .  .  .  .  .  .  .  .  .  .
>
> Then to defend the feeble in their right."

I.e., the obligations of rulers toward the ruled are here stressed.

78. *FQ* V. IX. 24.

79. *FQ* V. IX. 22.

80. *FQ* V. IX. 24.

81. *FQ* V. IX. 23.

82. *Loc. cit.*

83. Gray (*op. cit.*, p. 422) tries to show that, despite his advocacy of severe measures against the Irish, Spenser indicated that he had sympathy and pity for them.

84. *FQ* V. IV. 1.

85. In *FQ* V. XII. Cf. note 71, above.

86. *FQ* V. XII. 25.

87. *FQ* V. XII. 40.

88. *FQ* V. XII. 43.

89. *FQ* V. XII. 26.

90. *FQ* V. XII. 26.

91. E. Greenlaw ("The Influence of Machiavelli on Spenser," *Modern Philology*, VII [1909], 187–202) cites close parallels between the measures advocated by Spenser and those suggested by Machiavelli for a similar situation. "Spenser saw how entirely the principles laid down by Machiavelli for the governing of a turbulent foreign colony would fit the present case," and he applied them (p. 194). Greenlaw concludes that "the theories of Machiavelli are here applied as the great Italian intended" (p. 202)—which is probably true—and then proceeds to give his approval to Spenser's extremely harsh suggestions, apparently because they are reflections of "true" Machiavellianism on Spenser's part!

92. E. Greenlaw ("Spenser and British Imperialism," *Modern Philology*, IX [1912], 335) doubts whether in Spenser's time the lower classes in England itself would "have received a whit the more consideration." While I agree with this suggestion, I cannot follow Greenlaw when he claims that, in advocating this kind of action, Spenser follows "a course unswerving as it is lofty," representative of "Elizabethan political idealism," unless "idealism" and "imperialism"—Greenlaw says "the glorious vision of an imperial England"—are taken to mean the same thing (*ibid.*, pp. 369–70).

93. *FQ* VI. V. 29.

94. His defense of Lord Grey's activities in Ireland, particularly of the Smerwick massacre, and the suggestions for subduing the Irish (cf. *View*, ed. Gottfried, pp. 154–63, and a number of passages in *FQ* V) are the main cases in point. They have frequently been attacked—thus Pauline Henley, *Spenser in Ireland* (Cork, 1928). Gottfried has collected the major interpretations, criticisms of, and apologies for, the *View* in *Variorum*, Appendix III, 497–532. See the critical remarks of Legouis and de Selincourt reprinted there. Padelford's comment on the worst passage (p. 158, lines 3248–70 of the *View*) is that it is "a terrible proposal, uttered with cold deliberateness." The more recent tendency has been to exonerate Spenser from the charges of advocating and defending unusually cruel measures. The defense has argued, for instance, that Spenser's resolute plans were better than Elizabeth's vacillations, that his words have been misinterpreted, and that his measures were entirely in keeping with contemporary usage. Cf. Greenlaw, "Spenser and British Imperialism," *op. cit.*, pp. 360–64; R. Heffner, "Spenser's View of Ireland: Some Observations," *Modern Language Quarterly*, III (1942), 507–15; A. C. Judson, *Life of Edmund Spenser*, pp. 91–92. It would go beyond the scope of the present investigation to enter into a detailed discussion of the question. It seems, however, that Spenser would not have found it necessary to defend Lord Grey so vehemently if his activities had not been regarded as unusually and unduly cruel by many contemporaries; that Spenser would not have had to express fears that pity might prevent Elizabeth from approving his own proposals for dealing with the Irish (*View*, p. 159, lines 3293–3302) if he had not himself been aware that they were extraordinarily harsh; that the authorities would not have prevented the printing of his treatise—as they probably did (cf. Bradner, *op. cit.*, p. 46)—if the measures proposed in it had been nothing but current practice.

95. Davis (*op. cit.*, p. 74) finds that "the defence of politic expediency by the champion of Platonic justice is no more anomalous than the persecution of heretics by the author of *Utopia*." In "such inconsistency" he sees the "inevitable outcome of contemporary thought and conditions." I cannot see the "inevitability" of such inconsistency, and do not think that it could be found in a man like Erasmus. Cf. also Jones, *A Spenser Handbook*, p. 384. Gray (*loc. cit.*) has noted as a "curious characteristic of Spenser" this "seeming capacity for holding two beliefs, or experiencing two emotions which are incompatible with one another."

96. *FQ* V. 9–10.

97. *FQ* V. 10.

98. Spenser sometimes has very amusing ideas as to what constitutes "justice" in social life. Thus, any emancipation of women is simply based on usurpation, which means that it runs contrary to true justice. Only the restoration of women "to mens subiection" can reestablish justice (*FQ* V. VII. 42).

99. Bradner, *op. cit.*, p. 155: "Courtesy in Spenser's hand comes very close to being the virtue which embraces all the rest." "It surpasses justice because it adds love to law" (p. 152).

100. On Spenser's conception of the courtier, cf. also *Variorum, FQ* VI, 317–48, Appendix I, "The Plan and Conduct of Book VI."

101. *FQ* VI. II. 1.

102. *FQ* VI. X. 23.

103. *FQ* VI. I. 26. Typical manifestations of discourtesy are cowardice, treachery, lack of hospitality, slander, greed, envy, lust, ingratitude.

104. Cf. the remarks on Burbon, *FQ* V. XI. 52 ff., V. XII. 2, and those on Turpine, VI. VII. 1, where he who does "gentle deedes with franke delight" is contrasted with "a vile donghill mind"; also VI. VI. 33, where the unworthy knight is addressed as "vile cowheard dogge."

105. See *FQ* VI. III. 30 ff. for an example "of fowle discourtesie, vnfit for Knight."

106. *FQ* VI. III. 40.

107. Artegall, for instance, is brave but certainly not foolhardy, and his insuperable companion, Talus, gives him an almost too comfortable margin of safety. His opponents, Gerioneo, Grantorto, the Souldan all have great strength but fight recklessly and thus lose (cf. *Variorum, FQ* V, 292).

108. *FQ* VI. I. 41.

109. *Loc. cit.*: Nothing is worse "then the reproch of pride and cruelnesse." Spenser does make a point of showing that Talus is always restrained by his chivalrous master when in victory he becomes exceedingly cruel. Yet by modern standards, and even by the standards of some of his contemporaries, the kind of "just punishment" Spenser's knights are permitted to execute sometimes seems cruel rather than just.

110. Siegel (*op. cit.*, p. 209) identifies the "ape" with the "Italianates" at the English court, and contrasts it with Spenser's "Calvinist" gentleman. I do not think the distinction, and therefore the identification, is valid in these terms.—We are not primarily concerned with the actual political situation in which this poem originated and which it sought

to influence, but only with the political ideas to which it gives expression.

111. *MHT*, lines 1127–35.

112. *MHT*, line 1045. While Spenser in this passage evidently attacked what in his day were regarded as Machiavellian practices, he himself accepted Machiavelli's advice in his *View.* Cf. Henley, *op. cit.,* p. 179; Greenlaw, *Studies in Spenser's Historical Allegory,* pp. 162–63; and particularly Greenlaw, "The Influence of Machiavelli on Spenser," *op. cit.,* where Spenser's "conventional" anti-Machiavellian argument in *MHT* is contrasted with the "right" intrepretation and application of Machiavelli in the *View.* Greenlaw points to five "Machiavellian" traits castigated by Spenser in *MHT*, and introduces pertinent passages from the *Principe* and from Gentillet to prove his point.

113. *MHT*, line 1183.

114. *MHT*, line 1187.

115. *MHT*, line 1189.

116. *MHT*, line 1119.

117. *MHT*, line 1121.

118. *MHT*, line 825.

119. *MHT*, line 797.

120. *MHT*, line 823.

121. *MHT*, line 1193.

122. *MHT*, lines 1195–96.

123. *MHT*, line 1199.

124. *MHT*, lines 1191–92.

125. *MHT*, line 796.

126. *MHT*, line 829.

127. Similar thoughts on the vices of courtiers and courts are voiced in *Colin Clouts come home againe,* lines 701–30. The "arts of schoole" are there "counted but toyes to busie ydle braines,"

> "Whiles single Truth and simple honestie
> Do wander vp and downe despys'd of all."

128. *MHT*, lines 829–38.

129. *The Courtyer . . . done into Englyshe by T. Hoby* (London, 1561). For detailed comparisons of Castiglione and *MHT*, see *Variorum, The Minor Poems,* Vol. II, or W. L. Renwick's edition of Spenser's *Complaints* (London, 1928).

130. *MHT*, lines 717–93.

131. *MHT*, lines 727–29.

132. And, as J.L. Lievsay points out in *Variorum, FQ* VI, 192, from Guazzo's *Civile Conversation.* For a comparison of *FQ* VI. I. 2, and the manners prescribed for the *Cortegiano* by Castiglione, see Bhattacherje, *Studies in Spenser,* p. 85.

133. Pp. 191–92, *supra.*

134. *MHT*, lines 735–47.

135. *MHT*, lines 755–56.

136. *MHT*, lines 764–69. (Italics mine.) It is hardly necessary to point out that Spenser himself tried to kindle ambitious spirits by his tales of dreadful battles of knights in *The Faerie Queene.*

137. *MHT*, line 772.
138. "Not so much for to gaine or for to raise
    Himselfe to high degree. . . ."—*MHT*, lines 774–75.

Spenser, on the other hand, does not indicate that the courtier has to spend his own wealth in the prince's service—a complaint voiced by Elyot. Spenser himself derived considerable material profit from his services to the Crown.

139. *MHT*, line 776.
140. *MHT*, lines 780–82.
141. *MHT*, line 790.
142. First ed. (London, 1581). There were very numerous new editions which kept this standard manual up to date. Cf. also B. H. Putnam, *Early Treatises on the Practice of the Justices of the Peace in the Fifteenth and Sixteenth Centuries* (Oxford, 1924).
143. Artegall, the defender of justice, becomes acquainted with this wrong kind of government in his youth: Astraea, his teacher,

> "caused him to make experience
> Vpon wyld beasts, which she in woods did find
> With wrongfull powre oppressing others of their kind."
>
> *FQ* V. I. 7

This sounds like an allusion to Spenser's political teaching in the fable of *Mother Hubberds Tale:* The wickedness of tyranny as exemplified in the animal kingdom is one of Artegall's earliest lessons.

144. *FQ* V. II. 29–54. For commentaries see *Variorum, FQ* V, 336–47, Appendix III, "The Political Allegory of Canto II."
145. Bhattacherje (*Studies in Spenser*, pp. 11–15) shows the parallel between Plato's reasoning and Spenser's treatment of the theme.
146. He did see and describe the abuses of the system, especially at court (see *Mother Hubberds Tale*, for instance), and had personal grievances against it, but that did not change his basic convictions.
147. *FQ* V. II. 41. F. M. Padelford ("Spenser's Arraignment of the Anabaptists," *Journal of English and Germanic Philology*, XII [1913], 434–48) points out that these lines "voice the attitude of the English Church" in its condemnation of the Anabaptists, and quotes similar biblical texts as well as passages from official sermons of the time.
148. *FQ* V. II. 32. M. Y. Hughes ("Spenser and Utopia," *Studies in Philology*, XVII [1920], 132–46) sees a prototype for the giant's demagoguery and eventual downfall in Ket's rebellion of 1549, and connects Spenser's condemnation of the giant's teachings and activities with such tracts as Sir John Cheke's *The Hurt of Sedition*, written against Ket's rebellion.
149. *FQ* V. II. 33. Certainly a fitting and pointed description of demagoguery. "Uncontrolled freedome" and "licentious libertie" were always strongly condemned by Spenser, in whatever shape they might appear. Cf. *FQ* V. V. 25, where the latter term occurs to describe an amazonic society which has emancipated itself from male rule: women, like the vulgar, "were borne to base humilitie, Vnlesse"—and here he suddenly remembers his gracious sovereign—"the heauens them lift to lawfull soueraintie."

150. *FQ* V. II. 34.

151. *Loc. cit.*

152. For a discussion of Spenser's ideas on harmony, concord, and discord, and an enumeration of possible sources, see *Variorum, FQ* IV. 309–13.

153. *FQ* V. II. 36.

154. *Loc. cit.* This is certainly the epitome of ultraconservatism! Gough (*op. cit.,* p. 188) quotes a similar passage from the *View:* "all innovacion is perillous." Renwick (*Edmund Spenser: An Essay on Renaissance Poetry,* p. 171) discusses Spenser's belief in the "necessity of stability."

155. *FQ* V. II. 37.

156. *Loc. cit.*

157. *FQ* V. II. 38. The fox (in *MHT,* lines 129–49) similarly scorns "all seruile base subiection" and advocates equality of property:

> "For nowe a few haue all and all haue nought
>
> . . . . . . . . . . . . . . . . . . . . . .
>
> There is no right in this partition."

Padelford ("Spenser's Arraignment of the Anabaptists," *op. cit.*) considers these theories "part and parcel of the supposed Anabaptist program" which Spenser attacked.

158. Robert Crowley, *An Informacion and Peticion agaynst the Oppressours of the Pore Commons of this Realme* (London, 1548), is a major example of such social protest. On the whole subject, see Helen White, *Social Criticism in Popular Religious Literature of the Sixteenth Century* (New York, 1944).

159. *FQ* V. II. 39.

160. The giant can, of course, see nature and society, but he misinterprets them because he is unaware of the moving forces—the unseen things—behind them:

> "Sith of things subiect to thy daily vew
> Thou doest not know the causes, nor their courses dew."
>
> *FQ* V. II. 42

This lack of knowledge, insight, and piety is basically responsible for his social revolution.

161. *FQ* V. II. 41:

> "He pulleth downe, he setteth vy on hy:
> He giues to this, from that he takes away."

Padelford, "Spenser's Arraignment of the Anabaptists," *op. cit.,* and *Variorum, FQ* V, 178–79, establish the connection between this phrase and biblical teachings.

162. Kilcolman Castle, at least, was "built on a little knoll," but the location of the house that Spenser himself built on his estate has not been established (Judson, *Life,* p. 129).

163. For Spenser's acquisitions of Kilcolman and other properties, see Judson, *Life,* pp. 102–4, 110, 126–27; for his pension, *ibid.,* p. 155. Bradner (*op. cit.,* p. 186) speaks of Spenser's "distinctly practical ability to

deal with life and carve out a fortune," and says (*ibid.*, p. 3) that, with the grant of 3,000 acres from the forfeited estates of the Earl of Desmond, Spenser in 1589 became "one of the landed gentry."

164. Legouis (*op. cit.*, p. 206) has this to say: "Il ne tenta pas de supprimer les castes mais plutôt de s'élancer dans la plus haute."

165. W. G. Zeeveld, "Social Equalitarianism in a Tudor Crisis," *Journal of the History of Ideas*, VII (1946), 35–55. (Reprinted in his *Foundations of Tudor Policy* [Cambridge, Mass., 1948].)

166. Elyot, *Governour*, I, 3.

167. *FQ* V. II. 49–50.

168. *FQ* V. II. 49.

169. *FQ* V. II. 50.

170. *FQ* V. II. 52.

171. *FQ* V. II. 51.

172. *Arcadia* (London, 1590), ed. Feuillerat (Cambridge, 1922), pp. 315 ff.

173. *FQ* V. II. 52. "Spenser uses the word 'raskall' only to describe a mob or rout" (*Variorum, FQ* V, 262). Gough (*op. cit.*, p. 191) remarks that "Artegall's embarrassment is typical of the knights of romance." Gray (*op. cit.*, p. 415) maintains that "in medieval romance the knight rarely encounters the 'rascal many' " as he does in Spenser, and attributes this trait to Spenser's Irish experiences. It seems to me that the preoccupation with rebellious crowds is a more general sixteenth-century phenomenon.

174. *FQ* V. II. 53.

175. *FQ* V. XI. 44.

176. *FQ* V. XI. 38.

177. *FQ* V. XI. 47. References to similar biblical images in *Variorum* notes on this passage.

178. *FQ* V. XI. 58. Other similes of this kind in *The Faerie Queene* are mentioned in *Variorum* note on these lines.

179. *Loc. cit.* Gough (*op. cit.*, p. 315) explains "bils and glayues" as "infantry weapons with long wooden handles and an axe or knife at the head."

180. *FQ* V. XI. 57.

181. *Loc. cit.*

182. *FQ* V. XI. 59. Spenser seems to have enjoyed such comparisons. Another instance is *FQ* V. VIII. 50, where Artegall chases the enemy like "wyld goats."

183. *Loc. cit.*

184. *FQ* V. XI. 65.

185. *FQ* V. II. 54.

186. Renwick (*Edmund Spenser*, p. 171) has pointed to this similarity: "The rabble is crushed because it is a rabble, incapable of constant policy. . . . Spenser's political attitude is thus similar to that of Shakespeare, and for good cause."

187. Cf. also F. M. Padelford, "The Political, Economic, and Social Views of Spenser," *Journal of English and Germanic Philology*, XIV (1915), 417 ff., for his attitude toward the problems of the lower classes.

188. *FQ* V. II. 38.

189. In *FQ* V. VIII.

190. *FQ* V. VIII. 20.

191. *FQ* V. VIII. 30. "Tortious" means "wrongful" (Gough, *op. cit.*, p. 265).

192. While Spenser's authoritarianism can be explained as the repetition and logical development of the general line of thought of the English defenders of the established order, it is probable that in his political views he was also influenced by such works as Jean Bodin's *Six Livres de la République* (Paris, 1576), in which tolerant absolutism is advocated. W. L. Renwick, in his edition of *A View of the Present State of Ireland* (London, 1934), p. 248, argues that Spenser probably knew Bodin's book, and shows similarities in certain of Bodin's and Spenser's passages, but he believes that Spenser's views would have been much the same if he had not known Bodin's work. C. G. Smith (*Spenser's Theory of Friendship*, pp. 23–24) points to similarities between Spenser's ideas on harmony and those of Bodin and *Les Politiques*. Jones (*A Spenser Handbook*, pp. 380–84) lists a number of similarities in Spenser's *View* and in Bodin's work. Henley (*op. cit.*, p. 184) believes that Spenser's tolerant views on religion are derived from Bodin. Padelford ("The Political Economic, and Social Views of Spenser," *op. cit.*) also assumes Spenser's familiarity with Bodin's *République*. For a general treatment of Bodin's influence, cf. George L. Mosse, "The Influence of Jean Bodin's *République* on English Political Thought," *Medievalia et Humanistica*, V (1948), 73–83, and *The Struggle for Sovereignty in England from the Reign of Queen Elizabeth to the Petition of Right* (East Lansing, 1950). The relation of Spenser's political thought to that of Bodin and other French contemporaries, and to Raleigh's, Hooker's, and Sir Thomas Smith's ideas is beyond the scope of the present work.

193. Cf. White (*op. cit.*, p. 81): In the Elizabethan period, "the tendencies to social radicalism of More have been swallowed up in the prevailing concern for social order and stability."

## EPILOGUE

1. See Zera S. Fink, *The Classical Republicans: An Essay in the Recovery of a Pattern of Thought in Seventeenth Century England* (Evanston, 1945), p. ix.

2. Quoted *ibid.*, p. 95, from "Of Reformation in England," in *Prose Works* (London, 1848–53), II, 408.

3. Fink, *op. cit.*, p. 122.

4. See D. Brunton and D. H. Pennington, *Members of the Long Parliament* (London, 1954), pp. 3–7, 177.

# Index

⟦ PRINTED
IN U·S·A· ⟧